A TEXAS COMPANION FOR THE COURSE IN WILLS, TRUSTS, AND ESTATES 2015-2016

Joshua C. Tate
Associate Professor of Law
Southern Methodist University

ASPEN SELECT SERIES

A TEXAS COMPANION FOR THE COURSE IN WILLS, TRUSTS, AND ESTATES 2015-2016

Joshua C. Tate
Associate Professor of Law
Southern Methodist University

Wolters Kluwer

Published by Wolters Kluwer in New York.

Wolters Kluwer serves customers worldwide with CCH, Aspen Publishers, and Kluwer Law International products. (www.wolterskluwerlb.com)

To contact Customer Service, e-mail customer.service@wolterskluwer.com, call 1-800-234-1660, fax 1-800-901-9075, or mail correspondence to:

Wolters Kluwer
Attn: Order Department
PO Box 990
Frederick, MD 21705

Printed in the United States of America.

1 2 3 4 5 6 7 8 9 0

ISBN 978-1-4548-7068-5

About Wolters Kluwer Law & Business

Wolters Kluwer Law & Business is a leading global provider of intelligent information and digital solutions for legal and business professionals in key specialty areas, and respected educational resources for professors and law students. Wolters Kluwer Law & Business connects legal and business professionals as well as those in the education market with timely, specialized authoritative content and information-enabled solutions to support success through productivity, accuracy and mobility.

Serving customers worldwide, Wolters Kluwer Law & Business products include those under the Aspen Publishers, CCH, Kluwer Law International, Loislaw, Best Case, ftwilliam.com and MediRegs family of products.

CCH products have been a trusted resource since 1913, and are highly regarded resources for legal, securities, antitrust and trade regulation, government contracting, banking, pension, payroll, employment and labor, and healthcare reimbursement and compliance professionals.

Aspen Publishers products provide essential information to attorneys, business professionals and law students. Written by preeminent authorities, the product line offers analytical and practical information in a range of specialty practice areas from securities law and intellectual property to mergers and acquisitions and pension/benefits. Aspen's trusted legal education resources provide professors and students with high-quality, up-to-date and effective resources for successful instruction and study in all areas of the law.

Kluwer Law International products provide the global business community with reliable international legal information in English. Legal practitioners, corporate counsel and business executives around the world rely on Kluwer Law journals, looseleafs, books, and electronic products for comprehensive information in many areas of international legal practice.

Loislaw is a comprehensive online legal research product providing legal content to law firm practitioners of various specializations. Loislaw provides attorneys with the ability to quickly and efficiently find the necessary legal information they need, when and where they need it, by facilitating access to primary law as well as state-specific law, records, forms and treatises.

Best Case Solutions is the leading bankruptcy software product to the bankruptcy industry. It provides software and workflow tools to flawlessly streamline petition preparation and the electronic filing process, while timely incorporating ever-changing court requirements.

ftwilliam.com offers employee benefits professionals the highest quality plan documents (retirement, welfare and non-qualified) and government forms (5500/PBGC, 1099 and IRS) software at highly competitive prices.

MediRegs products provide integrated health care compliance content and software solutions for professionals in healthcare, higher education and life sciences, including professionals in accounting, law and consulting.

Wolters Kluwer Law & Business, a division of Wolters Kluwer, is headquartered in New York. Wolters Kluwer is a market-leading global information services company focused on professionals.

For my grandparents

Margaret Jean Leathers, Judson Roy Williams,

Mary Ruth Starr (1916-1975), and Erman Granville Tate (1915-1980),

for those who came before them,

and for those who follow

Summary of Contents

Table of Contents

Table of Contents

Table of Contents

Table of Contents

Table of Contents

Table of Contents

Preface to the 2015-2016 Edition

The past half-century has seen many changes in the Texas law of trusts and estates, some home-grown and some made in response to national reform efforts. Although Texas has not adopted the Uniform Probate Code or the Uniform Trust Code, we have incorporated many innovations from those uniform acts while rejecting others. When the Texas legislature has adopted uniform act provisions, it has often made changes to the statutory wording that can have important consequences in application. Law students who intend to become estate planners in Texas must master the distinctive features of relevant Texas statutes and case law. On the other hand, thanks to interstate migration, the increasing popularity of out-of-state trusts, and the understandable desire of many Texans to own a summer home in a state with a cooler climate, Texas estate planners should have some familiarity with rules and concepts not applied here but common elsewhere. For these reasons, Texas law students benefit from national casebooks on trusts and estates, even though those books devote significant coverage to topics that are not normally relevant to Texas estate planning practice.

This book is designed to fill in the gap for law teachers who wish to use a national casebook while giving their students a firm grounding in the Texas law of trusts and estates. The organization is based on Dukeminier and Sitkoff, Wills, Trusts, and Estates (Aspen Publishers, 9th ed. 2013). The structure of this book, however, makes it easy to teach the material in any order depending on the casebook and the preferences of the instructor. The materials in this edition have been updated to reflect changes made through the 2015 regular session of the Texas legislature, including revised rules concerning the revocation of nonprobate transfers on divorce, guidelines for trust protectors and directed trusts, and a new subchapter allowing for the judicial modification or reformation of wills in cases of mistake. The cases of *Ross v. Goldstein*, *Gilkey v. Chambers*, *San Antonio Area Foundation v. Lang*, and *Brinker v. Wobaco Trust Ltd.* have been omitted from this edition. On the other hand, *Rachal v. Reitz*, the 2013 Texas Supreme Court decision holding trust arbitration clauses enforceable, has been added, along with *Jordan v. Lyles*, a recent Texas Court of Appeals opinion on the fiduciary duties implicated by a power of attorney.

I thank Johnny Buckles, McKen Carrington, Matt Festa, Terri Helge, Helen Jenkins, Stanley Johanson, Bob Palmer, Aric Short, Mark Siegel, and Rob Sitkoff for sharing their course syllabi and offering advice. I am grateful to my wife Lisa and our children Charlie and Ellie for their continued patience and kindness.

Note: Footnotes are consecutive within each individual chapter. Editorial comments (mainly pointing out amendments to statutes discussed in the cases) are marked "—Ed."

Joshua C. Tate

July 2015

Chapter 1. Introduction: Freedom of Disposition

Section A. Ethical Considerations

Attorney owes no duty to intended beneficiaries of deceased client's estate plan

BARCELO v. ELLIOTT
Supreme Court of Texas
923 S.W.2d 575 (1996)

PHILLIPS, C.J. The issue presented is whether an attorney who negligently drafts a will or trust agreement owes a duty of care to persons intended to benefit under the will or trust, even though the attorney never represented the intended beneficiaries. The court of appeals held that the attorney owed no duty to the beneficiaries, affirming the trial court's summary judgment for the defendant-attorney. Because the attorney did not represent the beneficiaries, we likewise conclude that he owed no professional duty to them. We accordingly affirm the judgment of the court of appeals.

I

After Frances Barcelo retained attorney David Elliott to assist her with estate planning, Elliott drafted a will and inter vivos trust agreement for her. The will provided for specific bequests to Barcelo's children, devising the residuary of her estate to the inter vivos trust. Under the trust agreement, trust income was to be distributed to Barcelo during her lifetime. Upon her death, the trust was to terminate, assets were to be distributed in specific amounts to Barcelo's children and siblings, and the remainder was to pass to Barcelo's six grandchildren. The trust agreement contemplated that the trust would be funded by cash and shares of stock during Barcelo's lifetime, although the grandchildren contend that this never occurred. Barcelo signed the will and trust agreement in September 1990.

Barcelo died on January 22, 1991. After two of her children contested the validity of the trust, the probate court, for reasons not disclosed on the record before us, declared the trust to be invalid and unenforceable. Barcelo's grandchildren—the intended remainder beneficiaries under the trust—subsequently agreed to settle for what they contend was a substantially smaller share of the estate than what they would have received pursuant to a valid trust.

Barcelo's grandchildren then filed the present malpractice action against Elliott and his law firm (collectively "Elliott"). Plaintiffs allege that Elliott's negligence caused the trust to be invalid, resulting in foreseeable injury to the plaintiffs.[1] Elliott moved for summary judgment on the sole ground that he owed no professional duty to the grandchildren because he had never represented them. The trial court granted Elliott's motion for summary judgment. The court of appeals affirmed . . . .

II

The sole issue presented is whether Elliott owes a duty to the grandchildren that could give rise to malpractice liability even though he represented only Frances Barcelo, not the grandchildren, in preparing and implementing the estate plan.

A

At common law, an attorney owes a duty of care only to his or her client, not to third parties who may have been damaged by the attorney's negligent representation of the client. See Savings Bank v. Ward, 100 U.S. 195, 200, 25 L. Ed. L. 621 (1879); Annotation, Attorney's Liability, to One Other Than Immediate Client, for Negligence in Connection with Legal Duties, 61 A.L.R.4th 615, 624 (1988). Without this "privity barrier," the rationale goes, clients would lose control over the attorney-client relationship, and attorneys would be subject to almost unlimited liability. See Helen Jenkins, Privity—A Texas-Size Barrier to Third Parties for Negligent Will Drafting—An Assessment and Proposal, 42 Baylor L. Rev. 687, 689-90 (1990). Texas courts of appeals have uniformly applied the privity barrier in the estate planning context. See Thomas v. Pryor, 847 S.W.2d 303, 304-05 (Tex. App.-Dallas 1992), judgm't vacated by agr., 863 S.W.2d 462 (Tex. 1993); Dickey v. Jansen, 731 S.W.2d 581, 582-83 (Tex. App.-Houston [1st Dist.] 1987, writ ref'd n.r.e.); Berry v. Dodson, Nunley & Taylor, 717 S.W.2d 716, 718-19 (Tex. App.-San Antonio 1986), judgm't vacated by agr., 729 S.W.2d 690 (Tex. 1987).

---

[1] The plaintiffs alleged that Elliott acted negligently when he:

> A. provided in the trust agreement that it would not be effective until signed by the trustee, designated to be First City Bank of Houston, and then failed to obtain the execution of the trust document by the trustee;
>
> B. drafted Mrs. Barcelo's will so as to provide that the residuary of her estate would pass into the trust he sought to create for Mrs. Barcelo, and then provided in the trust agreement that the trust would terminate upon Mrs. Barcelo's death, leaving her residuary to pass by intestacy to her children instead of her six grandchildren, including Plaintiffs, as provided in the trust agreement; and
>
> C. failed to take the necessary steps on behalf of Mrs. Barcelo to fund the trust with the shares of stock . . . .

Introduction: Freedom of Disposition

Plaintiffs argue, however, that recognizing a limited exception to the privity barrier as to lawyers who negligently draft a will or trust would not thwart the rule's underlying rationales. They contend that the attorney should owe a duty of care to persons who were specific, intended beneficiaries of the estate plan. We disagree.

B

The majority of other states addressing this issue have relaxed the privity barrier in the estate planning context. See Lucas v. Hamm, 56 Cal. 2d 583, 15 Cal. Rptr. 821, 825, 364 P.2d 685, 689 (1961), cert. denied, 368 U.S. 987, 82 S. Ct. 603, 7 L. Ed. 2d 525 (1962); Stowe v. Smith, 184 Conn. 194, 441 A.2d 81, 83 (1981); Needham v. Hamilton, 459 A.2d 1060, 1062 (D.C. 1983); DeMaris v. Asti, 426 So. 2d 1153, 1154 (Fla. Dist. Ct. App. 1983); Ogle v. Fuiten, 102 Ill. 2d 356, 80 Ill. Dec. 772, 774-75, 466 N.E.2d 224, 226-27 (1984); Walker v. Lawson, 526 N.E.2d 968, 968 (Ind. 1988); Schreiner v. Scoville, 410 N.W.2d 679, 682 (Iowa 1987); Pizel v. Zuspann, 247 Kan. 54, 795 P.2d 42, 51 (1990); In re Killingsworth, 292 So. 2d 536, 542 (La. 1973); Hale v. Groce, 304 Or. 281, 744 P.2d 1289, 1292-93 (1987); Guy v. Liederbach, 501 Pa. 47, 459 A.2d 744, 751-53 (1983); Auric v. Continental Cas. Co., 111 Wis. 2d 507, 331 N.W.2d 325, 327 (1983). But see Lilyhorn v. Dier, 214 Neb. 728, 335 N.W.2d 554, 555 (1983); Viscardi v. Lerner, 125 A.D.2d 662, 510 N.Y.S.2d 183, 185 (1986); Simon v. Zipperstein, 32 Ohio St. 3d 74, 512 N.E.2d 636, 638 (1987).

While some of these states have allowed a broad cause of action by those claiming to be intended beneficiaries, see *Stowe*, 441 A.2d at 84; *Ogle*, 80 Ill. Dec. at 775, 466 N.E.2d at 227; *Hale*, 744 P.2d at 1293, others have limited the class of plaintiffs to beneficiaries specifically identified in an invalid will or trust. See Ventura County Humane Society v. Holloway, 40 Cal. App. 3d 897, 115 Cal. Rptr. 464, 468 (1974); *DeMaris*, 426 So. 2d at 1154; *Schreiner*, 410 N.W.2d at 683; Kirgan v. Parks, 60 Md. App. 1, 478 A.2d 713, 718-19 (1984) (holding that, if cause of action exists, it does not extend to situation where testator's intent as expressed in the will has been carried out); Ginther v. Zimmerman, 195 Mich. App. 647, 491 N.W.2d 282, 286 (1992) (same); *Guy*, 459 A.2d at 751-52. The Supreme Court of Iowa, for example, held that

> a cause of action ordinarily will arise only when as a direct result of the lawyer's professional negligence the testator's intent as expressed in the testamentary instruments is frustrated in whole or in part and the beneficiary's interest in the estate is either lost, diminished, or unrealized.

Schreiner v. Scoville, 410 N.W.2d 679, 683 (Iowa 1987).

C

We agree with those courts that have rejected a broad cause of action in favor of beneficiaries. These courts have recognized the inevitable problems with disappointed heirs attempting to prove that the defendant-attorney failed to implement the deceased testator's intentions. Certainly allowing extrinsic evidence would create a host of difficulties. In

DeMaris v. Asti, 426 So. 2d 1153, 1154 (Fla. Dist. Ct. App. 1983), for example, the court concluded that "[t]here is no authority—the reasons being obvious—for the proposition that a disappointed beneficiary may prove, by evidence totally extrinsic to the will, the testator's testamentary intent was other than as expressed in his solemn and properly executed will." Such a cause of action would subject attorneys to suits by heirs who simply did not receive what they believed to be their due share under the will or trust. This potential tort liability to third parties would create a conflict during the estate planning process, dividing the attorney's loyalty between his or her client and the third-party beneficiaries.

Moreover, we believe that the more limited cause of action recognized by several jurisdictions also undermines the policy rationales supporting the privity rule. These courts have limited the cause of action to beneficiaries specifically identified in an invalid will or trust. Under these circumstances, courts have reasoned, the interests of the client and the beneficiaries are necessarily aligned, negating any conflict, as the attorney owes a duty only to those parties which the testator clearly intended to benefit. See, e.g., *Needham*, 459 A.2d at 1062.

In most cases where a defect renders a will or trust invalid, however, there are concomitant questions as to the true intentions of the testator. Suppose, for example, that a properly drafted will is simply not executed at the time of the testator's death. The document may express the testator's true intentions, lacking signatures solely because of the attorney's negligent delay. On the other hand, the testator may have postponed execution because of second thoughts regarding the distribution scheme. In the latter situation, the attorney's representation of the testator will likely be affected if he or she knows that the existence of an unexecuted will may create malpractice liability if the testator unexpectedly dies.

The present case is indicative of the conflicts that could arise. Plaintiffs contend in part that Elliott was negligent in failing to fund the trust during Barcelo's lifetime, and in failing to obtain a signature from the trustee. These alleged deficiencies, however, could have existed pursuant to Barcelo's instructions, which may have been based on advice from her attorneys attempting to represent her best interests. An attorney's ability to render such advice would be severely compromised if the advice could be second-guessed by persons named as beneficiaries under the unconsummated trust.

In sum, we are unable to craft a bright-line rule that allows a lawsuit to proceed where alleged malpractice causes a will or trust to fail in a manner that casts no real doubt on the testator's intentions, while prohibiting actions in other situations. We believe the greater good is served by preserving a bright-line privity rule which denies a cause of action to all beneficiaries whom the attorney did not represent. This will ensure that attorneys may in all cases zealously represent their clients without the threat of suit from third parties compromising that representation.

We therefore hold that an attorney retained by a testator or settlor to draft a will or trust owes no professional duty of care to persons named as beneficiaries under the will or trust.[2]

D

Plaintiffs also contend that, even if there is no tort duty extending to beneficiaries of an estate plan, they may recover under a third-party-beneficiary contract theory. While the majority of jurisdictions that have recognized a cause of action in favor of will or trust beneficiaries have done so under negligence principles, some have allowed recovery in contract. . . . In Texas, however, a legal malpractice action sounds in tort and is governed by negligence principles. See Cosgrove v. Grimes, 774 S.W.2d 662, 664 (Tex. 1989); Willis v. Maverick, 760 S.W.2d 642, 644 (Tex. 1988). Cf. Heyer v. Flaig, 70 Cal. 2d 223, 74 Cal. Rptr. 225, 228, 449 P.2d 161, 164 (1969) (recognizing that third-party-beneficiary contract theory "is conceptually superfluous since the crux of the action must lie in tort in any case; there can be no recovery without negligence"). Even assuming that a client who retains a lawyer to draft an estate plan intends for the lawyer's work to benefit the will or trust beneficiaries, the ultimate question is whether, considering the competing policy implications, the lawyer's professional duty should extend to persons whom the lawyer never represented. For the reasons previously discussed, we conclude that the answer is no.

For the foregoing reasons, we affirm the judgment of the court of appeals.

OWEN, J., did not participate in the decision.

CORNYN, J., joined by ABBOTT, J., dissenting. With an obscure reference to "the greater good," 923 S.W.2d at 578, the Court unjustifiably insulates an entire class of negligent lawyers from the consequences of their wrongdoing, and unjustly denies legal recourse to the grandchildren for whose benefit Ms. Barcelo hired a lawyer in the first place. I dissent.

By refusing to recognize a lawyer's duty to beneficiaries of a will, the Court embraces a rule recognized in only four states, while simultaneously rejecting the rule in an overwhelming majority of jurisdictions. Notwithstanding the fact that in recent years the Court has sought to align itself with the mainstream of American jurisprudence, the Court inexplicably balks in this case.

The threshold question in a negligence action, including a legal malpractice suit, is duty. El Chico Corp. v. Poole, 732 S.W.2d 306, 311 (Tex. 1987); see Cosgrove v. Grimes, 774 S.W.2d 662, 664 (Tex. 1989) (holding that a legal malpractice action in Texas is

---

[2] We express no opinion as to whether the beneficiary of a trust has standing to sue an attorney representing the trustee for malpractice. Cf. Thompson v. Vinson & Elkins, 859 S.W.2d 617, 621-23 (Tex. App.-Houston [1st Dist.] 1993, writ denied) (holding that beneficiary lacked standing to sue trustee's attorney).

grounded in negligence). Whether a defendant owes a duty to the plaintiff depends on several factors, including risk, foreseeability, and likelihood of injury weighed against the social utility of the actor's conduct, the magnitude of the burden of guarding against injury, and the consequences of placing the burden on the defendant. Greater Houston Transp. Co. v. Phillips, 801 S.W.2d 523, 525 (Tex. 1990).

The foreseeability of harm in this case is not open to serious question. Because Ms. Barcelo hired Mr. Elliott to accomplish the transfer of her estate to her grandchildren upon her death, the potential harm to the beneficiaries if the testamentary documents were incorrectly drafted was plainly foreseeable. See *Lucas*, 15 Cal. Rptr. at 824, 364 P.2d at 688; see also Heyer v. Flaig, 70 Cal. 2d 223, 74 Cal. Rptr. 225, 228, 449 P.2d 161, 164-65 (1969) ("The attorney's actions and omissions will affect the success of the client's testamentary scheme; and thus the possibility of thwarting the testator's wishes immediately becomes foreseeable. Equally foreseeable is the possibility of injury to an intended beneficiary."). Foreseeability of harm weighs heavily in favor of recognizing a duty to intended beneficiaries.

Additionally, the Court's decision means that, as a practical matter, no one has the right to sue for the lawyer's negligent frustration of the testator's intent. A flaw in a will or other testamentary document is not likely be discovered until the client's death. And, generally, the estate suffers no harm from a negligently drafted testamentary document. *Heyer*, 74 Cal. Rptr. at 228, 449 P.2d at 165. Allowing beneficiaries to sue would provide accountability and thus an incentive for lawyers to use greater care in estate planning. Robert L. Rabin, Tort Recovery for Negligently Inflicted Economic Loss, 37 Stan. L. Rev. 1513, 1521 (1985). Instead, the Court decides that an innocent party must bear the burden of the lawyer's error. The Court also gives no consideration to the fair adjustment of the loss between the parties, one of the traditional objectives of tort law. See W. Page Keeton et al., Prosser and Keeton on the Law of Torts § 4, at 24-25 (5th ed. 1984); Robert E. Litan et al., The U.S. Liability System: Background and Trends, in Liability: Perspectives and Policy 1, 3 (Robert E. Litan and Clifford Winston eds., 1988). These grounds for the imposition of a legal duty in tort law generally, which apply to lawyers in every other context, are no less important in estate planning.

Nor do the reasons the Court gives for refusing to impose a duty under these circumstances withstand scrutiny. Contrary to the Court's view, recognizing an action by the intended beneficiaries would not extend a lawyer's duty to the general public, but only to a limited, foreseeable class. Because estate planning attorneys generally do not face *any* liability in this context, potential liability to the intended beneficiaries would not place them in a worse position than attorneys in any other setting.

The Court also hypothesizes that liability to estate beneficiaries may conflict with the attorney's duty to the client. Before the beneficiaries could prevail in a suit against the attorney, however, they would necessarily have to show that the attorney breached a duty to the decedent. This is because the lawyer's duty to the client is to see that the client's intentions are realized by the very documents the client has hired the lawyer to draft. No conflicting duty to the beneficiaries is imposed.

Searching for other hypothetical problems that might arise if a cause of action for the beneficiaries is recognized, the Court observes that a will not executed at the testator's death could in fact express the testator's true intentions. 923 S.W.2d at 578. Granted, such a scenario may be the result of either the testator's indecision or the attorney's negligence. Similarly, a family member might be intentionally omitted from a will at the testator's direction, or negligently omitted because of the drafting lawyer's mistake. In other words, what appears to be attorney negligence may actually reflect the testator's wishes.

But surely these are matters subject to proof, as in all other cases. Nothing distinguishes this class of cases from many others in this respect. The Court fails to consider that the beneficiaries will in each case bear the burden of establishing that the attorney breached a duty to the testator, which resulted in damages to the beneficiaries. Lawyers, wishing to protect themselves from liability, may document the testator's intentions.

In addition, Elliott suggests that allowing beneficiaries to sue the testator's attorney would interfere with the attorney-client privilege, by either encouraging attorneys to violate clients' confidences or by hindering attorneys' ability to defend their actions. This concern, too, is unfounded. Under Texas law, the attorney-client privilege does not survive the testator. . . . This is because the lawyer-client privilege applies only to confidential communications, which are "not intended to be disclosed to third persons." Texas Rule of Civil Evidence 503(a)(5). And, as Professor Wigmore has explained, "[a]s to the *tenor* and *execution* of the will, it seems hardly open to dispute that they are the very facts which the testator expected and intended to be disclosed after his death." Wigmore § 2314, at 613 (emphasis in original).

In sum, I would hold that the intended beneficiary of a will or testamentary trust may bring a cause of action against an attorney whose negligence caused the beneficiary to lose a legacy in whole or in part. Accordingly, I would reverse the judgment of the court of appeals and remand this case to the trial court.

SPECTOR, J., dissenting. The issue in this case is whether the attorney, David Elliott, owed a duty to Frances Barcelo's intended beneficiaries. The majority holds that he did not. The other dissenting justices would recognize a broad cause of action in favor of any person claiming to be an intended beneficiary, regardless of whether the plaintiff is identified in the will or trust instrument. Because I would recognize only a limited cause of action for the intended beneficiaries of wills and trusts, I write separately to dissent.

At common law, an attorney owes no duty to third parties who may have been damaged by the attorney's negligent representation of the attorney's client. See Savings Bank

v. Ward, 100 U.S. 195, 25 L. Ed. 621 (1879). As the majority notes, although Texas courts of appeals have consistently accepted this restriction in the estate planning context, most other states addressing this issue have lowered the privity barrier in this area. . . . I believe that recognizing such a cause of action would further public policy by requiring attorneys to exercise due care in implementing a testator's estate plan. Under current law, only the attorney's client has standing to sue for negligent preparation of the will or trust. Although the testator's personal representative would succeed to this cause of action upon the testator's death, the estate itself may suffer no damage from an invalid will or trust that frustrates the testator's intentions. See Heyer v. Flaig, 70 Cal. 2d 223, 74 Cal. Rptr. 225, 228, 449 P.2d 161, 165 (1969); *Guy*, 459 A.2d at 749. Consequently, an attorney who negligently drafts a will or trust that is discovered to be invalid after the testator's death is accountable to no one.

I would not go so far as to hold that attorneys who draft wills and trusts have a duty to persons who are not beneficiaries named in the will or trust. Recognizing such a broad cause of action is as likely to frustrate the testator's intent as it is to carry it out. I would, however, allow beneficiaries who are specifically identified on the face of an invalid will or trust to assert a claim.

Recognizing a limited cause of action would subject attorneys who prepare wills and trusts documents to the same standard of care governing attorneys generally. Because I believe that this is sound public policy, I dissent.

Personal representative may, on behalf of decedent's estate, sue drafting attorney for malpractice

BELT v. OPPENHEIMER, BLEND, HARRISON & TATE, INC.

Supreme Court of Texas
192 S.W.3d 780 (2006)

JEFFERSON, C.J. Kristin Terk Belt and Kimberly Terk Murphy (the Terks)—the joint, independent executors of their father David Terk's estate—sued several attorneys and their law firm, Oppenheimer, Blend, Harrison, & Tate, Inc. (collectively, the Attorneys) for legal malpractice. The Attorneys moved for summary judgment on the ground that estate planners owe no duty to the personal representatives of a deceased client's estate. The trial court granted the motion, and the court of appeals affirmed the judgment. We hold, to the contrary, that there is no legal bar preventing an estate's personal representative from maintaining a legal malpractice claim on behalf of the estate against the decedent's estate planners. Accordingly, we reverse the court of appeals' judgment and remand to the trial court for further proceedings.

Introduction: Freedom of Disposition

I

BACKGROUND

David Terk hired the Attorneys to prepare his will. After his death, the Terks became the joint, independent executors of their father's estate. As executors, the Terks sued the Attorneys for legal malpractice, alleging that the Attorneys were negligent in drafting their father's will and in advising him on asset management. They claim the estate incurred over $1,500,000 in tax liability that could have been avoided by competent estate planning.

In affirming the trial court's judgment for the Attorneys, the court of appeals cited *Barcelo v. Elliott*, in which we held that beneficiaries cannot maintain a malpractice cause of action against a decedent's estate-planning attorney because the attorney lacks privity with non-client beneficiaries and therefore owes them no duty. 141 S.W.3d 706, 708-09 (citing *Barcelo*, 923 S.W.2d 575 (Tex. 1996)). The Terks argue that the *Barcelo* rule bars only claims by beneficiaries suing for their own injuries and does not preclude suits brought by personal representatives on an estate's behalf. We granted the Terks' petition to consider whether personal representatives may bring legal malpractice claims on behalf of a decedent's estate. 48 Tex. Sup. Ct. J. 524 (Apr. 11, 2005).

II

DISCUSSION

Legal malpractice claims sound in tort. See Cosgrove v. Grimes, 774 S.W.2d 662, 664 (Tex. 1989). The plaintiff must demonstrate "that (1) the attorney owed the plaintiff a duty, (2) the attorney breached that duty, (3) the breach proximately caused the plaintiff's injuries, and (4) damages occurred." Peeler v. Hughes & Luce, 909 S.W.2d 494, 496 (Tex. 1995).

While an attorney always owes a duty of care to a client, no such duty is owed to non-client beneficiaries, even if they are damaged by the attorney's malpractice. See *Barcelo*, 923 S.W.2d at 577. In *Barcelo*, we considered whether beneficiaries dissatisfied with the distribution of estate assets may sue an estate-planning attorney for legal malpractice after a client's death. Id. at 576. In that case, the intended beneficiaries of a trust, which was declared invalid after the client's death, sued the attorney who drafted the trust agreement. Id. We held that the non-client beneficiaries could not maintain a suit against the decedent's estate planner because "the greater good is served by preserving a bright-line privity rule which denies a cause of action to all beneficiaries whom the attorney did not represent." Id. at 578.

Several policy considerations supported our *Barcelo* holding. First, the threat of suits by disappointed heirs after a client's death could create conflicts during the estate-planning process and divide the attorney's loyalty between the client and potential beneficiaries, generally compromising the quality of the attorney's representation. Id. at 578. We also noted that suits brought by bickering beneficiaries would necessarily require extrinsic evidence to prove how a decedent intended to distribute the estate, creating a "host of difficulties." Id. We therefore held that barring a cause of action for estate-planning malpractice by beneficiaries would help ensure that estate planners "zealously represent[ed]" their clients. Id. at 578-79.

Thus, in Texas, a legal malpractice claim in the estate-planning context may be maintained only by the estate planner's client. This is the minority rule in the United States—only eight other states require strict privity in estate-planning malpractice suits. In the majority of states, a beneficiary harmed by a lawyer's negligence in drafting a will or trust may bring a malpractice claim against the attorney, even though the beneficiary was not the attorney's client. . . .

The question in this case, however, is whether the *Barcelo* rule bars suits brought *on behalf of* the decedent client by his estate's personal representatives. Because most states allow beneficiaries to maintain estate-planning malpractice claims, only a handful of jurisdictions have considered this specific issue. We confront this question for the first time today.

Generally, in Texas an estate's personal representative[3] has the capacity to bring a survival action on behalf of a decedent's estate. See Austin Nursing Ctr., Inc. v. Lovato, 171 S.W.3d 845, 850 (Tex. 2005); see also Texas Probate Code § 233A (personal representative can institute suit for recovery of estate's personal property, debts or damages).[4] Therefore, if the Terks' legal malpractice claim is brought on behalf of the decedent's estate and survives the decedent, the Terks may maintain a suit against the Attorneys. . . .

A

We have never specifically considered whether a legal malpractice claim in the estate-planning context survives a deceased client. A claim that an estate planner's negligence resulted in the improper depletion of a client's estate involves injury to the decedent's property. . . . Moreover, when an attorney's malpractice results in financial loss, the aggrieved client is fully compensated by recovery of that loss; the client may not recover damages for mental anguish or other personal injuries. See Douglas v. Delp, 987 S.W.2d 879, 885 (Tex. 1999).

---

[3] The definition of "personal representative" includes an "executor, independent executor, administrator, independent administrator, [or] temporary administrator, together with their successors." Texas Probate Code § 3(aa).

[4] The Texas Probate Code has been repealed and replaced by a new Texas Estates Code effective January 1, 2014. This revision, which is "part of the state's continuing statutory revision program" is intended to be nonsubstantive, and has the goal of making the law "more accessible and understandable." Tex. Estates Code § 21.001 (effective 2014). The statutory excerpts in this book come from the Estates Code, although the cases refer to the earlier Probate Code provisions. —Ed.

Thus, estate-planning malpractice claims seeking recovery for pure economic loss are limited to recovery for property damage. See id. Therefore, in accordance with the long-standing, common-law principle that actions for damage to property survive the death of the injured party, we hold that legal malpractice claims alleging pure economic loss survive in favor of a deceased client's estate, because such claims are necessarily limited to recovery for property damage. . . . Even though an estate may suffer significant damages after a client's death, this does not preclude survival of an estate-planning malpractice claim. While the primary damages at issue here—increased tax liability—did not occur until after the decedent's death, the lawyer's alleged negligence occurred while the decedent was alive. Apex Towing Co. v. Tolin, 41 S.W.3d 118, 120 (Tex. 2001) (legal malpractice claim accrues "when facts have come into existence that authorize a claimant to seek a judicial remedy"). If the decedent had discovered this injury prior to his death, he could have brought suit against his estate planners to recover the fees paid to them. . . .

B

Because legal malpractice claims survive in favor of the decedent's estate, the estate has a justiciable interest in the controversy sufficient to confer standing. See Austin Nursing Ctr., Inc. v. Lovato, 171 S.W.3d 845, 850 (Tex. 2005). A decedent's estate, however "is not a legal entity and may not properly sue or be sued as such." Id. at 849. (citing Price v. Estate of Anderson, 522 S.W.2d 690, 691 (Tex. 1975)). Rather, certain individuals have the capacity to bring a claim on the estate's behalf. Id. Generally, "only the estate's personal representative has the capacity to bring a survival claim." Id. at 850-51 (noting that in certain circumstances, heirs may bring suit on behalf of the estate, such as when no administration is pending or necessary).

In this case, it is undisputed that the Terks are the independent executors of their father's estate. Thus, they may bring a claim on behalf of the estate in their capacity as personal representatives. . . . This holding is in accord with other jurisdictions, which have also recognized that, because the estate "stands in the shoes" of a decedent, it is in privity with the decedent's estate-planning attorney and, therefore, the estate's personal representative has the capacity to maintain the malpractice claim on the estate's behalf.

C

In holding for the Attorneys, the court of appeals noted that the policy concerns expressed in *Barcelo* concerning suits against estate planners by intended beneficiaries should also bar suits brought by personal representatives of an estate. 141 S.W.3d at 708. As noted above, in *Barcelo* we held that an attorney's ability to represent a client zealously would be compromised if the attorney knew that, after the client's death, he could be second-guessed by the client's disappointed heirs. 923 S.W.2d at 578. Accordingly, we held that estate-planning attorneys owe no professional duty to beneficiaries named in a trust or will. Id. at 578-79.

While this concern applies when disappointed heirs seek to dispute the size of their bequest or their omission from an estate plan, it does not apply when an estate's personal representative seeks to recover damages incurred by the estate itself. Cases brought by quarreling beneficiaries would require a court to decide how the decedent intended to apportion the estate, a near-impossible task given the limited, and often conflicting, evidence available to prove such intent. See id. at 578 (noting the problems associated with allowing extrinsic evidence to prove testator intent). In cases involving depletion of the decedent's estate due to negligent tax planning, however, the personal representative need not prove how the decedent intended to distribute the estate; rather, the representative need only demonstrate that the decedent intended to minimize tax liability for the estate as a whole.

Additionally, while the interests of the decedent and a potential beneficiary may conflict, a decedent's interests should mirror those of his estate. Thus, the conflicts that concerned us in *Barcelo* are not present in malpractice suits brought on behalf of the estate. See Nevin v. Union Trust Co., 726 A.2d 694, 701 (Me. 1999) (holding that the better rule is to allow only personal representatives, not beneficiaries, to sue for estate-planning malpractice, because what may be good for one beneficiary is not necessarily good for the estate as a whole).

We note, however, that beneficiaries often act as the estate's personal representative, and our holding today arguably presents an opportunity for some disappointed beneficiaries to recast a malpractice claim for their own "lost" inheritance, which would be barred by *Barcelo*, as a claim brought on behalf of the estate. The temptation to bring such claims will likely be tempered, however, by the fact that a personal representative who mismanages the performance of his or her duties may be removed from the position. See Texas Probate Code § 222(b)(4). Additionally, even assuming that a beneficiary serving as personal representative could prove, for example, that the deceased client intended to maximize the size of the entire estate by leaving a larger inheritance to the personal representative, he or she would not necessarily recover the lost inheritance should the malpractice claim succeed. Because the claim allowed under our holding today is for injuries suffered by the client's *estate*, any damages recovered would be paid to the estate and, only then, distributed in accordance with the decedent's existing estate plan. . . . Thus, the recovery would flow to the disappointed beneficiary only if the estate plan had provided for such a distribution, fulfilling the decedent's wishes. These factors prevent personal representatives who are also beneficiaries from using our holding today as an end run around *Barcelo*. . . .

Finally, we note that precluding both beneficiaries and personal representatives from bringing suit for estate-planning malpractice would essentially immunize estate-planning attorneys from liability for breaching their duty to their clients. As the *Barcelo* dissent noted, however, allowing estate-planning malpractice suits may help "provide accountability and thus an incentive for lawyers to use greater care in estate planning." 923 S.W.2d at 580 (Cornyn, J., dissenting). Limiting estate-planning malpractice suits to those brought by either the client or the client's personal representative strikes the appropriate balance between providing accountability for attorney negligence and protecting the sanctity of the attorney-client relationship.

III

CONCLUSION

The Terks—in their capacity as personal representatives of their father's estate—may maintain an estate-planning malpractice claim against the Attorneys. We therefore reverse the court of appeals' judgment and remand to the trial court for further proceedings consistent with this opinion.

Justice GREEN did not participate in the decision.

Personal representative may sue decedent's attorneys for malpractice relating to advice given to decedent as executor of his spouse's estate

SMITH v. O'DONNELL
Supreme Court of Texas
288 S.W.3d 417 (2009)

O'NEILL, J. Thomas O'Donnell, as executor of the estate of Corwin Denney, sued Cox & Smith, Corwin's attorneys, for legal malpractice, breach of fiduciary duty, and gross negligence/malice arising out of advice the attorneys gave Corwin while he was serving as executor of his wife's estate. The trial court granted summary judgment for the attorneys on all claims. The court of appeals reversed the summary judgment on the legal malpractice claim based on our holding in Belt v. Oppenheimer, Blend, Harrison & Tate, Inc., 192 S.W.3d 780 (Tex. 2006). In *Belt*, we held that an executor was in privity with the decedent's attorneys and could sue them for estate-planning malpractice. 192 S.W.3d at 787. A prior case, Barcelo v. Elliott, 923 S.W.2d 575 (Tex. 1996), barred estate-planning legal malpractice claims brought by third-party beneficiaries of the estate. This case asks us to consider whether an executor may bring suit against a decedent's attorneys for malpractice committed outside the estate-planning context. We hold that the executor should not be prevented from bringing the decedent's survivable claims on behalf of the estate, and affirm the court of appeals' judgment.

I. BACKGROUND

When Corwin Denney's wife, Des Cygne, died, Corwin served as executor of her estate. He retained Cox & Smith to advise him in the independent administration of her estate, and consulted the law firm regarding the separate versus community character of the couple's assets. According to Corwin, he and his wife had orally agreed that stock in Automation Industries, Inc., would be his separate property and stock in Gilcrease Oil Co. would be hers. Cox & Smith prepared a memorandum advising Corwin that the Automation and Gilcrease stock was presumed to be community property, and that additional information was necessary before classifying the assets. According to Cox & Smith, Corwin was also advised that he should probably pursue a declaratory judgment to properly classify the stock, which he declined to do. Cox & Smith, relying upon an analysis performed by Corwin's California accountant and without seeking a declaratory judgment, prepared an estate tax return that omitted any Automation stock from a list of Des Cygne's assets. Corwin died twenty-nine years later, leaving the bulk of his estate to charity. Approximately one month after his death, the Denney children, as beneficiaries of Des Cygne's trust, sued Corwin's estate alleging that Corwin had misclassified the Automation stock as his separate property, and as a result underfunded their mother's trust. O'Donnell, the executor of Corwin's estate, settled the children's claims for approximately $12.9 million, less than half of their estimated value.[5] O'Donnell then brought this suit for legal malpractice against Cox & Smith, alleging that the attorneys failed to properly advise Corwin about the serious consequences of mischaracterizing assets, and that their negligence caused damage to Corwin's estate.

II. PROCEDURAL HISTORY

At the trial court, Cox & Smith won a summary judgment on all claims. The trial court did not state a basis for its decision. The court of appeals initially affirmed the summary judgment, holding that no cause of action had accrued to Corwin during his lifetime, and thus O'Donnell lacked privity with the lawyers. We vacated and remanded for reconsideration in light of our decision in *Belt*, 192 S.W.3d 780. In *Belt*, we held that there was no accrual problem under similar circumstances. 192 S.W.3d at 785-86. There, the independent executrixes of an estate brought a legal malpractice claim on the estate's behalf alleging that a negligently-drafted will had increased the estate's tax liability. Id. at 782. We held that because the injury that formed the basis of the claim occurred when the will was drafted, the claim accrued prior to the decedent's death. 192 S.W.3d at 785-86. We further held that legal malpractice claims for pure economic loss are survivable and an estate's personal representative may bring survivable claims on behalf of the estate. Id. at 785-87.

In this case, the court of appeals held, on remand, that (1) a fact issue existed as to whether a malpractice cause of action accrued during Corwin's lifetime; (2) such a claim would survive in favor of the estate; and (3) no evidence supported O'Donnell's malice claim. Cox & Smith argued to the court of appeals that despite our holding in *Belt*, the summary judgment should have been affirmed because O'Donnell lacks privity with Cox & Smith. Cox & Smith based its argument on *Barcelo*, 923 S.W.2d 575, in which we held that estate-planning attorneys owe no duty to third-party beneficiaries, and are not subject to malpractice lawsuits brought by them. Cox & Smith contends legal malpractice claims cannot be brought by anyone but the client, and *Belt* merely created a narrow exception for executors bringing estate-planning legal malpractice claims. The court of appeals rejected this argument, and we consider it here.

---

[5] According to O'Donnell's attorney, the Des Cygne beneficiaries' claims against Corwin were worth at least $32 million and perhaps as much as $40 million.

III. PRIVITY BETWEEN ATTORNEYS AND EXECUTORS OF THE CLIENT'S ESTATE

An executor is a personal representative who "'stands in the shoes"' of the decedent. *Belt*, 192 S.W.3d at 787. As a general rule, an estate's personal representative may bring the decedent's survivable claims on behalf of the estate. Id. at 784; see also Texas Probate Code § 233A ("Suits for the recovery of personal property, debts, or damages . . . may be instituted by executors or administrators."). In *Belt*, we considered whether the executrixes' legal malpractice claim was survivable. 192 S.W.3d at 784. At common law, actions for damage to real or personal property survive the death of the owner. Id. Thus, we held that "legal malpractice claims alleging pure economic loss survive in favor of a deceased client's estate." Id. at 785.

Having identified these claims as survivable, we must consider whether there is any reason for an exception preventing executors from bringing them. Cox & Smith again relies on our holding in *Barcelo*, where we identified the longstanding privity rule barring non-clients from suing for legal malpractice. 923 S.W.2d at 577. In that case, the beneficiaries of a will and a trust agreement sued the estate-planning attorney for legal malpractice, alleging that negligent drafting had harmed their interests. Id. at 576. We refused to join the majority of states that relax the common-law privity barrier for intended beneficiaries, and held that third parties lack privity with a deceased's attorney and cannot sue for malpractice. Id. at 577-79.

We identified two policy considerations that supported our decision in *Barcelo*. First, allowing these suits could disrupt the attorney-client relationship. If third parties could sue for estate-planning legal malpractice, attorneys would be distracted by the threat of future lawsuits from disgruntled heirs, making them less able to serve their clients. Id. at 578. Second, third-party estate-planning malpractice suits would allow disappointed beneficiaries to seek a greater share of the estate by claiming the testator's true intent was different from what is expressed in a formally-executed will, and thus create "a host of difficulties." Id.

Cox & Smith contends *Barcelo* bars all legal malpractice suits brought by non-clients, with the exception of estate-planning malpractice claims brought by executors, like that in *Belt*. To adopt the rule Cox & Smith suggests would place us alone among the states, and would unnecessarily immunize attorneys who commit malpractice. None of the concerns we voiced about third-party malpractice suits apply to malpractice suits brought by an estate's personal representative. The threat of executor lawsuits will not impede the attorney-client relationship, because the estate's suit is based on injury to the deceased client, as opposed to any third party. The estate's suit is identical to one the client could have brought during his lifetime. An estate's interests, unlike a third-party beneficiary's, mirror those of the decedent. *Belt*, 192 S.W.3d at 787.[6]

---

[6] In *Belt*, we noted that several considerations should discourage beneficiaries who also act as an estate's personal representative from pursuing estate-planning malpractice claims in order to increase their own shares. First, mismanagement could subject the personal representative

Cox & Smith argues that the estate's interest in this suit is not truly in line with the decedent's because Corwin had always intended to keep the community-property stock out of the trust and treat it as his own property, and he did so without seeking the declaratory judgment Cox & Smith recommended.[7] This argument, though, goes to the weight of the legal malpractice claim and does not change the fact that O'Donnell "stands in the [deceased's] shoes" in assessing the claim's merit and deciding whether or not to assert it on the estate's behalf. Id. Of course, if the evidence demonstrates that Corwin would have ignored Cox & Smith's advice no matter how competently provided, the malpractice claim will fail for lack of proximate causation. But at this point in the proceedings, the merits of the malpractice claim are undeveloped. There is at least some evidence that Corwin would have followed his lawyers' advice to pursue a declaratory judgment if they had clearly advised him to do so or warned him adequately of the severe consequences of mischaracterizing community assets.

And although Cox & Smith suggests, and the dissenting justices assume, that O'Donnell colluded with the Denney children in settling their claims, there is nothing in the record that would support such a presumption. If Cox & Smith can in fact demonstrate collusion at trial, it would presumably negate causation and/or mitigate damages on the legal malpractice claim, and could subject O'Donnell to personal liability to Corwin's beneficiaries for violating his fiduciary duties as executor of Corwin's estate. We see no reason to create a rule that would deprive an estate of any remedy for wrongdoing that caused it harm by prohibiting the estate from pursuing survivable claims the decedent could have brought during his lifetime.

Cox & Smith argues that the court of appeals' decision creates an end-run around *Barcelo*, allowing disgruntled beneficiaries to sue to increase their inheritances. However, the Des Cygne beneficiaries' claims were not against Corwin's estate as beneficiaries of his will, but against Corwin as executor of their mother's estate. Had they known during his lifetime that Corwin had misallocated their mother's community property and brought suit while he was alive, as the dissenting justices say they should have, any judgment or settlement they might have obtained for damage to their mother's estate would have been collectable from Corwin, who then could have asserted a claim against Cox & Smith for legal malpractice. In such a case, under Cox & Smith's and the dissenting justices' view, *Barcelo* would extinguish Corwin's malpractice claim upon his death simply because the Des Cygne beneficiaries were

---

to removal. *Belt*, 192 S.W.3d at 787-88 (citing Texas Probate Code § 222(b)(4)). Second, any damages recovered would be paid to the estate, then distributed according to the existing estate plan. Id. at 788. These concerns are not present here because O'Donnell is not a beneficiary of Corwin's will or Des Cygne's, and furthermore, the claim is not for estate-planning malpractice.

[7] The dissent asks, "would the client be rooting for the executor and the beneficiaries?" The answer is almost certainly yes. The Des Cygne beneficiaries received fixed amounts under Corwin's will. The only beneficiaries that stand to benefit from the suit against Cox & Smith are the charity to which Corwin intended to leave the bulk of his estate and possibly Corwin's widow.

also beneficiaries of Corwin's estate. We do not believe *Barcelo* will bear such an expansive reading. To the contrary, when negligent legal advice depletes the decedent's estate in a manner that does not implicate how the decedent intended to apportion his estate, *Barcelo*'s concerns about quarreling beneficiaries and conflicting evidence do not arise. See *Barcelo*, 923 S.W.2d at 578. Here, the beneficiaries of Des Cygne's trust do not dispute Corwin's intent as expressed in his will. They have already been paid a settlement out of Corwin's estate for damage Corwin allegedly caused to their mother's trust; the outcome of O'Donnell's legal malpractice suit against Cox & Smith will have no impact on their recovery, and they have no interest in that suit.

Adopting the broad rule Cox & Smith proposes would preclude executors from recovering for any claims the estate has to pay potential beneficiaries due to bad legal advice the decedent received during his lifetime. For example, according to Cox & Smith and the dissenting justices, if Corwin had improperly handled co-owned property based on bad legal advice and then died, his estate would be liable to the co-owner and could sue for legal malpractice so long as the co-owner was not related to Corwin and therefore a potential beneficiary of his estate. If a judgment was entered against Corwin because counsel botched his defense in a personal injury action arising out of an automobile accident, and Corwin later died, his estate could not assert a malpractice claim for damages that his estate must pay if the injured party happened to be a beneficiary of his will. We see no reason to extend the *Barcelo* privity bar to survivable malpractice suits brought by an executor, and declined to do so in *Belt*. We do not read *Barcelo* to bar O'Donnell's suit against Cox & Smith.

The dissent contends our decision will somehow allow disgruntled beneficiaries to employ gamesmanship to recover more than they were devised and will open up new avenues for attorney liability. Under *Barcelo*, beneficiaries cannot sue a decedent's attorneys for estate-planning malpractice. Id. at 579. But this case does not involve a claim of estate-planning malpractice and it does not involve a suit by a decedent's beneficiaries against the decedent's attorneys. The Des Cygne beneficiaries did not sue Corwin's attorneys and have no interest in the outcome of the legal malpractice case. They did sue Corwin's estate, but did so in their capacity as the wronged beneficiaries of their mother's allegedly underfunded trust, not as disgruntled beneficiaries of Corwin's will. We see no reason to bar a completely separate lawsuit—that of the executor against Corwin's attorneys—simply because Des Cygne's beneficiaries sued the estate for Corwin's mishandling of their mother's trust.

IV. MALICE

O'Donnell has filed a cross-petition challenging the court of appeals' holding that O'Donnell presented no evidence of malice to support an award of exemplary damages. . . . Considering all the evidence, there is nothing to suggest that Cox & Smith had any intent to harm Corwin or consciously chose to not give him more detailed advice, and thus the court of appeals did not err in affirming the no-evidence summary judgment on malice.

V. CONCLUSION

For the foregoing reasons, the court of appeals' judgment is affirmed.

Justice HECHT and Justice GREEN did not participate in the decision.

WILLETT, J., joined by WAINWRIGHT, J., dissenting.

This legal-malpractice appeal turns on whether *Belt* or *Barcelo* should control. Decided a decade apart, both decisions have their place in our jurisprudence—*Barcelo* states the general rule (non-clients cannot file malpractice suits), *Belt* the exception (executors sometimes can). Unlike the Court, I believe today's case is governed by *Barcelo*'s general privity barrier, as it is rife with *Barcelo*-like concerns of divided loyalties and conflicts of interest. Indeed, this case presents exactly the sort of gamesmanship flagged in *Belt*, "an opportunity for some disappointed beneficiaries to recast a malpractice claim for their own 'lost' inheritance, which would be barred by *Barcelo*, as a claim brought on behalf of the estate."

A lawyer's focus should be stubbornly client-focused, concerned with today's representation of satisfied clients, not tomorrow's litigation from dissatisfied critics. The Court's decision, I fear, sends this troubling message: *caveat advocatus*—zealously represent your client at your own risk. It's hard to be zealous while nervous. For the concerns expressed in *Barcelo* (and echoed in *Belt*), I would affirm the trial court's summary judgment for Cox & Smith.

I. *BARCELO* AND *BELT* REVISITED

Barcelo held that trust beneficiaries lacked privity with the trustor's attorney and therefore had no claim for legal malpractice. The Court reaffirmed the general Texas rule that an attorney's professional duty of care extends only to his client, and declined to recognize an exception to the privity barrier applicable "in the estate planning context." The Court's chief rationale was that relaxing the privity rule might create conflicts of interest that would discourage lawsuit-wary attorneys from acting solely and zealously on behalf of their clients:

> Such a cause of action would subject attorneys to suits by heirs who simply did not receive what they believed to be their due share under the will or trust. This potential tort liability to third parties would create a conflict during the estate planning process, dividing the attorney's loyalty between his or her client and the third-party beneficiaries . . . .
>
> We believe the greater good is served by preserving a bright-line privity rule which denies a cause of action to all beneficiaries whom the attorney did not represent. This will ensure that attorneys may in all cases zealously represent their

> clients without the threat of suit from third parties compromising that representation.[8]

In *Barcelo*, we did not identify an actual conflict of interest between the third-party beneficiaries and the attorney. Our decision to adopt a bright-line rule must therefore be read as based on the mere *possibility* of conflicts of interest between the client trustor or testator and the third-party beneficiary.

Belt, on the other hand, held that independent executors of an estate could sue an estate-planning attorney for injury to the estate as a whole. The alleged injury to the estate in *Belt* was a substantial and avoidable estate-tax liability.

A critical distinction between *Belt* and *Barcelo* is that in *Belt* the interests of the testator, the estate, the executors, and the heirs were aligned. In *Belt*, we respected and reconciled *Barcelo* by emphasizing that the potential conflicts of interest that concerned us in that case were absent in *Belt*:

> [I]n *Barcelo*, we held that an attorney's ability to represent a client zealously would be compromised if the attorney knew that, after the client's death, he could be second-guessed by the client's disappointed heirs. Accordingly, we held that estate-planning attorneys owe no professional duty to beneficiaries named in a trust or will.
>
> While this concern applies when disappointed heirs seek to dispute the size of their bequest or their omission from an estate plan, it does not apply when an estate's personal representative seeks to recover damages incurred by the estate itself. Cases brought by quarreling beneficiaries would require a court to decide how the decedent intended to apportion the estate, a near-impossible task given the limited, and often conflicting, evidence available to prove such intent. In cases involving depletion of the decedent's estate due to negligent tax planning, however, the personal representative need not prove how the decedent intended to distribute the estate; rather, the representative need only demonstrate that the decedent intended to minimize tax liability for the estate as a whole.
>
> Additionally, while the interests of the decedent and a potential beneficiary may conflict, a decedent's interests should mirror those of his estate. Thus, the conflicts that concerned us in *Barcelo* are not present in malpractice suits brought on behalf of the estate.[9]

II. THE *BARCELO* PRIVITY BARRIER SHOULD GOVERN THIS CASE

Today's case should fall under the *Barcelo* privity barrier because conflicts of interest abound. While this case has a slightly altered procedural posture—suit filed by the executor, not the

---

[8] [923 S.W.2d] at 578-79.

[9] [192 S.W.3d] at 787 (footnote and citations omitted).

beneficiaries directly—there is little confusion that the executor is a pass-through, essentially bringing the children's claims in the estate's name. The trust beneficiaries had interests that directly conflicted with the interests of Corwin Denney, the client. The trust was established at the death of Denney's second wife, Des Cygne, pursuant to her will. Every asset that went into Des Cygne's trust was an asset that Denney could not treat as his separate property and spend or otherwise use as he wished. B*arcelo*'s central holding is that this conflict of interest necessarily means that trust beneficiaries do not share privity with the client's attorneys, who should focus solely on the client's best interests and wishes.

The trust beneficiaries, Denney's children, could have sued Denney during his lifetime for failing to adequately fund Des Cygne's trust with her rightful share of the couple's community property. The beneficiaries declined to do so, almost surely aware that Denney would have vigorously contested any characterization of the Automation Industries stock as community property and that he would have offered evidence of an oral agreement with Des Cygne that all the stock was his separate property. Nor did the beneficiaries sue Denney's attorneys after Denney's death. If they had, they would have lost under *Barcelo.* Instead, they waited thirty-four days after their father died and sued his estate. The executor, O'Donnell, raised no limitations defense but instead settled with the beneficiaries for generous sums.[10] He then sued Cox & Smith for malpractice, essentially taking the position that Denney's attorneys should have persuaded him, against his strong and repeated wishes, to surrender more assets to Des Cygne's trust. So we have a *Barcelo* suit draped in *Belt* garb. I would disallow the legal makeover.

The record is clear that Denney believed that all the Automation Industries stock was his separate property and that he opposed funding the trust with this prized asset. O'Donnell, with nothing to win or lose personally by settling with the trust beneficiaries, has now become a conduit for the trust beneficiaries' claim that Denney should have been more generous to the trust and less generous to himself. Under *Barcelo,* attorneys should not be forced to answer such claims. The privity rule should preempt lawsuits where the executor effectively serves as a pass-through for the beneficiaries' claims.

III. A BYPASS SUIT FOR EVERY BYPASS TRUST?

Because of the conflicts of interest inherent in expecting an attorney to safeguard the interests of clients and beneficiaries alike, claims by disappointed beneficiaries would discourage attorneys from focusing solely on the client's best interests, the essential teaching of *Barcelo.* I see no special significance to the fact that the beneficiaries here were beneficiaries to a trust that was not created by Denney's will. *Barcelo* also concerned a separate trust that allegedly was not properly funded. Regardless, the critical similarity with

---

[10] Affidavits submitted by the executor's experts assert that Denney failed to fund Des Cygne's trust with Automation Industries stock worth approximately $1.8 million at the time of her death, resulting in claims by the trust beneficiaries that O'Donnell settled years later for over $12.86 million. O'Donnell also paid the estate counsel who advised him $2.3 million for eight months of work that included one deposition.

Barcelo is that the interests of the beneficiaries whose claims led to the malpractice suit were not necessarily aligned with the interests of the deceased client, and the mere risk of divided loyalties compelled us to maintain a bright-line privity barrier that precluded legal malpractice suits filed by third parties.

I would not read *Belt* to apply whenever third parties manage to bring suit against the estate instead of the attorneys or the client directly. Again, the trust beneficiaries here could have brought suit against Denney or his attorneys but declined to do so. In *Barcelo*, the disappointed trust beneficiaries apparently could have pursued litigation against the executor of the client's estate, but instead settled with the estate "for what they contend[ed] was a substantially smaller share of the estate than what they would have received pursuant to a valid trust." Bypass trusts and other trusts are extremely common estate planning devices for couples wishing to minimize taxes or serve other estate planning goals. As happened here, the beneficiaries to the trust created by the will of the first spouse to die may have to wait until the surviving spouse dies, since the surviving spouse typically receives income from the trust until death, and the corpus of the trust then goes to the beneficiaries. If *Barcelo* can be circumvented in three simple steps—(1) beneficiaries sue the estate to resolve an objection to how the trust was funded or created; (2) executor settles with the beneficiaries; (3) executor then recoups the settlement by suing the attorneys who long-ago advised one or both spouses—*Barcelo*'s privity bar will prove porous indeed. I would limit *Belt* to cases where the court can safely assume that the interests of the client, the executor, and the disappointed heir or trust beneficiary are plainly and truly aligned, a situation we manifestly do not see here.

Further, if the only prerequisite to suit against a deceased client's attorney is that it must be brought by the executor, an endless variety of claims could be brought on the theory that the attorney's advice resulted in a smaller estate or trust. Every lawyer who advised a client to plead guilty or not, file for bankruptcy or not, settle a dispute or not, incorporate a business or not, and so on, would be fair game. I suspect that many experienced estate-planning attorneys have encountered a client who plans to "breathe his last breath and spend his last dollar," and who wishes not to be bothered with the paperwork, expense, meetings, or loss of control over assets involved in maximizing his estate. Today's decision arguably places a duty on attorneys to dissuade such a client from his carefree inclinations, and to steer him instead to altruism, a task, in my view, better left to those with divinity degrees instead of law degrees.

The distinction between this case and *Belt* is best captured with this question: would the client be rooting for the executor and the beneficiaries? In *Belt* we assumed the answer was "yes" so long as the client wanted his estate-tax liability minimized, thus leaving more to the chosen heirs. As the interests of the client-testator, estate, executor, and heirs were perfectly aligned, extending privity from the client to the executor made perfect sense.

In today's case, a "yes" answer is less clear. To put it mildly, the record does not suggest that Denney would be rooting for the trust beneficiaries, his six children, whom he wanted to inherit only nominal sums from himself and Des Cygne, with the bulk of his estate going to charity.[11] The California suit by the children directly precipitated the Texas

---

[11] The flavor of the relationship between Denney and his children is provided in a letter Denney wrote to daughter Carolyn in 1979, a copy of which was sent to all his children, in which he made clear that he wanted his children only to inherit modest amounts:

> As I look back over my life, I feel extremely fortunate to have been able to have started with absolutely nothing and end up with the potential, in some small way, to contribute to the world. . . .
>
> Now, I would like to discuss with you, each of my children, with your having the knowledge that each will receive a copy of this letter.
>
> . . . DesCygne and I made the trip to pay a visit on more than one occasion with your extending less than a warm welcome to DesCygne. . . . As I recall, not too many months later, you insisted that you be given a wedding almost immediately. Your mother was very much opposed to the wedding, but I sanctioned same, only because of my suspicion of the nature of the urgency, which later became substantiated.
>
> As you know, I soon became suspicious that [son in law] Gerry would never amount to anything. . . . The culmination of these episodes was the asking by you and Gerry that I loan to you $10,000.00 for the purchase of a gasoline filling station. The result, of which, was a complete squandering of the money. . . .
>
> DesCygne was very aware of the hatred you, [daughter] Mary, and [daughter] Anne felt for her. . . . DesCygne's estate was only nominal, and resulted exclusively from what I had given to her. . . . In my will, there is an equally nominal amount to be divided equally between the six children. . . . I know you abhor the thought of getting a job. . . .
>
> I was violently opposed to Mary marrying Gary; however, I gave them the best of weddings in Tulsa. Mary, was no better than you, in her hatred of DesCygne. . . . Anne is the only one of my children who has ever visited me. . . . With regard to [sons] Tommy and Pete, both of them were terrible problems for the several years following DesCygne's death. These problems involved rebellion against all moral standards, consumption of drugs, inabilities to hold a job, scrapes with the law, and squandering of money. . . .
>
> With regard to [daughter] Deci, as you know, she has achieved an extremely poor academic record every school year. We still do not believe that this record is caused by anything other than a complete lack of application and a selfish desire to do ever what she wants. . . . Her use of drugs and alcohol has contributed to her downfall. . . . At the time Deci made her decision, I explained to her that she was not going to inherit, except in a very nominal way, from her mother or me. . . .

legal malpractice suit. *Barcelo* endeavored to bar legal-malpractice suits by beneficiaries with a bright-line rule because conflicts might arise due to "concomitant questions as to the true intentions of the testator." *Belt* distinguished cases "when disappointed heirs seek to dispute the size of their bequest," and where the attorneys are being "second-guessed by the client's disappointed heirs," the situation here.

Cox & Smith advised Denney regarding Des Cygne's trust and her estate-tax filing. In the course of this advice the Cox & Smith attorneys advised Denney that the Automation Industries stock might, depending on choice-of-law questions, be deemed community property despite Denney's written representation to the attorneys that "DesCygne and I had a firm understanding that she had no interest in my stock in [Automation Industries]." Cox & Smith recommended that Denney seek a declaratory judgment regarding the proper characterization of the stock, but he refused, and instead "made a decision that it . . . was his separate property," according to the testimony of Cox & Smith attorney Jack Guenther. Denney always believed that the Automation Industries stock was his separate property, as he started the company in the 1940s, long before he married Des Cygne. Throughout his lifetime—through Des Cygne's death, three divorces, and a stock sale while married to his fifth wife—Denney insisted the stock was his alone. O'Donnell's testimony confirms Denney's consistent position for thirty years was "that he, not any of his wives, owned all the Automation Industries stock."

At bottom, the legal-malpractice claim is that Cox & Smith should have persuaded Denney to do something he believed was wrong and did not want to do. Denney's lawyers should not be subject to suit, decades after their representation, for implementing their client's express wishes to live out his life as a wealthier man, based on a then-defensible position that the stock was indeed his separate property and did not belong in Des Cygne's trust. The privity rule serves to tell lawyers in this situation to fight for Denney, not against him, and try to assure that he gets to keep his stock.

This case presents a conflict between client and trust beneficiary (Denney and his children) and also requires a presumption, against all record evidence, that Denney would cheer his estate's decision to settle with the children (who wanted the millions that Denney instead gave to charity) and then sue Cox & Smith for having carried out his wishes. Unlike the facts in *Belt*, what most benefits the living client who received the legal advice (treating the stock as separate property) and what the executor thought was in the estate's best

---

> Finally, I would like for you and the others to know, that upon my death the vast majority of my assets will go to the Denney Foundation.

Denney's last wife Nanci, in a deposition, summarized the suit that Denney's "horrible, odious, unattractive, disagreeable" children brought against the estate as follows: "They called him a liar and a fraud and a cheat. And I never understood why they really did it. I think they just wanted to get more money than he had left them."

interest (paying millions to settle claims that the stock was community property) are contradictory. These conflicting, misaligned interests were not present in *Belt*.

IV. CONCLUSION

On these facts, we cannot indulge *Belt*-like presumptions that Denney's interests while living "mirror those of his estate," that the estate's interests "are compatible with the client's interests," or that Denney would want to see his executor "standing in his shoes" by suing the attorneys whose work Denney praised. O'Donnell is trying to squeeze into Denney's shoes, but the fit is quite uncomfortable, and the Court should not allow it.

Section B. The Probate Process

Estates Code § 22.001. Applicability of Definitions

(a) Except as provided by Subsection (b), the definition for a term provided by this chapter applies in this code unless a different meaning of the term is otherwise apparent from the context in which the term is used.

(b) If Title 3 provides a definition for a term that is different from the definition provided by this chapter, the definition for the term provided by Title 3 applies in that title.

Estates Code § 22.008. Devise

"Devise":

(1) used as a noun, includes a testamentary disposition of real property, personal property, or both; and

(2) used as a verb, means to dispose of real property, personal property, or both, by will.

Estates Code § 22.009. Devisee

"Devisee" includes a legatee.

Estates Code § 22.018. Interested Person; Person Interested

"Interested person" or "person interested" means:

(1) an heir, devisee, spouse, creditor, or any other having a property right in or claim against an estate being administered; and

(2) anyone interested in the welfare of an incapacitated person, including a minor.

Estates Code § 22.031. Representative; Personal Representative

(a) "Representative" and "personal representative" include:

(1) an executor and independent executor;

(2) an administrator, independent administrator, and temporary administrator; and

(3) a successor to an executor or administrator listed in Subdivision (1) or (2).

(b) The inclusion of an independent executor in Subsection (a) may not be construed to subject an independent executor to the control of the courts in probate matters with respect to settlement of estates, except as expressly provided by law.

Estates Code § 22.034. Will

"Will" includes:

(1) a codicil; and

(2) a testamentary instrument that merely:

(A) appoints an executor or guardian;

(B) directs how property may not be disposed of; or

(C) revokes another will.

Estates Code § 55.001. Opposition in Probate Proceeding

A person interested in an estate may, at any time before the court decides an issue in a proceeding, file written opposition regarding the issue. The person is entitled to process for witnesses and evidence, and to be heard on the opposition, as in other suits.

Estates Code § 101.001. Passage of Estate on Decedent's Death

(a) Subject to Section 101.051, if a person dies leaving a lawful will:

(1) all of the person's estate that is devised by the will vests immediately in the devisees;

(2) all powers of appointment granted in the will vest immediately in the donees of those powers; and

(3) all of the person's estate that is not devised by the will vests immediately in the person's heirs at law.

(b) Subject to Section 101.051, the estate of a person who dies intestate vests immediately in the person's heirs at law.

Estates Code § 101.003. Possession of Estate by Personal Representative

On the issuance of letters testamentary or of administration on an estate described by Section 101.001, the executor or administrator has the right to possession of the estate as the estate existed at the death of the testator or intestate, subject to the exceptions provided by Section 101.051. The executor or administrator shall recover possession of the estate and hold the estate in trust to be disposed of in accordance with the law.

Estates Code § 101.051. Liability of Estate for Debts in General

(a) A decedent's estate vests in accordance with Section 101.001(a) subject to the payment of:

(1) the debts of the decedent, except as exempted by law; and

(2) any court-ordered child support payments that are delinquent on the date of the decedent's death.

(b) A decedent's estate vests in accordance with Section 101.001(b) subject to the payment of, and is still liable for:

(1) the debts of the decedent, except as exempted by law; and

(2) any court-ordered child support payments that are delinquent on the date of the decedent's death.

Estates Code § 202.002. Circumstances Under Which Proceeding to Declare Heirship Is Authorized

A court may conduct a proceeding to declare heirship when:

(1) a person dies intestate owning or entitled to property in this state and there has been no administration in this state of the person's estate;

(2) there has been a will probated in this state or elsewhere or an administration in this state of a decedent's estate, but:

(A) property in this state was omitted from the will or administration; or

(B) no final disposition of property in this state has been made in the administration; or

(3) it is necessary for the trustee of a trust holding assets for the benefit of a decedent to determine the heirs of the decedent.

Estates Code § 202.009. Attorney ad Litem

(a) The court shall appoint an attorney ad litem in a proceeding to declare heirship to represent the interests of heirs whose names or locations are unknown.

(b) The court may expand the appointment of the attorney ad litem appointed under Subsection (a) to include representation of an heir who is an incapacitated person on a finding that the appointment is necessary to protect the interests of the heir.

Estates Code § 202.201. Required Statements in Judgment

(a) The judgment in a proceeding to declare heirship must state:

(1) the names of the heirs of the decedent who is the subject of the proceeding; and

(2) the heirs' respective shares and interests in the decedent's property.

(b) If the proof in a proceeding to declare heirship is in any respect deficient, the judgment in the proceeding must state that.

Estates Code § 202.202. Finality and Appeal of Judgment

(a) The judgment in a proceeding to declare heirship is a final judgment.

(b) At the request of an interested person, the judgment in a proceeding to declare heirship may be appealed or reviewed within the same time limits and in the same manner as other judgments in probate matters.

Estates Code § 202.205. Effect of Certain Judgments on Liability to Creditors

(a) A judgment in a proceeding to declare heirship stating that there is no necessity for administration of the estate of the decedent who is the subject of the proceeding constitutes authorization for a person who owes money to the estate, has custody of estate property, acts as registrar or transfer agent of an evidence of interest, indebtedness, property, or right belonging to the estate, or purchases from or otherwise deals with an heir named in the judgment to take the following actions without liability to a creditor of the estate or other person:

(1) to pay, deliver, or transfer the property or the evidence of property rights to an heir named in the judgment; or

(2) to purchase property from an heir named in the judgment.

(b) An heir named in a judgment in a proceeding to declare heirship is entitled to enforce the heir's right to payment, delivery, or transfer described by Subsection (a) by suit.

(c) Except as provided by this section, this chapter does not affect the rights or remedies of the creditors of a decedent who is the subject of a proceeding to declare heirship.

Estates Code § 205.001. Entitlement to Estate Without Appointment of Personal Representative

The distributees of the estate of a decedent who dies intestate are entitled to the decedent's estate without waiting for the appointment of a personal representative of the estate to the extent the estate assets, excluding homestead and exempt property, exceed the known liabilities of the estate, excluding any liabilities secured by homestead and exempt property, if:

(1) 30 days have elapsed since the date of the decedent's death;

(2) no petition for the appointment of a personal representative is pending or has been granted;

(3) the value of the estate assets, excluding homestead and exempt property, does not exceed $50,000;

(4) an affidavit that meets the requirements of Section 205.002 is filed with the clerk of the court that has jurisdiction and venue of the estate;

(5) the judge approves the affidavit as provided by Section 205.003; and

(6) the distributees comply with Section 205.004.

Estates Code § 205.002. Affidavit Requirements

(a) An affidavit filed under Section 205.001 must:

(1) be sworn to by:

(A) two disinterested witnesses;

(B) each distributee of the estate who has legal capacity; and

(C) if warranted by the facts, the natural guardian or next of kin of any minor distributee or the guardian of any other incapacitated distributee;

(2) show the existence of the conditions prescribed by Sections 205.001(1), (2), and (3); and

(3) include:

(A) a list of all known estate assets and liabilities;

(B) the name and address of each distributee; and

(C) the relevant family history facts concerning heirship that show each distributee's right to receive estate money or other property or to have any evidence of money, property, or other right of the estate as is determined to exist transferred to the distributee as an heir or assignee.

(b) A list of all known estate assets under Subsection (a)(3)(A) must indicate which assets the applicant claims are exempt.

Estates Code § 205.003. Examination and Approval of Affidavit

The judge shall examine an affidavit filed under Section 205.001. The judge may approve the affidavit if the judge determines that the affidavit conforms to the requirements of this chapter.

Estates Code § 205.004. Copy of Affidavit to Certain Persons

The distributees of the estate shall provide a copy of the affidavit under this chapter, certified by the court clerk, to each person who:

(1) owes money to the estate;

(2) has custody or possession of estate property; or

(3) acts as a registrar, fiduciary, or transfer agent of or for an evidence of interest, indebtedness, property, or other right belonging to the estate.

Estates Code § 205.006. Title to Homestead Transferred Under Affidavit

(a) If a decedent's homestead is the only real property in the decedent's estate, title to the homestead may be transferred under an affidavit that meets the requirements of this chapter.

The affidavit used to transfer title to the homestead must be recorded in the deed records of a county in which the homestead is located.

(b) A bona fide purchaser for value may rely on an affidavit recorded under this section. A bona fide purchaser for value without actual or constructive notice of an heir who is not disclosed in the recorded affidavit acquires title to a homestead free of the interests of the undisclosed heir, but remains subject to any claim a creditor of the decedent has by law. A purchaser has constructive notice of an heir who is not disclosed in the recorded affidavit if an affidavit, judgment of heirship, or title transaction in the chain of title in the deed records identifies that heir as the decedent's heir.

(c) An heir who is not disclosed in an affidavit recorded under this section may recover from an heir who receives consideration from a purchaser in a transfer for value of title to a homestead passing under the affidavit.

Estates Code § 205.007. Liability of Certain Persons

(a) A person making a payment, delivery, transfer, or issuance under an affidavit described by this chapter is released to the same extent as if made to a personal representative of the decedent. The person may not be required to:

(1) see to the application of the affidavit; or

(2) inquire into the truth of any statement in the affidavit.

(b) The distributees to whom payment, delivery, transfer, or issuance is made are:

(1) answerable for the payment, delivery, transfer, or issuance to any person having a prior right; and

(2) accountable to any personal representative appointed after the payment, delivery, transfer, or issuance.

(c) Each person who executed the affidavit is liable for any damage or loss to any person that arises from a payment, delivery, transfer, or issuance made in reliance on the affidavit.

(d) If a person to whom the affidavit is delivered refuses to pay, deliver, transfer, or issue property as provided by this section, the property may be recovered in an action brought for that purpose by or on behalf of the distributees entitled to the property on proof of the facts required to be stated in the affidavit.

Introduction: Freedom of Disposition

Estates Code § 205.009. Construction of Certain References

A reference in this chapter to "homestead" or "exempt property" means only a homestead or other exempt property that would be eligible to be set aside under Section 353.051 if the decedent's estate was being administered.

Estates Code § 252.201. Will Delivery

On receiving notice of a testator's death, the person who has custody of the testator's will shall deliver the will to the clerk of the court that has jurisdiction of the testator's estate.

Estates Code § 252.202. Personal Service on Custodian of Estate Papers

On a sworn written complaint that a person has custody of the last will of a testator or any papers belonging to the estate of a testator or intestate, the judge of the court that has jurisdiction of the estate shall have the person cited by personal service to appear and show cause why the person should not deliver:

(1) the will to the court for probate; or

(2) the papers to the executor or administrator.

Estates Code § 252.203. Arrest; Confinement

On the return of a citation served under Section 252.202, if the judge is satisfied that the person served with the citation had custody of the will or papers at the time the complaint under that section was filed and the person does not deliver the will or papers or show good cause why the will or papers have not been delivered, the judge may have the person arrested and confined until the person delivers the will or papers.

Estates Code § 256.001. Will Not Effective Until Probated

Except as provided by Subtitle K with respect to foreign wills, a will is not effective to prove title to, or the right to possession of, any property disposed of by the will until the will is admitted to probate.

Estates Code § 256.201. Admission of Will to Probate

If the court is satisfied on the completion of hearing an application for the probate of a will that the will should be admitted to probate, the court shall enter an order admitting the will to probate. Certified copies of the will and the order admitting the will to probate, or of the record of the will and order, and the record of testimony, may be:

(1) recorded in other counties; and

(2) used in evidence, as the originals may be used, on the trial of the same matter in any other court when taken to that court by appeal or otherwise.

Estates Code § 256.204. Period for Contest

(a) After a will is admitted to probate, an interested person may commence a suit to contest the validity thereof not later than the second anniversary of the date the will was admitted to probate, except that an interested person may commence a suit to cancel a will for forgery or other fraud not later than the second anniversary of the date the forgery or fraud was discovered.

(b) Notwithstanding Subsection (a), an incapacitated person may commence the contest under that subsection on or before the second anniversary of the date the person's disabilities are removed.

Estates Code § 257.001. Probate of Will as Muniment of Title Authorized

A court may admit a will to probate as a muniment of title if the court is satisfied that the will should be admitted to probate and the court:

(1) is satisfied that the testator's estate does not owe an unpaid debt, other than any debt secured by a lien on real estate; or

(2) finds for another reason that there is no necessity for administration of the estate.

Estates Code § 257.101. Declaratory Judgment Construing Will

(a) On application and notice as provided by Chapter 37, Civil Practice and Remedies Code, the court may hear evidence and include in an order probating a will as a muniment of title a declaratory judgment:

(1) construing the will, if a question of construction of the will exists; or

(2) determining those persons who are entitled to receive property under the will and the persons' shares or interests in the estate, if a person who is entitled to property under the provisions of the will cannot be ascertained solely by reference to the will.

(b) A declaratory judgment under this section is conclusive in any suit between a person omitted from the judgment and a bona fide purchaser for value who purchased property after entry of the judgment without actual notice of the claim of the omitted person to an interest in the estate.

(c) A person who delivered the testator's property to a person declared to be entitled to the property under the declaratory judgment under this section or engaged in any other transaction with the person in good faith after entry of the judgment is not liable to any person for actions taken in reliance on the judgment.

Estates Code § 301.151. General Proof Requirements

An applicant for the issuance of letters testamentary or of administration of an estate must prove to the court's satisfaction that:

(1) the person whose estate is the subject of the application is dead;

(2) except as provided by Section 301.002(b) with respect to administration necessary to receive or recover property due a decedent's estate, and Section 501.006 with respect to a foreign will, four years have not elapsed since the date of the decedent's death and before the application;

(3) the court has jurisdiction and venue over the estate;

(4) citation has been served and returned in the manner and for the period required by this title; and

(5) the person for whom letters testamentary or of administration are sought is entitled by law to the letters and is not disqualified.

Estates Code § 304.001. Order of Persons Qualified to Serve as Personal Representative

(a) The court shall grant letters testamentary or of administration to persons qualified to act, in the following order:

(1) the person named as executor in the decedent's will;

(2) the decedent's surviving spouse;

(3) the principal devisee of the decedent;

(4) any devisee of the decedent;

(5) the next of kin of the decedent;

(6) a creditor of the decedent;

(7) any person of good character residing in the county who applies for the letters;

(8) any other person who is not disqualified under Section 304.003; and

(9) any appointed public probate administrator.

(b) For purposes of Subsection (a)(5), the decedent's next of kin:

(1) is determined in accordance with order of descent, with the person nearest in order of descent first, and so on; and

(2) includes a person and the person's descendants who legally adopted the decedent or who have been legally adopted by the decedent.

(c) If persons are equally entitled to letters testamentary or of administration, the court:

(1) shall grant the letters to the person who, in the judgment of the court, is most likely to administer the estate advantageously; or

(2) may grant the letters to two or more of those persons.

Estates Code § 304.002. Renouncing Right to Serve as Personal Representative

A decedent's surviving spouse, or, if there is no surviving spouse, the heirs or any one of the heirs of the decedent to the exclusion of any person not equally entitled to letters testamentary or of administration, may renounce the right to the letters in favor of another qualified person in open court or by a power of attorney authenticated and filed with the county clerk of the county where the application for the letters is filed. After the right to the letters has been renounced, the court may grant the letters to the other qualified person.

Estates Code § 304.003. Persons Disqualified to Serve as Executor or Administrator

A person is not qualified to serve as an executor or administrator if the person is:

(1) incapacitated;

(2) a felon convicted under the laws of the United States or of any state of the United States unless, in accordance with law, the person has been pardoned or has had the person's civil rights restored;

(3) a nonresident of this state who:

(A) is a natural person or corporation; and

(B) has not:

(i) appointed a resident agent to accept service of process in all actions or proceedings with respect to the estate; or

(ii) had that appointment filed with the court;

(4) a corporation not authorized to act as a fiduciary in this state; or

(5) a person whom the court finds unsuitable.

Estates Code § 308.002. Required Notice to Certain Beneficiaries After Probate of Will

(a) Except as provided by Subsection (c), not later than the 60th day after the date of an order admitting a decedent's will to probate, the personal representative of the decedent's estate, including an independent executor or independent administrator, shall give notice that complies with Section 308.003 to each beneficiary named in the will whose identity and address are known to the representative or, through reasonable diligence, can be ascertained. If, after the 60th day after the date of the order, the representative becomes aware of the identity and address of a beneficiary who was not given notice on or before the 60th day, the representative shall give the notice as soon as possible after becoming aware of that information.

(b) Notwithstanding the requirement under Subsection (a) that the personal representative give the notice to the beneficiary, the representative shall give the notice with respect to a beneficiary described by this subsection as follows:

(1) if the beneficiary is a trustee of a trust, to the trustee, unless the representative is the trustee, in which case the representative shall, except as provided by Subsection (b-1), give the notice to the person or class of persons first eligible to receive the trust income, to be determined for purposes of this subdivision as if the trust were in existence on the date of the decedent's death;

(2) if the beneficiary has a court-appointed guardian or conservator, to that guardian or conservator;

(3) if the beneficiary is a minor for whom no guardian or conservator has been appointed, to a parent of the minor; and

(4) if the beneficiary is a charity that for any reason cannot be notified, to the attorney general.

(b-1) The personal representative is not required to give the notice otherwise required by Subsection (b)(1) to a person eligible to receive trust income at the sole discretion of the trustee of a trust if:

(1) the representative has given the notice to an ancestor of the person who has a similar interest in the trust; and

(2) no apparent conflict exists between the ancestor and the person eligible to receive trust income.

(c) A personal representative is not required to give the notice otherwise required by this section to a beneficiary who:

(1) has made an appearance in the proceeding with respect to the decedent's estate before the will was admitted to probate;

(2) is entitled to receive aggregate gifts under the will with an estimated value of $2,000 or less;

(3) has received all gifts to which the beneficiary is entitled under the will not later than the 60th day after the date of the order admitting the decedent's will to probate; or

(4) has received a copy of the will that was admitted to probate or a written summary of the gifts to the beneficiary under the will and has waived the right to receive the notice in an instrument that:

(A) either acknowledges the receipt of the copy of the will or includes the written summary of the gifts to the beneficiary under the will;

(B) is signed by the beneficiary; and

(C) is filed with the court.

(d) The notice required by this section must be sent by registered or certified mail, return receipt requested.

Estates Code § 308.003. Contents of Notice

The notice required by Section 308.002 must include:

(1) the name and address of the beneficiary to whom the notice is given or, for a beneficiary described by Section 308.002(b), the name and address of the beneficiary for whom the notice is given and of the person to whom the notice is given;

(2) the decedent's name;

(3) a statement that the decedent's will has been admitted to probate;

(4) a statement that the beneficiary to whom or for whom the notice is given is named as a beneficiary in the will;

(5) the personal representative's name and contact information; and

(6) either:

(A) a copy of the will that was admitted to probate and of the order admitting the will to probate; or

(B) a summary of the gifts to the beneficiary under the will, the court in which the will was admitted to probate, the docket number assigned to the estate, the date the will was admitted to probate, and, if different, the date the court appointed the personal representative.

Estates Code § 308.051. Required Notice Regarding Presentment of Claims in General

(a) Within one month after receiving letters testamentary or of administration, a personal representative of an estate shall provide notice requiring each person who has a claim against the estate to present the claim within the period prescribed by law by:

(1) having the notice published in a newspaper printed in the county in which the letters were issued; and

(2) if the decedent remitted or should have remitted taxes administered by the comptroller, sending the notice to the comptroller by certified or registered mail.

(b) Notice provided under Subsection (a) must include:

(1) the date the letters testamentary or of administration were issued to the personal representative;

(2) the address to which a claim may be presented; and

(3) an instruction of the representative's choice that the claim be addressed in care of:

(A) the representative;

(B) the representative's attorney; or

(C) "Representative, Estate of __________" (naming the estate).

(c) If a newspaper is not printed in the county in which the letters testamentary or of administration were issued, the notice must be posted and the return made and filed as otherwise required by this title.

Estates Code § 308.052. Proof of Publication

A copy of the published notice required by Section 308.051(a)(1), together with the publisher's affidavit, sworn to and subscribed before a proper officer, to the effect that the notice was published as provided in this title for the service of citation or notice by publication, shall be filed in the court in which the cause is pending.

Estates Code § 308.053. Required Notice to Secured Creditor

(a) Within two months after receiving letters testamentary or of administration, a personal representative of an estate shall give notice of the issuance of the letters to each person the representative knows to have a claim for money against the estate that is secured by estate property.

(b) Within a reasonable period after a personal representative obtains actual knowledge of the existence of a person who has a secured claim for money against the estate and to whom notice was not previously given, the representative shall give notice to the person of the issuance of the letters testamentary or of administration.

(c) Notice provided under this section must be:

(1) sent by certified or registered mail, return receipt requested; and

(2) addressed to the record holder of the claim at the record holder's last known post office address.

(d) The following shall be filed with the clerk of the court in which the letters testamentary or of administration were issued:

(1) a copy of each notice and of each return receipt; and

(2) the personal representative's affidavit stating:

(A) that the notice was mailed as required by law; and

(B) the name of the person to whom the notice was mailed, if that name is not shown on the notice or receipt.

Estates Code § 308.054. Permissive Notice to Unsecured Creditor

(a) At any time before an estate administration is closed, a personal representative may give notice by certified or registered mail, return receipt requested, to an unsecured creditor who has a claim for money against the estate.

(b) Notice given under Subsection (a) must:

(1) expressly state that the creditor must present the claim before the 121st day after the date of the receipt of the notice or the claim is barred, if the claim is not barred by the general statutes of limitation; and

(2) include:

(A) the date the letters testamentary or of administration held by the personal representative were issued to the representative;

(B) the address to which the claim may be presented; and

(C) an instruction of the representative's choice that the claim be addressed in care of:

(i) the representative;

(ii) the representative's attorney; or

(iii) "Representative, Estate of ________" (naming the estate).

Estates Code § 355.001. Presentment of Claim to Personal Representative

A claim may be presented to a personal representative of an estate at any time before the estate is closed if suit on the claim has not been barred by the general statutes of limitation.

Estates Code § 355.060. Unsecured Claims Barred Under Certain Circumstances

If a personal representative gives a notice permitted by Section 308.054 to an unsecured creditor for money and the creditor's claim is not presented before the 121st day after the date of receipt of the notice, the claim is barred.

Estates Code § 355.061. Allowing Barred Claim Prohibited: Court Disapproval

(a) A personal representative may not allow a claim for money against a decedent or the decedent's estate if a suit on the claim is barred:

(1) under Section 355.060, 355.064, or 355.201(b); or

(2) by an applicable general statute of limitation.

(b) A claim for money that is allowed by the personal representative shall be disapproved if the court is satisfied that the claim is barred, including because the limitation has run.

Estates Code § 355.102. Claims Classification; Priority of Payment

(a) Claims against an estate shall be classified and have priority of payment as provided by this section.

(b) Class 1 claims are composed of funeral expenses and expenses of the decedent's last illness for a reasonable amount approved by the court, not to exceed a total of $15,000. Any excess shall be classified and paid as other unsecured claims.

(c) Class 2 claims are composed of expenses of administration, expenses incurred in preserving, safekeeping, and managing the estate, including fees and expenses awarded under Section 352.052, and unpaid expenses of administration awarded in a guardianship of the decedent.

(d) Class 3 claims are composed of each secured claim for money under Section 355.151(a)(1), including a tax lien, to the extent the claim can be paid out of the proceeds of the property subject to the mortgage or other lien. If more than one mortgage, lien, or security interest exists on the same property, the claims shall be paid in order of priority of the mortgage, lien, or security interest securing the debt.

(e) Class 4 claims are composed of claims:

(1) for the principal amount of and accrued interest on delinquent child support and child support arrearages that have been:

(A) confirmed as a judgment or a determination of arrearages by a court under Title 5, Family Code; or

(B), administratively determined by the Title IV-D agency, as defined by Section 101.033, Family Code, in a Title IV-D case, as defined by Section 101.034, Family Code; and

(2) for unpaid child support obligations under Section 154.015, Family Code.

(f) Class 5 claims are composed of claims for taxes, penalties, and interest due under Title 2, Tax Code, Chapter 2153, Occupations Code, former Section 81.111, Natural Resources Code, the Municipal Sales and Use Tax Act (Chapter 321, Tax Code), Section 451.404, Transportation Code, or Subchapter I, Chapter 452, Transportation Code.

(g) Class 6 claims are composed of claims for the cost of confinement established by the Texas Department of Criminal Justice under Section 501.017, Government Code.

(h) Class 7 claims are composed of claims for repayment of medical assistance payments made by the state under Chapter 32, Human Resources Code, to or for the benefit of the decedent.

(i) Class 8 claims are composed of any other claims not described by Subsections (b)-(h).

Estates Code § 355.103. Priority of Certain Payments

When a personal representative has estate funds in the representative's possession, the representative shall pay in the following order:

(1) funeral expenses and expenses of the decedent's last illness, in an amount not to exceed $15,000;

(2) allowances made to the decedent's surviving spouse and children, or to either the surviving spouse or children;

(3) expenses of administration and expenses incurred in preserving, safekeeping, and managing the estate; and

(4) other claims against the estate in the order of the claims' classifications.

Estates Code § 401.001. Expression of Testator's Intent in Will

(a) Any person capable of making a will may provide in the person's will that no other action shall be had in the probate court in relation to the settlement of the person's estate than the probating and recording of the will and the return of any required inventory, appraisement, and list of claims of the person's estate.

(b) Any person capable of making a will may provide in the person's will that no independent administration of his or her estate may be allowed. In such case the person's estate, if administered, shall be administered and settled under the direction of the probate court as other estates are required to be settled and not as an independent administration.

Estates Code § 401.002. Creation in Testate Estate by Agreement

(a) Except as provided in Section 401.001(b), if a decedent's will names an executor but the will does not provide for independent administration as provided in Section 401.001(a), all of the distributees of the decedent may agree on the advisability of having an independent administration and collectively designate in the application for probate of the decedent's will, or in one or more separate documents consenting to the application for probate of the decedent's will, the executor named in the will to serve as independent executor and request that no other action shall be had in the probate court in relation to the settlement of the decedent's estate other than the probating and recording of the decedent's will and the return of an inventory, appraisement, and list of claims of the decedent's estate. In such case the probate court shall enter an order granting independent administration and appointing the person, firm, or corporation designated by the distributees as independent executor, unless the court finds that it would not be in the best interest of the estate to do so.

(b) Except as provided in Section 401.001(b), in situations where no executor is named in the decedent's will, or in situations where each executor named in the will is deceased or is disqualified to serve as executor or indicates by affidavit filed with the application for administration of the decedent's estate the executor's inability or unwillingness to serve as executor, all of the distributees of the decedent may agree on the advisability of having an independent administration and collectively designate in the application for probate of the decedent's will, or in one or more separate documents consenting to the application for probate of the decedent's will, a qualified person, firm, or corporation to serve as independent administrator and request that no other action shall be had in the probate court in relation to the settlement of the decedent's estate other than the probating and recording of the decedent's will and the return of an inventory, appraisement, and list of claims of the decedent's estate. In such case the probate court shall enter an order granting independent administration and appointing the person, firm, or corporation designated by the distributees as independent administrator, unless the court finds that it would not be in the best interest of the estate to do so.

Estates Code § 401.003. Creation in Intestate Estate by Agreement

(a) All of the distributees of a decedent dying intestate may agree on the advisability of having an independent administration and collectively designate in the application for administration of the decedent's estate, or in one or more documents consenting to the application for administration of the decedent's estate, a qualified person, firm, or corporation to serve as independent administrator and request that no other action shall be had in the probate court in relation to the settlement of the decedent's estate other than the return of an inventory, appraisement, and list of claims of the decedent's estate. In such case the probate court shall enter an order granting independent administration and appointing the person, firm, or corporation designated by the distributees as independent administrator, unless the court finds that it would not be in the best interest of the estate to do so.

(b) The court may not appoint an independent administrator to serve in an intestate administration unless and until the parties seeking appointment of the independent administrator have been determined, through a proceeding to declare heirship under Chapter 202, to constitute all of the decedent's heirs.

Estates Code § 401.005. Bond; Waiver of Bond

(a) If an independent administration of a decedent's estate is created under Section 401.002 or 401.003, then, unless the probate court waives bond on application for waiver, the independent executor shall be required to enter into bond payable to and to be approved by the judge and the judge's successors in a sum that is found by the judge to be adequate under all circumstances, or a bond with one surety in a sum that is found by the judge to be adequate under all circumstances, if the surety is an authorized corporate surety.

(b) This section does not repeal any other section of this title.

Estates Code § 402.001. General Scope and Exercise of Powers

When an independent administration has been created, and the order appointing an independent executor has been entered by the probate court, and the inventory, appraisement, and list of claims has been filed by the independent executor and approved by the court or an affidavit in lieu of the inventory, appraisement, and list of claims has been filed by the independent executor, as long as the estate is represented by an independent executor, further action of any nature may not be had in the probate court except where this title specifically and explicitly provides for some action in the court.

Estates Code § 402.002. Independent Executors May Act Without Court Approval

Unless this title specifically provides otherwise, any action that a personal representative subject to court supervision may take with or without a court order may be taken by an independent executor without a court order. The other provisions of this subtitle are designed to provide additional guidance regarding independent administrations in specified situations, and are not designed to limit by omission or otherwise the application of the general principles set forth in this chapter.

Estates Code § 403.001. Setting Aside Exempt Property and Allowances

The independent executor shall set aside and deliver to those entitled exempt property and allowances for support, and allowances in lieu of exempt property, as prescribed in this title, to the same extent and result as if the independent executor's actions had been accomplished in, and under orders of, the court.

Estates Code § 403.051. Duty of Independent Executor

(a) An independent executor, in the administration of an estate, independently of and without application to, or any action in or by the court:

(1) shall give the notices required under Sections 308.051 and 308.053;

(2) may give the notice to an unsecured creditor with a claim for money permitted under Section 308.054 and bar a claim under Section 403.055; and

(3) may approve or reject any claim, or take no action on a claim, and shall classify and pay claims approved or established by suit against the estate in the same order of priority, classification, and proration prescribed in this title.

(b) To be effective, the notice prescribed under Subsection (a)(2) must include, in addition to the other information required by Section 308.054, a statement that a claim may be effectively presented by only one of the methods prescribed by this subchapter.

Estates Code § 403.059. Enforcement of Claims by Suit

Any person having a debt or claim against the estate may enforce the payment of the same by suit against the independent executor; and, when judgment is recovered against the independent executor, the execution shall run against the estate of the decedent in the possession of the independent executor that is subject to the debt. The independent executor shall not be required to plead to any suit brought against the executor for money until after six months after the date that an independent administration was created and the order appointing the executor was entered by the probate court.

Estates Code § 404.001. Accounting

(a) At any time after the expiration of 15 months after the date that the court clerk first issues letters testamentary or of administration to any personal representative of an estate, any person interested in the estate may demand an accounting from the independent executor. The independent executor shall furnish to the person or persons making the demand an exhibit in writing, sworn and subscribed by the independent executor, setting forth in detail:

(1) the property belonging to the estate that has come into the executor's possession as executor;

(2) the disposition that has been made of the property described by Subdivision (1);

(3) the debts that have been paid;

(4) the debts and expenses, if any, still owing by the estate;

(5) the property of the estate, if any, still remaining in the executor's possession;

(6) other facts as may be necessary to a full and definite understanding of the exact condition of the estate; and

(7) the facts, if any, that show why the administration should not be closed and the estate distributed.

(a-1) Any other interested person shall, on demand, be entitled to a copy of any exhibit or accounting that has been made by an independent executor in compliance with this section.

(b) Should the independent executor not comply with a demand for an accounting authorized by this section within 60 days after receipt of the demand, the person making the demand may compel compliance by an action in the probate court. After a hearing, the court shall enter an order requiring the accounting to be made at such time as it considers proper under the circumstances.

(c) After an initial accounting has been given by an independent executor, any person interested in an estate may demand subsequent periodic accountings at intervals of not less than 12 months, and such subsequent demands may be enforced in the same manner as an initial demand.

(d) The right to an accounting accorded by this section is cumulative of any other remedies which persons interested in an estate may have against the independent executor of the estate.

Estates Code § 404.003. Removal of Independent Executor Without Notice

The probate court, on the court's own motion or on the motion of any interested person, and without notice, may remove an independent executor appointed under this subtitle when:

(1) the independent executor cannot be served with notice or other processes because:

(A) the independent executor's whereabouts are unknown;

(B) the independent executor is eluding service; or

(C) the independent executor is a nonresident of this state without a designated resident agent; or

(2) sufficient grounds appear to support a belief that the independent executor has misapplied or embezzled, or is about to misapply or embezzle, all or part of the property committed to the independent executor's care.

Estates Code § 404.0035. Removal of Independent Executor With Notice

(a) The probate court, on the court's own motion, may remove an independent executor appointed under this subtitle after providing 30 days' written notice of the court's intent to remove the independent executor, by certified mail, return receipt requested, to the independent executor's last known address and to the last known address of the independent executor's attorney of record, if the independent executor:

(1) neglects to qualify in the manner and time required by law; or

(2) fails to return, before the 91st day after the date the independent executor qualifies, either an inventory of the estate property and a list of claims that have come to the independent executor's knowledge or an affidavit in lieu of the inventory, appraisement, and list of claims, unless that deadline is extended by court order.

(b) The probate court, on its own motion or on motion of any interested person, after the independent executor has been cited by personal service to answer at a time and place fixed in the notice, may remove an independent executor when:

(1) the independent executor fails to make an accounting which is required by law to be made;

(2) the independent executor fails to timely file the affidavit or certificate required by Section 308.004;

(3) the independent executor is proved to have been guilty of gross misconduct or gross mismanagement in the performance of the independent executor's duties;

(4) the independent executor becomes an incapacitated person, or is sentenced to the penitentiary, or from any other cause becomes legally incapacitated from properly performing the independent executor's fiduciary duties; or

(5) the independent executor becomes incapable of properly performing the independent executor's fiduciary duties due to a material conflict of interest.

Estates Code § 404.0036. Removal Order

(a) The order of removal of an independent executor shall state the cause of removal and shall direct by order the disposition of the assets remaining in the name or under the control of the removed independent executor. The order of removal shall require that letters issued to the removed independent executor shall be surrendered and that all letters shall be canceled of record.

(b) If an independent executor is removed by the court under Section 404.003 or 404.0035, the court may, on application, appoint a successor independent executor as provided by Section 404.005.

Estates Code § 404.0037. Costs and Expenses Related to Removal of Independent Executor

(a) An independent executor who defends an action for the independent executor's removal in good faith, whether successful or not, shall be allowed out of the estate the independent executor's necessary expenses and disbursements, including reasonable attorney's fees, in the removal proceedings.

(b) Costs and expenses incurred by the party seeking removal that are incident to removal of an independent executor appointed without bond, including reasonable attorney's fees and expenses, may be paid out of the estate.

Chapter 2. Intestacy: An Estate Plan by Default

Section A. The Basic Scheme

Estates Code § 201.001. Estate of an Intestate Not Leaving Spouse

(a) If a person who dies intestate does not leave a spouse, the estate to which the person had title descends and passes in parcenary to the person's kindred in the order provided by this section.

(b) The person's estate descends and passes to the person's children and the children's descendants.

(c) If no child or child's descendant survives the person, the person's estate descends and passes in equal portions to the person's father and mother.

(d) If only the person's father or mother survives the person, the person's estate shall:

(1) be divided into two equal portions, with:

(A) one portion passing to the surviving parent; and

(B) one portion passing to the person's siblings and the siblings' descendants; or

(2) be inherited entirely by the surviving parent if there is no sibling of the person or siblings' descendants.

(e) If neither the person's father nor mother survives the person, the person's entire estate passes to the person's siblings and the siblings' descendants.

(f) If none of the kindred described by Subsections (b)-(e) survive the person, the person's estate shall be divided into two moieties, with:

(1) one moiety passing to the person's paternal kindred as provided by Subsection (g); and

(2) one moiety passing to the person's maternal kindred as provided by Subsection (h).

(g) The moiety passing to the person's paternal kindred passes in the following order:

(1) if both paternal grandparents survive the person, equal portions pass to the person's paternal grandfather and grandmother;

(2) if only the person's paternal grandfather or grandmother survives the person, the person's estate shall:

(A) be divided into two equal portions, with:

(i) one portion passing to the surviving grandparent; and

(ii) one portion passing to the descendants of the deceased grandparent; or

(B) pass entirely to the surviving grandparent if no descendant of the deceased grandparent survives the person; and

(3) if neither the person's paternal grandfather nor grandmother survives the person, the moiety passing to the decedent's paternal kindred passes to the descendants of the person's paternal grandfather and grandmother, and so on without end, passing in like manner to the nearest lineal ancestors and their descendants.

(h) The moiety passing to the person's maternal kindred passes in the same order and manner as the other moiety passes to the decedent's paternal kindred under Subsection (g).

Estates Code § 201.002. Separate Estate of an Intestate

(a) If a person who dies intestate leaves a surviving spouse, the estate, other than a community estate, to which the person had title descends and passes as provided by this section.

(b) If the person has one or more children or a descendant of a child:

(1) the surviving spouse takes one-third of the personal estate;

(2) two-thirds of the personal estate descends to the person's child or children, and the descendants of a child or children; and

(3) the surviving spouse is entitled to a life estate in one-third of the person's land, with the remainder descending to the person's child or children and the descendants of a child or children.

(c) Except as provided by Subsection (d), if the person has no child and no descendant of a child:

(1) the surviving spouse is entitled to all of the personal estate;

(2) the surviving spouse is entitled to one-half of the person's land without a remainder to any person; and

(3) one-half of the person's land passes and is inherited according to the rules of descent and distribution.

(d) If the person described by Subsection (c) does not leave a surviving parent or one or more surviving siblings, or their descendants, the surviving spouse is entitled to the entire estate.

Estates Code § 201.102. No Distinction Based on Property's Source

A distinction may not be made, in regulating the descent and distribution of an estate of a person dying intestate, between property derived by gift, devise, or descent from the intestate's father, and property derived by gift, devise, or descent from the intestate's mother.

Estates Code § 201.103. Treatment of Intestate's Estate

All of the estate to which an intestate had title at the time of death descends and vests in the intestate's heirs in the same manner as if the intestate had been the original purchaser.

Estates Code § 201.057. Collateral Kindred of Whole and Half Blood

If the inheritance from an intestate passes to the collateral kindred of the intestate and part of the collateral kindred are of whole blood and the other part are of half blood of the intestate, each of the collateral kindred who is of half blood inherits only half as much as that inherited by each of the collateral kindred who is of whole blood. If all of the collateral kindred are of half blood of the intestate, each of the collateral kindred inherits a whole portion.

Estates Code § 201.058. Convicted Persons

(a) No conviction shall work corruption of blood or forfeiture of estate except as provided by Subsection (b).

(b) If a beneficiary of a life insurance policy or contract is convicted and sentenced as a principal or accomplice in wilfully bringing about the death of the insured, the proceeds of the insurance policy or contract shall be paid in the manner provided by the Insurance Code.

Estates Code § 201.060. Alienage

A person is not disqualified to take as an heir because the person, or another person through whom the person claims, is or has been an alien.

Estates Code § 201.061. Estate of Person who Dies by Suicide

The estate of a person who commits suicide descends or vests as if the person died a natural death.

Estates Code § 201.101. Determination of Per Capita with Representation Distribution

(a) The children, descendants, brothers, sisters, uncles, aunts, or other relatives of an intestate who stand in the first or same degree of relationship alone and come into the distribution of the intestate's estate take per capita, which means by persons.

(b) If some of the persons described by Subsection (a) are dead and some are living, each descendant of those persons who have died is entitled to a distribution of the intestate's estate. Each descendant inherits only that portion of the property to which the parent through whom the descendant inherits would be entitled if that parent were alive.

Property Code § 71.001. Escheat

(a) If an individual dies intestate and without heirs, the real and personal property of that individual is subject to escheat.

(b) "Escheat" means the vesting of title to property in the state in an escheat proceeding under Subchapter B.

Property Code § 71.003. Presumption of Intestacy

An individual is presumed to have died intestate if, on or before the seventh anniversary of the date of the individual's death, the individual's will has not been recorded or probated in the county where the individual's property is located.

Section B. Community Property

Texas Constitution art. XVI, § 15. Separate and community property of husband and wife

Sec. 15. All property, both real and personal, of a spouse owned or claimed before marriage, and that acquired afterward by gift, devise or descent, shall be the separate property of that spouse; and laws shall be passed more clearly defining the rights of the spouses, in relation to separate and community property; provided that persons about to marry and spouses, without the intention to defraud pre-existing creditors, may by written instrument from time to time partition between themselves all or part of their property, then existing or to be acquired, or exchange between themselves the community interest of one spouse or future spouse in any property for the community interest of the other spouse or future spouse in other community property then existing or to be acquired, whereupon the portion or interest set aside to each spouse shall be and constitute a part of the separate property and estate of such spouse or future spouse; spouses also may from time to time, by written instrument, agree between themselves that the income or property from all or part of the separate property then owned or which thereafter might be acquired by only one of them, shall be the separate property of that spouse; if one spouse makes a gift of property to the other that gift is presumed to include all the income or property which might arise from that gift of property; spouses may agree in writing that all or part of their community property becomes the property of the surviving spouse on the death of a spouse; and spouses may agree in writing that all or part of the separate property owned by either or both of them shall be the spouses' community property.

Texas Constitution art. XVI, § 52. Descent and distribution of homestead; restrictions on partition

Sec. 52. On the death of the husband or wife, or both, the homestead shall descend and vest in like manner as other real property of the deceased, and shall be governed by the same laws of descent and distribution, but it shall not be partitioned among the heirs of the deceased during the lifetime of the surviving husband or wife, or so long as the survivor may elect to use or occupy the same as a homestead, or so long as the guardian of the minor children of the deceased may be permitted, under the order of the proper court having the jurisdiction, to use and occupy the same.

Family Code § 3.001. Separate Property

A spouse's separate property consists of:

(1) the property owned or claimed by the spouse before marriage;

(2) the property acquired by the spouse during marriage by gift, devise, or descent; and

(3) the recovery for personal injuries sustained by the spouse during marriage, except any recovery for loss of earning capacity during marriage.

Family Code § 3.002. Community Property

Community property consists of the property, other than separate property, acquired by either spouse during marriage.

Family Code § 3.003. Presumption of Community Property

(a) Property possessed by either spouse during or on dissolution of marriage is presumed to be community property.

(b) The degree of proof necessary to establish that property is separate property is clear and convincing evidence.

Family Code § 4.102. Partition or Exchange of Community Property

At any time, the spouses may partition or exchange between themselves all or part of their community property, then existing or to be acquired, as the spouses may desire. Property or a property interest transferred to a spouse by a partition or exchange agreement becomes that spouse's separate property. The partition or exchange of property may also provide that future earnings and income arising from the transferred property shall be the separate property of the owning spouse.

Family Code § 4.202. Agreement to Convert to Community Property

At any time, spouses may agree that all or part of the separate property owned by either or both spouses is converted to community property.

Family Code § 4.203. Formalities of Agreement

(a) An agreement to convert separate property to community property:

(1) must be in writing and:

(A) be signed by the spouses;

(B) identify the property being converted; and

(C) specify that the property is being converted to the spouses' community property; and

(2) is enforceable without consideration.

(b) The mere transfer of a spouse's separate property to the name of the other spouse or to the name of both spouses is not sufficient to convert the property to community property under this subchapter.

Estates Code § 201.003. Community Estate of an Intestate

(a) If a person who dies intestate leaves a surviving spouse, the community estate of the deceased spouse passes as provided by this section.

(b) The community estate of the deceased spouse passes to the surviving spouse if:

(1) no child or other descendant of the deceased spouse survives the deceased spouse; or

(2) all of the surviving children and descendants of the deceased spouse are also children or descendants of the surviving spouse.

(c) If the deceased spouse is survived by a child or other descendant who is not also a child or descendant of the surviving spouse, one-half of the community estate is retained by the surviving spouse and the other one-half passes to the deceased spouse's children or descendants. The descendants inherit only the portion of that estate to which they would be entitled under Section 201.101. In every case, the community estate passes charged with the debts against the community estate.

Section C. Simultaneous Death

Estates Code § 121.052. Required Period of Survival for Intestate Succession and Certain Other Purposes

A person who does not survive a decedent by 120 hours is considered to have predeceased the decedent for purposes of the homestead allowance, exempt property, and intestate succession, and the decedent's heirs are determined accordingly, except as otherwise provided by this chapter.

Estates Code § 121.053. Intestate Succession: Failure to Survive Presumed Under Certain Circumstances

A person who, if the person survived a decedent by 120 hours, would be the decedent's heir is considered not to have survived the decedent for the required period if:

(1) the time of death of the decedent or of the person, or the times of death of both, cannot be determined; and

(2) the person's survival for the required period after the decedent's death cannot be established.

Estates Code § 121.101. Required Period of Survival for Devisee

A devisee who does not survive the testator by 120 hours is treated as if the devisee predeceased the testator unless the testator's will contains some language that:

(1) deals explicitly with simultaneous death or deaths in a common disaster; or

(2) requires the devisee to survive the testator, or to survive the testator for a stated period, to take under the will.

Estates Code § 121.102. Required Period of Survival for Contingent Beneficiary

(a) If property is disposed of in a manner that conditions the right of a beneficiary to succeed to an interest in the property on the beneficiary surviving another person, the beneficiary is considered not to have survived the other person unless the beneficiary survives the person by 120 hours, except as provided by Subsection (b).

(b) If an interest in property is given alternatively to one of two or more beneficiaries, with the right of each beneficiary to take being dependent on that beneficiary surviving the other beneficiary or beneficiaries, and all of the beneficiaries die within a period of less than 120 hours, the property shall be divided into as many equal portions as there are beneficiaries. The portions shall be distributed respectively to those who would have taken if each beneficiary had survived.

Estates Code § 121.151. Distribution of Community Property

(a) This section applies to community property, including the proceeds of life or accident insurance that are community property and become payable to the estate of either the husband or wife.

(b) If a husband and wife die leaving community property but neither survives the other by 120 hours, one-half of all community property shall be distributed as if the husband had survived, and the other one-half shall be distributed as if the wife had survived.

Estates Code § 121.152. Distribution of Property Owned by Joint Owners

If property, including community property with a right of survivorship, is owned so that one of two joint owners is entitled to the whole of the property on the death of the other, but neither survives the other by 120 hours, one-half of the property shall be distributed as if one joint owner had survived, and the other one-half shall be distributed as if the other joint owner had survived. If there are more than two joint owners and all of the joint owners die within a period of less than 120 hours, the property shall be divided into as many equal portions as there are joint owners and the portions shall be distributed respectively to those who would have taken if each joint owner survived.

Estates Code § 121.153. Distribution of Certain Insurance Proceeds

(a) If the insured under a life or accident insurance policy and a beneficiary of the proceeds of that policy die within a period of less than 120 hours, the insured is considered to have survived the beneficiary for the purpose of determining the rights under the policy of the beneficiary or beneficiaries as such.

(b) This section does not prevent the applicability of Section 121.151 to proceeds of life or accident insurance that are community property.

Section D. Negative Wills and Disinheritance

Estates Code § 251.002. Interests That May Pass by Will; Disinheritance

. . .

(b) A person who makes a last will and testament may:

(1) disinherit an heir; and

(2) direct the disposition of property or an interest passing under the will or by intestacy.

Section E. The Meaning of "Children"

Family Code § 161.206. Order Terminating Parental Rights

(a) If the court finds by clear and convincing evidence grounds for termination of the parent-child relationship, it shall render an order terminating the parent-child relationship.

(b) Except as provided by Section 161.2061 [relating to limited post-termination conduct], an order terminating the parent-child relationship divests the parent and the child of all legal rights and duties with respect to each other, except that the child retains the right to inherit from and through the parent unless the court otherwise provides.

(c) Nothing in this chapter precludes or affects the rights of a biological or adoptive maternal or paternal grandparent to reasonable access under Chapter 153.

. . .

Family Code § 162.507. Effect of Adoption

(a) The adopted adult is the son or daughter of the adoptive parents for all purposes.

(b) The adopted adult is entitled to inherit from and through the adopted adult's adoptive parents as though the adopted adult were the biological child of the adoptive parents.

(c) The adopted adult may not inherit from or through the adult's biological parent. A biological parent may not inherit from or through an adopted adult.

Estates Code § 22.004. Child

(a) "Child" includes an adopted child, regardless of whether the adoption occurred through:

(1) an existing or former statutory procedure; or

(2) acts of estoppel.

(b) The term "child" does not include a child who does not have a presumed father unless a provision of this code expressly states that a child who does not have a presumed father is included.

Estates Code § 22.026. Next of Kin

"Next of kin" includes:

(1) an adopted child or the adopted child's descendants; and

(2) the adoptive parent of the adopted child.

Estates Code § 201.054. Adopted Child

(a) For purposes of inheritance under the laws of descent and distribution, an adopted child is regarded as the child of the adoptive parent or parents, and the adopted child and the adopted child's descendants inherit from and through the adoptive parent or parents and their kindred as if the adopted child were the natural child of the adoptive parent or parents. The adoptive parent or parents and their kindred inherit from and through the adopted child as if the adopted child were the natural child of the adoptive parent or parents.

(b) The natural parent or parents of an adopted child and the kindred of the natural parent or parents may not inherit from or through the adopted child, but the adopted child inherits from and through the child's natural parent or parents, except as provided by Section 162.507(c), Family Code.

(c) This section does not prevent an adoptive parent from disposing of the parent's property by will according to law.

(d) This section does not diminish the rights of an adopted child under the laws of descent and distribution or otherwise that the adopted child acquired by virtue of inclusion in the definition of "child" under Section 22.004.

Estates Code § 201.056. Persons Not in Being

No right of inheritance accrues to any person unless the person is born before, or is in gestation at, the time of the intestate's death and survives for at least 120 hours. A person is:

(1) considered to be in gestation at the time of the intestate's death if insemination or implantation occurs at or before the time of the intestate's death; and

(2) presumed to be in gestation at the time of the intestate's death if the person is born before the 301st day after the date of the intestate's death.

Estates Code § 201.062. Treatment of Certain Parent-Child Relationships

(a) A probate court may enter an order declaring that the parent of a child under 18 years of age may not inherit from or through the child under the laws of descent and distribution if the court finds by clear and convincing evidence that the parent has:

(1) voluntarily abandoned and failed to support the child in accordance with the parent's obligation or ability for at least three years before the date of the child's death, and did not resume support for the child before that date;

(2) voluntarily and with knowledge of the pregnancy:

(A) abandoned the child's mother beginning at a time during her pregnancy with the child and continuing through the birth;

(B) failed to provide adequate support or medical care for the mother during the period of abandonment before the child's birth; and

(C) remained apart from and failed to support the child since birth; or

(3) been convicted or has been placed on community supervision, including deferred adjudication community supervision, for being criminally responsible for the death or serious injury of a child under the following sections of the Penal Code or adjudicated under Title 3, Family Code, for conduct that caused the death or serious injury of a child and that would constitute a violation of one of the following sections of the Penal Code:

(A) Section 19.02 (murder);

(B) Section 19.03 (capital murder);

(C) Section 19.04 (manslaughter);

(D) Section 21.11 (indecency with a child);

(E) Section 22.01 (assault);

(F) Section 22.011 (sexual assault);

(G) Section 22.02 (aggravated assault);

(H) Section 22.021 (aggravated sexual assault);

(I) Section 22.04 (injury to a child, elderly individual, or disabled individual);

(J) Section 22.041 (abandoning or endangering child);

(K) Section 25.02 (prohibited sexual conduct);

(L) Section 43.25 (sexual performance by a child); or

(M) Section 43.26 (possession or promotion of child pornography).

(b) On a determination under Subsection (a) that the parent of a child may not inherit from or through the child, the parent shall be treated as if the parent predeceased the child for purposes of:

(1) inheritance under the laws of descent and distribution; and

(2) any other cause of action based on parentage.

Estates Code § 201.051. Maternal Inheritance

(a) For purposes of inheritance, a child is the child of the child's biological or adopted mother, and the child and the child's issue shall inherit from the child's mother and the child's maternal kindred, both descendants, ascendants, and collateral kindred in all degrees, and they may inherit from the child and the child's issue. However, if a child has intended parents, as defined by Section 160.102, Family Code, under a gestational agreement validated under Subchapter I, Chapter 160, Family Code, the child is the child of the intended mother and not the biological mother or gestational mother unless the biological mother is also the intended mother.

(b) This section does not permit inheritance by a child for whom no right of inheritance accrues under Section 201.056 or by the child's issue.

Estates Code § 201.052. Paternal Inheritance

(a) For purposes of inheritance, a child is the child of the child's biological father if:

(1) the child is born under circumstances described by Section 160.201, Family Code;

(2) the child is adjudicated to be the child of the father by court decree under Chapter 160, Family Code;

(3) the child was adopted by the child's father; or

(4) the father executed an acknowledgment of paternity under Subchapter D, Chapter 160, Family Code, or a similar statement properly executed in another jurisdiction.

(a-1) Notwithstanding Subsection (a), if a child has intended parents, as defined by Section 160.102, Family Code, under a gestational agreement validated under Subchapter I, Chapter 160, Family Code, the child is the child of the intended father and not the biological father unless the biological father is also the intended father.

(b) A child described by Subsection (a) or (a-1) and the child's issue shall inherit from the child's father and the child's paternal kindred, both descendants, ascendants, and collateral kindred in all degrees, and they may inherit from the child and the child's issue.

(c) A person may petition the probate court for a determination of right of inheritance from a decedent if the person:

(1) claims to be a biological child of the decedent and is not otherwise presumed to be a child of the decedent; or

(2) claims inheritance through a biological child of the decedent who is not otherwise presumed to be a child of the decedent.

(d) If under Subsection (c) the court finds by clear and convincing evidence that the purported father was the biological father of the child:

(1) the child is treated as any other child of the decedent for purposes of inheritance; and

(2) the child and the child's issue may inherit from the child's paternal kindred, both descendants, ascendants, and collateral kindred in all degrees, and they may inherit from the child and the child's issue.

(e) This section does not permit inheritance by a purported father of a child, recognized or not, if the purported father's parental rights have been terminated.

(f) This section does not permit inheritance by a child for whom no right of inheritance accrues under Section 201.056 or by the child's issue.

Presumption that mother's husband is child's father may be rebutted

WILSON ex rel. C.M.W. v. Estate of WILLIAMS
Court of Appeals of Texas, Waco
99 S.W.3d 640 (2003)

VANCE, J. This appeal is from an order that found Derrick Williams to be the father of a child identified as D.W.W. and determined who are Derrick's heirs. To aid in an understanding of the issues, we must first identify in some detail the parties and others who will be discussed in this opinion:

- Derrick Williams ("Derrick")—died intestate, at the age of thirty-seven, on September 3, 1998, after an industrial accident;

- C.M.W.—born on June 10, 1988, and acknowledged by all parties to be Derrick's child and an heir to his estate;

- Teresa Wilson ("Teresa")—C.M.W.'s mother, and a party to the proceedings as next friend for C.M.W.;

- Loretta Seals ("Loretta")—a party to the proceedings in her own right, advancing her claim to be Derrick's surviving spouse at the time of his death and thus an heir to his estate, and as next friend for D.W.W.;

- D.W.W. —born on March 26, 1992, and claimed by Loretta to be Derrick's child and an heir to his estate;

- Marceal Williams ("Marceal") —Derrick's mother;

- Debra Williams ("Debra") —Derrick's twin sister;

- Terry Williams ("Terry") —Derrick's brother;

- Michael Childress—Loretta's former husband; she and Michael were married in 1989; they were married at the time D.W.W. was born, but divorced several weeks later;

- Tyler Seals—Tyler and Loretta entered into a ceremonial marriage in Oklahoma after she and Derrick separated; and

- Charles O. Grigson ("Grigson")—an attorney serving as the temporary administrator of Derrick's estate at the time of trial.

Intestacy: An Estate Plan by Default

Both Teresa, on behalf of C.M.W., and Loretta, for herself and on behalf of D.W.W., filed applications under the Probate Code to determine heirship. Texas Probate Code § 48; Id. § 49. Loretta also asked the court to establish the parent-child relationship between Derrick and D.W.W. under the Family Code. The disputed part of the probate proceeding was transferred to the District Court of Leon County. Texas Probate Code § 5(b). After a bench trial, the court signed an order that (a) found that Derrick died without a written will, (b) found that Derrick was the father of D.W.W. and that Loretta was his common-law wife at the time of his death, and (c) declared that C.M.W., D.W.W., and Loretta are Derrick's heirs.

Teresa filed a notice of appeal. We will review her four issues as two broad questions: (1) Does the evidence establish that Loretta had an informal marriage to Derrick, so that the court was justified in finding her to be an heir?; and (2) Does the evidence establish that the parent-child relationship existed between Derrick and D.W.W., so that the court was justified in finding D.W.W. to be an heir? Because we find that Loretta was not barred from proving the existence of her informal marriage to Derrick and that Derrick consented in writing to be named and was named as father on D.W.W.'s birth certificate, we will affirm the order.

BACKGROUND

In March 1992, Loretta, who was then married to Michael Childress, gave birth to D.W.W. Loretta testified, however, that she had been separated from Michael for more than a year before D.W.W.'s birth, and she had been living with Derrick for most of that time. Although she testified that on one occasion, about nine months prior to D.W.W.'s birth, she had slept with a man whose name she could not recall, she maintained throughout her testimony that Derrick was D.W.W.'s father.

As to the informal marriage, Loretta testified that after her divorce from Michael became final, about five weeks after D.W.W.'s birth, she and Derrick agreed to marry, lived together, and held each other out as husband and wife.[1] In support of this testimony, Loretta also offered her mother's testimony and numerous exhibits, including canceled checks and medical records.

In addition, Loretta offered evidence that Derrick acknowledged D.W.W. as his son: D.W.W.'s birth certificate, which names Derrick as the father; an acknowledgment-of-paternity form signed by Derrick; and her testimony that Derrick chose D.W.W.'s name. There was no evidence from any source that Derrick rescinded or attempted to rescind his acknowledgment of paternity, or that he renounced fathering D.W.W.

---

[1] The statutes regarding informal marriage are codified at Texas Family Code §§ 2.401-2.405. Informal marriage is the statutory term used to describe what is colloquially known as a common-law marriage. We will use these terms interchangeably throughout this opinion.

In 1994, Loretta moved out of the house she and Derrick shared. Several months later she married Tyler Seals in a ceremonial marriage in Oklahoma. On September 3, 1998, Derrick died after an industrial accident that occurred approximately two weeks earlier.[2]

On February 20, 2001, Loretta was appointed temporary administrator of Derrick's estate. After Marceal intervened, seeking to replace Loretta as temporary administrator, the probate court found that both Loretta and Marceal had conflicts of interest and appointed Charles O. Grigson, an attorney, to serve as temporary administrator of Derrick's estate. The court further ordered each potential heir to file an application for determination of heirship. As we have noted, the district court tried the issues and entered the order appealed from.

FINDINGS OF FACT AND CONCLUSIONS OF LAW

The court entered the following Findings of Fact and Conclusions of Law that are applicable to the issues in the appeal:

- Loretta met the appropriate burden of proof to establish her informal marriage to Derrick under section 2.401(2) of the Family Code;

- Even if this proceeding were not commenced by the second anniversary of the date on which Loretta and Derrick separated, Loretta rebutted the presumption created by section 2.401(2)(b) of the Family Code;

- The informal marriage was established after Loretta was divorced from Michael Childress in 1992, was never dissolved by divorce, and was existing at the time of Derrick's death in 1998;

- Loretta's marriage to Tyler Seals was void under section 6.602(a) of the Family Code because of her then-existing marriage to Derrick; any presumption of its validity was rebutted; and that marriage became valid under section 6.202(b) after Derrick's death;

- Loretta is Derrick's surviving spouse and is entitled to rights of inheritance under section 38(b) of the Probate Code;

- Derrick voluntarily executed a Statement of Paternity under section 160.201 of the Family Code; the Statement is valid under sections 160.211 and 160.213 of the Family Code;

---

[2] We note that wrongful death and survivor claims brought by Marceal, C.M.W., and Loretta are currently pending in federal district court. The federal court has stayed its proceedings pending our resolution of this appeal. These claims represent by far the largest potential asset in Derrick's estate.

- Derrick is a presumed father of D.W.W. under sections 151.002(a)(3)(A) and 151.002(a)(3)(B) of the Family Code; that presumption was not rebutted by the evidence;

- Derrick consented in writing to be named as D.W.W.'s father on the child's birth certificate; he voluntarily signed the birth certificate;

- Derrick is the father of D.W.W. and D.W.W. is Derrick's child for all purposes; the parent-child relationship between Derrick and D.W.W. has been established by the appropriate burden of proof;

- D.W.W. is an heir of Derrick under section 42(b) of the Probate Code, entitled to inheritance rights under section 38(b)(1) of the Probate Code;

- The presumption that Michael Childress is the father of D.W.W. was rebutted by clear and convincing evidence; and

- No person with standing, or any representative with standing, contested with evidence any presumption that Derrick is the father of D.W.W. or produced an express statement denying paternity under section 160.101 of the Family Code. . . .

INFORMAL MARRIAGE AND HEIRSHIP

Teresa argues in two issues that the trial court erred in declaring Loretta an heir of Derrick and in finding that Loretta was Derrick's common-law spouse at his death. Teresa urges us to apply a former provision of the Family Code that created a one-year statute of limitations on suits to prove the existence of an informal marriage. . . . We find that the court properly applied § 2.401(b) as it existed at the time of trial, which created a rebuttable presumption, not a statute of limitations. . . . Teresa's first and second issues are overruled.

PATERNITY AND HEIRSHIP

In her third and fourth issues, Teresa complains that the court erred by finding that Derrick was D.W.W.'s father and by declaring D.W.W. to be Derrick's heir. These issues are intertwined because without a determination that Derrick was D.W.W.'s father, D.W.W. will be unable to show any entitlement to Derrick's estate.

Statutes in force at the time of death govern the disposition of the decedent's estate. Dickson v. Simpson, 807 S.W.2d 726, 727 (Tex. 1991). On September 3, 1998, the date of Derrick's death, § 42(b) of the Probate Code established that a child is the child of his biological father if one of four conditions was satisfied: (1) the child is born under circumstances described by Family Code § 151.002; (2) the child is adjudicated to be the child of the father by court decree as provided by Family Code Chapter 160; (3) the child was adopted by his father; or (4) the father executed a statement of paternity as provided by Family Code § 160.202.

Under the Probate Code, an heir's property rights vest immediately upon the death of a decedent. Texas Probate Code § 37 ("all the estate of such person, not devised or bequeathed, shall vest immediately in his heirs at law"). Some provisions of the Family Code were revised or repealed after 1998 and before trial. Because a change in the Family Code should not affect the status of a person who was an "heir" of the decedent under then-existing law, we will apply the version of the Family Code that was in effect in 1998 to resolve the issue of parentage, which we will address first. . . .

Presumptions of Paternity

Under § 151.002 of the 1998 version of the Family Code . . . [a] man is presumed to be the biological father of a child if:

> (1) he and the child's biological mother are or have been married to each other and the child is born during the marriage or not more than 300 days after the date the marriage terminated by death, annulment, or divorce or by having been declared void;
>
> (2) before the child's birth, he and the child's biological mother attempted to marry each other by a marriage in apparent compliance with law, although the attempted marriage is or could be declared void, and the child is born during the attempted marriage or not more than 300 days after the date the attempted marriage terminated by death, annulment, or divorce or by having been declared void;
>
> (3) after the child's birth, he and the child's biological mother have married or attempted to marry each other by a marriage in apparent compliance with law, although the attempted marriage is or could be declared void or voided by annulment, and;
>
>> (A) he has filed a written acknowledgment of his paternity of the child under Chapter 160;
>>
>> (B) he consents in writing to be named and is named as the child's father on the child's birth certificate; or
>>
>> (C) he is obligated to support the child under a written voluntary promise or by court order;
>
> (4) without attempting to marry the mother, he consents in writing to be named as the child's father on the child's birth certificate; or

> (5) before the child reaches the age of majority, he receives the child into his home and openly holds out the child as his biological child.

Id.

Because Loretta's divorce from Michael Childress was finalized only after D.W.W.'s birth, Michael was D.W.W.'s presumed father. Id. § 151.002(a)(1). However, Loretta testified that she had been separated from Michael for at least a year before D.W.W. was born,[3] and the court found that she proved she and Derrick informally married after her divorce from Michael. Furthermore, she introduced two documents that evidenced Derrick's acknowledgment of D.W.W. as his son: a birth certificate naming Derrick as D.W.W.'s father, and a preprinted Texas Department of Health acknowledgment-of-paternity form signed by Derrick. Therefore, Derrick is also the presumed father of D.W.W. under the 1998 Family Code. Id.

Under the 1998 Family Code, a presumption of paternity under § 151.002 could be rebutted only as provided by section 160.110, which dealt with the presumptions of paternity and the burden of proof. . . . Section 160.110(a) of the 1998 Family Code provided: "In a suit in which there is a presumption of parentage under Chapter 151, the party denying a presumed father's paternity of the child has the burden of rebutting the presumption of paternity by clear and convincing evidence." Id. . . . Thus, in order for Loretta to "prevail" on her determination-of-parentage claim (for the court to determine that Derrick was D.W.W.'s father), she must have rebutted the presumption that Michael is the father—and have proven facts creating the presumption that Derrick is D.W.W.'s father—by clear and convincing evidence. . . .

Rebutting the Presumption That Michael Is D.W.W.'s Father

Loretta testified that she did not have sexual relations with Michael during the probable time of D.W.W.'s conception. She testified that she did have sexual relations with Derrick during that time, and she also admitted to having had sexual relations one time with a man whose name she could not recall, approximately nine months prior to D.W.W.'s birth. No other direct evidence was admitted about whether Michael could be D.W.W.'s father.[4] Moreover, in a bench trial the judge, as factfinder, is the sole judge of the credibility of the witnesses and weight to be given their testimony. Dubree v. Blackwell, 67 S.W.3d 286, 289 (Tex. App.-

---

[3] Her testimony was that she had not had conjugal relations with Michael during the probable time of conception of D.W.W.

[4] The court rejected testimony from Robert Collins, Teresa's expert witness on D.N.A. testing. He testified that based on the results of D.N.A. testing of D.W.W., Loretta, Marceal, Debra, and Terry, he agreed with the finding that there was a zero percent probability that Derrick was D.W.W.'s father. However, he also testified at one point, "So I have not determined the parentage of a child because that is not my job. My job is to find disease causing genes . . . ."

Amarillo 2001, no pet.); Leyva v. Pacheco, 163 Tex. 638, 358 S.W.2d 547, 549 (1962). If the judge found Loretta's testimony to be credible, he could have reasonably formed a firm belief or conviction about the truth of her claim that Derrick, not Michael, had fathered D.W.W. . . .

Derrick signed a statement of paternity that recited the following: "I, Derrick W. Williams, now residing at P.O. Box 575, Teague, Texas, 75860, acknowledge that I am the father of the following child: [D.W.W.] born 3-26-92 at Navarro, Texas to Loretta Jean Tate and request that I be named as the father of the child on the certificate of birth. I was not married to the mother of the child at the time of conception of the child or at any subsequent time. The child is not the biological child of any other man." It was signed and sworn to on March 27, 1992. Derrick's name appears as the father on the birth certificate. Both the statement of paternity and the birth certificate were admitted into evidence without objection. Based on this evidence the judge could have reasonably formed a firm belief or conviction about the truth of Loretta's claim . . . .

Because we have found (a) that Loretta rebutted the presumption that Michael was D.W.W.'s father, (b) that she presented sufficient evidence to create the presumption that Derrick was D.W.W.'s father, and (c) no one with standing rebutted that presumption, we find no fault with the judgment insofar as it found D.W.W. to be Derrick's child. Teresa's third issue is overruled. . . .

Heirship

Teresa contends, however, that even if D.W.W. is *presumed* to be Derrick's child under the Family Code, he is, nevertheless, precluded from inheriting from Derrick by the plain language of the Probate Code. Section 42(b) of the 1998 Probate Code provided: "Paternal Inheritance. (1) For the purpose of inheritance, a child is the child of his *biological* father if . . . ." ([e]mphasis added). Teresa reasons that in order for D.W.W. to inherit from Derrick, he must prove a biological connection. To that end, Teresa argues that the court erred by excluding a D.N.A. parentage test report, which Teresa claims disproves any biological link between Derrick and D.W.W. . . .

Error may be predicated on a ruling that excludes a party's evidence only if the substance of the evidence was made known to the court by offer. . . . An offer of proof is sufficient if it apprised the court of the substance of the testimony and may be presented in the form of a concise statement. Chance v. Chance, 911 S.W.2d 40, 51-52 (Tex. App.-Beaumont 1995, writ denied). Excluded evidence also may be preserved for appellate review by a post-trial bill of exception. Texas Rule of Appellate Procedure 33.2. . . . Teresa offered the report into evidence twice, and both times the court sustained Loretta's objections and excluded it. Teresa first offered the report during cross-examination of Loretta and again offered it during the testimony of Collins, the expert who testified about D.N.A. testing. Although some of the substance of the report is apparent in the record of Collins's testimony, there was no offer of proof of the report itself.[5] Therefore, Teresa has waived her complaint and the D.N.A. parentage test report is not before this court.[6]

Biological Father Under the Probate Code

Moreover, we note that we do not read the Probate Code to require proof of a biological link. Rather we interpret section 42(b) as *defining* what a biological father is. Under 42(b) a biological father includes a man who has adopted a child. We do not readily conceive of a situation where a father would adopt a child who is his biological child,[7] especially in light of the procedures in the Family Code that would allow such a man to maintain a suit to adjudicate his parentage of the child. See Texas Family Code §§ 160.201-.316. Therefore, we interpret section 42(b) to include all adoptions. Although adopting a child creates a relationship in law, it does not create a relationship in blood. Therefore, we conclude that D.W.W. did not need to establish an actual "biological" link to Derrick to be considered the "child of his biological father" and to be entitled to inherit from him. Derrick satisfied one of the provisions of section 42(b), and the court properly found him to be D.W.W.'s father. Accordingly, we hold that the court did not err in declaring D.W.W. to be an heir of Derrick. Teresa's fourth issue is overruled.

CONCLUSION

Having overruled each of Teresa's issues, we affirm the order of the district court.

Section F. Transfers to Children: Advancements

Estates Code § 201.151. Determination of Advancement; Date of Valuation

(a) If a decedent dies intestate as to all or part of the decedent's estate, property that the decedent gave during the decedent's lifetime to a person who, on the date of the decedent's death, is the decedent's heir, or property received by the decedent's heir under a nontestamentary transfer under Subchapter B, Chapter 111, or Chapter 112 or 113, is an advancement against the heir's intestate share of the estate only if:

---

[5] Although a copy of the D.N.A. parentage report is included in the bound reporter's record, our review of the record fails to disclose that Teresa made an offer of proof or post-trial bill of exception of the report itself.

[6] Subchapter F of Chapter 160 of the 2001 Family Code now provides specific guidance for genetic testing to determine parentage, including the testing of ancestors or collateral kindred when a putative parent is unavailable for testing. Texas Family Code §§ 160.501-.511.

[7] At oral argument, Teresa argued that in the context of section 42(b) adoption referred only to the situation where a father adopted his own child. We disagree.

(1) the decedent declared in a contemporaneous writing, or the heir acknowledged in writing, that the gift or nontestamentary transfer is an advancement; or

(2) the decedent's contemporaneous writing or the heir's written acknowledgment otherwise indicates that the gift or nontestamentary transfer is to be considered in computing the division and distribution of the decedent's intestate estate.

(b) For purposes of Subsection (a), property that is advanced is valued as of the earlier of:

(1) the time that the heir came into possession or enjoyment of the property; or

(2) the time of the decedent's death.

Estates Code § 201.152. Survival of Recipient Required

If the recipient of property described by Section 201.151 does not survive the decedent, the property is not considered in computing the division and distribution of the decedent's intestate estate unless the decedent's contemporaneous writing provides otherwise.

Section G. Disclaimer

Estates Code § 122.002. Who May Disclaim

(a) A person who may be entitled to receive property as a beneficiary who on or after September 1, 1977, intends to irrevocably disclaim all or any part of the property shall evidence the disclaimer as provided by this chapter.

(b) Subject to Subsection (c), the legally authorized representative of a person who may be entitled to receive property as a beneficiary who on or after September 1, 1977, intends to irrevocably disclaim all or any part of the property on the beneficiary's behalf shall evidence the disclaimer as provided by this chapter.

(c) A disclaimer made by a legally authorized representative described by Subsection (d)(1), (2), or (3), other than an independent executor, must be made with prior court approval of the court that has or would have jurisdiction over the legally authorized representative. A disclaimer made by an independent executor on behalf of a decedent may be made without prior court approval.

(d) In this section, "legally authorized representative" means:

(1) a guardian if the person entitled to receive the property as a beneficiary is an incapacitated person;

(2) a guardian ad litem if the person entitled to receive the property as a beneficiary is an unborn or unascertained person;

(3) a personal representative, including an independent executor, if the person entitled to receive the property as a beneficiary is a decedent; or

(4) an attorney in fact or agent appointed under a durable power of attorney authorizing disclaimers if the person entitled to receive the property as a beneficiary executed the power of attorney as a principal.

Estates Code § 122.003. Effective Date; Creditors' Claims.

(a) A disclaimer evidenced as provided by this chapter is effective for all purposes as of the date of the decedent's death.

(b) Property disclaimed in accordance with this chapter is not subject to the claims of a creditor of the disclaimant.

Estates Code § 122.051. Form and Contents

(a) A disclaimer of property receivable by a beneficiary must be evidenced by written memorandum acknowledged before:

(1) a notary public; or

(2) another person authorized to take acknowledgments of conveyances of real estate.

(b) A disclaimer of property receivable by a beneficiary must include a statement regarding whether the beneficiary is a child support obligor described by Section 122.107.

Estates Code § 122.055. Filing Deadline

(a) Except as provided by Subsection (c), a written memorandum of disclaimer of a present interest must be filed not later than nine months after the date of the decedent's death.

(b) Except as provided by Subsection (c), a written memorandum of disclaimer of a future interest may be filed not later than nine months after the date of the event determining that the taker of the property or interest is finally ascertained and the taker's interest is indefeasibly vested.

(c) If the beneficiary is a charitable organization or a governmental agency of the state, a written memorandum of disclaimer of a present or future interest must be filed not later than the later of:

(1) the first anniversary of the date the beneficiary receives the notice required by Subchapter A, Chapter 308; or

(2) the expiration of the six-month period following the date the personal representative files:

(A) the inventory, appraisement, and list of claims due or owing to the estate; or

(B) the affidavit in lieu of the inventory, appraisement, and list of claims.

Estates Code § 122.056. Notice

(a) Except as provided by Subsection (b), a copy of the written memorandum of disclaimer shall be delivered in person to, or mailed by registered or certified mail to and received by, the legal representative of the transferor of the interest or the holder of legal title to the property to which the disclaimer relates not later than nine months after:

(1) the date of the decedent's death; or

(2) if the interest is a future interest, the date the person who will receive the property or interest is finally ascertained and the person's interest is indefeasibly vested.

(b) If the beneficiary is a charitable organization or a governmental agency of this state, notice of a disclaimer required by Subsection (a) must be filed not later than the later of:

(1) the first anniversary of the date the beneficiary receives the notice required by Subchapter A, Chapter 308; or

(2) the expiration of the six-month period following the date the personal representative files:

(A) the inventory, appraisement, and list of claims due or owing to the estate; or

(B) the affidavit in lieu of the inventory, appraisement, and list of claims.

Estates Code § 122.101. Effect

Unless the decedent's will provides otherwise:

(1) property subject to a disclaimer passes as if the person disclaiming or on whose behalf a disclaimer is made had predeceased the decedent; and

(2) a future interest that would otherwise take effect in possession or enjoyment after the termination of the estate or interest that is disclaimed takes effect as if the disclaiming beneficiary had predeceased the decedent.

Estates Code § 122.102. Ineffective Disclaimer

(a) Except as provided by Subsection (b), a disclaimer that does not comply with this chapter is ineffective.

(b) A disclaimer otherwise ineffective under Subsection (a) is effective as an assignment of the disclaimed property to those who would have received the property had the person attempting the disclaimer died before the decedent.

Estates Code § 122.104. Disclaimer after Acceptance

A disclaimer is not effective if the person making the disclaimer has previously accepted the property by taking possession or exercising dominion and control of the property as a beneficiary.

Estates Code § 122.107. Attempted Disclaimers by Certain Child Support Obligors Ineffective

(a) A disclaimer made by a beneficiary who is a child support obligor of estate property that could be applied to satisfy the beneficiary's child support obligation is not effective if the beneficiary owes child support arrearages that have been:

(1) administratively determined by the Title IV-D agency as defined by Section 101.033, Family Code, in a Title IV-D case as defined by Section 101.034, Family Code; or

(2) confirmed and reduced to judgment as provided by Section 157.263, Family Code.

(b) After distribution of estate property to a beneficiary described by Subsection (a), the child support obligee to whom the child support arrearages are owed may enforce the child support obligation by a lien or by any other remedy provided by law.

Chapter 3. Wills: Formalities and Forms

Section A. Attested Wills

Estates Code § 251.001. Who May Execute Will

Under the rules and limitations prescribed by law, a person of sound mind has the right and power to make a last will and testament if, at the time the will is made, the person:

(1) is 18 years of age or older;

(2) is or has been married; or

(3) is a member of the armed forces of the United States, an auxiliary of the armed forces of the United States, or the United States Maritime Service.

Estates Code § 251.051. Written, Signed, and Attested

Except as otherwise provided by law, a last will and testament must be:

(1) in writing;

(2) signed by:

(A) the testator in person; or

(B) another person on behalf of the testator:

(i) in the testator's presence; and

(ii) under the testator's direction; and

(3) attested by two or more credible witnesses who are at least 14 years of age and who subscribe their names to the will in their own handwriting in the testator's presence.

Estates Code § 251.053. Exception for Foreign and Certain Other Wills

Section 251.051 does not apply to a written will executed in compliance with:

(1) the law of the state or foreign country where the will was executed, as that law existed at the time of the will's execution; or

(2) the law of the state or foreign country where the testator was domiciled or had a place of residence, as that law existed at the time of the will's execution or at the time of the testator's death.

Estates Code § 251.101. Self-Proved Will

A self-proved will is a will:

(1) to which a self-proving affidavit subscribed and sworn to by the testator and witnesses is attached or annexed; or

(2) that is simultaneously executed, attested, and made self-proved as provided by Section 251.1045.

Estates Code § 251.102. Probate and Treatment of Self-Proved Will

(a) A self-proved will may be admitted to probate without the testimony of any subscribing witnesses if:

(1) the testator and witnesses execute a self-proving affidavit; or

(2) the will is simultaneously executed, attested, and made self-proved as provided by Section 251.1045.

(b) A self-proved will may not otherwise be treated differently than a will that is not self-proved.

Estates Code § 251.103. Period for Making Attested Wills Self-Proved

A will or testament that meets the requirements of Section 251.051 may be made self-proved at:

(1) the time of the execution of the will or testament; or

(2) a later date during the lifetime of the testator and the witnesses.

Estates Code § 251.104. Requirements for Self-Proving Affidavit

(a) An affidavit that is in form and content substantially as provided by Subsection (e) is a self-proving affidavit.

(b) A self-proving affidavit must be made by the testator and by the attesting witnesses before an officer authorized to administer oaths. The officer shall affix the officer's official seal to the self-proving affidavit.

(c) The self-proving affidavit shall be attached or annexed to the will or testament.

(d) An affidavit that is in substantial compliance with the form of the affidavit provided by Subsection (e), that is subscribed and acknowledged by the testator, and that is subscribed and sworn to by the attesting witnesses is sufficient to self-prove the will. No other affidavit or certificate of a testator is required to self-prove a will or testament other than the affidavit provided by Subsection (e).

(e) The form and content of the self-proving affidavit must be substantially as follows:

THE STATE OF TEXAS
COUNTY OF ________________
Before me, the undersigned authority, on this day personally appeared ________________, ________________, and ________________, known to me to be the testator and the witnesses, respectively, whose names are subscribed to the annexed or foregoing instrument in their respective capacities, and, all of said persons being by me duly sworn, the said ________________, testator, declared to me and to the said witnesses in my presence that said instrument is [his/her] last will and testament, and that [he/she] had willingly made and executed it as [his/her] free act and deed; and the said witnesses, each on [his/her] oath stated to me, in the presence and hearing of the said testator, that the said testator had declared to them that said instrument is [his/her] last will and testament, and that [he/she] executed same as such and wanted each of them to sign it as a witness; and upon their oaths each witness stated further that they did sign the same as witnesses in the presence of the said testator and at [his/her] request; that [he/she] was at that time eighteen years of age or over (or being under such age, was or had been lawfully married, or was then a member of the armed forces of the United States, or an auxiliary of the armed forces of the United States, or the United States Maritime Service) and was of sound mind; and that each of said witnesses was then at least fourteen years of age.

____
Testator

____
Witness

____
Witness
Subscribed and sworn to before me by the said ____________, testator, and by the said ________________ and ________________, witnesses, this ______ day of ________________ A.D. ________________.
(SEAL)
(Signed) ________________________________
(Official Capacity of Officer)

Estates Code § 251.1045. Simultaneous Execution, Attestation, and Self-Proving

(a) As an alternative to the self-proving of a will by the affidavits of the testator and the attesting witnesses as provided by Section 251.104, a will may be simultaneously executed, attested, and made self-proved before an officer authorized to administer oaths, and the testimony of the witnesses in the probate of the will may be made unnecessary, with the inclusion in the will of the following in form and contents substantially as follows:

I, ________________________, as testator, after being duly sworn, declare to the undersigned witnesses and to the undersigned authority that this instrument is my will, that I willingly make and execute it in the presence of the undersigned witnesses, all of whom are present at the same time, as my free act and deed, and that I request each of the undersigned witnesses to sign this will in my presence and in the presence of each other. I now sign this will in the presence of the attesting witnesses and the undersigned authority on this ______ day of __________, 20________________.

____

Testator
The undersigned, __________ and __________, each being at least fourteen years of age, after being duly sworn, declare to the testator and to the undersigned authority that the testator declared to us that this instrument is the testator's will and that the testator requested us to act as witnesses to the testator's will and signature. The testator then signed this will in our presence, all of us being present at the same time. The testator is eighteen years of age or over (or being under such age, is or has been lawfully married, or is a member of the armed forces of the United States or of an auxiliary of the armed forces of the United States or of the United States Maritime Service), and we believe the testator to be of sound mind. We now sign our names as attesting witnesses in the presence of the testator, each other, and the undersigned authority on this __________ day of __________, 20______________.

____

Witness

____

Witness
Subscribed and sworn to before me by the said __________, testator, and by the said ______________ and ______________, witnesses, this _____ day of __________, 20_____________.
(SEAL)
(Signed)___________________
(Official Capacity of Officer)

(b) A will that is in substantial compliance with the form provided by Subsection (a) is sufficient to self-prove a will.

Estates Code § 251.105. Effect of Signature on Self-Proving Affidavit

A signature on a self-proving affidavit is considered a signature to the will if necessary to prove that the will was signed by the testator or witnesses or both, except that, in that case, the will may not be considered a self-proved will.

Estates Code § 251.106. Contest, Revocation, or Amendment of Self-Proved Will

A self-proved will may be contested, revoked, or amended by a codicil in the same manner as a will that is not self-proved.

Estates Code § 254.002. Bequests to Certain Subscribing Witness

(a) Except as provided by Subsection (c), if a devisee under a will is also a subscribing witness to the will and the will cannot be otherwise established:

(1) the bequest is void; and

(2) the subscribing witness shall be allowed and compelled to appear and give the witness's testimony in the same manner as if the bequest to the witness had not been made.

(b) Notwithstanding Subsection (a), if the subscribing witness described by that subsection would have been entitled to a share of the testator's estate had the testator died intestate, the witness is entitled to as much of that share as does not exceed the value of the bequest to the witness under the will.

(c) If the testimony of a subscribing witness described by Subsection (a) proving the will is corroborated by at least one disinterested and credible person who testifies that the subscribing witness's testimony is true and correct:

(1) the bequest to the subscribing witness is not void under Subsection (a); and

(2) the subscribing witness is not regarded as an incompetent or noncredible witness under Subchapters B and C, Chapter 251.

Estates Code § 256.153. Proof of Execution of Attested Will

(a) An attested will produced in court that is not self-proved as provided by this title may be proved in the manner provided by this section.

(b) A will described by Subsection (a) may be proved by the sworn testimony or affidavit of one or more of the subscribing witnesses to the will taken in open court.

(c) If all the witnesses to a will described by Subsection (a) are nonresidents of the county or the witnesses who are residents of the county are unable to attend court, the will may be proved:

(1) by the sworn testimony of one or more of the witnesses by written or oral deposition taken in accordance with Section 51.203 or the Texas Rules of Civil Procedure;

(2) if no opposition in writing to the will is filed on or before the date set for the hearing on the will, by the sworn testimony or affidavit of two witnesses taken in open court, or by deposition as provided by Subdivision (1), to the signature or the handwriting evidenced by the signature of:

(A) one or more of the attesting witnesses; or

(B) the testator, if the testator signed the will; or

(3) if it is shown under oath to the court's satisfaction that, after a diligent search was made, only one witness can be found who can make the required proof, by the sworn testimony or affidavit of that witness taken in open court, or by deposition as provided by Subdivision (1), to a signature, or the handwriting evidenced by a signature, described by Subdivision (2).

(d) If none of the witnesses to a will described by Subsection (a) are living, or if each of the witnesses is a member of the armed forces or the armed forces reserves of the United States, an auxiliary of the armed forces or armed forces reserves, or the United States Maritime Service and is beyond the court's jurisdiction, the will may be proved:

(1) by two witnesses to the handwriting of one or both of the subscribing witnesses to the will or the testator, if the testator signed the will, by:

(A) sworn testimony or affidavit taken in open court; or

(B) written or oral deposition taken in the same manner and under the same rules as depositions are taken in other civil actions; or

(2) if it is shown under oath to the court's satisfaction that, after a diligent search was made, only one witness can be found who can make the required proof, by the sworn testimony or affidavit of that witness taken in open court, or by deposition as provided by Subdivision (1), to a signature or the handwriting described by Subdivision (1).

(e) A witness being deposed for purposes of proving the will as provided by Subsection (c) or (d) may testify by referring to a certified copy of the will, without the judge requiring the original will to be removed from the court's file and shown to the witness.

Section B. Curative Doctrines

Texas does not apply doctrine of substantial compliance to improperly attested wills

Estate of IVERSEN
Court of Appeals of Texas, Fort Worth
150 S.W.3d 824 (2004)

McCOY, J. Appellants Jorgen Nylund, Linda Nylund Klev, and Wendy Nylund ("Nylund") appeal from the probate court's judgment admitting to probate the purported will of Lars Ingerman Iversen a/k/a Lars Ingermann Iversen ("Iversen") and appointing Anna E. Iversen Schoenwandt ("Schoenwandt") as independent administratrix. In a single point, Nylund complains that the will is not competent under section 59(a) of the Texas Probate Code ("the Code") to direct distribution of Iversen's property and to designate a legal representative of his estate. We will reverse and remand to the probate court.

I. FACTUAL AND PROCEDURAL BACKGROUND

Iversen was twice married. His first marriage ended in divorce in 1975, and likewise, the second marriage to Schoenwandt ended in divorce in 1993. Thereafter, Iversen remained unmarried until the time of his death on August 27, 2003 in Lewisville, Texas at the age of fifty-nine. The Nylund appellants are children of his first marriage. In a document dated April 2, 2000, which is the subject of this appeal, Iversen bequeathed all of his possessions to Schoenwandt as his sole beneficiary, giving her full power of attorney in all of his affairs. The one-page typed document contains Iversen's signature, which is notarized. The purported will was admitted to probate in the Denton County Probate Court, and Schoenwandt was appointed independent administratrix. Nylund subsequently filed an Opposition to Probate Will and to Issuance of Letters Testamentary and Petition for a Determination of Heirship, asserting that the purported will is not valid due to the lack of two attesting witnesses as required by the Code and that the decedent's property should therefore pass intestate. Nylund further asserted that Schoenwandt is not a proper person to serve in the capacity as independent administratrix.

It is undisputed that the purported will does not contain the signatures of two attesting witnesses. Nevertheless, affidavits of Schoenwandt's stepdaughter Catherine Tincher and daughter-in-law Melody Schoenwandt were admitted, wherein they testified that they saw Iversen sign the will and that he declared his property should pass to Schoenwandt. The probate court found that the affidavit testimony reflected Iversen's testamentary intent and constituted "substantial compliance" with section 59(a) of the Code, id., ordered the will admitted to probate, and appointed Schoenwandt as independent administratrix. This appeal followed.

II. LEGAL ANALYSIS

The requirements of section 59(a) of the Code are straight-forward. Subsection (a) requires that a written, nonholographic will (1) be signed by the testator in person or by another person for him at his direction and in his presence, and (2) be attested by two or more credible witnesses above the age of fourteen "who shall subscribe their names thereto in their own handwriting in the presence of the testator." Texas Probate Code § 59(a). While a notary has been held to account for one attesting witness, see Reagan v. Bailey, 626 S.W.2d 141, 142 (Tex. App.-Fort Worth 1981, writ ref'd n.r.e.), it is undisputed that the requirement of two attesting witnesses was not met in this case. The same section of the Code also allows the will to be self-proven; that is, the testimony of the attesting witnesses becomes unnecessary in the probate of the will if affidavits of the testator and the witnesses are made in "substantial compliance" with an affidavit form prescribed in section 59(b) of the Code. Subsection (b) reads as follows:

> An affidavit in *form* and content *substantially* as provided by Subsection (a) of this section is a "self-proving affidavit." A will with a self-proving affidavit subscribed and sworn to by the testator and witnesses attached or annexed to the will is a "self-proved will."[1] *Substantial compliance* with the *form* of such affidavit shall suffice to cause the will to be self-proved. For this purpose, an affidavit that is subscribed and acknowledged by the testator and subscribed and sworn to by the witnesses would suffice as being in substantial compliance. A signature on a self-proving affidavit is considered a signature to the will if necessary to prove that the will was signed by the testator or witnesses, or both, but in that case, the will may not be considered a self-proved will.

Texas Probate Code § 59(b) (emphasis supplied). Nowhere in this section, or any other, is there any mention of "substantial compliance" with the attesting signature requirements of the will itself contained in section 59(a). Further, no self-proving affidavits were offered in this case.

None of the cases cited by Schoenwandt stand for the principle that "substantial compliance" is sufficient for the attesting witness requirement of a written nonholographic will not accompanied by a self-proving affidavit.

---

[1] The Texas legislature has since changed the law to allow wills to be simultaneously executed, attested, and made self-proved. See Tex. Estates Code § 251.1045 (effective 2014). — Ed.

III. CONCLUSION

Therefore, we hold that the probate court erred in ruling that "substantial compliance" in the form of affidavit testimony is sufficient to satisfy the attesting witness requirements of section 59(a) of the Code. We sustain Nylund's issue, reverse the probate court's judgment, and remand the case for proceedings consistent with this opinion.

Section C. Notarized Wills

Notary may serve as a subscribing witness to a will

Estate of TEAL
Court of Appeals of Texas, Corpus Christi-Edinburg
135 S.W.3d 87 (2002)

YANEZ, J. This appeal is brought to challenge the admission of the will of Ronald Teal to probate. We affirm.

BACKGROUND

On August 4, 1987, Ronald Teal signed the will at issue in this appeal. In 1990, Teal married appellant, and he remained married to her until his death in October, 1999. Appellant was in California at the time of Teal's death, and when she arrived at Teal's home several days later, the proponent of the will and several other people were already at Teal's residence, sorting and boxing his property for storage. The will was not found in the initial search, but was discovered some time later by the proponent of the will. On February 22, 2000, the proponent filed an application for probate of the will, which was contested by the appellant. Following a bench trial, the will was admitted to probate. Appellant challenges the judgment of the trial court with six issues, contending that the trial court erred in: (1) admitting the will to probate; (2) awarding $8,000 in expenses and fees to the executor of the will; and (3) the manner in which the fees were paid to the executor. Appellant further contends that the trial judge should be recused from hearing any of the matters still pending in this case.

In her first issue, appellant argues that the will is void on its face because it lacks the statutory requisites of a will; the proponent failed to prove that the will was attested to by two witnesses; the proponent failed to prove the will as required by Texas law; the will was not executed with the requisite formalities and solemnities; and finally, the proponent failed to meet the burden of proving the will had not been revoked. We will address this issue by first discussing the will, then we will examine those requirements of a will under Texas law which are relevant to this case.

THE WILL

The instrument in dispute is a two-page, type-written document drafted by the deceased, dated August 4, 1987. The front of the first page and front of the second page set out the testator's disposition of his property. At the bottom of the second page is the following statement:

> The foregoing instrument consisting of two (2) pages, including this page, was signed, sealed, published, and declared by *Ronald Curtis Teal* as his Last Will and Testament, in the presence of witnesses, who at his request and in his presence and in the presnece [sic] of one another, subscribe our names, hereto as witnesses on the date hereof; and we declare that at the time of the execution of this instrument, *Ronald Curtis Teal*, according to best knowledge and belief, was of sound and disposing mind and memory and under no constraint.

The will contains no designated lines for witnesses; however, beneath this provision is the signature of Maria H. Anzaldua, a notary public. Anzaldua also sealed the will with her notary seal. On the back of the second page of the document are two signatures, with the word "witness" hand-printed beneath each. There is nothing written on the back of the first page. One signature is illegible, the other appears to read "Jane Martinez."

WILL REQUIREMENTS

Under Texas law, a will must:

> be in writing and signed by the testator in person or by another person for him by his direction and in his presence, and shall, if not wholly in the handwriting of the testator, be attested by two or more credible witnesses above the age of fourteen years who shall subscribe their names thereto in their own handwriting in the presence of the testator.

Texas Probate Code § 59(a). There is no requirement that a will be notarized. See id. If a will is not self-proved, an attested will may be proved by the sworn testimony or affidavit of one or more of the subscribing witnesses, taken in open court. Texas Probate Code § 84(b).[2] The proponent of a will must also prove that the will was not revoked. Texas Probate Code § 88(b)(3).

At the trial, the will proponent produced testimony showing that he had been unable to locate either of the two people whose signatures are found on the back of the

---

[2] A will can be made self-proved, thus avoiding the need for the witnesses to testify in the probating of the will, by having the testator and witnesses sign a "self-proving affidavit" before "an officer authorized to administer oaths under the laws of this State." Texas Probate Code § 59(a). The will in the instant case was not self-proved.

second page of the document. The proponent argued Anzaldua had acted as a subscribing witness, and produced her in that capacity. Appellant argues that Anzaldua was not a subscribing witness, and further, that she was "not credible." Thus, this Court must answer the question: can a notary, who did not intend to sign the will in the capacity of subscribing witness, serve as a witness for the purposes of proving a will? To answer this question, we must consider the role of a witness to a will, and determine if Anzaldua served in that role.

THE ROLE OF THE WILL WITNESS

A witness to a will serves to prove the will was executed with the formalities and solemnities and under the circumstances required to make the will valid. See Texas Probate Code § 84(b). To prove a will requires the sworn testimony or affidavit of one or more of the subscribing witnesses. Texas Probate Code § 84(b)(1). The witness must testify in court, or by affidavit, that the testator declared that the instrument was his last will and testament, that he had willingly and freely made and executed the instrument, that he was over eighteen years old, and that he was of sound mind and body. See Texas Probate Code § 59(a) (setting out necessary contents for an affidavit to prove will without testimony of witness in open court). The witnesses must sign their names in the testator's presence. Id.; Jones v. Whiteley, 533 S.W.2d 881, 883 (Tex. App.-Fort Worth 1976, writ ref'd, n.r.e.). However, there is no requirement that the testator sign the instrument in the presence of the witnesses. See Texas Probate Code § 59(a); *Jones*, 533 S.W.2d at 883.

We will now examine Anzaldua's involvement in the execution of Teal's will to determine if she fulfilled the role of a witness.

ANZALDUA'S TESTIMONY

Anzaldua was familiar with Teal because he had been her teacher when she graduated from high school. Before he brought his will to her, Teal briefly visited Anzaldua and discussed having a will made. Anzaldua was unable to type the will at that time, and advised Teal that he should "go through a lawyer" to have his will prepared; however, Teal did not want to have his will drafted by an attorney. Teal returned to Anzaldua's home on August 4, 1987, about two weeks after their first meeting, with the will now in dispute. Teal brought two people with him, both of whom were older than Anzaldua, who graduated from high school in 1971. Teal and the two other people signed the document in front of Anzaldua, who then signed it herself. Anzaldua stated that she had recorded the names of the two other people in her notary log, but that she had since discarded her notary records. Anzaldua testified that she asked Teal some questions about his will, which confirmed that he was familiar with the contents of the will, knew "who he was leaving everything to," and was signing it of his own free will. To Anzaldua's knowledge, Teal never revoked the will.

On cross-examination, Anzaldua stated that she signed the will "to witness to the signature on the will," not as "a subscribing witness." She also stated that a notary's function is only to acknowledge that the people signing a document were actually present and did, in fact, sign the document. Anzaldua testified that she asked Teal if he was certain the will reflected his desired disposition of his estate and further asked him, "What if you decide to remarry some day?" Teal replied that, should he remarry, "the will will stand."

ANZALDUA'S ROLE IN THE EXECUTION OF THE WILL

We now hold that, under the facts in this case, the notary, although she did not intend to sign as a subscribing witness, did in fact serve as a subscribing witness. She spoke to the testator, ascertained that he was of sound mind and body, was aware of the contents of the will and was executing it of his own free will. She signed the will in the presence of the testator. Because there is no requirement that a will be notarized, Anzaldua's signature served no purpose other than as a witness. Her actions, in questioning the testator about his intentions and the contents of the will are more consistent with the actions of a witness, than with the actions of a notary public. See Texas Government Code §§ 406.014, 406.016 (setting out actions for which a notary public has authority and recording requirements). Under the facts of this case, Anzaldua served as a witness.

This ruling is consistent with that of the San Antonio Court of Appeals in Saathoff v. Saathoff, 101 S.W.2d 910, 912 (Tex. Civ. App.-San Antonio 1937, writ ref'd). In *Saathoff*, the testator executed an affidavit, rather than making a will. Id. at 911. The affidavit was testamentary in nature, and was signed by a witness as well as the attorney who prepared the affidavit, who signed as a notary public. Id. The San Antonio court held that the affidavit was in fact a will, and the attorney, although he signed as a notary public, was a witness to the will as required by law. Id. at 912.

Having determined that Anzaldua was a witness to Teal's will, we now address the remaining contentions in appellant's first issue.

APPELLANT'S REMAINING CHALLENGES TO THE WILL

Was the will executed with the requisite formalities and solemnities? The will at issue is in writing, was signed by the testator, and was attested to by three witnesses above the age of fourteen who subscribed their names to the will in the presence of the testator. Thus, the will was executed with the requisite formalities and solemnities under Texas law. See Texas Probate Code § 59(a).

Was the will proved as required by Texas law? Although a will must be witnessed by at least two witnesses, only one subscribing witness must testify. Texas Probate Code § 84(b)(1). Anzaldua's testimony was sufficient to prove the will because, as discussed above, she served as a subscribing witness to the will. Appellant argues that Anzaldua was not a credible witness and therefore her testimony should be disregarded. The trier of fact is the sole judge of a witness's credibility and the weight to be given their testimony . . . . The trial court implicitly found Anzaldua to be credible and we will not question that finding. Further, when a will provides no pecuniary benefit to the witness, the will itself constitutes evidence that the witness was credible to attest to the will at the time the will was executed.

Triestman v. Kilgore, 838 S.W.2d 547 (Tex. 1992). The will in the instant case includes no pecuniary benefit to Anzaldua.

Was the will revoked? Finally, the proponent of the will met his burden of proving the will had not been revoked. See Texas Probate Code § 88(b)(3) (to obtain probate of a will, proponent must prove will was not revoked). Once a proponent has proven that a will is otherwise valid and was executed with the requisite formalities and solemnities, a rebuttable "presumption of continuity" arises and, absent evidence of revocation, the will proponent need not produce direct evidence of non-revocation. Harkins v. Crews, 907 S.W.2d 51, 59 (Tex. App.-San Antonio 1995, writ denied); In re Estate of Page, 544 S.W.2d 757, 760 (Tex. Civ. App.-Corpus Christi 1976, writ ref'd n.r.e.). The testimony of a witness that, to her knowledge or belief, the testator did not revoke the will is sufficient evidence of non-revocation to support probate of the will. Bryant v. Hamlin, 373 S.W.2d 837, 840 (Tex. Civ. App.-Dallas 1963, writ ref'd n.r.e.). The record contains no evidence of revocation. Anzaldua testified that, to her knowledge, Teal never revoked the will.

Appellant argues that a marriage subsequent to the execution of a will raises a presumption that prior wills are revoked, unless the beneficiaries of the will would have inherited notwithstanding the marriage. It has long been recognized that, in Texas, the statutory method of revoking a will is exclusive. . . . A subsequent marriage does not revoke a will. Texas Probate Code § 63.

We overrule appellant's first issue.

APPELLANT'S REMAINING ISSUES

In her second and third issues, appellant challenges the award of $8,000 to the executor of the will for expenses and attorneys fees. In her fourth issue, appellant argues that the trial court erred in allowing the $8,000 to be withdrawn from the "Estate Safe Guard Account" without "a further specific order regarding such account." In her fifth and sixth issues, appellant argues that Judge Robert Vargas erred by refusing to recuse himself "as to the pending probate matters after the WILL was admitted." In her sixth issue, appellant argues that the trial court that heard the motion to recuse erred by failing to recuse Judge Vargas for all pending matters. We hold that appellant does not have standing to raise these issues.

STANDING

A person must have an interest in an estate to bring a suit protecting an interest in the estate. See Oldham v. Keaton, 597 S.W.2d 938, 943-44 (Tex .Civ. App.-Texarkana 1980, writ ref'd n.r.e.) (assignees of a remainder interest in an estate had standing because they had an interest in the estate). A party must show that its interest has been prejudiced to have standing to appeal. Gorman v. Gorman, 966 S.W.2d 858, 864 (Tex. App.-Houston [1st Dist.] 1998, pet. denied). The appellant bears the burden of making a *prima facie* showing of prejudice. Id. An appealing party may not complain of errors that do not affect its rights. . . .

Appellant is not a devisee under the will. Therefore, she has no interest in the estate of which the will disposes. Because she has no interest in the estate, appellant has no interest which has been prejudiced by the court's decisions affecting the disposition of the estate. Without an interest in the estate, appellant lacks standing to challenge the disposition of the estate. Similarly, she is not prejudiced by the fact that Judge Vargas was not recused. Because we hold that appellant does not have standing to challenge the will disposition, we dismiss her issues challenging the distribution of funds from the estate, and her issues challenging the denial of her motion to recuse Judge Vargas on all pending matters pertaining to the administration of the will.

Section D. Holographic Wills

Estates Code § 251.052. Exception for Holographic Wills

Notwithstanding Section 251.051, a will written wholly in the testator's handwriting is not required to be attested by subscribing witnesses.

Estates Code § 251.107. Self-Proved Holographic Will

Notwithstanding any other provision of this subchapter, a will written wholly in the testator's handwriting may be made self-proved at any time during the testator's lifetime by the attachment or annexation to the will of an affidavit by the testator to the effect that:

(1) the instrument is the testator's last will;

(2) the testator was 18 years of age or older at the time the will was executed or, if the testator was younger than 18 years of age, that the testator:

(A) was or had been married; or

(B) was a member of the armed forces of the United States, an auxiliary of the armed forces of the United States, or the United States Maritime Service at the time the will was executed;

(3) the testator was of sound mind; and

(4) the testator has not revoked the will.

Estates Code § 256.154. Proof of Execution of Holographic Will

(a) A will wholly in the handwriting of the testator that is not self-proved as provided by this title may be proved by two witnesses to the testator's handwriting. The evidence may be by:

(1) sworn testimony or affidavit taken in open court; or

(2) if the witnesses are nonresidents of the county or are residents who are unable to attend court, written or oral deposition taken in accordance with Section 51.203 or the Texas Rules of Civil Procedure.

(b) A witness being deposed for purposes of proving the will as provided by Subsection (a)(2) may testify by referring to a certified copy of the will, without the judge requiring the original will to be removed from the court's file and shown to the witness.

Contingent will is not effective if contingency fails to occur

In re Estate of PEREZ
Court of Appeals of Texas, San Antonio
155 S.W.3d 599 (2004)

MARION, J. In this appeal, we must determine whether a will admitted to probate in Texas was contingent upon the death of the testator during heart surgery, or whether the heart surgery was merely the inducement to the making of the will. Because we conclude the will was contingent upon the testator's death during surgery and he did not die during surgery, the will is not subject to probate. Accordingly, we reverse the trial court's judgment and remand.

BACKGROUND

Appellants are the daughters of Dr. Mario Delgado Perez from his first marriage. Dr. Perez died in Mexico on December 7, 2000 at his sister's home. Appellee is Dr. Perez's second wife. On June 20, 2000, Dr. Perez executed a document in Mexico that purports to be his last will and testament. Shortly after Dr. Perez's death, one of the appellants filed an application for the administration of Dr. Perez's estate in Mexico, indicating that he died without a valid will. On February 9, 2001, appellee filed an application to probate Dr. Perez's will in Texas in the Webb County court. On February 26, 2001, appellee appeared before the Mexican court in the intestate proceedings. Appellee filed a claim for payment of debts in those proceedings, and she ultimately settled her interests in Mexico with the estate's administrator. Appellee did not produce the will in the Mexican proceedings. On May 9, 2001, the Texas court admitted the will to probate. On June 7, 2001, appellants filed their contest in the Texas proceedings. On September 15, 2003, appellants filed a motion for a partial traditional summary judgment and for a partial no-evidence summary judgment, which the trial court denied, and this appeal ensued.

ANALYSIS

Dr. Perez's will reads, in pertinent part, as follows:

> To Whom It May Concern:
>
> I, Dr. Mario Delgado Perez, Mexican, married, over 21 years of age, and neighbor of this city, make the following disposition:
>
> That during my life, I have acquired various properties in different sections in this city and out of it; and *because I am sick and waiting for a heart surgery, and providing ahead of any emergency, I make the following disposition to be fulfilled* ***in case my death occurs during the surgery,*** hoping it will be fulfilled as it is my wish by my heirs, my wife . . . [and] my children, . . .
>
> I wish and dispose that the properties acquired by me be divided in the following manner: [the will then makes nine bequests].

(Emphasis added). The certification attached to the will states, in pertinent part, as follows: "This document is the will of Dr. Mario Delgado Perez, in which he expresses the way in which he wants his wealth and properties to be divided and distributed *in case of his death at the moment he undergoes heart surgery.*" (Emphasis added). The certification is signed by Dr. Perez, a witness, and a notary public.

As their first grounds for summary judgment, appellants assert the effectiveness of Dr. Perez's will was contingent upon his death during heart surgery. They contend that because there is no evidence he died during surgery, and in fact he died later at his sister's home, the contingency never occurred, rendering the will inoperative. Appellee counters that Dr. Perez's heart illness and the impending surgery were merely the inducement to his making the will; therefore, the will is subject to probate.

A "contingent will" is a will that will take effect only upon the happening of a specified contingency. Bagnall v. Bagnall, 148 Tex. 423, 225 S.W.2d 401, 402 (1949); Dougherty v. Holscheider, 40 Tex. Civ. App. 31, 88 S.W. 1113, 1114 (1905, writ dism'd). The operation of a contingent will is defeated by the nonoccurrence of the contingency. Id. In determining whether a will is contingent, courts must determine whether the happening of the contingency is a condition precedent to the operation of the will, or whether the possibility of the contingency was only a statement of the motive or inducement that led to the preparation and execution of the instrument. *Bagnall*, 225 S.W.2d at 402. "If the contingency mentioned is a condition precedent to the validity of the will, such contingency must have taken place in order to entitle the will to probate; if the possibility mentioned is only the inducement which prompted the making of the will, then such will is effective upon the testator's death even though such event does not take place." Id.

For a will to be contingent, it must "reasonably appear that the testator affirmatively intended the will not to take effect unless the given contingency did or did not happen, as the case might be." Ferguson v. Ferguson, 121 Tex. 119, 45 S.W.2d 1096, 1097 (1931). The condition must be clearly expressed by appropriate language or by necessary implication. Id. at 1099. The character of the bequests may be examined to determine whether a contingent will was intended. Id. at 1098.

Appellee relies on *Ferguson* for her argument that a will is not contingent upon a certain event unless that contingency is stated in every paragraph of the will. Appellee asserts that because each paragraph of Dr. Perez's will does not state a contingency, the will is ambiguous. We disagree with appellee's interpretation of *Ferguson. I*n that case, the Court stated the testatrix's intention must be determined based the following two sentences: "I am going on a journey and I may never come back alive so I make this Will, but I expect to make changes if I live. First, I want a Hospital built in Haskell in memory of my husband Francis Marion to cost $50,000 (Fifty Thousand Dollars), if I live I expect to have it done myself." Id. at 1096. The document then continued with other bequests. The Court noted that the testatrix did not state in her will, "This Will is to be effective if I die on this trip." Id. at 1097. Because the will contained no express provision that it was contingent upon the testatrix's death during a journey, the Court determined the will was ambiguous. Id. at 1096-97.

Because the will was ambiguous, the *Ferguson* Court applied the following rules to discern the testatrix's intention: (1) the fact that testatrix left a will implies that she did not intend to die intestate; (2) a will is construed to be a general, and not a contingent, will, unless the intention to the contrary clearly appears either expressly or by necessary implication from a reading of the language of the will as a whole; (3) if the event mentioned in the will merely indicates the inducement which caused the testatrix to make the will, and her intent to make it contingent is not apparent, the will is entitled to probate as a general will; and (4) if the will is open to two constructions, that interpretation will be given it which will prevent intestacy. Id. at 1097. After examining the will, the Court determined the will "indicates that her main desire was to dispose of her property herself and not to die intestate." Id. at 1098.

The *Ferguson* case is clearly distinguishable. First, that Court determined the language in the will was ambiguous, while we do not consider the language in Dr. Perez's will to be ambiguous. Second, in *Ferguson*, there were "no express words expressing a condition in Mrs. Morton's will such as: 'If I die on this trip,' 'If anything happens,' or the like." Id. at 1099. Here, Dr. Perez's will states that disposition of his property "be fulfilled in case [his] death occurs during the surgery." The certification emphasizes this contingency with the statement that his "wealth and properties . . . be divided and distributed in case of his death at the moment he undergoes heart surgery."

In *Bagnall*, which was decided by the Supreme Court after *Ferguson*, the Court held that the use of the word "if" expressed a condition: "The use of this word implies a condition; it means 'provided' or 'in case that.'" 225 S.W.2d at 402.[3] The *Dougherty* court noted that "most of the cases holding wills dependent on the happening of the condition named, the words 'if I never get back,' referring to a certain journey, or 'should anything happen to me,' referring to a particular time or event, were used." 88 S.W. at 1115. Similarly, in Dr. Perez's will and certification, he twice uses the phrase "in case" when referring to the disposition of his property. This language unambiguously indicates Dr. Perez's intention that his will was contingent upon his death during the impending heart surgery. This contingency did not occur; therefore, the will never became effective.

CONCLUSION

Because we conclude Dr. Perez's contingent will is not subject to probate, we need not address appellants' remaining issues on appeal. See Texas Rule of Appellate Procedure 47.1. We reverse the trial court's judgment and remand the case for further proceedings.

Section E. Revocation of Wills: Writing or Physical Act

Estates Code § 253.002. Revocation of Will

A written will, or a clause or devise in a written will, may not be revoked, except by a subsequent will, codicil, or declaration in writing that is executed with like formalities, or by the testator destroying or canceling the same, or causing it to be destroyed or canceled in the testator's presence.

Estates Code § 256.156. Proof of Will Not Produced in Court

(a) A will that cannot be produced in court must be proved in the same manner as provided in Section 256.153 for an attested will or Section 256.154 for a holographic will, as applicable. The same amount and character of testimony is required to prove the will not produced in court as is required to prove a will produced in court.

(b) In addition to the proof required by Subsection (a):

(1) the cause of the nonproduction of a will not produced in court must be proved, which must be sufficient to satisfy the court that the will cannot by any reasonable diligence be produced; and

---

[3] In *Bagnall*, the will stated, "Remember me W.W. Bagnall by this. If any thing happens to me. While gone. All my belongings and estate goes to James B. Bagnall Brother of mine." 225 S.W.2d at 401.

(2) the contents of the will must be substantially proved by the testimony of a credible witness who has read either the original or a copy of the will, has heard the will read, or can identify a copy of the will.

Will proponents may rebut presumption of revocation for will last seen in testator's possession but not found at death

In re Estate of TURNER
Court of Appeals of Texas, Eastland
265 S.W.3d 709 (2008)

STRANGE, J. This is a will contest arising from an application to probate the photocopy of a missing will. The trial court conducted a bench trial and ordered the photocopy admitted to probate. Finding no error, we affirm.

I. BACKGROUND FACTS

Clifton Lewis Turner[4] fatally shot himself on March 2, 2006. His sister, Betty Glaze, filed an application to probate a will not produced in court and attached a photocopy of a will that she contended Lewis executed in 1990. The will named Glaze executrix and sole beneficiary of Lewis's estate. Glaze advised the court that she had diligently searched for Lewis's original will but had been unable to locate it, that Lewis gave her a copy of his will after executing the original, and that the attached photocopy was an accurate copy of the original. Glaze identified herself, her brother Jack Turner, and her sister Yvonne Cottrell as the individuals who would inherit Lewis's estate in the absence of a valid will. Jack and Yvonne opposed Glaze's application, contending that Lewis revoked the 1990 will before his death. The trial court granted Glaze's application and admitted the photocopied will to probate.

II. ISSUES ON APPEAL

Jack and Yvonne challenge the trial court's order with three issues. They contend that Glaze produced legally and factually insufficient evidence to overcome the presumption of revocation and that the trial court erred by excluding a statement Lewis made to his daughter indicating his intention to leave his estate to her.

---

[4] Mr. Turner went by "Lewis." To avoid confusion, we will refer to him as Lewis and to his brother Jack Turner as Jack.

III. ANALYSIS

A. Evidentiary Challenge

Jack and Yvonne called Courtney Stegemoller as a witness. Stegemoller was Lewis's daughter. She had also opposed Glaze's application for probate, but the trial court dismissed her contest for lack of standing. The trial court found that the parent-child relationship between Stegemoller and Lewis was terminated by court order in 1987 and that she had no right to inherit any portion of his estate.

Stegemoller testified that she and her father did not have a significant relationship until she was eighteen. She invited him to her high school graduation and thereafter began seeing him. Lewis discussed his estate planning during one of their visits. When she began to repeat Lewis's statement, Glaze asserted a hearsay objection. Jack and Yvonne responded that Stegemoller's testimony was not hearsay because it was not offered for the truth of the matter asserted or, alternatively, that it was admissible to show Lewis's state of mind. The trial court sustained the objection and Stegemoller made a bill of review. Stegemoller testified that the conversation took place last October and that Lewis told her "he had taken care of everything, and if he ever did pass away everything would be [hers]." This was the last time she ever spoke with him. . . .

Stegemoller's testimony is clearly hearsay. It was not offered to prove an operative fact, such as the fact that a conversation occurred, but was offered to show that Lewis had revoked his will because his statement—if believed—indicated a new testamentary intent. The trial court did not err by finding that Stegemoller's testimony was hearsay.

Jack and Yvonne argue . . . that Stegemoller's testimony was admissible under the state of mind exception . . . . Commentators have noted that, when this exception is applied to statements made by a testator, it "applies only to a testator's statement that 'relates to the execution, revocation, identification, or terms' of his will." 2A Steven Goode et al., Texas Practice: Courtroom Handbook on Texas Evidence 515 (2007 ed.) (citing Barnum v. State, 7 S.W.3d 782, 789-90 & n. 5 (Tex. App.-Amarillo 1999, pet. ref'd)).

The trial court did not err by finding this exception inapplicable. The challenged testimony may have been considered relevant to establish that Lewis had executed a new will naming Stegemoller as his sole beneficiary, but Jack and Yvonne's position was that Lewis died intestate. Consequently, its exclusion was not harmful to them. Alternatively, even though the excluded testimony did not directly refer to a prior will, the testimony may have been considered relevant to establish revocation since a bequest to Stegemoller would have been inconsistent with the terms of Lewis's 1990 will. But its exclusion cannot be considered harmful on this basis either.

Two uninterested witnesses testified that they saw Lewis's will shortly before his death and well after Stegemoller and Lewis's last conversation. Betty Webb was Lewis's longtime girlfriend. She testified that Lewis showed her his will several times including the day of his death. Lewis also showed his will to Webb's niece, Lisa Sliger, a few days before his death. Stegemoller's excluded testimony does not directly support Jack and Yvonne's position that Lewis had no will but suggest that he had a new one. Consequently, for Jack and Yvonne to prevail on their objection, the trial court necessarily had to disregard Glaze's, Webb's, and Sliger's testimony that Lewis showed them his will shortly before his death, believe Stegemoller's testimony that Lewis intended to leave her his estate, and disbelieve Stegemoller's testimony that Lewis had already taken care of everything. The record does not allow us to conclude that the admission of Stegemoller's testimony would have probably led to such a result. Issue No. Three is overruled.

B. Legal and Factual Sufficiency Challenges

Jack and Yvonne requested and the trial court entered findings of fact. Jack and Yvonne contest only the finding that Lewis did not revoke his 1990 will contending that the evidence is legally and factually insufficient to overcome the presumption of revocation.

1. Presumption of Revocation

When the original will cannot be located and the will was last seen in the testator's possession, a presumption arises that the testator destroyed the will with the intent of revoking it. Hibbler v. Knight, 735 S.W.2d 924, 927 (Tex. App.-Houston [1st Dist.] 1987, writ ref'd n.r.e.). The proponent must overcome this presumption by a preponderance of the evidence. In re Estate of Glover, 744 S.W.2d 939, 940 (Tex. 1988). This can be accomplished with proof of circumstances contrary to the presumption or with evidence that some other person fraudulently destroyed the will. In re Capps, 154 S.W.3d 242, 245 (Tex. App.-Texarkana 2005, no pet.). Courts have held that evidence the decedent recognized his will's continued validity and had continued affection for the chief beneficiary of his will, without evidence that he was dissatisfied with the will or had any desire to cancel or change it, is sufficient proof of circumstances contrary to the presumption. See Id. at 245-46; Sparkman v. Massey's Estate, 297 S.W.2d 308, 311 (Tex. Civ. App.-Dallas 1956, writ ref'd n.r.e.).

2. Standard of Review

A trial court's findings of fact in a bench trial are reviewed for legal and factual sufficiency under the same standards used to review a jury's verdict on jury questions. Girdner v. Rose, 213 S.W.3d 438, 445 (Tex. App.-Eastland 2006, no pet.). In considering a legal sufficiency challenge, we review all the evidence in the light most favorable to the prevailing party, indulging every inference in their favor. City of Keller v. Wilson, 168 S.W.3d 802, 822 (Tex. 2005). In reviewing a factual sufficiency challenge, we consider all of the evidence and uphold the finding unless the evidence is too weak to support it or the finding is so against the overwhelming weight of the evidence as to be manifestly unjust. Pool v. Ford Motor Co., 715 S.W.2d 629, 635 (Tex. 1986).

3. The Evidence

Lewis was divorced and lived alone. He and his former wife had one daughter but his parental rights were terminated in 1987. The parties stipulated that Lewis executed a valid will in 1990 and that the photocopied will attached to Glaze's application was a true and correct copy of that will. Lewis showed his will to a number of people. Glaze saw it less than one week before his death. Webb saw it the day he died. Sliger saw and read it in late February.

Webb was with Lewis for several hours the day that he shot himself. She arrived at his house at three o'clock in the afternoon. They went and checked his cattle, stopped at her brother's house, and were back at his home at seven. Lewis showed her his will and then returned it to its usual storage location: a three-shelf wall unit typically used for items such as letters and bills. He sat down in his recliner and watched television for one and one-half hours before going to his bedroom. When Webb went to check on him, he asked her to leave. She heard a shot. She ran back into the bedroom. When she realized what had happened, she called 911 and Glaze.

When police and emergency personnel arrived, Webb was taken outside and was not allowed to reenter Lewis's house. Glaze and her husband Bill Glaze went to Lewis's house in response to Webb's call but were not allowed to enter either. Lewis was taken to the Brownwood hospital and was then airlifted to San Angelo. Glaze and her husband drove to San Angelo. Jack and Yvonne were called, and they too went to the San Angelo hospital. Lewis shot himself Thursday night and was pronounced dead late Friday night. Everyone returned home early Saturday morning after completing paperwork. Webb, Glaze, and Bill went to a local funeral home that morning to arrange for Lewis's burial. While they were there, Jack called and asked to borrow Lewis's house key. Jack went inside Lewis's house and looked around. He noticed that Lewis's gun cabinet was empty. The cabinet had been locked and contained several guns when the police were there. Jack also noticed that there was no evidence of the shooting. Jack testified that Bill arrived while he was still there and told him that he had cleaned up Lewis's bedroom and that there were no guns in the cabinet because Lewis had previously sold them. Bill, however, denied being in Lewis's house, denied cleaning up the shooting, denied knowing anything about Lewis's guns, and denied telling anyone otherwise.

Stegemoller admitted entering Lewis's house after the funeral. She testified that she and her husband Josh briefly looked around and that they took Lewis's dog, but she denied taking anything else. Other testimony put her there days sooner. Robert Johnson, Lewis's neighbor and friend, testified that he saw an unknown man and woman at Lewis's house on Saturday. They introduced themselves as Lewis's daughter and "Jack." Johnson also testified that he saw three or four teenagers or young adults rummaging around in Lewis's house the day he shot himself. They arrived after the police had left and were there for at least one-half hour before he went to bed.

Glaze discovered on Saturday that Lewis's will was not in the folder where he normally kept it. She searched the remainder of the house and a second house that he owned and had previously lived in. Bill looked through two boxes of Lewis's paperwork. Glaze then went through Lewis's trash. They were unable to locate the will.

When all the evidence is reviewed in the light most favorable to the trial court's order, it is legally sufficient to overcome the presumption of revocation. There was testimony of a close relationship between Lewis and Glaze but not Jack and Yvonne, and no evidence of a "falling out" or other recent discord. Lewis's will left everything to Glaze. Lewis also named her his beneficiary on non-testamentary assets including a bank account and an investment account. What happened to the original will is unclear, but there was no evidence that he physically destroyed it. In fact, several witnesses testified that Lewis showed it to them shortly before his death. There was also no evidence that he made any changes to his non-testamentary asset beneficiary designations. Issue No. One is overruled.

The evidence is also factually sufficient. The question of what happened to the original will has understandably bedeviled the parties. Jack and Yvonne spend much of their brief directing our attention to evidence that indicates they did not destroy it and to evidence that contradicts the testimony of other witnesses. For example, they question Johnson's testimony about four teenagers being in Lewis's house after the police left, pointing out that nothing was broken into and that the teenagers would not have turned on the lights as Johnson described if they were attempting to vandalize the house. They point to evidence that Webb, Glaze, and Bill had immediate access to Lewis's house but that they did not. They note that, according to Jack's testimony, Lewis's bedroom had already been cleaned and Lewis's guns taken before he ever entered the house and contend that Bill was lying to the court. They also contend that Webb's credibility is questionable because of alleged inconsistencies between her trial testimony and her conduct shortly after Lewis's death.

Jack and Yvonne's argument invites this court to reassess the credibility of the witnesses. This we may not do. In a bench trial, the trial court, as factfinder, is the sole judge of the credibility of the witnesses and the weight to be given their testimony. Nat'l Freight, Inc. v. Snyder, 191 S.W.3d 416, 425 (Tex. App.-Eastland 2006, no pet.). The court may accept or reject all or any part of that testimony. Nordstrom v. Nordstrom, 965 S.W.2d 575, 580-81 (Tex. App.-Houston [1st Dist.] 1997, pet. denied).

The trial court could reasonably find the presumption of revocation was rebutted with evidence of fraudulent destruction or with proof of circumstances contrary to the presumption. If Johnson's testimony is believed, four teenagers were in Lewis's house the night he shot himself and Stegemoller and her husband were there shortly after Lewis's death. The trial court could reasonably accept this testimony and conclude that the will was taken as part of a robbery or vandalism or that Stegemoller took it because it did not name her as a beneficiary. The court could have also concluded that Bill's testimony was more credible than Jack's and determined that Jack took the will when he was alone in Lewis's house Saturday morning.

Alternatively, the court could have found Webb's, Sliger's, and Glaze's testimony credible and concluded that the surrounding circumstances were inconsistent with revocation. No witness questioned the relationship between Glaze and Lewis. The trial court could consider the lack of any significant discord between them, the fact that Lewis showed his will to at least three people in the week before his death, and that Lewis made no changes to any of his non-testamentary asset beneficiary designations and could have reasonably concluded that Lewis did not revoke the 1990 will.

The trial court was presented with conflicting evidence on what Lewis may have said or done with regard to his estate planning, on who had access to his house and when, and on whether individual witness's testimony was credible. The trial court's resolution of this conflicting evidence in favor of probating the will was predicated upon factually sufficient evidence. Issue No. Two is overruled.

IV. Holding

The trial court's order admitting the will to probate is affirmed.

Section F. Revocation By Operation of Law

Estates Code § 123.001. Will Provisions Made Before Dissolution of Marriage

(a) In this section:

(1) "Irrevocable trust" means a trust:

(A) for which the trust instrument was executed before the dissolution of a testator's marriage; and

(B) that the testator was not solely empowered by law or by the trust instrument to revoke.

(2) "Relative" means an individual related to another individual by:

(A) consanguinity, as determined under Section 573.022, Government Code; or

(B) affinity, as determined under Section 573.024, Government Code.

(b) If, after the testator makes a will, the testator's marriage is dissolved by divorce, annulment, or a declaration that the marriage is void, unless the will expressly provides otherwise:

(1) all provisions in the will, including all fiduciary appointments, shall be read as if the former spouse and each relative of the former spouse who is not a relative of the testator had failed to survive the testator; and

(2) all provisions in the will disposing of property to an irrevocable trust in which a former spouse or a relative of a former spouse who is not a relative of the testator is a beneficiary or is nominated to serve as trustee or in another fiduciary capacity or that confers a general or special power of appointment on a former spouse or a relative of a former spouse who is not a relative of the testator shall be read to instead dispose of the property to a trust the provisions of which are identical to the irrevocable trust, except any provision in the irrevocable trust:

(A) conferring a beneficial interest or a general or special power of appointment to the former spouse or a relative of the former spouse who is not a relative of the testator shall be treated as if the former spouse and each relative of the former spouse who is not a relative of the testator had disclaimed the interest granted in the provision; and

(B) nominating the former spouse or a relative of the former spouse who is not a relative of the testator to serve as trustee or in another fiduciary capacity shall be treated as if the former spouse and each relative of the former spouse who is not a relative of the testator had died immediately before the dissolution of the marriage.

(c) Subsection (b)(2) does not apply if one of the following provides otherwise:

(1) a court order; or

(2) an express provision of a contract relating to the division of the marital estate entered into between the testator and the testator's former spouse before, during, or after the marriage.

Estates Code § 123.002. Treatment of Decedent's Former Spouse

A person is not a surviving spouse of a decedent if the person's marriage to the decedent has been dissolved by divorce, annulment, or a declaration that the marriage is void, unless:

(1) as the result of a subsequent marriage, the person is married to the decedent at the time of death; and

(2) the subsequent marriage is not declared void under Subchapter C.

Estates Code § 123.052. Revocation of Certain Nontestamentary Transfers; Treatment of Former Spouse as Beneficiary Under Certain Policies or Plans

(a) The dissolution of the marriage revokes a provision in a trust instrument that was executed by a divorced individual before the divorced individual's marriage was dissolved and that:

(1) is a revocable disposition or appointment of property made to the divorced individual's former spouse or any relative of the former spouse who is not a relative of the divorced individual;

(2) revocably confers a general or special power of appointment on the divorced individual's former spouse or any relative of the former spouse who is not a relative of the divorced individual; or

(3) revocably nominates the divorced individual's former spouse or any relative of the former spouse who is not a relative of the divorced individual to serve:

(A) as a personal representative, trustee, conservator, agent, or guardian; or

(B) in another fiduciary or representative capacity.

(b) Subsection (a) does not apply if one of the following provides otherwise:

(1) a court order;

(2) the express terms of a trust instrument executed by the divorced individual before the individual's marriage was dissolved; or

(3) an express provision of a contract relating to the division of the marital estate entered into between the divorced individual and the individual's former spouse before, during, or after the marriage.

(c) Sections 9.301 and 9.302, Family Code, govern the designation of a former spouse as a beneficiary of certain life insurance policies or as a beneficiary under certain retirement benefit plans or other financial plans.

Estates Code § 123.151. Designation of Former Spouse or Relative of Former Spouse on Certain Multiple-Party Accounts

(a) In this section:

(1) "Beneficiary," "multiple-party account," "P.O.D. account," and "P.O.D. payee" have the meanings assigned by Chapter 113.

(2) "Public retirement system" has the meaning assigned by Section 802.001, Government Code.

(3) "Relative" has the meaning assigned by Section 123.051.

(b) If, after a decedent designates a spouse or a relative of a spouse who is not a relative of the decedent as a P.O.D. payee or beneficiary, including alternative P.O.D. payee or beneficiary, on a P.O.D. account or other multiple-party account, the decedent's marriage is dissolved by divorce, annulment, or a declaration that the marriage is void, the designation provision on the account is not effective as to the former spouse or the former spouse's relative unless:

(1) the court decree dissolving the marriage designates the former spouse or the former spouse's relative as the P.O.D. payee or beneficiary;

(2) the decedent redesignated the former spouse or the former spouse's relative as the P.O.D payee or beneficiary after the marriage was dissolved; or

(3) the former spouse or the former spouse's relative is designated to receive the proceeds or benefits in trust for, on behalf of, or for the benefit of a child or dependent of either the decedent or the former spouse.

(c) If a designation is not effective under Subsection (b), a multiple-party account is payable to the named alternative P.O.D. payee or beneficiary or, if an alternative P.O.D. payee or beneficiary is not named, to the estate of the decedent.

(d) A financial institution or other person obligated to pay an account described by Subsection (b) that pays the account to the former spouse or the former spouse's relative as P.O.D. payee or beneficiary under a designation that is not effective under Subsection (b) is liable for payment of the account to the person provided by Subsection (c) only if:

(1) before payment of the account to the designated P.O.D. payee or beneficiary, the payor receives written notice at the home office or principal office of the payor from an interested person that the designation of the P.O.D. payee or beneficiary is not effective under Subsection (b); and

(2) the payor has not interpleaded the account funds into the registry of a court of competent jurisdiction in accordance with the Texas Rules of Civil Procedure.

(e) This section does not affect the right of a former spouse to assert an ownership interest in an undivided multiple-party account described by Subsection (b).

(f) This section does not apply to the disposition of a beneficial interest in a retirement benefit or other financial plan of a public retirement system.

Family Code § 9.301. Pre-Decree Designation of Ex-Spouse as Beneficiary of Life Insurance

(a) If a decree of divorce or annulment is rendered after an insured has designated the insured's spouse as a beneficiary under a life insurance policy in force at the time of rendition, a provision in the policy in favor of the insured's former spouse is not effective unless:

(1) the decree designates the insured's former spouse as the beneficiary;

(2) the insured redesignates the former spouse as the beneficiary after rendition of the decree; or

(3) the former spouse is designated to receive the proceeds in trust for, on behalf of, or for the benefit of a child or a dependent of either former spouse.

(b) If a designation is not effective under Subsection (a), the proceeds of the policy are payable to the named alternative beneficiary or, if there is not a named alternative beneficiary, to the estate of the insured.

(c) An insurer who pays the proceeds of a life insurance policy issued by the insurer to the beneficiary under a designation that is not effective under Subsection (a) is liable for payment of the proceeds to the person or estate provided by Subsection (b) only if:

(1) before payment of the proceeds to the designated beneficiary, the insurer receives written notice at the home office of the insurer from an interested person that the designation is not effective under Subsection (a); and

(2) the insurer has not interpleaded the proceeds into the registry of a court of competent jurisdiction in accordance with the Texas Rules of Civil Procedure.

Family Code § 9.302. Pre-Decree Designation of Ex-Spouse as Beneficiary in Retirement Benefits and Other Financial Plans

(a) If a decree of divorce or annulment is rendered after a spouse, acting in the capacity of a participant, annuitant, or account holder, has designated the other spouse as a beneficiary under an individual retirement account, employee stock option plan, stock option, or other form of savings, bonus, profit-sharing, or other employer plan or financial plan of an employee or a participant in force at the time of rendition, the designating provision in the plan in favor of the other former spouse is not effective unless:

(1) the decree designates the other former spouse as the beneficiary;

(2) the designating former spouse redesignates the other former spouse as the beneficiary after rendition of the decree; or

(3) the other former spouse is designated to receive the proceeds or benefits in trust for, on behalf of, or for the benefit of a child or dependent of either former spouse.

(b) If a designation is not effective under Subsection (a), the benefits or proceeds are payable to the named alternative beneficiary or, if there is not a named alternative beneficiary, to the designating former spouse.

(c) A business entity, employer, pension trust, insurer, financial institution, or other person obligated to pay retirement benefits or proceeds of a financial plan covered by this section who pays the benefits or proceeds to the beneficiary under a designation of the other former spouse that is not effective under Subsection (a) is liable for payment of the benefits or proceeds to the person provided by Subsection (b) only if:

(1) before payment of the benefits or proceeds to the designated beneficiary, the payor receives written notice at the home office or principal office of the payor from an interested person that the designation of the beneficiary or fiduciary is not effective under Subsection (a); and

(2) the payor has not interpleaded the benefits or proceeds into the registry of a court of competent jurisdiction in accordance with the Texas Rules of Civil Procedure.

(d) This section does not affect the right of a former spouse to assert an ownership interest in an undivided pension, retirement, annuity, or other financial plan described by this section as provided by this subchapter.

(e) This section does not apply to the disposition of a beneficial interest in a retirement benefit or other financial plan of a public retirement system as defined by Section 802.001, Government Code.

Section G. Components of a Will

Unattested handwritten memorandum cannot validate prior unattested typewritten instrument

HINSON v. HINSON
Supreme Court of Texas
280 S.W.2d 731 (1955)

WALKER, J. Respondent is the widow, and petitioner is the child by a former marriage, of J.W. Hinson, Sr., who died in Harris County on September 16, 1952. We are required to determine whether two instruments executed by the decedent are entitled to probate, either separately or together, as his last will and testament.

On April 20, 1951, the decedent signed a printed and typewritten instrument, containing a formal introductory paragraph declaring the same to be his last will and testament, wherein he directed the payment of his debts, devised and bequeathed all of his property to respondent for her lifetime, and at her death to be divided equally between petitioner and two other named persons, provided that one-third of the estate should be given to petitioner in the event of respondent's remarriage, conferred upon respondent the power of sale, appointed executors, and revoked all former wills. This instrument also bears the signature and seal of a notary public but is not otherwise attested.

Thereafter the decedent wrote his own handwriting and signed the following on a sheet of hotel stationery:

> Aug. 24, 1951
>
> Supplementary to my Last Will, it still stands as is.
>
> to my wife Ethel Mae Hinson. my will is in brief case zipper comp. Copy to wife. Copy to my son J.W. Hinson Jr. Everything is yours Darling. Pay the Home off. Sell my car. Have will probated at once. Go to Judge Ewing Boyd, tell him who you are. He will give you all legal advice needed. He is my friend. Sell all of my guns & things you do not need. Sell the Home if you like. But buy another one where you wish to live. Take care of everything I leave you will need it all.
>
> I love you Darling so much more than my own life. Bye. J.W. Hinson.

After the death of her husband, respondent filed in the County Court an application to probate in which she prayed that both writings, or in the alternative the handwritten instrument alone, be admitted to probate as the last will and testament of the decedent. Petitioner contested the application, contending that neither instrument is entitled to probate, because the first is not attested as required by law and because the second was not executed by the decedent with testamentary intent. The judgment of the County Court admitting both instruments to probate having been appealed, the cause was tried de novo in the District Court without the intervention of a jury, the only evidence introduced being the two instruments and certain facts stipulated by the parties. Testamentary capacity was admitted, and there was no question of fraud or undue influence. The parties agreed that the typewritten instrument dated April 20th was in existence in its present form at all times since that date, was found in a separate compartment of decedent's brief case after his death exactly as indicated in the handwritten instrument, and is the document to which reference is made in the latter instrument. The District Court sustained petitioner's contentions with respect to the formal typewritten document, and entered a judgment probating only the holographic instrument dated August 24th. This judgment has been affirmed by the Court of Civil Appeals. 273 S.W.2d 116. It is our opinion that neither instrument can be probated.

An instrument is not a will unless it is executed with testamentary intent. The animus testandi does not depend upon the maker's realization that he is making a will, or upon his designation of the instrument as a will, but upon his intention to create a revocable disposition of his property to take effect after his death. It is essential, however, that the maker shall have intended to express his testamentary wishes in the particular instrument offered for probate. . . .

We agree with respondent that the decedent intended to make a testamentary disposition of his property. It is our opinion, however, that the holographic instrument of August 24th was not intended as a declaration of the manner in which he would have his property pass and vest at his death. He had previously signed an instrument which he expressly declared to be his last will and testament and which the parties agree is the "will" referred to in the informal memorandum. The latter instrument begins with the words "Supplementary to my last will and testament, it still stands as is." This clearly negatives any intention to revoke or modify any of the provisions of the typewritten instrument. At the very outset, the decedent conveys the idea that he has something in mind other than the making of a testamentary disposition of his property. He has already executed an instrument which he thinks is a legal will, and "it still stands as is." He then tells his wife "my will is in brief case zipper comp.," which obviously was not intended to refer to the instrument which he was then writing. Later he advises her to have the will probated at once and suggests that she go to Judge Ewing Boyd for legal advice.

It should also be observed that the decedent had some knowledge of the form and wording of a will. The introduction to the typewritten instrument expressly declares the same to be his last will and testament. In the body of this "will" he used the words "give, devise and bequeath" and "it is my will," directed the payment of debts, appointed executors and revoked former wills. The holographic instrument does not affirmatively state that it is intended or declared to be a will and does not contain language ordinarily used to make a disposition of property. While this circumstance is not controlling, it tends to support our conclusion as to the decedent's purpose in executing the informal memorandum.

The statement "Everything is yours Darling" in an instrument properly executed and intended as a will might be effectual to pass the decedent's property. We are not permitted, however, to lift such statement out of context, but must consider the same in the light of all the provisions of the instrument. The introductory sentence clearly indicates that the decedent intended that his property should pass and vest under and in accordance with the provisions of the typewritten instrument. By the terms of that "will," his wife took a life estate with power of sale. It is not reasonable to believe, therefore, that the statement "Everything is yours Darling" was intended to operate as a devise of the property to her. We think it is apparent from a reading of the entire instrument that this sentence was written by the decedent for the purpose of informing the respondent that he had devised his property to her. The remaining provisions regarding the preservation of the property and the sale of various items thereof are in the nature of suggestions and advice to the wife for her guidance in the management of the estate he had attempted to devise to her by the "will."

Respondent argues that the existence of testamentary intent presents a question of fact, and that we are bound by the implied finding of the trial judge that the holographic instrument was intended as a will. . . . It is our opinion, however, that the evidence in this case conclusively establishes as a matter of law that the decedent intended that his property should pass and vest not by the provisions of the informal memorandum but under and in accordance with the terms of typewritten instrument. Under these circumstances the holographic instrument standing alone cannot be admitted to probate.

Respondent also contends that the typewritten instrument is republished by, or incorporated by reference in, the holographic writing and thus is validated, and that the two instruments, taken together, should be admitted to probate as the decedent's will. Petitioner concedes that the handwritten document evidences the intention of the decedent to republish or incorporate by reference the earlier typewritten instrument.

The doctrine of incorporation by reference has been recognized by at least one Court of Civil Appeals and by a statement in one of our early opinions, but we do not find that it has been expressly approved by a decision of this court. See Allday v. Cage, Tex. Civ. App., 148 S.W. 838, wr. ref.; Heidenheimer v. Bauman, 84 Tex. 174, 19 S.W. 382. It is well settled, however, that a properly executed and valid codicil which contains a sufficient reference to a prior will, operates as a republication of the will in so far as it is not altered or revoked by the codicil; the will and codicil are then to be regarded as one instrument speaking from the date of the codicil. Most jurisdictions in which the question has arisen also hold that a properly executed codicil validates a prior will which was inoperative or invalid because of defective execution, lack of testamentary capacity or undue influence. We note that the latter rule is recognized by implication in Campbell v. Barrera, Tex. Civ. App., 32 S.W. 724, no writ, and will assume for the purpose of this opinion that such rule does obtain in Texas. This brings us to the question which we regard as controlling in the present case.

Art. 8283, Vernon's Ann. Tex. Civ. Stat., provides that a will "shall, if not wholly in the handwriting of the testator, be attested by two or more credible witnesses above the age of fourteen years, subscribing their names thereto in their own handwriting in the presence of the testator." The handwritten instrument of August 24th appears on its face to be attested by three witnesses, but the parties have stipulated that the signatures of two of the witnesses were placed on the instrument after the decedent's death and the record is silent as to when or under what circumstances the other witness signed. The writing is simply a signed but unattested holograph. We must decide, therefore, whether an unattested non-holographic instrument may be validated by a subsequently executed and unattested holographic document. . . .

This is not a case in which the extrinsic-document is referred to simply for the purpose of identifying the beneficiaries of the will or the property devised thereby, or of ascertaining the intention of the testator in some collateral matter, or of resolving an ambiguity resulting from the language used in the will. The typewritten paper of April 20th is the operative testamentary instrument; without it no part of the decedent's scheme or plan for the disposition of his property can be ascertained. We must look to that document to determine the very substance of his testamentary wishes, including the property devised, the identity of the beneficiaries, the estates devised to each, the powers of the life tenant, and the names of the executors. Even if such instrument is regarded as having been incorporated in or republished by the later handwritten memorandum and the two documents are considered together, we are still confronted with the fact that the instrument offered for probate is not wholly in the handwriting of the decedent and is not attested as required by statute. It is our conclusion, therefore, that under the clear provisions of our statute the two instruments involved in this case cannot be admitted to probate.

The judgments of the trial court and of the Court of Civil Appeals are reversed, the judgment is here rendered that the probate of either instrument separately or the two instruments together be denied.

Estates Code § 255.001. Definitions

In this subchapter:

(1) "Contents" means tangible personal property, other than titled personal property, found inside of or on a specifically devised item. The term includes clothing, pictures, furniture, coin collections, and other items of tangible personal property that:

(A) do not require a formal transfer of title; and

(B) are located in another item of tangible personal property such as a cedar chest or other furniture.

(2) "Titled personal property" includes all tangible personal property represented by a certificate of title, certificate of ownership, written label, marking, or designation that signifies ownership by a person. The term includes a motor vehicle, motor home, motorboat, or other similar property that requires a formal transfer of title.

Estates Code § 255.002. Certain Personal Property Excluded from Devise of Real Property

A devise of real property does not include any personal property located on, or associated with, the real property or any contents of personal property located on the real property unless the will directs that the personal property or contents are included in the devise.

Estates Code § 255.003. Contents Excluded from Legacy of Personal Property

A legacy of personal property does not include any contents of the property unless the will directs that the contents are included in the legacy.

Section H. Contracts Relating to Wills

Estates Code § 254.004. Contracts Concerning Wills or Devises; Joint or Reciprocal Wills

(a) A contract executed or entered into on or after September 1, 1979, to make a will or devise, or not to revoke a will or devise, may be established only by:

(1) a written agreement that is binding and enforceable; or

(2) a will stating:

(A) that a contract exists; and

(B) the material provisions of the contract.

(b) The execution of a joint will or reciprocal wills does not constitute by itself sufficient evidence of the existence of a contract.

Chapter 4. Wills: Capacity and Contests

Section A. Mental Capacity

Estates Code § 55.002. Trial By Jury

In a contested probate or mental illness proceeding in a probate court, a party is entitled to a jury trial as in other civil actions.

Estates Code § 256.151. General Proof Requirements

An applicant for the probate of a will must prove to the court's satisfaction that:

(1) the testator is dead;

(2) four years have not elapsed since the date of the testator's death and before the application;

(3) the court has jurisdiction and venue over the estate;

(4) citation has been served and returned in the manner and for the period required by this title; and

(5) the person for whom letters testamentary or of administration are sought is entitled by law to the letters and is not disqualified.

Estates Code § 256.152. Additional Proof Required for Probate of Will

(a) An applicant for the probate of a will must prove the following to the court's satisfaction, in addition to the proof required by Section 256.151, to obtain the probate:

(1) the testator did not revoke the will; and

(2) if the will is not self-proved, the testator:

(A) executed the will with the formalities and solemnities and under the circumstances required by law to make the will valid; and

(B) at the time of executing the will, was of sound mind and:

(i) was 18 years of age or older;

(ii) was or had been married; or

(iii) was a member of the armed forces of the United States, an auxiliary of the armed forces of the United States, or the United States Maritime Service.

(b) A will that is self-proved as provided by Subchapter C, Chapter 251, or, if executed in another state or a foreign country, is self-proved in accordance with the laws of the state or foreign country of the testator's domicile at the time of the execution is not required to have any additional proof that the will was executed with the formalities and solemnities and under the circumstances required to make the will valid.

. . .

Will proponents may obtain summary judgment when contestants fail to prove elements of various challenges to capacity and volition of testator

Estate of GRAHAM
Court of Appeals of Texas, Corpus Christi
69 S.W.3d 598 (2002)

DORSEY, J. This is a will contest. Frances Graham died in 1998 at the age of 83 years. His wife predeceased him, and he had no children. Two years before his death, Mr. Graham executed a will leaving his entire estate to the two daughters of his full sister. After Mr. Graham's will was admitted to probate, his seven remaining nieces and nephews brought suit to challenge the will. Those nieces and nephews are the children of Mr. Graham's half-sister. The two nieces who are beneficiaries under the will are the "will proponents," and the seven nieces and nephews who brought this are the "will contestants."

In their suit, the will contestants asserted that the will was invalid for the following reasons:

(1) it was not executed with the formalities and solemnities required by the Texas Probate Code;

(2) Mr. Graham lacked testamentary capacity when he executed it;

(3) it was executed as a result of the undue influence and fraud;

(4) Mr. Graham did not intend the document to be a will; and,

(5) Mr. Graham was mistaken as to the contents of the instrument.[1]

The will proponents moved for summary judgment on all causes of action. . . . The trial court granted the motion . . . and entered an order that the will contestants take nothing by their suit. . . . In a traditional summary judgment proceeding, the standard of review on appeal is whether the movant at the trial level carried the burden of showing that no genuine issue of material fact existed as to one or more elements of the nonmovant's cause or claim and that judgment should be granted as a matter of law. See Texas Rule of Civil Procedure 166a(c); Nixon v. Mr. Prop. Mgmt. Co., Inc., 690 S.W.2d 546, 548 (Tex. 1985). In resolving the issue of whether the movant has carried this burden, all evidence favorable to the nonmovant must be taken as true and all reasonable inferences, including any doubts, must be resolved in the nonmovant's favor. *Nixon*, 690 S.W.2d at 548-49.

FAILURE TO PROPERLY EXECUTE THE WILL

We first address the will contestants' claim that Mr. Graham's will was not executed with the "formalities and solemnities required by the Texas Probate Code." Section 59 of the Texas Probate Code sets forth the requisites of a will. See Texas Probate Code § 59(a). It states that, except where otherwise provided by law, a will must be (1) in writing, (2) signed by the testator and (3) be attested by two or more credible witnesses above the age of fourteen years who shall subscribe their names thereto in their own handwriting in the presence of the testator. Id. The will proponents provided summary judgment evidence establishing that Mr. Graham's will met those requirements. . . .

Section 59 also provides a method for self-proving a will. See id. § 59(a)-(c). A will which is self-proved needs no further proof of its execution with the formalities and solemnities and under the circumstances required to make it a valid will. See id. § 84(a). While a self-proved will can still be challenged, the self-proving affidavit constitutes prima facie evidence of the will's execution. See Gasaway v. Nesmith, 548 S.W.2d 457, 458 (Tex. Civ. App.-Houston [1st Dist.] 1977, writ ref'd n.r.e.). . . . [T]he will proponents' summary judgment evidence establishes that the will was self-proven. Thus, prima facie validity of its execution was established. . . .

The will contestants failed to offer any evidence that raises a genuine issue of material fact regarding whether Francis Graham's will was executed with appropriate formalities. In fact, the entire depositions of all seven of the will contestants were offered by the movant, as were excerpts of those depositions offered by the will contestants themselves. None of them had any knowledge regarding the circumstances surrounding the execution of Mr. Graham's will. Thus, summary judgment was properly granted on that basis.

---

[1] They also made a claim for constructive trust. Constructive trust is an equitable remedy that is imposed upon property obtained by fraudulent means. Thigpen v. Locke, 363 S.W.2d 247, 250 (Tex. 1962). Because we have found no fraud, constructive trust is not available.

LACK OF TESTAMENTARY CAPACITY

Next, the will contestants alleged that Mr. Graham did not have testamentary capacity when he executed his will. In order to execute a valid will,

> [T]he testator must have been of sound mind at its execution; and by this is meant that he must have been capable of understanding the nature of the business he was engaged in, the nature and extent of his property, the persons to whom he meant to devise and bequeath it, the persons dependent upon his bounty, and the mode of distribution among them; that he must have had memory sufficient to collect in his mind the elements of the business to be transacted, and to hold them long enough to perceive, at least, their obvious relations to each other, and be able to form a reasonable judgment as to them; and that he was not under the influence of an insane delusion, either in regard to his property or the natural and proper objects of his bounty, which affected the disposition he was about to make.

Prather v. McClelland, 76 Tex. 574, 13 S.W. 543, 547 (1890). This definition of testamentary capacity remains the benchmark in Texas. . . .

While even the proponent of a self-proven will retains the burden of proving testamentary capacity when offering the will for probate, once the will has been admitted to probate, the burden shifts to any contestant to establish a *lack* of testamentary capacity. See Texas Probate Code § 88(b) (stating that to obtain the probate of a will, the applicant must prove to the satisfaction of the court that the testator was "of sound mind"); Croucher v. Croucher, 660 S.W.2d 55, 57 (Tex. 1983) (fact that will is self-proved does not relieve applicant for probate of the burden of establishing testamentary capacity of testator); Woods' Estate, 542 S.W.2d 845, 846 (Tex. 1976) (burden is on contestant); Lee v. Lee, 424 S.W.2d 609, 612 n. 1 (Tex. 1968) (after will admitted to probate, burden is on will contestants to establish incapacity by a preponderance of the evidence).

The Texas Supreme Court has said that the proper inquiry in a will contest on grounds of testamentary incapacity is the condition of the testator's mind on the day the will was executed. *Lee*, 424 S.W.2d at 611. If there is no direct testimony of acts, demeanor or condition indicating that the testator lacked testamentary capacity on the date of execution, the testator's mental condition on that date may be determined from lay opinion testimony based upon the witnesses' observations of testator's conduct either prior or subsequent to the execution. Id. However, that evidence has probative force only if some evidence exists demonstrating that the condition persists and has some probability of being the same condition that existed at the time the will was made. Id. Thus, to successfully challenge a testator's mental capacity with circumstantial evidence from time periods other than the day on which the will was executed, the will contestants must establish (1) that the evidence offered indicates a lack of testamentary capacity; (2) that the evidence is probative of the testator's capacity (or lack thereof) on the day the will was executed; and (3) that the evidence provided is of a satisfactory and convincing character, because probate will not be set aside on the basis of evidence that creates only a suspicion of mental incapacity. See Horton v. Horton, 965 S.W.2d 78, 85 (Tex. App.-Fort Worth 1998, no pet.).

The will proponents established as a matter of law that Mr. Graham possessed testamentary capacity at the time he signed his will. Cynthia Baumgardner stated in her affidavit that Mr. Graham approached her at her job and asked her to type up his will for him. He then executed the will in front of her and two other witnesses. She stated that Mr. Graham had written out the terms of his will and asked her to type them up exactly as he had written. This indicates Mr. Graham knew what he was doing and desired to dispose of his estate in the manner outlined in the will. Baumgardner also stated that Mr. Graham told her that day that he wanted his property to go to his two nieces, Theresa A. Carollo and Bernadette P. Jaswith, the will proponents. She also stated that Graham "was acting solely on his own without influence or presence of any family member or any other person, and he stated that he just wanted to have things done in a legal and proper way so that his Estate would go to his two nieces as set out in the Will." This evidence indicates that Mr. Graham possessed the testamentary capacity required to make a valid will.

The will proponents also attached to their motion the affidavit of Rachel Jimenez. Rachel Jimenez stated that she was acquainted with Mr. Graham for over twenty-four years, saw him almost on a daily basis during the last year of his life, and that he was "alert and coherent and knew exactly what he was doing from the time [she] first met him through his hospitalization and stay in the nursing home here in Corpus Christi just prior to his death." She stated that during the time she knew Graham, there was never a time when he was not mentally alert and capable of taking care of his own affairs. She also stated that he was "afraid of" one of his nephews that lived in Corpus Christi and would not allow that nephew to enter his property. (The nephew referred to is one of the will contestants.) She also stated that she had to use a special phone code to contact Mr. Graham because he did not want to inadvertently answer the phone and have to talk to one of his nephews, whom he feared would be soliciting money from him. Jimenez stated that Mr. Graham disliked his nephews who lived in Corpus very much and considered them dangerous. She said Mr. Graham told her that after one of them stole money from his wallet, he had nothing more to do with them. Finally, Jimenez stated that, to her knowledge, none of the contestants visited Mr. Graham when he was in the nursing home and hospital prior to his death.

Also attached to the summary judgment was the affidavit of Alice Jimenez, who stated that she knew Mr. Graham for approximately twenty years, saw him several times during the last year of his life including one visit while he was in the nursing home, and that he was always mentally alert and of sound mind. She stated that he was capable of handling his own financial affairs from the time she met him until his death.

The affidavit of Altagracia Garcia, the notary who acknowledged Mr. Graham's will, was also attached to the proponents' motion. Garcia stated that although she only met Mr. Graham the one time, he seemed to her to know exactly what he was doing and seemed to be fully mentally competent. She also stated that as he was getting ready to leave her office, he commented that he had some nephews he did not care for.

Also attached to proponents' motion was the affidavit of Joe Adame, a neighbor of Mr. Graham's from 1982 until the time he died. Adame stated that he spoke to Mr. Graham as recently as a few months before his death and that he seemed "fully competent." He also said that although he visited with the Grahams regularly—though not frequently—Mr. Graham never mentioned any nephews or nieces.

The affidavit of Mona Baen, a long-time friend of Mr. Graham's, was also provided. Ms. Baen stated that Mr. Graham was a family friend for years, and that she lived near the Grahams while growing up. She said that when her mother was alive, she, too, used the telephone code system with Mr. Graham so that he could avoid certain phone calls. Ms. Baen stated that she knew that Mr. Graham cared "particularly" about a niece in Chicago named Theresa, but she did not remember his mentioning any other niece in that area. She stated that Mr. Graham had related he had other nephews and nieces for whom he did not care. Ms. Baen stated that she and her mother visited Mr. Graham often when he was in the hospital suffering from his last illness. After he died, either she or her mother called Theresa in Chicago and met her plane when Theresa and her husband arrived in Corpus. She said that although Mr. Graham was "somewhat eccentric, he was always of sound mind and knew exactly what he was doing and saying, even right up until the time of his death."

That evidence negates the will contestants' allegation that Mr. Graham did not have the requisite testamentary capacity to execute a valid will in 1998. He was fully aware that he was making a will bequeathing his entire estate to his two nieces and not leaving anything to the contestants. See *Prather*, 13 S.W. at 547. By all accounts, Mr. Graham was lucid and comprehended what he was doing when he executed his will.

In contrast, the will contestants did not submit a scintilla of evidence raising a fact issue on the question of whether Mr. Graham possessed testamentary capacity at the time he executed his will. . . . In fact, they made no argument whatever regarding testamentary capacity in their response and produced no evidence in that regard. Accordingly, we affirm the trial court's judgment in favor of the will proponents on the testamentary capacity cause of action.

LACK OF INTENT TO MAKE A WILL

Next, the will contestants alleged that Mr. Graham did not possess the required testamentary intent when he executed his March 1996 will. A document is not a will unless it is executed with testamentary intent. Hinson v. Hinson, 154 Tex. 561, 280 S.W.2d 731, 733 (1955). "To give the instrument the legal effect either of a will or other revocation of former wills it must be written and signed with the present intention to make it a will or revocation." Brackenridge v. Roberts, 114 Tex. 418, 267 S.W. 244, 246 (1924); see also *Hinson*, 280 S.W.2d at 733. "It is essential . . . that the maker shall have intended to express his testamentary wishes in the particular instrument." *Hinson*, 280 S.W.2d at 733. This concept has been explained to mean that in order for a document to possess the requisite testamentary intent, it must be evident that the testator intended that the very document at issue to be the instrument that actually makes the disposition of the testator's estate. See id., show his free agency was overcome by such influence. See *Rothermel*, 369 S.W.2d at 922. "The exertion of influence that was undue cannot be inferred alone from opportunity, but there must be some testimony, direct or circumstantial, to show that influence was not only present but that it was in fact exerted with respect to the making of the testament itself." See id. at 923. This is not enough to defeat a motion for traditional summary judgment when the movants have offered ample evidence establishing the absence of undue influence. We affirm the trial court's grant of summary judgment on this cause of action as well.

FRAUD

Finally, the will contestants alleged that Mr. Graham's will was executed as a result of fraud. A claim that a will was procured through fraud requires proof of some kind of misrepresentation. See *Guthrie*, 934 S.W.2d at 832-33. The will proponents offered ample evidence to show that Mr. Graham's will was not the result of any type of fraud. The will contestants offered no controverting evidence showing any type of misrepresentation. Accordingly, we affirm summary judgment on the fraud claim.

The will proponents' motion for summary judgment is hereby AFFIRMED in all respects.

Direct evidence of testator's general mental condition may support finding of testamentary capacity

Estate of ARRINGTON

Court of Appeals of Texas, Houston
365 S.W.3d 463 (2012)

BLAND, J. This is a will contest case. The testator's wife, Brenda Arrington, challenges the trial court's judgment, rendered on a jury verdict, admitting the will to probate and appointing the testator's daughter, Patricia Daley, the executrix of the will. The jury found that the disputed will was validly executed and the testator, Gerald Pat Arrington, possessed testamentary capacity. On appeal, Brenda contends that no evidence supports the jury's findings. We affirm.

BACKGROUND

Two days after doctors diagnosed him with an inoperable brain tumor, Gerald Pat Arrington ("Pat") executed a self-proved will naming his daughter, Patricia, as the independent executrix and sole beneficiary of his estate. See Texas Probate Code § 59(a), (b) (allowing for wills to be self-proved by affidavits of testator and subscribing witnesses meeting certain requirements). As recited in his will, Pat was married at the time to Brenda Arrington, but they were separated pending a divorce. The couple had no children together. Pat's will names his children from previous relationships: Michael Lee Arrington, Blake Jon Arrington, Patricia Jacqueline Arrington Daley, Lora Lara, and Jennifer Gale Arrington. Although Pat's final will acknowledges each of his children and his wife Brenda, Pat made no provision for any of them save Patricia.

Pat executed his final will at a bank, on December 27, 2004, in the presence of two subscribing witnesses and a notary. Appended to Pat's will are sworn affidavits from Rachael Wells and Deanie Vezurk, the two subscribing witnesses, averring to the requirements set forth in section 59(a) of the Texas Probate Code for self-proving affidavits. See Texas Probate Code § 59(a). The subscribing witnesses and the notary, Sarah Nobles, testified at trial to the facts set forth in the affidavits: that Pat signed his will in the presence of two subscribing witnesses, the witnesses signed the will in his presence, and the subscribing witnesses were over the age of fourteen. See id.

The witnesses and the notary also testified to Pat's mental capacity on the date he executed his will. Vezurk recounted that Pat had lived near her and, based on her interactions with him, he appeared of sound mind the day he executed his will. Wells testified that she was not well acquainted with Pat, but that Pat understood that he was executing his final will. Finally, Nobles testified that she had frequently interacted with Pat during her twenty years as a bank employee and, based on her familiarity with him, nothing about Pat's demeanor was out of the ordinary the day he executed his will. Nobles recalled that Pat had told her that he needed to get his last will and testament notarized that day.

Pat suffered from headaches as a result of his tumor and took steroids to allay his symptoms. Despite his diagnosis, witnesses testified that Pat was mentally competent in December 2004, and he had not experienced memory loss as a result of his condition. Pat's sisters testified that Pat had maintained his mental faculties until his death.

In addition to the brain tumor, Pat had been suffering from the effects of an electric shock accident in 1983. Pat had difficulty speaking and an unsteady gait following the accident. Pat's condition improved over time. Rehabilitative therapy had enabled Pat to work cattle, ride horses, and drive. He continued to engage in these activities until 2005, when treatment for his tumor began to impede his daily activities. Pat died in December 2005.

Witnesses also testified about the nature of Pat's family relations. The executrix, Patricia, had lived with Pat since her birth. After she married David Daley, the couple resided at Pat's home. The Daleys helped Pat care for his land and work cattle. Pat's son, Blake, testified that Pat had told him that Pat would will his entire estate to Patricia. Blake reasoned that Pat did so because Patricia was Pat's only "stable" child, acted as the family matriarch, and could be depended on to keep Pat's land in the family. Blake testified that Pat did not devise his separate property to his wife Brenda because Brenda had not lived with Pat during the four years preceding his death; Pat had become certain that Brenda would sell his property if he left it to her.

After Pat's death, Patricia applied to probate his final will. Brenda contested the application. A jury found in favor of Patricia, determining that (1) the proffered will was the will that Pat had executed in December 2004, (2) Pat validly executed the will, and (3) Pat possessed testamentary capacity on the day he executed it. Brenda moved for judgment notwithstanding the verdict and a new trial. The trial court denied Brenda's motions and admitted the will to probate. On appeal, Brenda maintains that the trial court erred in admitting the will to probate because no evidence supports the jury's findings that the proffered will was valid and that Pat had testamentary capacity on the day he executed it.

STANDARD OF REVIEW

A trial court may disregard a jury's verdict and render a judgment notwithstanding that verdict if the evidence is legally insufficient to support the jury's findings or a directed verdict would have been proper because a legal principle precludes recovery. . . .

VALIDITY OF THE WILL

To admit a will to probate, a trial court must find that it is valid. Guthrie v. Suiter, 934 S.W.2d 820, 829 (Tex. App.-Houston [1st Dist.] 1996, no writ). Patricia, the proponent of the will, had the burden to establish validity. See Croucher v. Croucher, 660 S.W.2d 55, 57 (Tex. 1983); Douthit v. McLeroy, 539 S.W.2d 351, 352 (Tex. 1976) (per curiam).

To be valid, a will must conform to the requirements set forth in section 59(a) of the Probate Code. Texas Probate Code § 59(a). With exceptions inapplicable here, section 59(a) provides that a will is valid if it is (1) in writing, (2) signed by the testator, and (3) attested by two or more credible witnesses above the age of fourteen years, who write their signatures in the testator's presence. Id. Section 59(a) further provides that a will may be made "self-proved, and the testimony of the witnesses in the probate thereof may be made unnecessary, by the affidavits of the testator and attesting witnesses, made before an officer authorized to administer oaths." Id. A self-proved will is prima facie evidence that the will was properly executed. See *Guthrie*, 934 S.W.2d at 829; see also Bracewell v. Bracewell, 20 S.W.3d 14, 26 (Tex. App.-Houston [14th Dist.] 2000, no pet.). Accordingly, a self-proved will may be admitted to probate without the testimony of any subscribing witnesses. Texas Probate Code § 59(c); *Guthrie*, 934 S.W.2d at 829.

Pat executed his final will in the presence of two witnesses and a notary. Appended to his will are affidavits from Rachael Wells and Deanie Vezurk, the two subscribing witnesses, averring to the language provided by section 59(a) for self-proving affidavits. See Texas Probate Code § 59(a), (b). Because Pat's will contains affidavits from the subscribing witnesses reciting the language set forth in section 59(a), it is a self-proved will. Id. Thus, Patricia's proffer of the will itself was prima facie evidence that the will was validly executed; she needed no further proof to demonstrate its validity. Texas Probate Code § 59(c). Nevertheless, Patricia presented testimony at trial from both subscribing witnesses. They confirmed the facts set forth in their affidavits, recalling that they had affixed their signatures to Pat's will in his presence and that Pat had signed his will in their presence. Both witnesses confirmed that they were over the age of fourteen.

Brenda challenges the jury's finding of valid execution because the subscribing witnesses did not testify that Pat signed each page of the proffered will nor did they read the contents of the will. But the statute does not require that a will's contents be published to its witnesses. See Texas Probate Code § 59(a); Brown v. Traylor, 210 S.W.3d 648, 664 (Tex. App.-Houston [1st Dist.] 2006, no pet.) (publication not prerequisite to validity; contents must be proved only if will cannot be produced in court). Nor does the Probate Code require testimony that the testator initialed every page of his final will. See Texas Probate Code § 59(a) (will not wholly in testator's handwriting shall be signed). Both witnesses executed affidavits that track the format within Chapter 59, and testified that Pat declared that they were witnesses to his last will, which Pat executed on December 27, 2004. Although Brenda implies in her reply brief that the will Patricia sought to admit to probate was not the December 27 will, the jury expressly found that it was. The affidavits and testimony of the testamentary witnesses support the jury's finding.

The proffered will complies with all statutory requirements for a self-proved will. As the will was executed in compliance with the solemnities prescribed by the Probate Code, we hold that it was validly executed.

TESTAMENTARY CAPACITY

Testamentary capacity means that the testator has possession of sufficient mental ability at the time of execution of the will (1) to understand the effect of making a will and the general nature and extent of the testator's property, (2) to know the testator's next of kin and the natural objects of his bounty, and (3) to have sufficient memory to assimilate the elements of executing a will, to hold those elements long enough to perceive their obvious relation to each other, and to form a reasonable judgment as to them. Prather v. McClelland, 76 Tex. 574, 584-85, 13 S.W. 543, 545-46 (1890); *Guthrie*, 934 S.W.2d at 829; Wilkinson v. Moore, 623 S.W.2d 662, 663-64 (Tex. Civ. App.-Houston [1st Dist.] 1981, writ dism'd). In a will contest challenging testamentary capacity, the issue is the condition of the testator's mind on or around the date he executed the will. *Wilkinson*, 623 S.W.2d at 663-64. A challenger to the will's validity may also rely on evidence of incompetence on occasions both before and after the execution date if the condition persisted and had some probability of being "the same condition which obtained at the time of the will's making." *Guthrie*, 934 S.W.2d at 830; *Croucher*, 660 S.W.2d at 57.

The jury in this case heard both kinds of evidence. The jury heard direct evidence of Pat's mental condition on the date the will was executed. Both subscribing witnesses testified that Pat was of sound mind when he signed his will at the bank. One subscribing witnesses had known Pat for twenty years. She testified that nothing about Pat's demeanor was out of the ordinary that day. The notary also provided direct evidence of Pat's mental condition. She testified that, on the date Pat signed his will, Pat was of sound mind, was capable of conversation, and answered her questions. She further recounted that Pat told her that he was signing his will and that it needed to be notarized.

The jury in this case also heard testimony about Pat's health problems, including testimony about a 1983 electric shock accident, his headaches, and his declining health in 2005. Brenda conceded that Pat performed his daily work after the accident; he worked cattle on horseback. Members of Pat's family testified that Pat possessed all his mental faculties after the accident, noticing no change in his daily behavior beyond some difficulty walking. The jury heard testimony that, in December 2004, Pat suffered from headaches and was taking steroids to treat the symptoms of his brain tumor. Pat's sisters, a son, a daughter, and a co-worker each testified that, despite this condition, Pat acted like himself during that time. They recalled that Pat provided them with driving directions to his doctor's office. After doctors biopsied his tumor in 2005, Pat became partially paralyzed. Pat no longer cared for himself but relied on his family to care for him. Nevertheless, Pat's sisters testified that he maintained his mental faculties until his death.

Brenda argues that the evidence that Patricia adduced is legally insufficient. She claims that, because no evidence demonstrates that Pat discussed his children or the approximate nature of his property with the witnesses on the date he executed his will, Pat lacked the capacity to make a judgment about bequeathing his property. She asserts that Pat did not know who his children were because his will names a child whom he never adopted in a legal proceeding, and it omits an alleged sixth child. But a finding of testamentary capacity does not hinge entirely on direct evidence that the testator discussed the details of his children, wealth, or disposition at the time he signed his will. See *Prather*, 13 S.W. at 545-46. The jury heard direct evidence of Pat's general mental condition on the day he executed his will and the attending months before and after: this evidence supports its determination that Pat knew that he was executing his will and that he had deliberately chosen Patricia to be his sole beneficiary. . . .

We hold that the evidence is legally sufficient to support the jury's finding of testamentary capacity. See Collins v. Smith, 53 S.W.3d 832, 843 (Tex. App.-Houston [1st Dist.] 2001, no pet.) (testimony that testator was of sound mind and knew what he was doing when he executed will was sufficient to remove any suspicion surrounding wills execution); Horton v. Horton, 965 S.W.2d 78, 86 (Tex. App.-Fort Worth 1998, no pet.) (evidence testator had taken pain medication and experienced hallucinations was not sufficient to show incapacity where witnesses testified testator was of sound mind when he executed will and no direct evidence demonstrated he experienced hallucinations at time he signed will).

CONCLUSION

The trial court properly upheld the jury's findings on validity and testamentary capacity. It properly admitted the will to probate. We therefore affirm the judgment of the trial court.

Perceived "lack of family love" not basis for insane delusion challenge

BAUER v. Estate of BAUER
Court of Appeals of Texas, Houston
687 S.W.2d 410 (1985)

BROWN, C.J. This is an appeal from the trial court's refusal to give a jury instruction on insane delusion in a will contest. Roger Bauer, thirty-one years old and on the verge of economic success, was visiting his mother, the appellant in this case, in Green Valley, Arizona during the Christmas holidays of 1983. On December 30 he wrote a holographic will in the form of a letter to his girlfriend, Lai Lee. A few minutes later he committed suicide.

The letter contains the following statement:

> "My primary reason for doing this a near complete lack of family love. It is something that will always be missing from my life. I will never be able to compensate for it no matter what."

In later paragraphs Roger calls upon Lai to take certain actions with regard to his burial, his car, his debts, his investment properties, and the gun with which he shot himself. Among the debts he ask[s] her to pay out of his holdings is one of $5000 to his mother (the appellant). He suggests that this money can be used to pay for an eye operation for his sister Linda which would make contacts or glasses unnecessary. The last sentence of the letter states simply, "I will everything I own to Lai W. Lee."

The appellant/contestant claims in her sole ground of error that Roger's belief that he had "a near complete lack of family love" was not only false or unfounded, but amounted to an insane delusion. In support of her claim she points to proof at trial that Roger suffered from "intermittent explosive disorder," a psychological disorder. According to the expert testimony, the intermittent explosive disorder caused the several instances of violent behavior he displayed toward his mother, sister and father over a period of years. It does not cause hallucinations, but instead can cause one to build up in his mind an interpretation of a relationship with another, or of something said by that person, which could be so totally unfounded as to amount to a delusion. We affirm.

We agree with appellant that if the issue of an insane delusion is raised, and the trial court submits nothing more than the general issue of testamentary capacity, such action is reversible error. See Goans v. Green, 464 S.W.2d 104 (Tex. 1970). However, it is also true that a failure to submit a jury issue is reversible only if the complaining party offered the missing special issue in substantially correct form. Texas Rule of Civil Procedure 279.

At the conclusion of the evidence, appellant requested the following instruction:

> "You are instructed that an insane delusion as respects testamentary capacity is a belief in a state of circumstances that no rational person would accept as true.
>
> "You are further instructed that when testator's false belief amounts in law to insane delusions *in terms of his will or influence thereby*, testamentary capacity is lacking even though testator might know the nature and extent of his property, effect of his will, and the natural objects of his bounty and might be able to handle complex business matters." (Emphasis added).

An insane delusion has been defined in Texas as "the belief of a state of supposed facts that do not exist, and which no rational person would believe." The contestant of a will is entitled to an instruction on insane delusion if there is any evidence of probative force which, with the inferences that may reasonably be drawn therefrom, will support a finding that the testator was laboring under such a delusion which *affected the terms of his will.* Lindley v. Lindley, 384 S.W.2d 676, 679 (Tex. 1964) (emphasis added).

We do not believe that appellant's issue was submitted in substantially correct form. The question is anything but trivial. The general rule is that where insanity is not shown, but only some insane delusion or monomania, the will is valid unless the terms of it appear to have been directly influenced by the infirmity. Gulf Oil Corp. v. Walker, 288 S.W.2d 173, 180 (Tex. Civ. App.-Beaumont 1956, no writ). The *Gulf Oil* case further elaborates the test to be followed in setting aside a will:

> "A man may believe himself to be the supreme ruler of the universe and nevertheless make a perfectly sensible disposition of his property, and the courts will sustain it when it appears that his mania did not dictate its provisions." Id. at 180. . . .

Nowhere in the record of this case does the testimony suggest that Roger would have made a different disposition of his property if he had not suffered from the intermittent explosive disorder. He and Lai had maintained a close relationship for six years before his death. They lived together for several years. She worked alongside him making repairs on his rental properties. When his father died he substituted Lai for his father as the primary beneficiary of his life insurance policy, listing her in his application as his "fiancee." He told his colleagues at work that Lai was his common-law wife. He also made a specific disposition of money to his mother in his will. In view of these facts, the jury was entitled to an issue which would present an either/or choice whether Roger's delusion in any way "affected the terms of his will," Lindley v. Lindley, supra, or "dictated its provisions," Gulf Oil v. Walker, supra. "Insane delusions in terms of his will or influence thereby," the "test" offered by appellant, masks the issue to be decided behind a flaccid and uncertain phrase which fails to state a proposition.

We believe, moreover, that even if appellant had submitted a proper instruction, this case does not present the kind of false belief which amounts to an insane delusion as that term is defined in law. No mere mistake, or prejudice or ill-founded conclusion, can ever be the basis of setting aside a will. Navarro v. Rodriquez, 235 S.W.2d 665, 667 (Tex. Civ. App.-San Antonio 1950, no writ). A finding of insane delusion is conditioned on the testator's belief in a state of supposed *facts;* the existence or non-existence of "family love" is a comparatively subjective phenomenon not well suited to proof within our legal system.

Appellant and Linda Bauer (Roger's sister) claim that they loved Roger. Appellant testified that she made sacrifices over the years in his behalf. We do not doubt the sincerity of these statements. Yet we must ask: where, from Roger's point of view, could family love have existed except in his mind? Thus if, as he reported in his will and many times before to friends, he did not feel it, if it did not express itself in him, how can we then say that he possessed it?

A distinction between facts and ideas, then, while too rough to serve as a general rule, is the proper guide to the disposition of this case. Black's Law Dictionary 531-2 (5th ed. 1979) defines "fact" as "[a] thing done; an action performed or an incident transpiring; an event or circumstance; an actual occurence." We think that the tenor of this definition and of existing Texas precedents exclude the idea of "family love" from consideration as the basis of an insane delusion. Perhaps the classic Texas case on insane delusion is Rodgers v. Fleming, 3 S.W.2d 77 (Tex. Comm. App. 1928, holding adopted). In *Rodgers* the testator believed that his nephew was going to kill him for his property. The testator had taken up carrying a pistol as a consequence of his belief. He also believed that astronomers were on the verge of discovering the location of the gates of heaven.

The false beliefs in *Rodgers*, then, concerned the nephew's intent to commit a specific act and the capacity of University of Texas astronomers to locate a specific place, heaven; in other words, to perform a specific action, to cause an actual occurrence. Thus precedent only exists for declaring as an insane delusion a belief which can be judged true or false by reference to the physical world or to the realm of specific acts and intentions.

In keeping with the spirit of *Rodgers* is Green v. Goans, 458 S.W.2d 705 (Tex. Civ. App.-El Paso, writ ref'd n.r.e. 464 S.W.2d 104 (Tex. 1970). The testator, in *Green*, who had moved in to a room adjoining the house of his close friends, suddenly developed the belief that these friends were trying to kill him. Similarly, in Lindley v. Lindley, 384 S.W.2d 676 (Tex. 1964), the testatrix's son had suffered a complete mental breakdown. He was taken to a hospital where it became necessary to tie him to his bed. The testatrix, who was 93 years old, saw this happen, and when the son died shortly thereafter, she developed the notion that the hospital and her two other children had caused the son's death and adjusted her will accordingly. The court in *Lindley* held that appellant was, under those facts, entitled to an instruction on insane delusion. In Spruance v. Northway, 601 S.W.2d 153 (Tex. Civ. App.-Waco 1980, writ ref'd n.r.e.), also cited by appellant, the testatrix believed that the appellee had put her in the hospital and was trying to get her property.

Unlike the insane delusions in the above cases, the term "family love" refers to an intangible sensation, an idea; it is a feeling which cannot exist independently of a positive belief in its existence. It is somewhat analogous to a gift under the law of property, which cannot be transferred—and thus cannot be a gift—unless it is actually received or delivered. A better analogy, perhaps, is provided by the law of libel, which distinguishes between facts and opinions. Facts, which can be proved true or false, are actionable; on the other hand, there is no such thing as a false idea. A.H. Belo Corp. v. Rayzor, 644 S.W.2d 71, 79 (Tex. App.-Fort Worth 1982, writ ref'd n.r.e.). In sum, a belief in a "near complete lack of family love" simply does not fall within that class of beliefs about which a judgment as to insane delusion can reasonably be made. Appellant's point of error is overruled.

The judgment of the trial court is affirmed.

Section B. Undue Influence

Estates Code § 254.003. Devises to Certain Attorneys and Other Persons

(a) A devise of property in a will is void if the devise is made to:

(1) an attorney who prepares or supervises the preparation of the will;

(2) a parent, descendant of a parent, or employee of the attorney described by Subdivision (1); or

(3) the spouse of a person described by Subdivision (1) or (2).

(b) This section does not apply to:

(1) a devise made to a person who:

(A) is the testator's spouse;

(B) is an ascendant or descendant of the testator; or

(C) is related within the third degree by consanguinity or affinity to the testator; or

(2) a bona fide purchaser for value from a devisee in a will.

Estates Code § 254.005. Forfeiture Clause

(a) A provision in a will that would cause a forfeiture of or void a devise or provision in favor of a person for bringing any court action, including contesting a will, is enforceable unless in a court action determining whether the forfeiture clause should be enforced, the person who brought the action contrary to the forfeiture clause establishes by a preponderance of the evidence that:

(1) just cause existed for bringing the action; and

(2) the action was brought and maintained in good faith.

(b) This section is not intended to and does not repeal any law recognizing that forfeiture clauses generally will not be construed to prevent a beneficiary from seeking to compel a fiduciary to perform the fiduciary's duties, seeking redress against a fiduciary for a breach of the fiduciary's duties, or seeking a judicial construction of a will or trust.

Property Code § 112.038. Forfeiture Clause

A provision in a trust that would cause a forfeiture of or void an interest for bringing any court action, including contesting a trust, is enforceable unless in a court action determining whether the forfeiture clause should be enforced, the person who brought the action contrary to the forfeiture clause establishes by a preponderance of the evidence that:

(1) just cause existed for bringing the action; and

(2) the action was brought and maintained in good faith.

Bequest to drafting attorney's in-office "independent contractor" is void

JONES v. KROWN
Court of Appeals of Texas, Fort Worth
218 S.W.3d 746 (2007)

I. INTRODUCTION

WALKER, J. This is an appeal from a declaratory judgment voiding a will's bequests and devises to Appellant Tilde Jones (Belenki). The primary issue we address in this appeal is whether a paralegal employed as an in-office independent contractor is nonetheless an employee for purposes of the application of Texas Probate Code section 58b. Because we hold that an in-office independent contractor is an employee within the meaning of the statute, we will affirm the trial court's declaratory judgment and the trial court's award of attorney's fees to Appellee Linda Krown, the testator's sister.

II. FACTUAL AND PROCEDURAL BACKGROUND

Attorney John Corbin prepared the Last Will and Testament of Michele I. Zorn. Zorn signed the will on May 5, 2003. Zorn's will named Belenki as executrix and as a beneficiary of Zorn's estate. Belenki worked in Corbin's office as an independent contractor for several years, including the time during which Corbin drafted Zorn's will and when Zorn executed the will. Belenki also performed work for several other attorneys who office-shared with Corbin; she kept track of her time, and each attorney paid her for the time she spent on their cases.

After Zorn passed away, Belenki filed Zorn's will for probate. Krown, Zorn's sister and heir at law, filed a motion for declaratory judgment, arguing that all devises and bequests to Belenki were void under Texas Probate Code section 58b, which provided that "a devise or bequest of property in a will to an heir or employee of the attorney who prepares or supervises the preparation of the will is void." See Texas Probate Code § 58b(a)(2). The trial court held an evidentiary hearing on Krown's motion for declaratory judgment, found that all bequests and devises to Belenki were void, and ordered that the bequests to Belenki be delivered to Zorn's intestate heirs. The trial court's declaratory judgment also ordered Belenki to pay Krown's costs and attorney's fees. . . . Belenki perfected this appeal and complains, in a single issue, that the trial court misconstrued and misapplied Texas Probate Code section 58b and erred by awarding attorney's fees and costs to Krown.

III. VOID BEQUESTS

Belenki contends that the trial court improperly construed Probate Code section 58b in a manner that voids Zorn's testamentary intent and void's Zorn's valid bequests to her. Specifically, Belenki argues that Zorn's bequests to her do not violate Probate Code section 58b because no evidence exists that Corbin, directly or indirectly through an employee or heir, sought to obtain all or a portion of Zorn's estate and because she, Belenki, was not Corbin's employee.

Belenki testified that she had worked for Corbin as an in-office independent contractor for several years; she worked for Corbin in this capacity when he drafted Zorn's will and on the date that Zorn signed her will. Belenki explained, however, that she did not draft Zorn's will and was not present in the room when Zorn signed the will. Belenki testified that she did contract work for Corbin from February 2003 to September 2004 and that she mainly worked on Corbin's personal injury cases. Belenki explained that she could come and go from the office as she pleased, that she was paid contract wages, that Corbin issued a Form 1099 to her, and that Corbin did not provide her with any benefits.

Corbin also testified that he prepared Zorn's will. He said that Belenki worked for him at his office as a legal assistant. Corbin confirmed that Belenki was an independent contractor, she could come and go as she pleased, and he did not provide benefits to her. Corbin stated that Belenki freely used his office internet and, except for some computer glitches, had access to his computer files; she shared his network.

Based on this evidence, the trial court found—in what is labeled as finding of fact number one—that Belenki "was an employee, within the meaning of 58b of the Texas Probate Code, of the attorney who prepared the Last Will and Testament filed herein, at both the time of drafting said Will and at the time of execution of said Will." In finding of fact number two, the trial court found that Belenki "is not the spouse of the testator, an ascendant or descendent of the testator, related within the third degree by consanguinity or affinity to the testator, or a bona fide purchaser for value from a devisee in the Will."

Because the evidence concerning Belenki's status as an in-office independent contractor as well as her relationship to Zorn was undisputed, the issue before us is whether the trial court properly applied the law, specifically Probate Code section 58b, to the undisputed facts. Thus, the issue presented is one of statutory construction, and we review matters of statutory construction de novo. City of San Antonio v. City of Boerne, 111 S.W.3d 22, 25 (Tex. 2003); City of Harlingen v. Alvarez, 204 S.W.3d 452, 459 (Tex. App.-Corpus Christi 2005, no pet.). Our primary objective in construing a statute is to give effect to the Legislature's intent. McIntyre v. Ramirez, 109 S.W.3d 741, 745 (Tex. 2003). If the statutory language is unambiguous, we will interpret the statute according to the "plain and common meaning of the statute's words." State ex rel. State Dep't of Highways & Pub. Transp. v. Gonzalez, 82 S.W.3d 322, 327 (Tex. 2002) (quoting Fitzgerald v. Advanced Spine Fixation Sys., Inc., 996 S.W.2d 864, 865 (Tex. 1999)). However, we must also consider the entire act, its nature and object, and the consequences that would follow from each construction. Atascosa County v. Atascosa County Appraisal Dist., 990 S.W.2d 255, 258 (Tex. 1999). Thus, we read the statute as a whole and interpret it to give effect to every part. City of San Antonio, 111 S.W.3d at 25.

At the time the will was executed, Texas Probate Code section 58b stated that "a devise or bequest of property in a will to an heir or employee of the attorney who prepares or supervises the preparation of the will is void." Texas Probate Code § 58b(a). The statute specified that it did not apply to a bona fide purchaser for value from a devisee in a will or to a devise or bequest made to a person who (1) is the testator's spouse, (2) is an ascendant or descendant of the testator, or (3) is related within the third degree by consanguinity or affinity to the testator. Id. § 58b(b). No other exceptions are listed.

The term "employee" is not defined in the Probate Code. See generally id. § 3. Because the language of Probate Code section 58b is unambiguous and Belenki has not argued that the language is ambiguous, we apply the plain and common meaning of the word "employee." At its simplest, an "employee" is "[o]ne who works for an employer; a person working for salary or wages." Black's Law Dictionary 525 (6th ed. 1990). Here, the evidence demonstrated that Corbin paid Belenki for legal services that she performed for him in his office; thus, under the above definition Belenki was Corbin's employee. She worked for Corbin for wages. Neither Probate Code section 58b nor any other Probate Code section draws a distinction between workers employed as independent contractors earning hourly wages and workers employed as traditional employees earning a salary.

Moreover, the application of section 58b to void Zorn's bequests to Belenki is consistent with the Legislature's intent in drafting the section, which was to avoid having an interested person use his position of trust to benefit himself. See Stanley M. Johanson, Johanson's Texas Probate Code Annotated § 58b cmt. (1998 ed.) (stating, "With a growing elderly population in Texas, there has been an increase in attorneys who have, unknowingly to the testator or rightful heirs, written themselves into wills."); see also Brown v. Traylor, 210 S.W.3d 648, 677 (Tex. App.-Houston [1st Dist.] 2006, no pet. h.) (supp. op. on reh'g) (Keyes, J., dissenting from denial of en banc reconsideration) (stating that under section 58b, a person who drafts a will is an interested person who may not use that position of trust to benefit either himself or a close relative).

Concerning Belenki's argument that no evidence exists that Corbin, directly or indirectly through an employee or heir, sought to obtain all or a portion of Zorn's estate, such a finding is not a prerequisite to the application of Probate Code section 58b. See Texas Probate Code § 58b. Consequently, we cannot hold that the absence of evidence of this fact precludes application of Probate Code section 58b.

The bottom line is that Belenki was working in Corbin's office, performing duties as a legal assistant for him during the time period when Corbin drafted Zorn's will—which made devises and bequests to Belenki—and when Zorn executed that will. The plain language of Probate Code section 58b, the stated legislative purpose in enacting section 58b, and a review of the Probate Code as a whole, all dictate the conclusion that Belenki was Corbin's employee for purposes of the application of Probate Code section 58b. The evidence is undisputed that Belenki's relationship with Zorn did not fall within one of the statutory exceptions to the application of Probate Code section 58b; that is, Belenki was not a bona fide purchaser for value, she is not Zorn's spouse, she is not an ascendant or descendant of Zorn, and she is not related within the third degree by consanguinity or affinity to Zorn. Id. § 58b(b). Because the trial court properly found that Belenki was Corbin's employee under Probate Code section 58b and because the evidence conclusively established that Belenki did not fall within any of the exceptions to section 58b, the trial court correctly applied Probate Code section 58b to the present facts to void Zorn's will's devises and bequests to Belenki. We overrule this portion of Belenki's issue.

IV. ATTORNEY'S FEES

Belenki next argues that the trial court erred and abused its discretion by awarding attorney's fees to Krown. Belenki contends that the trial court was not required to assess attorney's fees against her under the Declaratory Judgment Act and that she defended her friend's will in the trial proceeding in good faith. . . .

Here, the trial court made findings of fact that the amount of attorney's fees granted were just and reasonable. Belenki's only argument on appeal is that the trial court unfairly assessed attorney's fees against her. But, the trial court granted declaratory judgment in Krown's favor by voiding the bequests to Belenki. Therefore, we cannot say that the trial court's award of attorney's fees to Krown was unnecessary or unequitable; Krown prevailed in her declaratory action. See id. Because Belenki failed to demonstrate that the trial court abused its discretion by awarding attorney's fees, we overrule this portion of Belenki's issue.

V. CONCLUSION

Having addressed both of the challenges asserted in Belenki's sole issue and having overruled the issue, we affirm the trial court's declaratory judgment declaring all devises and gifts to Belenki void and assessing attorney's fees against Belenki.

Chapter 5. Wills: Construction

Section A. Mistaken or Ambiguous Language in Wills

Estates Code § 255.451. Circumstances Under Which Will May Be Modified or Reformed

(a) On the petition of a personal representative, a court may order that the terms of the will be modified or reformed, that the personal representative be directed or permitted to perform acts that are not authorized or that are prohibited by the terms of the will, or that the personal representative be prohibited from performing acts that are required by the terms of the will, if:

(1) modification of administrative, nondispositive terms of the will is necessary or appropriate to prevent waste or impairment of the estate's administration;

(2) the order is necessary or appropriate to achieve the testator's tax objectives or to qualify a distributee for government benefits and is not contrary to the testator's intent; or

(3) the order is necessary to correct a scrivener's error in the terms of the will, even if unambiguous, to conform with the testator's intent.

(b) An order described in Subsection (a)(3) may be issued only if the testator's intent is established by clear and convincing evidence.

Estates Code § 255.452. Judicial Discretion

The court shall exercise the court's discretion to order a modification or reformation under this subchapter in the manner that conforms as nearly as possible to the probable intent of the testator.

Estates Code § 255.453. Retroactive Effect

The court may direct that an order described by this subchapter has retroactive effect.

Estates Code § 255.454. Powers Cumulative

This subchapter does not limit a court's powers under other law, including the power to modify, reform, or terminate a testamentary trust under Section 112.054, Property Code.

Estates Code § 255.455. Duties and Liability of Personal Representative under Subchapter

(a) This subchapter does not create or imply a duty for a personal representative to:

(1) petition a court for modification or reformation of a will, to be directed or permitted to perform acts that are not authorized or that are prohibited by the terms of the will, or to be the will;

(2) inform devisees about the availability of relief under this subchapter; or

(3) review the will or other evidence to determine whether any action should be taken under this subchapter.

(b) A personal representative is not liable for failing to file a petition under Section 255.451.

Section B. Death of Beneficiaries

Estates Code § 255.151. Applicability of Subchapter

This subchapter applies unless the testator's last will and testament provides otherwise. For example, a devise in the testator's will stating "to my surviving children" or "to such of my children as shall survive me" prevents the application of Sections 255.153 and 255.154.

Estates Code § 255.152. Failure of Devise; Effect on Residuary Estate

(a) Except as provided by Sections 255.153 and 255.154, if a devise, other than a residuary devise, fails for any reason, the devise becomes a part of the residuary estate.

(b) Except as provided by Sections 255.153 and 255.154, if the residuary estate is devised to two or more persons and the share of one of the residuary devisees fails for any reason, that residuary devisee's share passes to the other residuary devisees, in proportion to the residuary devisee's interest in the residuary estate.

(c) Except as provided by Sections 255.153 and 255.154, the residuary estate passes as if the testator had died intestate if all residuary devisees:

(1) are deceased at the time the testator's will is executed;

(2) fail to survive the testator; or

(3) are treated as if the residuary devisees predeceased the testator.

Estates Code § 255.153. Disposition of Property to Certain Devisees who Predecease Testator

(a) If a devisee who is a descendant of the testator or a descendant of a testator's parent is deceased at the time the will is executed, fails to survive the testator, or is treated as if the devisee predeceased the testator by Chapter 121 or otherwise, the descendants of the devisee who survived the testator by 120 hours take the devised property in place of the devisee.

(b) Devised property to which Subsection (a) applies shall be divided into the number of shares equal to the total number of surviving descendants in the nearest degree of kinship to the devisee and deceased persons in the same degree of kinship to the devisee whose descendants survived the testator. Each surviving descendant in the nearest degree of kinship to the devisee receives one share, and the share of each deceased person in the same degree of kinship to the devisee whose descendants survived the testator is divided among the descendants by representation.

Estates Code § 255.154. Devisee under Class Gift

For purposes of this subchapter, a person who would have been a devisee under a class gift if the person had survived the testator is treated as a devisee unless the person died before the date the will was executed.

Estates Code § 255.401. Posthumous Class Gift Membership

(a) A right to take as a member under a class gift does not accrue to any person unless the person is born before, or is in gestation at, the time of the testator's death and survives for at least 120 hours. A person is:

(1) considered to be in gestation at the time of the testator's death if insemination or implantation occurs at or before the time of the testator's death; and

(2) presumed to be in gestation at the time of the testator's death if the person was born before the 301st day after the date of the testator's death.

(b) A provision in the testator's will that is contrary to this section prevails over this section.

Devise to testator's "living brothers and sisters" prevents application of antilapse statute

ALLEN v. TALLEY
Court of Appeals of Texas, Eastland
949 S.W.2d 59 (1997)

WRIGHT, J. This is a will construction case. The question presented is whether the decedent's will contains words of survivorship which preclude application of the anti-lapse statute.[1] The trial court held that it did and granted summary judgment accordingly. We affirm.

The facts are not disputed. The controversy results from the will of Mary B. Boase Shoults, deceased, which provides in relevant part:

> I give, devise and bequeath unto my *living brothers and sisters:* John Allen, Claude Allen, Lewis Allen, Lera Talley, and Juanita Jordan, to share and share alike, all of the property, real, personal and mixed, of which I may die seized and possessed or be entitled to at my death. (Emphasis added.)

At the time she executed her will, Mary had 3 brothers and 2 sisters who were alive. However, by the time that Mary died, all of her brothers and sisters had predeceased her except for her brother, Claude Allen, and her sister, Lera Talley. Each of the siblings who predeceased Mary left surviving children. Lewis Eugene Allen, Jr. is a surviving child of Lewis Allen, Sr. He filed an application to probate Mary's will. He also asked for the issuance of letters of administration and opposed Lera's request that letters of administration be

---

[1] Texas Probate Code § 68 provides in relevant part:

> (a) If a devisee who is a descendant of the testator or a descendant of a testator's parent is deceased at the time of the execution of the will, fails to survive the testator, or is treated as if the devisee predeceased the testator by Section 47 of this code or otherwise, the descendants of the devisee who survived the testator by 120 hours take the devised property in place of the devisee. The property shall be divided into as many shares as there are surviving descendants in the nearest degree of kinship to the devisee and deceased persons in the same degree whose descendants survived the testator. Each surviving descendant in the nearest degree receives one share, and the share of each deceased person in the same degree is divided among his descendants by representation. For purposes of this section, a person who would have been a devisee under a class gift if the person had survived the testator is treated as a devisee unless the person died before the date the will was executed.
>
> (e) This section applies unless the testator's last will and testament provides otherwise. For example, a devise or bequest in the testator's will such as "to my surviving children" or "to such of my children as shall survive me" prevents the application of Subsection (a) of this section.

issued to her. The court admitted the will to probate, but the order did not appoint an administrator.

Both Lewis, Jr. and Lera filed petitions for declaratory judgment. Lera argued that Mary intended that her estate pass to her brothers and sisters who were living at the time of her death and that the phrase "I give, devise and bequeath unto my living brothers and sisters: [naming them], to share and share alike" operates as words of survivorship precluding the application of the anti-lapse statute. On the other hand, Lewis, Jr. maintained that those words are not words of survivorship, that they do not create a class gift, and that the anti-lapse statute applies. If Lera is correct, then she and her brother, Claude, Mary's only living siblings as of the date of Mary's death, will share the entire estate. If Lewis, Jr.'s position is correct, then three-fifths of the estate will be shared by the survivors of Mary's deceased siblings because of the anti-lapse statute. Under Lewis, Jr.'s theory of the case, the remaining two-fifths would be shared equally by Claude and Lera. Both Lewis, Jr. and Lera filed motions for summary judgment. The trial court agreed with the position taken by Lera and granted her motion for summary judgment. In two points of error, Lewis, Jr. argues that the trial court erred in granting Lera's motion for summary judgment and in denying his motion for summary judgment.[2]

The primary concern of the court in the construction of a will is to determine the testator's intent. Henderson v. Parker, 728 S.W.2d 768, 770 (Tex. 1987). The intent of the testator must be ascertained by reviewing the will in its entirety. *Henderson v. Parker*, supra.

Neither party argues that the will is ambiguous, although both parties offer differing constructions of the will based on the same language. In the absence of ambiguity, we must construe the will based on the express language used. *Henderson v. Parker*, supra. We must determine what Mary meant by what she actually said, and not by what she should have said, giving the words used in the will their common and ordinary meaning absent a contrary expression in the will. White v. Taylor, 155 Tex. 392, 286 S.W.2d 925 (1956). If the court can give a "certain or definite legal meaning or interpretation" to the words of an instrument, the instrument is unambiguous; and the court may construe it as a matter of law. Coker v. Coker, 650 S.W.2d 391, 393 (Tex. 1983).

Lewis, Jr. argues that Mary intended for her estate to pass to her brothers and sisters who were living at the time the will was executed. He cites *Henderson v. Parker*, supra, as support for his contention. Lera distinguishes *Henderson* and, instead, relies, in part, upon Perry v. Hinshaw, 633 S.W.2d 503 (Tex. 1982).

---

[2] Other children of Mary's deceased siblings filed answers in the trial court, but Lewis Eugene Allen, Jr. is the only such child who perfected an appeal to this court.

The questioned clauses from *Perry*, from *Henderson*, and from Mary's will are:

Perry v. Hinshaw Will

> THIRD: Upon the death of HATTIE PETERSON, I direct that the real property from which the said HATTIE PETERSON, was receiving the rentals during her life time, be divided among the surviving sisters and brothers of myself and my beloved husband in the following manner: to my sister, MRS. HATTIE HOHHOF of Chicago, Illinois, one-half (1/2); and the remaining half to be divided equally, share and share alike, among the surviving brothers and sisters of my beloved husband, D.E. HINSHAW, the same being WILLIAM HINSHAW, FANNIE STEELE, COSA FRENSLY, LUDA JONES, and VERA PERRY, share and share alike.

Henderson v. Parker Will

> [T]hen in that event we give, devise and bequeath unto our surviving children of this marriage, all of our property and estates, of every nature and description, real, personal, and mixed, and wherever situated, in fee simple, as follows:
>
> TO DONALD E. PARKER 28 1/3 acres on the east end of our 95 acre tract, to MARVIN N. PARKER the center 33 1/3 acre tract with all improvements; and WILLIAM ALFRED PARKER the west 33 1/3 acres. Our will is that the land be divided equally between our three sons after deducting five acres heretofore given to DONALD E. PARKER.

Mary's Will

> I give, devise and bequeath unto my living brothers and sisters: John Allen, Claude Allen, Lewis Allen, Lera Talley, and Juanita Jordan, to share and share alike, all of the property, real, personal and mixed, of which I may die seized and possessed or be entitled to at my death.

In *Henderson*, the testators executed joint and reciprocal wills containing three alternative dispositions of their estate. The first two dispositions were to operate in the event one spouse survived the other and devised the entirety of the testators' estate to the survivor. The testators were survived by two sons, Donald and Marvin. The testators' son, William, predeceased the testators. He was survived by two daughters, Aline and Betty. Aline argued that the testators intended to create individual gifts to each of the three brothers and that the devise to William did not lapse but, instead, vested in his children, Aline and Betty.

The trial court granted the sisters' motion for summary judgment dividing the property to Donald and Marvin as provided under the wills, and the sisters each received an equal share of the property devised to their father, William. The court of appeals reversed the judgment of the trial court, found that the language created a class gift, and held that the two surviving brothers were entitled to the entire estate. The supreme court reversed, holding that the statement "[o]ur will is that the land be divided equally between our three sons" evidenced an intent to devise specific gifts to each son and that those gifts would inure to Aline and Betty to the extent of their deceased father's share. The court noted that the earlier survivorship provision was merely a general statement and that it was controlled by the subsequent, more specific provision which contained no words of survivorship. The court stated:

> Because a testator's intent is determined as of the time the will is executed, we read the phrase "surviving children of this marriage" to mean children "surviving" at the time the will was executed. Winkler v. Pitre, 410 S.W.2d 677, 679 (Tex. Civ. App.-San Antonio 1966, writ ref'd n.r.e.). The absence of survivorship language in the subsequent, more specific provision supports such a construction.

In *Perry*, all of D.E. Hinshaw's siblings had predeceased him except for Vera Perry. The supreme court held that Vera was entitled to one-half of the estate as the only surviving sibling:

> Lydia Hinshaw's will contains words of survivorship. Clearly, Vera Perry, as sole survivor of the brothers and sisters of D.E. Hinshaw, is entitled to an undivided 1/2 interest in the rental property. The fact Lydia Hinshaw [the testatrix] named her husband's brothers and sisters and also referred to them in terms of a class creates no ambiguity which would force this Court to resort to rules of construction. Any ambiguity is avoided by the clause: "share and share alike, among the surviving brothers and sisters."

Perry v. Hinshaw, supra at 505.

Here, Mary's will contained one general provision devising her entire estate to her "living brothers and sisters." There were no other specific provisions. Logically, Mary would not have devised any property owned at her death to any brothers or sisters who were deceased at the time the will was executed. Moreover, when the phrase "living brothers and sisters" is construed in light of the entire sentence, it is clear that Mary intended that it was her brothers and sisters who were living at the time of her death who were to participate in the ownership of her estate. Otherwise, the phrase "share and share alike," followed by no specific provisions to the contrary, would add nothing to the meaning of the will. We construe "living brothers and sisters," as used in the entire context of Mary's will, to be words of survivorship. Therefore, neither those who did not survive Mary nor their heirs are entitled to take under Mary's will. As Mary's only surviving siblings, Lera Talley and Claude Allen are entitled to share equally in the entire estate. Appellant's points of error are overruled.

The judgment of the trial court is affirmed.

Section C. Changes in Property: Ademption and Abatement

Estates Code § 255.101. Certain Lifetime Gifts Considered Satisfaction of Devise

Property that a testator gives to a person during the testator's lifetime is considered a satisfaction, either wholly or partly, of a devise to the person if:

(1) the testator's will provides for deduction of the lifetime gift from the devise;

(2) the testator declares in a contemporaneous writing that the lifetime gift is to be deducted from, or is in satisfaction of, the devise; or

(3) the devisee acknowledges in writing that the lifetime gift is in satisfaction of the devise.

Estates Code § 255.102. Valuation of Property

Property given in partial satisfaction of a devise shall be valued as of the earlier of:

(1) the date the devisee acquires possession of or enjoys the property; or

(2) the date of the testator's death.

Estates Code § 255.251. Definitions

(1) "Securities" has the meaning assigned by Section 4, The Securities Act (Article 581-4, Vernon's Texas Civil Statutes).

(2) "Stock" means securities.

Estates Code § 255.252. Increase in Securities; Accessions

Unless the will of a testator clearly provides otherwise, a devise of securities that are owned by the testator on the date the will is executed includes the following additional securities subsequently acquired by the testator as a result of the testator's ownership of the devised securities:

(1) securities of the same organization acquired because of an action initiated by the organization or any successor, related, or acquiring organization, including stock splits, stock dividends, and new issues of stock acquired in a reorganization, redemption, or exchange, other than securities acquired through the exercise of purchase options or through a plan of reinvestment; and

(2) securities of another organization acquired as a result of a merger, consolidation, reorganization, or other distribution by the organization or any successor, related, or acquiring organization, including stock splits, stock dividends, and new issues of stock acquired in a reorganization, redemption, or exchange, other than securities acquired through the exercise of purchase options or through a plan of reinvestment.

Estates Code § 255.253. Cash Distribution Not Included in Devise

Unless the will of a testator clearly provides otherwise, a devise of securities does not include a cash distribution relating to the securities that accrues before the testator's death, regardless of whether the distribution is paid before the testator's death.

Estates Code § 255.301. No Right to Exoneration of Debts

Except as provided by Section 255.302, a specific devise passes to the devisee subject to each debt secured by the property that exists on the date of the testator's death, and the devisee is not entitled to exoneration from the testator's estate for payment of the debt.

Estates Code § 255.302. Exception

A specific devise does not pass to the devisee subject to a debt described by Section 255.301 if the will in which the devise is made specifically states that the devise passes without being subject to the debt. A general provision in the will stating that debts are to be paid is not a specific statement for purposes of this section.

Estates Code § 355.151. Option to Treat Claim as Matured Secured Claim or Preferred Debt and Lien

(a) If a secured claim for money against an estate is presented, the claimant shall specify in the claim, in addition to all other matters required to be specified in the claim, whether the claimant desires to have the claim:

(1) allowed and approved as a matured secured claim to be paid in due course of administration, in which case the claim shall be paid in that manner if allowed and approved; or

(2) allowed, approved, and fixed as a preferred debt and lien against the specific property securing the indebtedness and paid according to the terms of the contract that secured the lien, in which case the claim shall be so allowed and approved if it is a valid lien.

(b) Notwithstanding Subsection (a)(2), the personal representative may pay a claim that the claimant desired to have allowed, approved, and fixed as a preferred debt and lien as described by Subsection (a)(2) before maturity if that payment is in the best interest of the estate.

Estates Code § 355.152. Period for Specifying Treatment of Secured Claim

(a) A secured creditor may present the creditor's claim for money and shall specify within the later of six months after the date letters testamentary or of administration are granted, or four months after the date notice required to be given under Section 308.053 is received, whether the claim is to be allowed and approved under Section 355.151(a)(1) or (2).

(b) A secured claim for money that is not presented within the period prescribed by Subsection (a) or that is presented without specifying how the claim is to be paid under Section 355.151 shall be treated as a claim to be paid in accordance with Section 355.151(a)(2).

Estates Code § 355.153. Payment of Matured Secured Claim

(a) A claim allowed and approved as a matured secured claim under Section 355.151(a)(1) shall be paid in due course of administration, and the secured creditor is not entitled to exercise any other remedy in a manner that prevents the preferential payment of claims and allowances described by Sections 355.103(1), (2), and (3).

(b) If a claim is allowed and approved as a matured secured claim under Section 355.151(a)(1) for a debt that would otherwise pass with the property securing the debt to one or more devisees in accordance with Section 255.301, the personal representative shall:

(1) collect from the devisees the amount of the debt; and

(2) pay that amount to the claimant in satisfaction of the claim.

(c) Each devisee's share of the debt under Subsection (b) is an amount equal to a fraction representing the devisee's ownership interest in the property securing the debt, multiplied by the amount of the debt.

(d) If the personal representative is unable to collect from the devisees an amount sufficient to pay the debt under Subsection (b), the representative shall, subject to Chapter 356, sell the property securing the debt. The representative shall:

(1) use the sale proceeds to pay the debt and any expenses associated with the sale; and

(2) distribute the remaining sale proceeds to each devisee in an amount equal to a fraction representing the devisee's ownership interest in the property, multiplied by the amount of the remaining sale proceeds.

(e) If the sale proceeds under Subsection (d) are insufficient to pay the debt and any expenses associated with the sale, the difference between the sale proceeds and the sum of the amount of the debt and the expenses associated with the sale shall be paid in the manner prescribed by Subsection (a).

Estates Code § 355.154. Preferred Debt and Lien

When a claim for a debt is allowed and approved under Section 355.151(a)(2):

(1) a further claim for the debt may not be made against other estate assets;

(2) the debt thereafter remains a preferred lien against the property securing the debt; and

(3) the property remains security for the debt in any distribution or sale of the property before final maturity and payment of the debt.

Estates Code § 355.109. Abatement of Bequests

(a) Except as provided by Subsections (b), (c), and (d), a decedent's property is liable for debts and expenses of administration other than estate taxes, and bequests abate in the following order:

(1) property not disposed of by will, but passing by intestacy;

(2) personal property of the residuary estate;

(3) real property of the residuary estate;

(4) general bequests of personal property;

(5) general devises of real property;

(6) specific bequests of personal property; and

(7) specific devises of real property.

(b) This section does not affect the requirements for payment of a claim of a secured creditor who elects to have the claim continued as a preferred debt and lien against specific property under Subchapter D.

(c) A decedent's intent expressed in a will controls over the abatement of bequests provided by this section.

(d) This section does not apply to the payment of estate taxes under Subchapter A, Chapter 124.

Chapter 6. Trusts: Characteristics and Creation

Section A. General Principles and Intent

Use of incorrect or nontechnical language does not preclude creation of trust

THATCHER v. CONWAY
Court of Civil Appeals of Texas, Beaumont
296 S.W.2d 790 (1956)

MURRAY, C.J. Appellees, A. W. Conway, Jr., et ux., filed suit in the District Court of Orange County . . . complaining of Leona Thatcher, guardian of the person and estate of Gary Leo Thatcher, a minor. The suit was brought to construe the will of Clyde S. Thatcher, deceased, and to define the rights, powers and duties of the trustees and executors and instruct them as to the management and control of such estate. The petition alleged, in effect, that Clyde S. Thatcher died intestate in Orange County, Texas, December 7, 1954; that the will appointed plaintiffs executor and executrix of his estate; a copy of the will was attached to the petition and made a part thereof; that said will was duly admitted to probate in Orange County; that the plaintiffs had qualified as executor and executrix. They further alleged that Leona Thatcher, the appellant, had been appointed guardian of the person and estate of Gary Leo Thatcher, a minor, and had qualified as such.

They further alleged that Gary Leo Thatcher is the minor son of Clyde S. Thatcher and Leona Thatcher and that said father and mother had been divorced at some date unknown to the pleader; that in said divorce decree the joint property of the parties had been divided between them and Leona Thatcher had been awarded the custody and control of the minor child. They further alleged that by the terms of the will they were appointed executor and executrix of the will of the said Clyde S. Thatcher, deceased, and also appointed as trustees for Gary Leo Thatcher, the minor, of the entire estate and beneficiary of the proceeds of three life insurance policies held by Clyde S. Thatcher upon his life; that they had accepted such trust and are willing to act as trustees. The petition also alleges that the entire estate of Clyde S. Thatcher included various interests in land, household goods, automobile, cash in bank and lists three insurance policies, one in the amount of $1,000 and two others totaling $4,000. The petition also alleged that the appellant Leona Thatcher, as guardian, has asserted a claim to proceeds of the said insurance policies and has indicated that she will seek control of all the remaining estate of Clyde S. Thatcher, deceased. In the petition it is prayed that due to the conflicting claims of the parties concerning the construction of said will and the respective rights, powers and duties, the court is requested to construe the will and determine if the appellees, A. W. Conway, Jr., and wife, were appointed trustees of the estate of Gary Leo Thatcher, and define the rights, powers and duties of the parties.

The will, which is the center of this controversy, was a holographic will, written entirely in the handwriting of the testator and is in the form of a letter to his son, Gary Leo Thatcher, who was four years of age at the time the will was written in 1954. The will is as follows:

> "Orange, Texas
> "Sunday, September-19-1954
> "Gary Leo Thatcher,
>
> "Dear Son
>
> "This is my last will and it takes the form of a letter to you. First I want to thank you for being the kind of a boy that you are. You have been everything to me. I have had lots of heartaches but you allways came along to cheer me up. I want you to grow up to be a real fine fellow. And what little real estate and insurance policies I have will be yours I have asked Mr and Mrs A. W. Conway Jr. who live on the Newton road out of Orange Tex to act as your guardian. They are a fine couple and will see that you get a good education. Everything you receive from me real estate and money and household furnishing will go to Mr and Mrs Conway to be used as they think best for you. Under no circumstances will they give your Mother Leona Thatcher any money or property of yours. I would like a very ordinary burial in some little cemetery out from Orange Texas. I have 3 other children besides Gary Leo Thatcher. Names are Thelma Faye Thatcher, Bobby Hugh Thatcher Marjorie Clyde Thatcher Brewer, each one of these children are given two dollars each of my estate. I understand the law requires they be given I dollar or more. These 3 children will understand why this was done. I will never understand why children will do to a parent what these 3 did to me. Gary Leo please allways be honest and fair with all your dealings. When I was in Ohio this year a lawyer told me that the Thatchers were good people but would not stick together. Well Gary you try to change all this and be a man who will stand for right. Gary please dont follow in your uncle Wilburs footsteps. Now Gary here are listed the real and personal property I have that is to be yours at my death. All except 6 dollars that is to be paid 2 dollars each to Thelma Faye Thatcher daughter, Bobby Hugh Thatcher, son Marjorie Clyde Thatcher Brewer daughter. 3 insurance Policies 1 for 1000 dollars, American National Life insurance Co. policy # 503636 1 for 3000 dollars. Equitable Life Assurance Cociety of the United states of America Group Insurance policy # 990010-09-452-07-9729. 1 policy for 1000 dollars The Equitable Life Assurance Society of the United States, Policy # 11.338.273 And Gary dont forget you will draw some benefits from Social Security payments. My Social Security # is 452-07-9729 then you will have a half interest in a home at 3587 East Lucas st.

Beaumont, Texas. This home is where you now live and occupies Lots # 2 & 3 — Block 217 Glenwood Addition, Beaumont, Texas. this property is subject to a court ruling that was made at the time of your Mothers divorce from me And is to be handled by Mr and Mrs Conway whom I have named is this letter. Then you will receive 3 lots #s 51-52-53 Block 217 Glenwood Addition Beaumont Texas these lots are all yours and no settlement of any kind is involved. You may pay the taxes and keep them or sell them and the money be paid to Mr and Mrs Conway to be used for your education. It will be up to them to do as they think best for you. Then Gary at the time of your Mothers divorce I was given one half of all the household furnishings of the home at 3587 Lucas st in Glenwood Addition, Beaumont Texas. Your Mother would not comply with this ruling so I never received anything I chereshed a beautiful collection of Furniture, China, and Glassware. These I had collected over the years I hope you can get and allways keep these Antiques of mine. Then there is a 1949 Pontiac Club Coupe I am buying not paid for at this date. You may sell it for the market price at the time of my death and keep the money for your self. Then there is a small checking account at the Orange National Bank. Name, Clyde S. Thatcher. this will also be yours Now Gary allways be nice to every one. And may god bless and keep you. Your father
"Clyde S. Thatcher.

"This letter will be authority for Mr and Mrs. A. W. Conway Jr. address Newton County road Orange Texas to assume full responsibility for my burial also to collect all money from insurance policys and handle all business that has to do with the estate of Clyde S. Thatcher and his Heir Gary Leo Thatcher. Age 4 years.
"signed. Clyde S. Thatcher."

The appellant answered the suit by plea in abatement, alleging that the will obviously does not convey anything to Conway and wife, nor refer to any other instrument which could be construed to be a conveyance to said people as trustees, therefore there is no necessity for any judicial construction of the will. The plea in abatement also alleged that the three life insurance policies were admitted in plaintiffs' petition to be payable to Gary Leo Thatcher, as beneficiary; that the proceeds of such policies were payable to the beneficiary named in the policies and therefore constituted no part of the estate of Clyde S. Thatcher, deceased; that the petition attempts to have the court decide that Clyde S. Thatcher, deceased, could and did by his will change the beneficiary in said policies from Gary Leo Thatcher, the minor boy, to the appellees Conway and wife as trustees under the will; that this is not correct and the petition should be dismissed. She also alleged that real estate devised in the will is an undivided one-half interest in a homestead of the appellant and her minor son, and the appellees in their petition attempt to have the court decree that they, as trustees, would be co-owners of such homestead. The plea in abatement also alleges that the holographic will of Clyde S. Thatcher, deceased, does not meet the requirements of the Texas Trust Act, Article 7425b-7, Revised Civil Statutes of Texas, to create a trust.

The trial court overruled the plea in abatement. The appellant also answered by special exception as to the identity of the parties, that the pleading did not allege that the will appointed Conway and wife trustees, nor that the deceased conveyed anything to them in any capacity. She also made various exceptions as to the effect of the will as alleged in the petition.

Appellant further answered by general denial and specially pleaded facts to the effect that the appellees had not acted with diligence in administering the estate of Clyde S. Thatcher, deceased. She specially pleaded that Gary Leo Thatcher, minor son, was beneficiary in the will and that under such designation as beneficiary the proceeds of such insurance policies should be paid only to the guardian of the minor named as beneficiary. She further pleaded various deficiencies of the will in its alleged failure to create a trust and appoint trustees.

The American National Insurance Company intervened by bill of interpleader, and alleged that it issued a life insurance policy on the life of Clyde S. Thatcher, deceased, in the sum of $1,000; that the proceeds of the policy is one of the matters in controversy; that with the filing of its intervention it deposited with the clerk of the court the money it owes under the insurance contract and asked the court to determine the party or parties entitled to receive such amount. It also prayed for its attorneys' fees and costs.

The trial was to the court without a jury. There was introduced in evidence the will and the envelope in which it was contained with the handwriting thereon and these instruments were brought up by photostatic copies in the statement of facts. The order of probate was introduced and the parties stipulated that appellees A. W. Conway, Jr., and wife were appointed executor and executrix of the estate of Clyde S. Thatcher, deceased; that Leona Thatcher, the appellant, was appointed legal guardian of the minor child, Gary Leo Thatcher; that Clyde S. Thatcher died December 7, 1954; that Gary Leo Thatcher, the minor son of the deceased and Leona Thatcher, the appellant, and that he was born December 3, 1949.

The parties then stipulated that Clyde S. Thatcher owned at his death 'that property and those claims described as follows'. The stipulation then describes an undivided half interest in real property in Beaumont, three lots in the City of Beaumont, an undivided half interest in furniture, china and silverware located in the house in Beaumont, an automobile, checking account in the bank and three insurance policies, two policies for $2,000 and one policy for $3,000. It also lists unpaid wages in the amount of $90. It further stipulated that Gary Leo Thatcher was named as beneficiary under the policies of insurance issued on the life of Clyde S. Thatcher, deceased.

The statement of facts contains no other facts.

The trial court rendered judgment, holding that it appeared to the court by the terms of the will that it was the intention of Clyde S. Thatcher to pass all of said property, including the proceeds of the life insurance policies, to Mr. and Mrs. A. W. Conway, Jr., as trustees of such property and that it was the intention of Clyde S. Thatcher that Leona Thatcher should not receive in any capacity any property or any of the proceeds of the life insurance policies; that it was his further intention for Mr. and Mrs. A. W. Conway, Jr., to hold all the property, including the proceeds of the life insurance policies, for the use and benefit of Gary Leo Thatcher and that Gary Leo Thatcher would be the only beneficiary named in said will to receive the property left to the exclusive control, care and management of Mr. and Mrs. A. W. Conway, Jr., and that Mr. and Mrs. A. W. Conway, Jr., are to hold and manage said property, including the proceeds of the life insurance policies, for the benefit of the minor for the purpose of giving him an education, and that the will of Clyde S. Thatcher created a trust for all such property, naming Mr. and Mrs. A. W. Conway, Jr., as trustees, and naming Gary Leo Thatcher exclusive beneficiary of the trust and that the trust is for the education of Gary Leo Thatcher. The judgment then decreed the above holdings and decreed that Mr. and Mrs. A. W. Conway, Jr., are trustees of all such property and that they shall hold such property in trust for Gary Leo Thatcher to the exclusion of the guardian, Leona Thatcher, and provided that in event of their resignation or removal that their substitute in trust shall have the same powers and duties as they have under the will. The judgment set bond at $5,000 to be executed by the trustees. It further decreed that the trust should cease to exist when Gary Leo Thatcher reached the age of 21 years or before such time and in event all of such property has been used for the purpose of said trust or for expenses incidental to carrying out this trust. It also provided that the intervenor, American National Life Insurance Company, be allowed their attorneys' fees and costs and that the money paid into the registry of the court by it should be paid to the appellees, Mr. and Mrs. A. W. Conway, Jr. It also provided that the appellant Leona Thatcher shall deliver to appellees, Mr. and Mrs. A. W. Conway, Jr., all property belonging to Clyde S. Thatcher before his death, including the proceeds of any insurance policies.

The appellant has duly perfected her appeal and has filed a supersedeas bond, superseding the judgment.

The appellant makes a long statement as to the nature of the case, which contains many matters of fact which are not shown by the record. The appellees have assailed such portions of the proof and say that they should not be considered by the court. We will determine this appeal only from our statement above, taken from the transcript and statement of facts.

By her Point No. 2 the appellant contends that the court erred in holding that the will in question created a trust and that the appellees were named as trustees. By her Point No. 4 appellant contends that the trial court erred in holding that the proceeds of the three policies of life insurance constituted a part of the estate of Clyde S. Thatcher, deceased, and that such proceeds be turned over to appellees to be administered by them as trustees. We think these two matters are the principal points in controversy, that they are presented here by appellant's points in her brief, and we will consider them in determining this appeal.

The above will of Clyde S. Thatcher, deceased, created a trust for the benefit of his minor son as sole beneficiary and appointed the appellees as trustees to carry out his wishes as expressed in the instrument. Even though the testator in writing his will often used terms and words mistakenly and apparently used the word 'guardian' when he obviously meant 'trustee', nevertheless his intention to create a trust and appoint these appellees as trustees is clear from the entire instrument. There is nothing in the will, when considered as creating a trust, which is in conflict with the Texas Trust Act, Article 7425b-7. It constitutes a transfer by will by the testator to other persons as trustees for another, his son. It is in writing and subscribed by him. While it is true that the will creating a trust does not provide for a definite time for the expiration of the trust, still the purpose of the trust is stated to be the care and education of the minor son and the trial court's decree in its judgment that the trust should terminate when the minor son has completed his education or has attained his majority is reasonable under those circumstances. When we consider the fact that the testator was obviously not a lawyer and did not know the exact legal meaning of some of the words he used in his will when considered alone, still from the whole instrument the testator's meaning and intention is clear. To effectuate an intention, trusts are often declared as a matter of inference from powers expressly granted and duties expressly imposed, and the courts will take into consideration the manifest purposes of an instrument which cannot be accomplished except through such an instrument made effective as a trust. Cruse v. Reinhard, Tex. Civ. App., 208 S.W.2d 598; Rich v. Witherspoon, Tex. Civ. App., 208 S.W.2d 674; Bell v. Board of Directors of Pythian Widows & Orphans Home, Tex. Civ. App., 219 S.W.2d 93; Gilkey v. Chambers, 146 Tex. 355, 207 S.W.2d 70.

We do not believe that the will of Clyde S. Thatcher, deceased, could have or would have the effect of conveying to the appellees as trustees the proceeds of insurance policies which named Gary Leo Thatcher, the minor boy, as beneficiary. A testator, of course, has the right to dispose of all his property by will. The testator here had no power or authority to change the beneficiary in his life insurance policies by will. His attempt to cause the proceeds of policies to be paid to the trustees named in his will was of no effect, because upon his death his estate and the executors and trustees thereunder had no interest in the proceeds of the life insurance policies. The insurance proceeds became the property of another at the time of his death. They became payable to the beneficiary named therein. Wipff v. Wipff, Tex. Civ. App., 209 S.W.2d 947.

Of course, the insured named in the policies of life insurance could have changed the beneficiary from his son to his estate, which is usually done by having the policy paid to the insured's executors, administrators and heirs. In such instances the proceeds of such life insurance policy would be disposed of by the will of the insured or by the law of descent and distribution in case he left no will. There is no showing in this record, and no intimation from the briefs of either party, that any effort was ever made to change the name of the beneficiary in any of the three policies except by the directions and provisions in the will itself. The authorities cited and relied upon by the appellees, Eaton v. Husted, 141 Tex. 349, 172 S.W.2d 493; Hughes v. Jackson, 125 Tex. 130, 81 S.W.2d 656 and Dunn v. Second National Bank of Houston, 131 Tex. 198, 113 S.W.2d 165, are not in point here. They deal with the impressment of a trust upon the proceeds of life insurance policies at the time of making the insured contract. In Dunn v. Second National Bank of Houston, supra, for instance the life insurance policy named a creditor of the insured as beneficiary for the purpose of paying a debt due him by the insured, and the policy itself was in the hands of such creditor beneficiary. We do not believe that these cases are authority in support of the contention of the appellees that they were entitled to receive the proceeds of the life insurance policies involved in this suit under the facts.

The judgment of the trial court insofar as it decrees a trust and appointment of the appellees as trustees thereunder is affirmed. Insofar as the judgment of the trial court decreeing that the proceeds of the insurance policies on the life of the deceased were a part of the trust and should be paid to such trustees is reversed and judgment rendered that the proceeds of such insurance policies were not a part of such trust, but were payable to the appellant as guardian of the person and estate of his minor son, Gary Leo Thatcher, the beneficiary named in such policies of insurance. The judgment in all other respects is affirmed.

The other points of error presented by the appellant present matters of procedure which do not affect the determination of this appeal on the principal points involved, and they are overruled without discussion.

The costs of this appeal are assessed one-fifth against the appellant and four-fifths against the appellees.

Property Code § 111.001. Short Title

This subtitle may be cited as the Texas Trust Code.

Property Code § 111.0035. Default and Mandatory Rules; Conflict Between Terms and Statute

(a) Except as provided by the terms of a trust and Subsection (b), this subtitle governs:

(1) the duties and powers of a trustee;

(2) relations among trustees; and

(3) the rights and interests of a beneficiary.

(b) The terms of a trust prevail over any provision of this subtitle, except that the terms of a trust may not limit:

(1) the requirements imposed under Section 112.031;

(2) the applicability of Section 114.007 to an exculpation term of a trust;

(3) the periods of limitation for commencing a judicial proceeding regarding a trust;

(4) a trustee's duty:

(A) with regard to an irrevocable trust, to respond to a demand for accounting made under Section 113.151 if the demand is from a beneficiary who, at the time of the demand:

(i) is entitled or permitted to receive distributions from the trust; or

(ii) would receive a distribution from the trust if the trust terminated at the time of the demand; and

(B) to act in good faith and in accordance with the purposes of the trust;

(5) the power of a court, in the interest of justice, to take action or exercise jurisdiction, including the power to:

(A) modify or terminate a trust or take other action under Section 112.054;

(B) remove a trustee under Section 113.082;

(C) exercise jurisdiction under Section 115.001;

(D) require, dispense with, modify, or terminate a trustee's bond; or

(E) adjust or deny a trustee's compensation if the trustee commits a breach of trust; or

(6) the applicability of Section 112.038.

(c) The terms of a trust may not limit any common-law duty to keep a beneficiary of an irrevocable trust who is 25 years of age or older informed at any time during which the beneficiary:

(1) is entitled or permitted to receive distributions from the trust; or

(2) would receive a distribution from the trust if the trust were terminated.

Property Code § 112.001. Methods of Creating Trust

A trust may be created by:

(1) a property owner's declaration that the owner holds the property as trustee for another person;

(2) a property owner's inter vivos transfer of the property to another person as trustee for the transferor or a third person;

(3) a property owner's testamentary transfer to another person as trustee for a third person;

(4) an appointment under a power of appointment to another person as trustee for the donee of the power or for a third person; or

(5) a promise to another person whose rights under the promise are to be held in trust for a third person.

Property Code § 112.002. Intention to Create Trust

A trust is created only if the settlor manifests an intention to create a trust.

Property Code § 112.003. Consideration

Consideration is not required for the creation of a trust. A promise to create a trust in the future is enforceable only if the requirements for an enforceable contract are present.

Property Code § 112.006. Additions to Trust Property

Property may be added to an existing trust from any source in any manner unless the addition is prohibited by the terms of the trust or the property is unacceptable to the trustee.

Property Code § 112.007. Capacity of Settlor

A person has the same capacity to create a trust by declaration, inter vivos or testamentary transfer, or appointment that the person has to transfer, will, or appoint free of trust.

Property Code § 112.008. Capacity of Trustee

(a) The trustee must have the legal capacity to take, hold, and transfer the trust property. If the trustee is a corporation, it must have the power to act as a trustee in this state.

(b) Except as provided by Section 112.034, the fact that the person named as trustee is also a beneficiary does not disqualify the person from acting as trustee if he is otherwise qualified.

(c) The settlor of a trust may be the trustee of the trust.

Property Code § 112.009. Acceptance by Trustee

(a) The signature of the person named as trustee on the writing evidencing the trust or on a separate written acceptance is conclusive evidence that the person accepted the trust. A person named as trustee who exercises power or performs duties under the trust is presumed to have accepted the trust, except that a person named as trustee may engage in the following conduct without accepting the trust:

(1) acting to preserve the trust property if, within a reasonable time after acting, the person gives notice of the rejection of the trust to:

(A) the settlor; or

(B) if the settlor is deceased or incapacitated, all beneficiaries then entitled to receive trust distributions from the trust; and

(2) inspecting or investigating trust property for any purpose, including determining the potential liability of the trust under environmental or other law.

(b) A person named as trustee who does not accept the trust incurs no liability with respect to the trust.

(c) If the person named as the original trustee does not accept the trust or if the person is dead or does not have capacity to act as trustee, the person named as the alternate trustee under the terms of the trust or the person selected as alternate trustee according to a method prescribed in the terms of the trust may accept the trust. If a trustee is not named or if there is no alternate trustee designated or selected in the manner prescribed in the terms of the trust, the court shall appoint a trustee on a petition of any interested person.

Property Code § 112.031. Trust Purposes

A trust may be created for any purpose that is not illegal. The terms of the trust may not require the trustee to commit a criminal or tortious act or an act that is contrary to public policy.

Property Code § 112.032. Active and Passive Trusts; Statute of Uses

(a) Except as provided by Subsection (b), title to real property held in trust vests directly in the beneficiary if the trustee has neither a power nor a duty related to the administration of the trust.

(b) The title of a trustee in real property is not divested if the trustee's title is not merely nominal but is subject to a power or duty in relation to the property.

Section B. Trust Property (The Res)

Property Code § 112.005. Trust Property

A trust cannot be created unless there is trust property.

Section C. A Beneficiary

Property Code § 112.037. Trust for Care of Animal

(a) A trust may be created to provide for the care of an animal alive during the settlor's lifetime. The trust terminates on the death of the animal or, if the trust is created to provide for the care of more than one animal alive during the settlor's lifetime, on the death of the last surviving animal.

(b) A trust authorized by this section may be enforced by a person appointed in the terms of the trust or, if a person is not appointed in the terms of the trust, by a person appointed by the court. A person having an interest in the welfare of an animal that is the subject of a trust authorized by this section may request the court to appoint a person to enforce the trust or to remove a person appointed to enforce the trust.

(c) Except as provided by Subsections (d) and (e), property of a trust authorized by this section may be applied only to the property's intended use under the trust.

(d) Property of a trust authorized by this section may be applied to a use other than the property's intended use under the trust to the extent the court determines that the value of the trust property exceeds the amount required for the intended use.

(e) Except as otherwise provided by the terms of the trust, property not required for the trust's intended use must be distributed to:

(1) if the settlor is living at the time the trust property is distributed, the settlor; or

(2) if the settlor is not living at the time the trust property is distributed:

(A) if the settlor has a will, beneficiaries under the settlor's will; or

(B) in the absence of an effective provision in a will, the settlor's heirs.

(f) For purposes of Section 112.036, the lives in being used to determine the maximum duration of a trust authorized by this section are:

(1) the individual beneficiaries of the trust;

(2) the individuals named in the instrument creating the trust; and

(3) if the settlor or settlors are living at the time the trust becomes irrevocable, the settlor or settlors of the trust or, if the settlor or settlors are not living at the time the trust becomes irrevocable, the individuals who would inherit the settlor or settlors' property under the law of this state had the settlor or settlors died intestate at the time the trust becomes irrevocable.

Agreement to care for animals is a contract, not a trust, when intent to create a trust is absent

SARAH v. PRIMARILY PRIMATES, INC.
Court of Appeals of Texas, San Antonio
255 S.W.3d 132 (2008)

ANGELINI, J. Appellants appeal from the trial court's order dismissing their case for lack of standing. On appeal, they argue that (1) an agreed order between them and Appellee Primarily Primates, Inc. entered into during the pendency of the underlying lawsuit gave them standing, and (2) they have standing pursuant to section 112.037 of the Texas Trust Code, which allows the creation of trusts to provide for the care of animals. We affirm the trial court's order dismissing the case for lack of standing.

BACKGROUND

In January 2006, Primarily Primates, Inc. ("PPI") and Ohio State University[1] entered into an agreement whereby Ohio State "transfer[ed] nine chimpanzees and three new world monkeys utilized in research at its Chimpanzee Center ('the Chimps and Monkeys')" to PPI, and PPI in turn agreed "to accept ownership of the Chimps and Monkeys and to provide for their lifetime care." The agreement lists the following as PPI's responsibilities:

(1) PPI agrees to accept ownership of the Chimps and Monkeys and to provide for their lifetime care in a humane environment that complies with all relevant state and federal regulations. PPI will not breed the Chimps and Monkeys, will not use them in research

[1] Ohio State University was not a party in the underlying lawsuit and is not a party in this appeal.

projects of any kind, and will not euthanize any of them except for humane reasons relating to a health condition.

(2) PPI will construct facilities for the housing of the Chimps and Monkeys in accordance with the specifications set forth in Attachment A.

(3) PPI will provide personnel and other assistance in connection with the shipment of the Chimps and Monkeys to PPI, in accordance with the Shipment Schedule set forth in Attachment B. The Parties will mutually agree on a shipping date.

(4) PPI will construct a temporary enclosure to house the Chimps and Monkeys pending completion of a permanent facility. PPI acknowledges receipt of $14,944.00 from Ohio State to cover the cost of constructing the temporary enclosure.

The agreement also lists the following as Ohio State's responsibilities:

(1) Ohio State will pay facility construction costs in the total amount of $236,483.00 as set forth in Attachment A. This amount will be paid upon execution of this Agreement.

(2) Ohio State will provide personnel and other assistance in connection with the shipment of the Chimps and Monkeys to PPI, and will pay the shipping costs in accordance with the Shipping Schedule set forth in Attachment B.

(3) Ohio State will provide an endowment to PPI in the amount of $8,000 per chimpanzee for a total of $72,000. A check for this amount, payable to Primarily Primates, Inc. will be delivered no later than 60 days after the Point of Transfer. Ohio State is not required to pay an endowment for the New World Monkeys.

The agreement, under a section titled "Ownership," also discusses that Ohio State "warrants that it is the owner of all rights, title and interest in the Chimps and Monkeys" and "transfers all rights, title and interest in the Chimps and Monkeys to PPI." In return, PPI "agrees to accept such transfer" effective at the "Point of Transfer." Further, according to the agreement, if "a lawsuit is initiated against Ohio State or PPI after the Point of Transfer challenging Ohio State's ownership," "its authority to transfer ownership," or "the validity of the ownership rights conveyed to PPI under this Agreement," then ownership of the Chimps and Monkeys will revert to Ohio State, but Ohio State will be responsible for all legal fees.

The agreement also provides that it "shall be governed by and construed in accordance with the laws of the State of Ohio" and that "[e]ither party may, at any time, and for any reason, terminate this Agreement by giving 7 days written notice to the other party."

In February of 2006, the primates were shipped from Ohio to PPI's facilities in Texas. Shortly after their arrival, two of them died, and a third escaped from a cage.

On April 27, 2006, attorneys purporting to act on behalf of "Sarah, Harper, Emma, Keeli, Ivy, Sheba, Darrell, Rain, and Ulysses" (the surviving primates) filed suit against PPI, alleging breach of contract. In the alternative, they brought a declaratory judgment action, asking the trial court to declare that "the contract [between PPI and Ohio State] is void because it violates Texas law." They also sought "removal from PPI and transfer to an appropriate sanctuary that will provide them with appropriate care as is described in the contract." Additionally, "[i]n the alternative, and in the unlikely event that the court does not order specific performance," they requested the "creation" of a trust and "an award of damages in the amount of $236,483.00 (the full contract price) to be held in trust and applied towards the acquisition of shelter and care at a suitable facility." They attached a copy of the contract to their petition.

On May 4, 2006, they filed a "Second Amended Original Petition," adding Henry Melvyn Richardson, Stephany Harris, and Klaree Boose, "people interested in Plaintiffs' welfare," as plaintiffs. This amended petition retained the same claims as the original one: breach of contract, declaratory judgment, and "recognition" (instead of "creation") of a trust.

In response to the lawsuit, PPI filed a motion to dismiss for lack of standing. After several hearings, the trial court dismissed the case for lack of standing. "Sarah, Harper, Emma, Keeli, Ivy, Sheba, Darrell, Rain, and Ulysses" (the surviving primates), along with Henry Melvyn Richardson, Stephany Harris, and Klaree Boose (the interested persons), filed a notice of appeal, seeking review of the trial court's order.[2]

DISCUSSION

A. Did the agreed order to appoint a master in chancery give appellants standing?

Richardson, Harris, and Boose ("appellants") argue that even if they did not initially have standing, they gained standing when PPI agreed to the [trial court's agreed] order appointing a master in chancery. We disagree. . . . PPI was not agreeing to have the master in chancery resolve the parties' dispute; it was agreeing only to the appointment of the master, who would then report to the trial court, which would then either accept or reject the master's recommendations. . . . We, therefore, hold that the agreed order to appoint a master in chancery did not confer standing upon appellants.

B. Do appellants have standing pursuant to section 112.037 of the Texas Trust Code?

A party must have standing to bring a lawsuit. Coastal Liquids Transp., L.P. v. Harris County Appraisal Dist., 46 S.W.3d 880, 884 (Tex. 2001). "Standing" is a party's justiciable interest in

---

[2] Although the notice of appeal states that, in addition to Richardson, Harris, and Boose, the surviving primates are seeking review of the trial court's order, no one argues on appeal that the surviving primates have standing. Thus, on appeal, we are considering only whether Richardson, Harris, and Boose, have standing.

the suit. Nootsie, Ltd. v. Williamson County Appraisal Dist., 925 S.W.2d 659, 661-62 (Tex. 1996). The test for standing requires that there be a real controversy between the parties that will actually be determined by the judicial declaration sought. Austin Nursing Ctr., Inc. v. Lovato, 171 S.W.3d 845, 849 (Tex. 2005). A plaintiff has standing when it is personally aggrieved, regardless of whether it is acting with legal authority. *Nootsie*, 925 S.W.2d at 661. If a party lacks standing, a trial court lacks subject-matter jurisdiction to hear the case. *Lovato*, 171 S.W.3d at 849. Thus, standing cannot be waived and can be raised for the first time on appeal. Id. And, whether a court has subject-matter jurisdiction is a question of law. Tex. Dep't of Parks & Wildlife v. Miranda, 133 S.W.3d 217, 226 (Tex. 2004).

1. Do we look to the petition or to the contract?

According to appellants, they have standing because their petition alleged sufficient facts by requesting that the trial court recognize the existence of a trust created for the care of the primates pursuant to section 112.037 of the Texas Trust Code. See Texas Property Code § 112.037(a) ("A trust may be created to provide for the care of an animal alive during the settlor's lifetime."). Subsection 112.037(b) allows "[a] person having an interest in the welfare of an animal that is the subject of a trust authorized by this section [to] request the court to appoint a person to enforce the trust or to remove a person appointed to enforce the trust." Id. § 112.037(b). According to Plaintiffs, their petition sufficiently alleged that Dr. Mel Richardson, Stephany Harris, and Klaree Boose were such "interested persons."

In response, PPI argues the following: (1) animals lack standing to bring suit under any applicable law; thus, the primates had no standing to bring the petition;[3] and (2) Richardson, Harris, and Boose have no justiciable interest in this lawsuit. According to PPI, Richardson, Harris, and Boose were not parties to the contract between PPI and Ohio State; they do not claim to be third-party beneficiaries to the contract; and they do not claim ownership rights to the primates. PPI also argues that the trial court could not hold that the contract between PPI and Ohio State created a trust to provide for the care of the primates pursuant to section 112.037 of the Texas Trust Code because the contract provided that it would be construed in accordance with Ohio law, and at the time the parties entered into the contract, Ohio law did not permit the creation of a trust to provide for the care of an animal.

In their reply brief, appellants argue that we should not consider the contract between PPI and Ohio State, but should instead look solely to their petition and take all the allegations in the petition as true. We disagree.

Generally, a trial court looks to the allegations of a plaintiff's petition to determine standing. See Tex. Dep't of Parks & Wildlife v. Miranda, 133 S.W.3d 217, 226 (Tex. 2004) (explaining that whether a pleader has alleged facts that affirmatively demonstrate a trial court's subject-matter jurisdiction is a question of law reviewed de novo); see id. (explaining that whether undisputed evidence of jurisdictional facts establishes a trial court's jurisdiction

---

[3] Appellants do not appear to dispute this fact as they focus their arguments on the contract creating a trust to provide for the benefit of the primates.

is also a question of law).... However, under certain circumstances, when deciding a jurisdictional challenge, a trial court may go beyond the allegations in the pleadings and consider evidence. Id. For example, if a plea to jurisdiction challenges the existence of jurisdictional facts and those facts are necessary to resolve the jurisdictional issue, the trial court is required to consider relevant evidence submitted by the parties. . . .

Here, at the hearing on the motion to dismiss, appellants' own trial counsel entered the contract between PPI and Ohio State in evidence. Thus, the contract is undisputed evidence that the court considered in deciding the motion, and, because we consider it to be necessary to resolve the jurisdictional issue, we will consider it on appeal. See id. at 227.

2. Did the contract between PPI and Ohio State create a trust to provide for the care of the primates?

The contract between PPI and Ohio State clearly states that it will be governed by Ohio law: "This Agreement shall be governed by and construed in accordance with the laws of the State of Ohio." PPI argues that because Ohio law did not recognize the creation of a trust to provide for the care of an animal at the time PPI and Ohio State entered into the contract, the contract cannot be construed as creating a trust. In response, appellants argue that "PPI's choice of law theory . . . is a matter of affirmative defense, which has no impact on subject matter jurisdiction," and that PPI waived this affirmative defense by failing to plead it. Thus, they argue that we must look to Texas law in considering whether the contract created a trust to provide for the care of the primates. Because we hold that the contract did not create a trust under Texas law, we need not decide whether Ohio law should apply.

Section 112.037 of the Texas Trust Code allows a trust to "be created to provide for the care of an animal alive during the settlor's lifetime." Texas Property Code § 112.037(a). Such a trust terminates on the death of the animal and may be enforced by a person appointed in the terms of the trust or, if a person is not appointed, by a person appointed by the court. See id. § 112.037(a)-(b).[4] However, although section 112.037 allows the creation of a trust to provide for the care of an animal, that does not necessarily mean that every contract relating to animals creates such a trust. Thus, we must consider whether the contract between PPI and Ohio State created a trust. Pursuant to the Texas Trust Code, there are many methods of creating an express trust. A trust may be created by:

> (1) a property owner's declaration that the owner holds the property as trustee for another person;
>
> (2) a property owner's inter vivos transfer of the property to another person as trustee for the transferor or a third person;

---

[4] Section 112.037(b) further allows a "person having an interest in the welfare of an animal that is the subject of a trust authorized by this section [to] request the court to appoint a person to enforce the trust or to remove a person appointed to enforce the trust." Texas Property Code § 112.037(b).

(3) a property owner's testamentary transfer to another person as trustee for a third person;

(4) an appointment under a power of appointment to another person as trustee for the donee of the power or for a third person; or

(5) a promise to another person whose rights under the promise are to be held in trust for a third person.

Texas Property Code § 112.001.

In arguing that the contract does not create a trust, PPI first emphasizes that the only types of trusts governed by the Texas Trust Code are express trusts—not resulting trusts, constructive trusts, business trusts, or deeds of trust. See id. § 111.003 ("For purposes of this subtitle, a 'trust' is an express trust only and does not include: (1) a resulting trust; (2) a constructive trust; (3) a business trust; or (4) a security instrument such as a deed of trust, mortgage, or security interest as defined by the Business & Commerce Code."). PPI then argues that the contract between Ohio State and PPI does not create an express trust; instead, it transfers title of the primates in fee from Ohio State to PPI.

"A trust is created only if the settlor manifests an intention to create a trust." Id. § 112.002. According to PPI, the contract here does not manifest such an intention; it does not indicate that PPI or Ohio State intended to create a trust. For example, an express trust requires a person be named as trustee. See id. § 112.001; Perfect Union Lodge No. 10 v. Interfirst Bank, 748 S.W.2d 218, 220 (Tex. 1988) (explaining that implicit in the statutory definition of trust "is the requirement of a trustee with administrative powers and fiduciary duties"); Humane Soc'y v. Austin Nat'l Bank, 531 S.W.2d 574, 577 (Tex. 1975) ("An express devise of property to another as trustee for named beneficiaries is required for creation of an express trust."). PPI emphasizes that the contract here does not name anyone as trustee for the primates. Indeed, the word "trustee" does not appear anywhere in the contract. PPI further points out that the contract also does not mention the terms "trust," "beneficiaries," "settlor," "grantor," or "donor." According to PPI, if it and Ohio State had intended for their agreement to create a trust, then the agreement would have included these terms. Instead, the contract uses terms like "transfer" and "ownership" to describe their agreement. For example, the contract states that Ohio State is "the owner of all rights, title and interest in the Chimps and Monkeys" and that it "hereby transfers all rights, title and interest in the Chimps and Monkeys to PPI and PPI agrees to accept such transfer, effective when the PPI veterinarian and the Ohio State veterinarian mutually agree that the Chimps and Monkeys have recovered from all pre-shipment procedures and are ready for actual shipment ('the Point of Transfer')." According to PPI, the use of these terms "plainly indicate that the agreement is a bilateral contract under which Ohio State transferred ownership of the chimpanzees and monkeys to PPI and PPI agreed to house and care for them."

In their reply brief, appellants make clear that they are arguing that the contract between PPI and Ohio State created an express trust. An "express trust" is "a fiduciary relationship with respect to property which arises as a manifestation by the settlor of an intention to create the relationship and which subjects the person holding title to the property to equitable duties to deal with the property for the benefit of another person." Id. § 111.004. Although acknowledging that the contract does not contain the terms "trust" or "trustee," appellants emphasize that such technical words of expression are not necessary to create a trust relationship. They argue that all that is required is that the beneficiary, the res, and the trust purpose be reasonably clear based on the entire instrument when construed in light of the circumstances surrounding its execution. According to appellants, here, the contract provides for Ohio State funds to be transferred to PPI "with the intent that the funds be used exclusively for the animals' benefit" and that "PPI accepted the trust property and agreed to be bound to provide the animals with lifetime care." Thus, appellants argue that the "material terms and the trust purpose are clear in light of the circumstances surrounding the execution of the agreement."

It is true that technical words of expression are not essential for the creation of a trust. *Perfect Union*, 748 S.W.2d at 220. A trust is a method used to transfer property. Jameson v. Bain, 693 S.W.2d 676, 680 (Tex. App.-San Antonio 1985, no writ). Thus, the trustee holds legal title and possession for the benefit of the beneficiaries. Faulkner v. Bost, 137 S.W.3d 254, 258 (Tex. App.-Tyler 2004, no pet.). "To create a trust by a written instrument, the beneficiary, the res, and the trust purpose must be identified." *Perfect Union*, 748 S.W.2d at 220. "It is not absolutely necessary that legal title be granted to the trustee in specific terms." Id. "Therefore, a trust by implication may arise, notwithstanding the testator's failure to convey legal title to the trustee, *when the intent to create a trust appears reasonably clear from the terms of the will*, construed in light of the surrounding circumstances." Id. (emphasis added).

For example, in Dulin v. Moore, 96 Tex. 135, 137, 70 S.W. 742, 742 (1902), the supreme court construed a will in which the testator, after devising real property in fee simple, provided that another person would be "trustee to receive and control the property" during the lives of the devisees. "The court recognized the issue as being whether the testator intended to confer mere 'naked powers' upon the trustee or to invest him with legal title for the purposes of the trust." *Perfect Union*, 748 S.W.2d at 221 (explaining *Dulin*'s reasoning). The court concluded that "although the will contains no words which expressly convey legal title to Dulin, the intention that he should take the legal title is as clearly manifested as if express terms had been employed." *Dulin*, 96 Tex. at 139, 70 S.W. at 743.

Similarly, in Heironimus v. Tate, 355 S.W.2d 76 (Tex. Civ. App.-Austin 1962, writ ref'd n.r.e.), the Austin Court of Appeals construed a will in which there were no express words giving the executor legal title to any property. "The will bequeathed property to two beneficiaries but further provided that the executors had discretion in making distributions to the beneficiaries during their lives, and upon their deaths the remainder passed to their lineal descendants." *Perfect Union*, 748 S.W.2d at 221 (explaining *Heironimus*). "The court concluded that a trust had been created with legal title vested in the executors." Id. (citing *Heironimus*, 355 S.W.2d at 80).

In Perfect Union Lodge No. 10 v. Interfirst Bank, 748 S.W.2d at 221, the supreme court noted that "[a]s in *Dulin* and *Heironimus*, we must construe a will which lacks specific language conferring legal title upon the executors." The court concluded that "[f]rom the provisions of the will as a whole, A.H. Lumpkin's intent to create a testamentary trust can be ascertained." Id. The will "devised all the residue of [Lumpkin's] estate to his wife for her life, with the remainder to Perfect Union Lodge." Id. It then provided that "my said executors shall handle my estate during the life of my wife." Id. According to the court, this language indicated that "Lumpkin intended to provide for more than a mere settlement of his business affairs and distribution of assets." Id. Furthermore, the court reasoned that "the provision granting the executors the powers found under the Trust Act authorized Moursund to exercise greater control over the property than was necessary for administration of the estate." Id. Therefore, pursuant to the language of the will, the court reasoned that Lumpkin "clearly intended to separate the management and control of his residual estate from the beneficial interest conferred upon his wife." Id. Thus, the court held that the will "created a testamentary trust for the life of his wife, which would terminate upon her death." Id.

Unlike the facts presented in *Dulin*, *Heironimus*, and *Perfect Union Lodge*, there is no clear intent in the contract between PPI and Ohio State to create a trust to provide for the care of the primates. While appellants emphasize that pursuant to the contract Ohio State transferred funds to PPI with the intent that the funds would be used for the primates' benefit and that PPI agreed to provide for their lifetime care, the contract also states that PPI agrees to accept "ownership" of the primates, that Ohio State "warrants that it is the owner of all *rights, title and interest*" in the primates, that Ohio State "*transfers* all rights, title, and interest" in the primates to PPI and that PPI agrees to accept "such transfer, effective" at "the Point of Transfer," and that if a lawsuit is initiated against Ohio State or PPI after "the Point of Transfer" challenging Ohio State's ownership of the primates, its authority to transfer ownership to PPI or the validity of the "*ownership rights conveyed to PPI*" under the contract, then "ownership" of the primates "shall revert to Ohio State." After reviewing the language used in the contract, we see no intention by Ohio State to create a trust; therefore, we hold that the contract between Ohio State and PPI did not create a trust to provide for the care of the primates.

CONCLUSION

Because the contract between Ohio State and PPI did not create a trust to provide for the care of the primates, appellants have no standing under section 112.037 of the Texas Trust Code to bring their claims. We, therefore, affirm the trial court's order dismissing the cause for lack of standing.

Section D. A Writing?

Oral trust cannot be created when property owner fails to relinquish dominion or control

AYERS v. MITCHELL

Court of Appeals of Texas, Texarkana
167 S.W.3d 924 (2005)

ROSS, J. Roy A. Ayers and his wife, Lorayne, deposited funds in an account at a bank where they, along with two of their children, Gail Mitchell and Larry Ayers, were signatories on the account. Mitchell eventually gained sole control over the funds. Roy testified that he demanded a return of the funds. When Mitchell refused, Roy filed suit against her, alleging, among other things, breach of contract, conversion, breach of fiduciary duty, and fraud. Roy also sued for "a declaratory judgment that all monies in issue are owned by Roy A. Ayers and should be returned to Roy A. Ayers." Mitchell counterclaimed, seeking a declaratory judgment as to the existence of a trust, terms of the trust, and her status as trustee. The funds at issue were ultimately deposited in the registry of the court.

The case was tried to the court and resulted in a judgment that Roy take nothing by his suit, that the funds at issue were held in an irrevocable trust for the benefit of Roy, and that Mitchell was the sole trustee of that trust. The court filed findings of fact and conclusions of law in support of its judgment. Roy appeals, challenging the material findings and conclusions made by the court. Because we hold the trial court erred in finding the existence of a valid trust, we reverse and render judgment that Roy is entitled to have the funds returned to him. We remand to the trial court the question of Roy's reasonable and necessary attorney's fees.

BACKGROUND

In 1998, Roy and Lorayne became concerned about their future health and living care needs. According to Mitchell's testimony, her parents asked her to take charge of their life savings to provide for their future healthcare needs. She said that her parents wanted to "shelter [these funds] . . . from Medicaid." So, on December 18, 1998, Roy and Lorayne created a savings account at a bank in Winnsboro, depositing approximately $48,000.00. There were four signatories on the account: Roy, Lorayne, Mitchell, and Larry. Mitchell's social security number was shown on the account, and she paid the taxes on the income from the account. Mitchell testified Roy instructed her to keep her siblings from misusing any of this money. Mitchell's siblings are: Larry, Marsha Kull, and Paul Ayers.

Lorayne died sometime after the creation of the savings account. In January 2003, Roy had surgery to amputate one of his legs. Following Roy's surgery, Mitchell and Kull broached the subject of Roy living in a nursing home. Larry was opposed to this idea and took Roy home to live with him. Larry testified he "gutted" his home and did significant remodeling to make the home accessible for Roy. There was also testimony that Larry isolated Roy from the rest of the family. Larry, a single person, hired care providers to come into the house to help with Roy's needs and with the cooking and other household chores. One caregiver testified it was her understanding from the other caregivers that Roy was not to be left alone with other members of the family. Jeff Ayers, Larry's son, testified Larry told him not to associate with Mitchell or Kull, or any of their children. Jeff also testified that Larry had coached Roy on how to answer questions in court.

In June 2003, Mitchell became aware that Larry had been writing checks of increasing value on Roy's checking account (not the account the subject of this suit). Mitchell then removed the funds in question from the savings account and opened a new account, with herself and Kull as signatories. Kull's name was removed from the account, at her request, leaving Mitchell as the only signatory. Mitchell testified she viewed herself as trustee of these funds and felt responsible to protect the money and see to it that the money was used for Roy's reasonable medical needs and for his "comfortable living expenses."

TRIAL COURT'S FINDINGS AND CONCLUSIONS

In its written findings of fact, the trial court found, among other things, that the bank account in question did not reflect that Mitchell was a trustee; that Roy and Lorayne intended that Mitchell hold the account subject to their requirements for comfortable living and medical needs; that Roy, Lorayne, Mitchell, and Larry were permitted to withdraw from the account; that Larry exerted undue influence over Roy; that the only withdrawal from the account made by Mitchell was for the construction of a bridge requested by Roy; that Roy was disoriented on the day of trial; that Roy was unable to care for himself; that Roy and Lorayne intended to completely divest themselves of any legal interests in the account in question; that Roy never made a demand on Mitchell for return of the account before filing suit; and that Roy and Lorayne intended for Mitchell to have complete control over the account subject only to their needs for healthcare and comfortable living.

In its conclusions of law, the trial court concluded that Mitchell is the trustee of the funds in the account in question; that the trust was intended to be irrevocable; that the trust became irrevocable on the death of Lorayne; that Roy is in need of a guardian; that, should any of the trust fund remain after the death of Roy, the trust terminates and the funds shall be paid out equally to the children of Roy and Lorayne; and that Roy and Lorayne intended to and did divest themselves of any interest in the trust fund except as beneficiaries thereof.

ROY'S CONTENTIONS

Roy contends the evidence established as a matter of law that Roy revoked the trust, and that failing to so find was against the great weight and preponderance of the evidence. He also contends the evidence established that Roy and Lorayne intended Larry and Mitchell to be joint trustees, and failing to so find was likewise against the great weight and preponderance of the evidence. Roy further contends the trial court erred in enforcing an oral trust and in ordering the trust *res* be divided equally among Roy's children following his death. Finally, Roy contends the trial court should have awarded him attorney's fees. . . .

EVIDENCE OF ORAL TRUST NOT LEGALLY SUFFICIENT

We begin our analysis with Roy's contention the trial court erred in enforcing an oral trust. In general, a trust must be in writing to be enforceable. Texas Property Code § 112.004. That statute requires a trust in either real or personal property to be created with a written document. However, a trust in personal property may be created, and the trust enforced, where there is a) a transfer of the trust property; b) to a trustee; c) who is neither settlor; d) nor beneficiary; e) if the transferor expresses at the time or before the transfer his or her intent to create a trust. Texas Property Code § 112.004(1). A trust meeting these requirements need not be in writing.

Mitchell contends, and the trial court found, that Roy, as settlor, transferred the funds in question to her as trustee. The Texas Property Code defines "beneficiary" as "a person for whose benefit property is held in trust, regardless of the nature of the interest." Texas Property Code § 111.004. Mitchell does not contend, and the evidence does not show, that Mitchell is a beneficiary of the alleged trust. The evidence does show that, at the time or before the bank account in question was created, Roy made statements to Mitchell consistent with creating a trust. Fatal to Mitchell's contention that an oral trust was established, however, is the absence of a complete transfer of the alleged trust property.

As it pertains to trusts, the Texas Property Code does not contain a definition of "transfer." See Texas Property Code § 111.004. However, in a case construing, in part, certain bank savings accounts opened by the account holder "in trust" for others, the Texas Supreme Court held that such trusts are governed in general by the rules applicable to gifts and explained that:

> The principal difference between such a trust and a gift lies in the fact that in the case of a gift the thing given passes to the donee, while in the case of a voluntary trust only the equitable or beneficial title passes to the cestui qui trust. In each case the equitable title must pass immediately and unconditionally and the transfer thereof must be so complete that the donee might maintain an action for the conversion of the property. Absent a completed gift of the equitable title, no trust is created, for an imperfect gift will not be enforced as a trust merely because of its imperfection. . . .

Fleck v. Baldwin, 141 Tex. 340, 172 S.W.2d 975, 978 (1943) (holding insufficient evidence of trust creation, particularly, lack of evidence of original owner's intent to yield control over funds in question). . . .

Applying these principles applicable to gifts, we hold that, to have a "transfer of the trust property to a trustee," as contemplated by Section 112.004(1), the transfer must divest the trustor of all dominion and control over the trust *res*.

In the instant case, there is evidence that, at or before the time the funds in question were placed in the savings account, Roy and Lorayne instructed Mitchell to take charge of such funds to provide for their future healthcare needs. Further, Roy's niece, Irene Ayers (daughter of Roy's brother) testified Roy told her that Mitchell was in charge of Roy's finances. However, the evidence further shows that neither Roy nor Lorayne ever divested themselves of all dominion and control over these funds. They both remained as signatories on the account where the funds were located. As such, they expressed their intent to retain control over such funds. It is axiomatic that, when an order to pay from an account has been signed by an authorized signer on the account, the order is to be paid. Roy and Lorayne remaining as signatories on the account defeats any claim that the funds in that account were transferred away from them.

Roy's continued control over the account is also shown by Mitchell's own testimony that her father instructed her to deduct $2,425.00 from the account to reimburse Mitchell for the cost of a bridge she had built on Roy's property. Roy's authorization of this expenditure shows his continued control over these funds and is inconsistent with the view that a complete transfer of those funds away from himself ever took place. Roy's continued control of the funds is also shown by evidence that he made one or more loans to Larry from those funds.

The undisputed evidence shows that Roy had control over these funds until Mitchell moved them, without Roy's knowledge or consent, into an account where she had sole control. We hold, as a matter of law, there was never a "transfer of the trust property to a trustee" as contemplated by Section 112.004(1). In the absence of a writing representing the creation of a trust, and in the further absence of a complete transfer of the funds, we hold that, as a matter of law, no valid trust was created. Accordingly, we sustain Roy's point that the trial court erred in enforcing an oral trust.

ANY TRUST CREATED WAS REVOCABLE

Notwithstanding our conclusion that no valid trust was created, we will address Roy's contention that the evidence established, as a matter of law, that Roy revoked any trust created and that the trial court's failure to so find was against the great weight and preponderance of the evidence. Even if a valid trust had been created, we hold that, as a matter of law, any such trust was revocable and that it was revoked by Roy.

The trial court found the alleged trust to be irrevocable. That finding, however, is not supported by the evidence and is contrary to law. Trusts created under Texas law are revocable, unless made specifically irrevocable. Westerfeld v. Huckaby, 462 S.W.2d 324, 327 (Tex. Civ. App.-Houston [1st Dist.] 1970), aff'd, 474 S.W.2d 189 (Tex. 1971). The irrevocability of a trust must appear from the terms and language of the instrument creating the trust. Texas Property Code § 112.051(a). Otherwise, the trust is revocable. See Texas Property Code § 112.051(a), (b). Here, there was no written document establishing the trust and stating its purposes, duration, or whether it was revocable. The alleged oral trust was, as a matter of law, revocable.

Mitchell contends, and the trial court concluded, that the supposed trust was intended to be irrevocable and became irrevocable when Lorayne died. Mitchell cites Citizens Nat'l Bank v. Allen, 575 S.W.2d 654, 658 (Tex. Civ. App.-Eastland 1978, writ ref'd n.r.e.), in support of her position that a trust becomes irrevocable on the death of the trustor. That case, however, dealt with only one settlor, and the Eastland court qualified its holding with the following language:

> [W]hen a valid inter vivos revocable trust is established and not revoked during the lifetime of the trustor, it becomes irrevocable upon his death, *and there being no other unfulfilled purposes of the trust expressed*, the trust terminates and is enforceable by the beneficiary.

Id. (Emphasis added.)

Obviously, where there is only one settlor of a trust, and he or she dies, that settlor is no longer capable of revoking the trust and, there being no other purpose, the trust becomes irrevocable. Where, however, there are multiple settlors, and one dies, but there are purposes of the trust yet unfulfilled, such trust does not become irrevocable on the death of one settlor. That is the situation here. Any trust that existed did not become irrevocable at Lorayne's death, because Roy survived Lorayne and at least part of the trust's purpose—providing for Roy's healthcare needs—remained unfulfilled. Further, none of the evidence showed that Ray and Lorayne intended the alleged trust to be irrevocable. We hold, therefore, that, even if a valid trust was created, it was revocable as a matter of law.

We also hold that, as a matter of law, Roy revoked any such trust. In so holding, we recognize the testimony on this issue was conflicting. Roy testified he made demand on Mitchell for return of the funds. Mitchell testified Roy did not request a return of the funds. The trial court, believing Mitchell and disbelieving Roy, found that Roy never made a demand on Mitchell for a return of the funds before filing suit. The trial court further found that Roy was "disoriented" at the time of trial and that he was incapable of managing his financial affairs. The trial court concluded, as a matter of law, Roy was in need of a guardian.

The trial court, as fact-finder, was the sole judge of the credibility of the witnesses and the weight to be given their testimony. As such, it was the court's prerogative to believe Mitchell's testimony and disbelieve Roy's. However, the issue of guardianship was not before the court. Indeed, the trial of this cause was abated pending a judicial determination of Roy's need for a guardian by a district court in Titus County. The application for such guardianship (filed by Kull) was denied December 11, 2003. This case was reinstated April 8, 2004, and went to trial April 30, 2004. The trial court also found that Larry exerted undue influence over Roy, but that finding is not linked to any specific conduct by Larry or Roy, and the effect of that finding is not stated.

Aside from the conflict in the testimony concerning whether Roy revoked the alleged trust, Roy contends, and we agree, that the act of filing suit was itself a demand by Roy for a return of the funds and a revocation of the alleged trust. We find it significant that the trial court, in its finding that Roy never made a demand on Mitchell for a return of the funds, limited its finding to the period "before filing suit." Further, Roy's testimony at trial made it unmistakably clear he was demanding a return of his funds. We hold that, even if Roy's funds were held in trust, as a matter of law, he revoked that trust by his act of filing suit and by his testimony at trial that he was demanding a return of his funds. The trial court's failure to so find was against the great weight and preponderance of the evidence. . . .

SUMMARY AND CONCLUSION

Because we hold that no valid trust was created in this case and that, even if such trust was created, it was, as a matter of law, a revocable trust and was revoked, we find it unnecessary to address Roy's other points of error.

We reverse and render judgment that Roy owns all the funds in issue and that such funds should be immediately returned to him. We remand to the trial court the determination of Roy's reasonable and necessary attorney's fees under Section 37.009 of the Texas Civil Practice and Remedies Code.

Property Code § 112.004. Statute of Frauds

A trust in either real or personal property is enforceable only if there is written evidence of the trust's terms bearing the signature of the settlor or the settlor's authorized agent. A trust consisting of personal property, however, is enforceable if created by:

(1) a transfer of the trust property to a trustee who is neither settlor nor beneficiary if the transferor expresses simultaneously with or prior to the transfer the intention to create a trust; or

(2) a declaration in writing by the owner of property that the owner holds the property as trustee for another person or for the owner and another person as a beneficiary.

Chapter 7. Nonprobate Transfers and Planning for Incapacity

Section A. Introduction to Will Substitutes

Estates Code § 111.051. Definitions

In this subchapter:

(1) "Contracting third party" means a financial institution, insurance company, plan custodian, plan administrator, or other person who is a party to an account agreement, insurance contract, annuity contract, retirement account, beneficiary designation, or other similar contract the terms of which control whether a nontestamentary transfer has occurred or to whom property passes as a result of a possible nontestamentary transfer. The term does not include a person who is:

(A) an owner of the property subject to a possible nontestamentary transfer; or

(B) a possible recipient of the property subject to a possible nontestamentary transfer.

(1-a) "Employees' trust" means:

(A) a trust that forms a part of a stock-bonus, pension, or profit-sharing plan under Section 401, Internal Revenue Code of 1954 (26 U.S.C. Section 401 (1986));

(B) a pension trust under Chapter 111, Property Code; and

(C) an employer-sponsored benefit plan or program, or any other retirement savings arrangement, including a pension plan created under Section 3, Employee Retirement Income Security Act of 1974 (29 U.S.C. Section 1002 (1986)), regardless of whether the plan, program, or arrangement is funded through a trust.

(2) "Financial institution" has the meaning assigned by Section 113.001.

(3) "Individual retirement account" means a trust, custodial arrangement, or annuity under Section 408(a) or (b), Internal Revenue Code of 1954 (26 U.S.C. Section 408 (1986)).

(4) "Retirement account" means a retirement-annuity contract, an individual retirement account, a simplified employee pension, or any other retirement savings arrangement.

(5) "Retirement-annuity contract" means an annuity contract under Section 403, Internal Revenue Code of 1954 (26 U.S.C. Section 403 (1986)).

(6) "Simplified employee pension" means a trust, custodial arrangement, or annuity under Section 408, Internal Revenue Code of 1954 (26 U.S.C. Section 408 (1986)).

Estates Code § 111.052. Validity of Certain Nontestamentary Instruments and Provisions

(a) This code does not invalidate:

(1) any provision in an insurance policy, employment contract, bond, mortgage, promissory note, deposit agreement, employees' trust, retirement account, deferred compensation arrangement, custodial agreement, pension plan, trust agreement, conveyance of property, security, account with a financial institution, mutual fund account, or any other written instrument effective as a contract, gift, conveyance, or trust, stating that:

(A) money or other benefits under the instrument due to or controlled or owned by a decedent shall be paid after the decedent's death, or property that is the subject of the instrument shall pass, to a person designated by the decedent in the instrument or in a separate writing, including a will, executed at the same time as the instrument or subsequently; or

(B) money due or to become due under the instrument shall cease to be payable if the promisee or promissor dies before payment or demand; or

(2) an instrument described by Subdivision (1).

(b) A provision described by Subsection (a)(1) is considered nontestamentary.

Property Code § 112.008. Capacity of Trustee

(a) The trustee must have the legal capacity to take, hold, and transfer the trust property. If the trustee is a corporation, it must have the power to act as a trustee in this state.

(b) Except as provided by Section 112.034, the fact that the person named as trustee is also a beneficiary does not disqualify the person from acting as trustee if he is otherwise qualified.

(c) The settlor of a trust may be the trustee of the trust.

Property Code § 112.033. Reservation of Interests and Powers by Settlor

If during the life of the settlor an interest in a trust or the trust property is created in a beneficiary other than the settlor, the disposition is not invalid as an attempted testamentary disposition merely because the settlor reserves or retains, either in himself or another person who is not the trustee, any or all of the other interests in or powers over the trust or trust property, such as:

(1) a beneficial life interest for himself;

(2) the power to revoke, modify, or terminate the trust in whole or in part;

(3) the power to designate the person to whom or on whose behalf the income or principal is to be paid or applied;

(4) the power to control the administration of the trust in whole or in part;

(5) the right to exercise a power or option over property in the trust or over interests made payable to the trust under an employee benefit plan, life insurance policy, or otherwise; or

(6) the power to add property or cause additional employee benefits, life insurance, or other interests to be made payable to the trust at any time.

Property Code § 112.034. Merger

(a) If a settlor transfers both the legal title and all equitable interests in property to the same person or retains both the legal title and all equitable interests in property in himself as both the sole trustee and the sole beneficiary, a trust is not created and the transferee holds the property as his own. This subtitle does not invalidate a trust account validly created and in effect under Chapter XI, Texas Probate Code.

(b) Except as provided by Subsection (c) of this section, a trust terminates if the legal title to the trust property and all equitable interests in the trust become united in one person.

(c) The title to trust property and all equitable interests in the trust property may not become united in a beneficiary, other than the settlor, whose interest is protected under a spendthrift trust, and in that case the court shall appoint a new trustee or cotrustee to administer the trust for the benefit of the beneficiary.

Section B. Revocable Trusts as Will Substitutes

Reference to "forever" in special warranty deed does not make trust irrevocable

VELA v. GRC LAND HOLDINGS, LTD.

Court of Appeals of Texas, San Antonio
383 S.W.3d 248 (2012)

SIMMONS, J. This appeal arises from a suit to partition a 1,889.87 acre ranch, known as Matambo Ranch, located in Zapata County. The trial court granted summary judgment in favor of appellee GRC Land Holdings, Ltd. and denied appellant Antonio M. Vela Jr.'s motion for summary judgment. Antonio Jr. contends on appeal that the trial court erroneously determined that a trust settlor may deed real property to a revocable *inter vivos* trust and may subsequently amend the trust to change the beneficiaries. We affirm the trial court's judgment.

BACKGROUND

The relevant facts underlying this appeal are undisputed. In 1985, Antonio M. Vela Sr. died testate, leaving a one-half undivided interest in the Matambo Ranch to his wife, Herminia C. Vela. The remaining one-half undivided interest was devised to their four children, Grizelda, Rose, Cordelia, and Antonio Jr., with each of the children holding a 12.5% undivided interest. In 1997, Herminia established the Herminia C. Vela Living Trust (the Trust) and listed as beneficiaries four heritage trusts—one for each of her four children. Six months later, she conveyed by special warranty deed (the Deed) her 50% interest in the ranch to the Trust. Following this conveyance, Herminia amended the Trust on three separate occasions. The final amendment, in 2001, removed the Antonio M. Vela, Jr. Heritage Trust as a beneficiary.

Herminia passed away in 2003. In the years following her death, Grizelda, Rose, and Cordelia formed GRC Land Holdings, Ltd. (GRC) and conveyed all of their collective interests in the Matambo Ranch to the limited partnership, including the 37.5% undivided interest from their father and the 50% undivided interest from the Trust. Thus by 2006, GRC ostensibly held 87.5% interest in the Matambo Ranch, leaving Antonio Jr. with the 12.5% interest he received from his father.

In 2008, GRC brought suit against Antonio Jr. to partition the ranch. Both parties moved for summary judgment. GRC's motion sought a declaration that the Trust, as amended, required the following partition: a 12.5% undivided interest to Antonio Jr. and an 87.5% undivided interest to GRC. Antonio Jr.'s motion sought a declaration that the Trust was made irrevocable by the Deed and, therefore, he owned an undivided 25% interest in the ranch and GRC owned the remaining 75% undivided interest. The trial court granted GRC's motion, denied Antonio Jr.'s motion, and ordered partition of the ranch. . . .

REVOCABLE *INTER VIVOS* TRUSTS

The issue on appeal is whether Herminia could amend the Trust to remove a beneficiary after the conveyance of real property into the Trust. Under the specific facts presented and the language of the applicable Trust and Deed, we conclude that the trial court did not err in granting summary judgment in favor of GRC.

A. Right to Revoke and Amend a Living Trust

As settlor, Herminia had the authority to revoke the Trust unless it was made irrevocable by "the express terms of [either] the instrument creating it or of an instrument modifying it." See Texas Property Code § 112.051(a); see also Moon v. Lesikar, 230 S.W.3d 800, 804 (Tex. App.-Houston [14th Dist.] 2007, pet. denied). The right to revoke a trust is coupled with the right to modify or amend its terms. See Texas Property Code § 112.051(b). No specific words of art are needed to create an irrevocable trust. See McCauley v. Simmer, 336 S.W.2d 872, 881 (Tex. Civ. App.-Houston 1960, writ dism'd). However, the instrument must clearly reflect the settlor's intent to make the trust irrevocable. See Austin Lake Estates Recreation Club, Inc. v. Gilliam, 493 S.W.2d 343, 347 (Tex. Civ. App.-Austin 1973, writ ref'd n.r.e.); see also Soefje v. Jones, 270 S.W.3d 617, 628 (Tex. App.-San Antonio 2008, no pet.) (asserting that construing an unambiguous trust is a matter of law, and the settlor's intent in creating the trust is ascertained "from the language in the four corners of the instrument").

B. The Trial Court Did Not Err

Antonio Jr. does not dispute that the Trust was originally revocable. He contends, however, that the Deed executed by Herminia manifested her intent to make the trust irrevocable. We must therefore look to the express language of the Deed to determine Herminia's intent. See Texas Property Code § 112.051; *Moon*, 230 S.W.3d at 804.

1. The Deed

The grantor listed in the special warranty deed is "Herminia C. Vela"; the grantee is listed as "Herminia C. Vela Living Trust." The conjoined granting and habendum clauses state:

> Grantor . . . grants, sells and conveys to Grantee the property . . . to have and hold it to Grantee, Grantee's heirs, executors, administrators, successors, or assigns forever.

The warranty clause reads:

> Grantor binds Grantor and Grantor's heirs, executors, administrators and successors to warrant and forever defend all and singular the property to Grantee and Grantee's heirs, executors, administrators, successors and claim the same or any part thereof; by,

through or under Grantor, but not otherwise and subject to the reservations from and exceptions to conveyance and warranty.

Antonio Jr. contends that the phrase in the Deed that grants to "Grantee [(the Trust)] and Grantee's heirs, executors, administrators and successors or assigns *forever*" indicates Herminia's intent to make the trust irrevocable. (emphasis added). In support of this contention, he relies on three Austin court of appeals cases[1] as well as the concept of equitable title. However, these cases are distinguishable and the principle of equitable title does not apply.[2]

2. Case Law Relied Upon by Appellant

In *Butler*, the court held that a real property conveyance by way of general warranty deed to a trust did not make the trust irrevocable. See Butler v. Shelton, 408 S.W.2d 530, 534 (Tex. Civ. App.-Austin 1966, writ ref'd n.r.e.). While the court highlighted the fact that the general warranty deed did not include the term "forever," the court noted, "It would be a strained and unwarranted construction to hold that the statutory form of general warranty in a trust deed has the effect of expressly making it irrevocable." See id.[3] Because the Deed executed by Herminia used statutory granting and warranty language, see Texas Property Code § 5.022, Antonio Jr.'s reliance on Butler is tenuous.

In *Austin Lake Estates*, a corporation conveyed property by quitclaim deed to "trustees, 'their heirs and assigns forever, *so that neither said corporation* [(as trust settlor and deed grantor)] *nor its successors and assigns shall have any right or title to or interest in such property, premises or appurtenances or any part thereof at any time hereafter*.'" *Austin Lake Estates*, 493 S.W.2d at 347 (emphasis added). The court held that the quitclaim deed created an irrevocable trust. Id. *Austin Lake Estates* is distinguishable from our case in at least three respects. First, in *Austin Lake Estates*, the deed itself was the instrument that created the trust; in our case, the trust and the special warranty deed conveying the ranch to the Trust were separate instruments. Cf. id. Second, the quitclaim deed in *Austin Lake Estates* contained not only statutory conveyance and warranty language, but it also incorporated language limiting revocability by the settlor. See id. Third, the trust in *Austin Lake Estates* made no provision for the settlor to modify, amend, or use the principal of the trust; rather, the trust conveyed title to the

---

[1] See Sheffield v. Ellison, No. 03–97–00050–CV, 1997 WL 334949 (Tex. App.-Austin June 19, 1997, no writ) (per curiam) (not designated for publication); Austin Lake Estates Recreation Club, Inc. v. Gilliam, 493 S.W.2d 343 (Tex. Civ. App.-Austin 1973, writ ref'd n.r.e.); Butler v. Shelton, 408 S.W.2d 530 (Tex. Civ. App.-Austin 1966, writ ref'd n.r.e.).

[2] We note that the grantee listed in the Deed was the Trust itself. We expressly distinguish this situation from an instance where trust beneficiaries (rather than a trust or a trustee) are specifically named as grantees in a special warranty deed.

[3] See generally Texas Property Code § 5.022 (providing the form of a covenant of general warranty including the phrase, "To have and to hold the above described premises, together with all and singular the rights and appurtenances thereto in any wise belonging, unto the said ________________, his heirs or assigns *forever*." (emphasis added)).

trustees forever without the possibility of ownership or modification by the settlor. See id.; see also Snyder v. Cowell, No. 08–01–00444–CV, 2003 WL 1849145, at *5 (Tex. App.-El Paso Apr. 10, 2003, no pet.) (mem. op.) (emphasizing the significance of the extra-statutory language used in the granting clause in *Austin Lake Estates*). Conversely, the Trust created by Herminia provides: "This trust is revocable by Settlor during Settlor's life. Settlor shall have the power and right to amend, modify and revoke, in whole or in part, this agreement or any terms or provisions thereof by notice in writing delivered to the Trustees." Importantly, it also provides: "So long as Settlor shall live, there shall be distributed to or for the benefit of Settlor so much of the trust income and principal as Settlor shall from time to time direct in writing."

Finally, Antonio Jr. cites an unpublished opinion to support his contention that use of the word "forever" in the special warranty deed caused the trust to become irrevocable. In *Sheffield*, the instrument creating the trust was a warranty deed. Sheffield v. Ellison, No. 03–97–00050–CV, 1997 WL 334949, at *1 (Tex. App.-Austin June 19, 1997, no writ) (per curiam) (not designated for publication). The court noted that the use of the word "forever" in the combined granting and habendum clause, as well as the phrase "ever defend" in the warranty clause, indicated an intent on behalf of the settlor to create an irrevocable trust. Id. at *3. There are two notable distinctions between *Sheffield* and the present appeal. First, there was no separate trust instrument in Sheffield that clearly indicated an intent on behalf of the settlor to create a revocable trust. Cf. id. at *1. Second, there was no applicable language that allowed the settlor to take the property out of the trust for the settlor's own use. Cf. id. at *1–3.

a. The Deed Did Not Make the Trust Irrevocable

The plain language of the special warranty deed does not indicate that Herminia, as settlor of the trust, intended to make the Trust irrevocable.[4] See *Soefje*, 270 S.W.3d at 628-29. Because section 112.051(a) requires express language of irrevocability, we conclude that the use of the term "forever" in the special warranty deed did not cause the Trust to become irrevocable. See *Snyder*, 2003 WL 1849145, at *5 (noting that use of the word "forever" in a general warranty deed did not, by itself, create an irrevocable trust); cf. *Soefje*, 270 S.W.3d at 628-29 (noting that for an amendment to revoke a trust, the amendment must contain express language indicating a settlor's intent to revoke the trust).

b. Equitable Title

Antonio Jr. also supports his contention that the trust became irrevocable by relying on the concept that equitable title in property immediately passes to a beneficiary when a trust is created. See Cutrer v. Cutrer, 334 S.W.2d 599, 605 (Tex. Civ. App.-San Antonio 1960), *aff'd*, 162 Tex. 166, 345 S.W.2d 513 (1961); see also Shearrer v. Holley, 952 S.W.2d 74, 78 (Tex.

---

[4] We note that the grantee listed in the Deed was the Trust itself. We expressly distinguish this situation from an instance in which trust beneficiaries (rather than a trust or a trustee) are specifically named as grantees in a special warranty deed.

App.-San Antonio 1997, no writ). Thus, he contends that because his heritage trust was vested with equitable title in the Matambo Ranch at the time Herminia conveyed her 50% interest into the Trust by special warranty deed, he could not be divested of the interest by Herminia's amendment to the Trust.

This contention ignores the defeasible nature of interests held by the beneficiaries of a revocable trust. See Cisneros v. San Miguel, 640 S.W.2d 327, 330 (Tex. App.-San Antonio 1982, writ ref'd n.r.e.) (noting that a beneficiary's interest is defeasible—i.e., capable of being divested—when the trust's settlor revokes the trust or uses up the entirety of a trust's corpus); see also Westerfeld v. Huckaby, 474 S.W.2d 189, 193 (Tex. 1971). Because the Trust was revocable and susceptible to amendment or modification by Herminia as settlor, Antonio Jr.'s interest in the ranch under the Trust was defeasible. As Antonio Jr.'s interest in the trust was properly divested by Herminia's written amendment to the Trust, the trial court did not err in declaring GRC's total interest in the ranch was an 87.5% undivided interest and Antonio Jr.'s total interest in the ranch was 12.5%.

CONCLUSION

The trial court did not err in granting summary judgment in favor of GRC Land Holdings, Ltd. and in denying Antonio Vela Jr.'s motion for summary judgment. Because GRC was entitled to summary judgment as a matter of law, we affirm the trial court's judgment.

Section C. Brokerage and Bank Accounts

Estates Code § 113.151. Establishment of Right of Survivorship in Joint Account; Ownership on Death of Party

(a) Sums remaining on deposit on the death of a party to a joint account belong to the surviving party or parties against the estate of the deceased party if the interest of the deceased party is made to survive to the surviving party or parties by a written agreement signed by the party who dies.

(b) Notwithstanding any other law, an agreement is sufficient under this section to confer an absolute right of survivorship on parties to a joint account if the agreement contains a statement substantially similar to the following: "On the death of one party to a joint account, all sums in the account on the date of the death vest in and belong to the surviving party as his or her separate property and estate."

(c) A survivorship agreement may not be inferred from the mere fact that the account is a joint account or that the account is designated as JT TEN, Joint Tenancy, or joint, or with other similar language.

(d) If there are two or more surviving parties to a joint account that is subject to a right of survivorship agreement:

(1) during the parties' lifetimes respective ownerships are in proportion to the parties' previous ownership interests under Sections 113.102, 113.103, and 113.104, as applicable, augmented by an equal share for each survivor of any interest a deceased party owned in the account immediately before that party's death; and

(2) the right of survivorship continues between the surviving parties if a written agreement signed by a party who dies provides for that continuation.

Estates Code § 113.152. Ownership of P.O.D. Account on Death of Party

(a) If the account is a P.O.D. account and there is a written agreement signed by the original payee or payees, on the death of the original payee or on the death of the survivor of two or more original payees, any sums remaining on deposit belong to:

(1) the P.O.D. payee or payees if surviving; or

(2) the survivor of the P.O.D. payees if one or more P.O.D. payees die before the original payee.

(b) If two or more P.O.D. payees survive, no right of survivorship exists between the surviving P.O.D. payees unless the terms of the account or deposit agreement expressly provide for survivorship between those payees.

(c) A guardian of the estate or an attorney in fact or agent of an original payee may sign a written agreement described by Subsection (a) on behalf of the original payee.

Estates Code § 112.051. Agreement for Right of Survivorship in Community Property

At any time, spouses may agree between themselves that all or part of their community property, then existing or to be acquired, becomes the property of the surviving spouse on the death of a spouse.

Estates Code § 112.052. Form of Agreement

(a) A community property survivorship agreement must be in writing and signed by both spouses.

(b) A written agreement signed by both spouses is sufficient to create a right of survivorship in the community property described in the agreement if the agreement includes any of the following phrases:

(1) "with right of survivorship";

(2) "will become the property of the survivor";

(3) "will vest in and belong to the surviving spouse"; or

(4) "shall pass to the surviving spouse."

(c) Notwithstanding Subsection (b), a community property survivorship agreement that otherwise meets the requirements of this chapter is effective without including any of the phrases listed in that subsection.

(d) A survivorship agreement may not be inferred from the mere fact that an account is a joint account or that an account is designated as JT TEN, Joint Tenancy, or joint, or with other similar language.

Estates Code § 112.054. Revocation of Agreement

(a) A community property survivorship agreement made in accordance with this chapter may be revoked as provided by the terms of the agreement.

(b) If a community property survivorship agreement does not provide a method of revocation, the agreement may be revoked by a written instrument:

(1) signed by both spouses; or

(2) signed by one spouse and delivered to the other spouse.

(c) A community property survivorship agreement may be revoked with respect to specific property subject to the agreement by the disposition of the property by one or both spouses if the disposition is not inconsistent with specific terms of the agreement and applicable law.

Estates Code § 112.152. Nontestamentary Nature of Transfers Under Agreement

(a) Transfers at death resulting from community property survivorship agreements made in accordance with this chapter are effective by reason of the agreements involved and are not testamentary transfers.

(b) Except as expressly provided otherwise by this title, transfers described by Subsection (a) are not subject to the provisions of this title applicable to testamentary transfers.

Issuance of securities certificates from account containing community property with right of survivorship does not revoke survivorship agreement

HOLMES v. BEATTY

Supreme Court of Texas
290 S.W.3d 852 (2009)

JEFFERSON, C.J. After decades of debate in the bench, bar, and the Legislature about the ability of spouses to obtain rights of survivorship in community property, Texas citizens changed the constitution to confirm that right. The 1987 amendment provides that "spouses may agree in writing that all or part of their community property becomes the property of the surviving spouse on the death of a spouse." Texas Constitution art. XVI, § 15. Two years later, the Legislature enacted Probate Code sections 451 through 462 to address the formalities necessary to . . . create a survivorship arrangement. See Texas Probate Code §§ 451-62. Today we are asked to determine how these sections operate with respect to rights of survivorship in certain brokerage accounts and securities certificates issued from those accounts. We conclude that the account agreements and certificates at issue here created rights of survivorship. Accordingly, we reverse and render in part and affirm in part the court of appeals' judgment.

I

FACTUAL AND PROCEDURAL BACKGROUND

Thomas and Kathryn Holmes married in 1972. During their marriage, Thomas and Kathryn amassed over ten million dollars in brokerage accounts and acquired securities certificates issued from those accounts. Kathryn died in 1999. Her will appointed Douglas Beatty, her son from a previous marriage, as the independent executor of her estate. Thomas died approximately nine months later. His son, Harry Holmes II ("Holmes"), also from a previous marriage, was appointed independent executor of his estate. The accounts and certificates were variously listed as "JT TEN"; "JT TEN *defined as* 'joint tenants with right of survivorship and not as tenants in common'"; "JTWROS"; and "Joint (WROS)." If those acronyms and definitions establish a right of survivorship, then Thomas acquired 100% upon Kathryn's death, and upon his death, the holdings would have passed under his will, which left nothing to Kathryn's children. If those designations were insufficient to create survivorship interests then, as community property, only 50% would have passed to Thomas, with the remaining 50% of the accounts and certificates passing under Kathryn's will, which left nothing to Thomas's children.

Beatty sought a declaration that all of the assets were community property; Holmes countered that the assets passed to Thomas through survivorship, and then to Thomas's beneficiaries following his death. On competing motions for summary judgment, the trial court concluded that some of the assets were held jointly with survivorship rights and others were community property. In two opinions, the court of appeals affirmed in part, reversed and rendered in part, and remanded for further proceedings. Holmes and Beatty petitioned this Court for review, which we granted. Because these two appeals involve "substantially similar facts, arguments, and briefing," we have consolidated them into a single opinion and judgment.

II

DEVELOPMENT OF RIGHTS OF SURVIVORSHIP IN COMMUNITY PROPERTY IN TEXAS

A

The *Hilley* Era

Texas has not always allowed spouses to create rights of survivorship in community property. In Hilley v. Hilley, 161 Tex. 569, 342 S.W.2d 565, 568 (1961), we held that it was unconstitutional for spouses to hold community property with rights of survivorship. . . . We noted that to hold otherwise would directly contravene the constitution's community property provision. . . . After *Hilley*, the Legislature amended the Probate Code in an attempt to recognize survivorship rights in community property. Act of April 27, 1961, 57th Leg., R.S., ch. 120, § 1, 1961 Tex. Gen. Laws 233, amended by Act of May 22, 1969, 61st Leg., R.S., ch. 641, § 3, 1969 Tex. Gen. Laws 1922, 1922 ("It is specifically provided that any husband and his wife may, by written agreement, create a joint estate out of their community property, with rights of survivorship."). In Williams v. McKnight, 402 S.W.2d 505, 508 (Tex. 1966), we considered the amendment's constitutionality. Citing *Hilley*, we held that any statutory attempt to grant survivorship rights in community property would be unconstitutional. Id. ("Constitutional limitations are as binding upon the Legislature as they are upon the Judiciary."). We reaffirmed that the only way for a couple to create survivorship rights was to partition their community property into separate property, then execute survivorship agreements for that separate property. Id. at 508. This process came to be known among practitioners as the "Texas Two-Step." See, e.g., Robert N. Virden, Joint Tenancy with Right of Survivorship & Community Property with Right of Survivorship, 53 Tex. B.J. 1179, 1179 (1990). Subsequent decisions echoed this result. . . .

B

The 1987 Constitutional Amendment and Subsequent Legislation

In 1987, the Legislature passed, and the Texas voters approved, a constitutional amendment authorizing rights of survivorship in community property. Tex. S.J. Res. 35, 70th Leg., R.S., 1987 Tex. Gen. Laws 4114, 4114-15. The amendment provided that "spouses may agree in writing that all or part of their community property becomes the property of the surviving spouse on the death of a spouse." Texas Constitution art. XVI, § 15. Two years later, the Legislature passed Senate Bill 1643, which added Part 3 to Chapter XI of the Probate Code concerning non-testamentary transfers. Act of May 26, 1989, 71st Leg., R.S., Ch. 655, § 2, 1989 Tex. Gen. Laws 2159, 2159-63. This new section governs "[a]greements between spouses regarding rights of survivorship in community property." Texas Probate Code § 46(b).

Probate Code sections 451 and 452 are at issue in this case. Section 451 states: "At any time, spouses may agree between themselves that all or part of their community property, then existing or to be acquired, becomes the property of the surviving spouse on the death of a spouse." Id. § 451. Section 452 lays out these requirements:

> An agreement between spouses creating a right of survivorship in community property must be in writing and signed by both spouses. If an agreement in writing is signed by both spouses, the agreement shall be sufficient to create a right of survivorship in the community property described in the agreement if it includes any of the following phrases:
>
> 1. (1) "with right of survivorship";
> 2. "will become the property of the survivor";
> 3. "will vest in and belong to the surviving spouse"; or
> 4. (1) "shall pass to the surviving spouse."
>
> An agreement that otherwise meets the requirements of this part, however, shall be effective without including any of those phrases.[5]

Id. § 452. The Legislature stated that these agreements do not change the nature of community property: "Property subject to an agreement between spouses creating a right of survivorship in community property remains community property during the marriage of the spouses." Id. § 453.

With this constitutional amendment and legislation, the Legislature hoped to finally resolve the battle over survivorship rights in community property. The proponents urged that these sorts of agreements were common in other states and simplified the transfer of certain assets to surviving spouses. See Gerry W. Beyer, 10 Texas Practice Series: Texas Law of Wills § 60.1 (3d ed. 2002). As Professor Beyer noted, a community property survivorship agreement "is a simple, convenient and inexpensive method for many married people to

---

[5] In 2011, the Texas legislature amended section 452 of the Probate Code (and section 112.052 of the Estates Code) to provide that "[a] survivorship agreement will not be inferred from the mere fact that the account is a joint account or that the account is designated as JT TEN, Joint Tenancy, or joint, or with other similar language." The amending statute explained that "[t]he changes in law made by this article to Section 452, Texas Probate Code, apply only to agreements created or existing on or after the effective date of this Act [Sept. 1, 2011], and are intended to overturn the ruling of the Texas Supreme Court in Holmes v. Beatty, 290 S.W.3d 852 (Tex. 2009)." —Ed.

achieve an at-death distribution of their community property that is in accord with their intent." Id. § 60.9.

As the amendment's drafters noted at the time, "[m]any Texas spouses hold a substantial amount of assets in a form that is ineffective to achieve their desired purpose." Senate Judiciary Comm., Resolution Analysis, Tex. S.J. Res. 35, 70th Leg., R.S. (1987). Supporters argued that the proposed constitutional amendment would "eliminate a trap for the unwary married couple who would execute a signature card provided by a financial institution and believe, mistakenly, that they have created an effective joint tenancy with right of survivorship in relation to their community property." Texas Legislative Council, Analyses of Proposed Constitutional Amendments and Referenda, Info. Report No. 87-2 at 36 (Sept. 1987).

The purpose of the amendment and accompanying legislation, then, was to provide "[a] simple means . . . by which both spouses by a written instrument can provide that the survivor of them may be entitled to all or any designated portion of their community property without the necessity of making a will for that purpose." Senate Judiciary Comm., Resolution Analysis, Tex. S.J. Res. 35, 70th Leg., R.S. (1987). As the committee observed, "many banks and savings and loans associations have often failed to provide forms by which their customers can create effective joint tenancies out of community property." Id. The amendment addressed these concerns by removing the constitutional hurdles to creating rights of survivorship in community property.

III

APPLICATION

The assets at issue in this case fall into two categories: (1) securities accounts and (2) securities certificates issued from those accounts. These two categories of assets are affected by distinct legal analyses, so we address each in turn.

A

The Securities Accounts

Thomas and Kathryn Holmes maintained investment accounts with multiple financial institutions. Each of them was governed by an account agreement that dictated terms, such as who could manage the accounts and whether the accounts were held with rights of survivorship.

Nonprobate Transfers and Planning for Incapacity

1

Accounts Agreements With a "JT TEN" Designation

At the time of Kathryn's death, the Holmeses held two investment accounts whose agreements included the designation "JT TEN": one with Dain Rauscher, Inc. and another with First Southwest Company. Thomas and Kathryn opened the Dain Rauscher account in 1994. The account agreement, titled "JOINT ACCOUNT AGREEMENT" was styled "THOMAS J. HOLMES AND KATHRYN V. HOLMES, JT TEN." The agreement gave the account holders an option to strike through "paragraph (a) or (b) whichever is inapplicable." Paragraph (a) stated "it is the express intention of the undersigned to create an estate or account as joint tenants with rights of survivorship and not as tenants in common." Paragraph (b) gave the account holders the option to designate who would receive the interest in the account upon their death and the percentages each recipient would receive. The Holmeses struck neither provision. They both signed the agreement, and "Jt. Ten" appeared next to Kathryn's name on the signature line.

The Holmeses opened the First Southwest Account in 1997. The account agreement listed their names as "THOMAS J. HOLMES, KATHRYN V. HOLMES JT TEN." The agreement did not define "JT TEN" and did not include any further discussion of survivorship rights. Both Thomas and Kathryn signed the First Southwest account, as well.

The court of appeals held that neither of these agreements "clearly reflect[ed] intent to own the account with a right of survivorship." 233 S.W.3d 475, 481; see also 233 S.W.3d 494, 505. As to the Dain Rauscher account, the court noted that because the couple did not strike through paragraph (a) or (b), the agreement "did not affirmatively reflect any intent to effect a non-testamentary transfer-through a right of survivorship or otherwise." 233 S.W.3d 475, 481. The court also rejected Holmes's argument that the "JT TEN" designation on the agreements satisfied section 452's requirements: the "mere inclusion of 'JT TEN' next to Kathryn's and Thomas's names in the account title did not sufficiently convey intent to create a right of survivorship." Id. at 483. The court agreed with Beatty's argument that "parties may own property as joint tenants without being subject to a right of survivorship." Id.; 233 S.W.3d 494, 505.

We disagree with the court of appeals on each point. A joint tenancy carries rights of survivorship. See, e.g., U.S. v. Craft, 535 U.S. 274, 280, 122 S. Ct. 1414, 152 L. Ed. 2d 437 (2002) ("The main difference between a joint tenancy and a tenancy in common is that a joint tenant also has a right of automatic inheritance known as 'survivorship.' Upon the death of one joint tenant, that tenant's share in the property does not pass through will or the rules of intestate succession; rather, the remaining tenant or tenants automatically inherit it."); 2 William Blackstone, Commentaries on the Laws of England 183 (3rd ed. 1768) ("[The] remaining grand incident of joint estates [is] the doctrine of survivorship . . . ."); Littleton's Tenures, Book III, ch. III, § 280 (Eugene W. Wambaugh ed., 1903) ("And it is to be understood, that the nature of joint-tenancy is, that he which surviveth shall have only the entire tenancy according to such estate as he hath . . . ."); 7 Richard R. Powell, Powell on Real Property § 51.03[3] (Michael Allan Wolf ed., 2000) ("Survivorship is central to a joint tenancy."). Contrary to Beatty's and the court of appeals' assertion then, a joint tenancy cannot be held without rights of survivorship; such a joint agreement would be a tenancy in common. See *Craft*, 535 U.S. at 280, 122 S. Ct. 1414; 7 Powell on Real Property § 51.01 [1] ("[A joint tenancy] is distinguished from a tenancy in common principally by the right of survivorship."). The financial industry's use of "joint tenancy" is also consistent with this view. See, e.g., Sec. Transfer Assoc., Guidelines of the Securities Transfer Association AV-1 (Oct. 2005) (defining "Joint Tenancy" as a "[f]orm of ownership where two or more individuals hold shares as joint tenants with right of survivorship. When one tenant dies, the entire tenancy remains to the surviving tenants. JOHN BROWN & MARY BROWN JT TEN.").

Citing Stauffer v. Henderson, 801 S.W.2d 858, 865 (Tex. 1990), the court of appeals held that it could not consider information that is not explicitly referenced in the agreement itself. 233 S.W.3d 494, 507. It therefore evaluated the designations "JT TEN" and "Jt. Ten" without reference to guidelines, codes, or custom. Id. at 509-13. In *Stauffer*, we held that under Probate Code section 439(a), concerning survivorship rights between non-spouses, parties could only establish survivorship using the statute's language (or language "substantially" similar to it), and a court could not consider other evidence to ascertain the parties' intent. S*tauffer*, 801 S.W.2d at 863-65 (citing Texas Probate Code § 439(a)). Applying this holding to the current case, the court of appeals stated:

> [W]e are addressing a situation in which Texas law dictates parties do not even have a certain type of agreement—a survivorship agreement—unless they have executed a written instrument complying with statutory formalities, including expression of their intent to create a right of survivorship. Therefore, if we must look outside the written instrument to determine that a term used therein means "right of survivorship," the parties have not expressed their intent within the written instrument.

233 S.W.3d 494, 511.

The court of appeals' reliance on *Stauffer*, however, was misplaced. Section 439(a) requires that a survivorship agreement between non-spouses use either the statute's language or a substitute that is "in substantially the [same] form." Texas Probate Code § 439(a). Section 452 is less restrictive, presumably because agreements between spouses are less vulnerable to fraud. The constitutional amendment permitting survivorship agreements in community property was intended to facilitate the creation of such agreements, see, e.g., Senate Judiciary Comm., Resolution Analysis, Tex. S.J. Res. 35, 70th Leg., R.S. (1987), and the Legislature's use of less confining language comports with that goal. Moreover, *Stauffer* precludes outside evidence, not reference to the common law or trade usage. Cf. Restatement (Second) of Contracts § 222 cmt. b ("There is no requirement that an agreement be ambiguous before evidence of a usage of trade can be shown . . . .").

Precedent, trade usage, and seminal treatises make clear that joint tenancies carry rights of survivorship, and the Holmeses' agreement included this designation. This does not fully answer, however, the inherent tension in owning community property as "joint tenants." Professor Reed Quilliam noted in an article published shortly after the constitutional amendment and statutes were adopted that "[j]oint tenancy is a form of separate property ownership and is wholly incompatible with community property concepts." See W. Reed Quilliam, Jr., A Requiem for Hilley: Is Survivorship Community Property a Solution Worse than the Problem?, 21 Tex. Tech. L. Rev. 1153, 1167 (1990). In the same discussion, though, Professor Quilliam predicted that situations like this case were likely to arise:

> It is likely that misconceptions about the new form of property ownership will result in instances of spouses agreeing to hold community property "as joint tenants with right of survivorship" rather than merely "with right of survivorship." What will be the effect of such designation?
>
> Manifestly the property will remain community, although the spouses' agreement to hold with right of survivorship should be given effect to impress *this* characteristic on it. The property *cannot* be joint tenancy property, a form of separate property ownership, unless it has first been rendered separate by partition. The agreement of the spouse violates the constitution insofar as it seeks to establish a joint tenancy in community property. But the agreement to hold such property with right of survivorship is now constitutionally sanctioned.

Id. at 1168-69 (emphasis in original). We agree with Professor Quilliam. A "joint tenancy" or "JT TEN" designation on an account is sufficient to create rights of survivorship in community property under section 452. The Dain Rauscher and First Southwest accounts included this designation, and we "give effect to the written expression of the parties' intent." Balandran v. Safeco Ins. Co. of Am., 972 S.W.2d 738, 741 (Tex. 1998). Because the "JT TEN" designation was sufficient to indicate the Holmeses' intent to hold those accounts with rights of survivorship, we reverse the court of appeals' judgment on the Dain Rauscher and First Southwest accounts.

2

The Raymond James Account

The Holmeses opened an investment account with Raymond James & Associates in 1995. The "New Account Form" gave Thomas and Kathryn the option to check a box for the "Account Classification." They chose "Joint (WROS)." The form also listed their names as "THOMAS J. HOLMES & KATHRYN V. HOLMES JTWROS." The trial court held that this account did not carry rights of survivorship, but the court of appeals reversed, holding "the Raymond James account agreement sufficiently conveyed Kathryn's and Thomas's intent to create a right of survivorship." 233 S.W.3d 494, 515.

The court of appeals reached this decision primarily based on the Holmeses' affirmative act of checking the "Joint (WROS)" box:

> Kathryn and Thomas affirmatively selected an "Account Classification." They were presented with fourteen options for the account classification and selected "Joint (WROS)" to the exclusion of all other options. Significantly, Kathryn and Thomas rejected "tenancy in common"—the very designation that Beatty attempts to assign to this account. We can conceive of no other meaning Kathryn and Thomas could have contemplated for "Joint (WROS)," considering that none of the other options can possibly be construed as meaning joint tenancy with rights of survivorship.

Id. at 515.

We agree with the court of appeals that "Joint (WROS)" means "joint tenancy with rights of survivorship." As such, this indicated the Holmeses' intent to obtain rights of survivorship in this account. This designation, along with Thomas's and Kathryn's signatures on the form, satisfy section 452's requirements. We therefore affirm the court of appeals' judgment on the Raymond James account.

B

The Securities Certificates

Securities issued in certificate form represent the other category of assets in dispute. Kathryn and Thomas opened accounts with several brokerage companies during their marriage, investing in a combination of stocks and bonds. Over time, the respective brokerage companies distributed some of these individual securities, in certificate form, to the Holmeses. The certificates themselves had various designations, such as "JT TEN"; "JT TEN—as joint tenants with right of survivorship and not as tenants in common"; and "JT WROS."

None of the certificates were signed by Kathryn or Thomas. As the court of appeals pointed out, it would have been unusual for them to do so. 233 S.W.3d 475, 484 ("None of the certificates at issue were signed by Kathryn or Thomas because owners do not typically sign stocks or bonds until they are ready to sell or redeem them."). Beatty contends that these individual certificates must satisfy the requirements of section 452 on their own, and because they were unsigned, they fail to do so. Holmes posits two alternative theories for establishing rights of survivorship in the certificates: (1) the survivorship language on the certificates is valid under section 450 of the Probate Code, and alternatively, (2) the survivorship language in the underlying account agreements govern the securities themselves. The court of appeals disagreed with Holmes on both theories and held that none of the certificates were held with rights of survivorship. 233 S.W.3d 475, 483, 233 S.W.3d 494, 522. We agree that section 450 is inapplicable to these assets, but we disagree with the court of appeals on Holmes's second argument. Because we hold that the agreements' survivorship language conferred survivorship rights in the certificates until the Holmeses disposed of them, the certificates passed to Thomas pursuant to those rights.

1

Texas Probate Code Section 450

Texas Probate Code section 450 falls under Part 2 of the chapter dealing with nontestamentary transfers. Texas Probate Code § 450. Section 450 states, in relevant part:

> (a) Any of the following provisions in [a] . . . bond, [or] . . . securities . . . is deemed to be nontestamentary, and this code does not invalidate the instrument or any provision:
>
> > (1) that money or other benefits theretofore due to, controlled, or owned by a decedent shall be paid after his death to a person designated by the decedent in either the instrument or a separate writing, including a will, executed at the same time as the instrument or subsequently . . . .

Id. Holmes argues that this language controls the securities certificates, and that the various designations found on the certificates (e.g. "JT TEN") establish rights of survivorship in those assets, and that section 452's requirements cannot "invalidate" this agreement. The court of appeals disagreed, holding that Part 3 of Chapter XI controlled, and Holmes, therefore, could not rely on section 450 to establish rights of survivorship in the certificates. 233 S.W.3d 475, 490. We agree with the court of appeals.

Probate Code section 46(b) states that "[a]greements between spouses regarding rights of survivorship in community property are governed by Part 3 of Chapter XI of this code." Texas Probate Code § 46(b). The court of appeals correctly noted that this provision makes it clear that "section 450 irreconcilably conflicts with Part 3." 233 S.W.3d 475, 489. To hold otherwise would allow parties to circumvent section 452's writing and signature requirements. By enacting section 46(b) at the same time as sections 451 through 462 (Chapter XI, Part 3 of the Probate Code), the Legislature provided that Part 3 is the exclusive means to establish rights of survivorship in community property.

2

Texas Probate Code Section 455

Holmes also argues that the certificates issued from the Holmeses' investment accounts retained the survivorship rights established by their respective account agreements pursuant to section 455. Section 455 falls within the Probate Code's discussion of survivorship rights in community property. Texas Probate Code § 455. Section 455, titled "Revocation," states:

> An agreement between spouses made in accordance with this part of this code may be revoked in accordance with the terms of the agreement. If the agreement does not provide a method for revocation, the agreement may be revoked by a written instrument signed by both spouses or by a written instrument signed by one spouse and delivered to the other spouse. The agreement may be revoked with respect to specific property subject to the agreement by the disposition of such property by one or both of the spouses if such disposition is not inconsistent with specific terms of the agreement and applicable law.

Id. Holmes argues that because Thomas and Kathryn never executed a revocation agreement pursuant to this section, and because the certificates were never disposed of, the account agreements govern the certificates. Beatty argues that the act of alienating the certificates from the accounts acted as a "disposition." We disagree.

Once the survivorship agreement was in place, the only means of revoking it was pursuant to the statute, i.e., through a subsequent written agreement or a disposition of the assets covered by the agreement. Section 455 does not define what constitutes a "disposition." Therefore, we give it its "ordinary meaning." Texas Government Code § 312.002. Black's Law Dictionary defines "disposition" as "[t]he act of transferring something to another's care or possession, esp. by deed or will; the relinquishing of property." Black's Law Dictionary 505 (8th ed. 2004). Webster's defines "disposition" as "a giving over to the care or possession of another, or a relinquishing." Webster's Third New Int'l Dictionary 654 (2002).

The issuance of securities in certificate form is not a "disposition" under the statute. The certificates were issued in the Holmeses' names, so ownership never changed; there was no "relinquishment" of the assets. As the court of appeals observed, "Kathryn and Thomas may have intended to own the securities in certificate form with a right of survivorship because they received the same property they had purchased through the accounts—just in a different form." 233 S.W.3d 494, 519. We agree that this was likely the Holmeses' expectation, especially because survivorship designations appeared on each of the certificates themselves, among them "JT WROS," "JT TEN," and "JT TEN—as joint tenancy with right of survivorship and not as tenancy in common."

Because we hold that issuing these certificates did not revoke the accounts' survivorship agreements, the certificates retained survivorship rights. We held above that the Dain Rauscher, First Southwest, and Raymond James accounts were held with rights of survivorship, so the certificates that were issued from those accounts carried the rights of survivorship established by those accounts' agreements. We therefore reverse the court of appeals judgment as to those certificates.

At the time of Kathryn's death, the Holmeses also held securities in certificate form issued from accounts once held with Kemper Securities and Principal/Eppler, Guerin & Turner. We must determine, then, whether the Kemper Securities and Principal account agreements established rights of survivorship. The Kemper account agreement was titled

"JOINT ACCOUNT WITH RIGHT OF SURVIVORSHIP" and was signed by both spouses. This meets the test we established above to create rights of survivorship in an investment account. The agreement for the account held with Principal/Eppler, Guerin & Turner listed the Holmeses' names as "Thomas J. Holmes & Kathryn V. Holmes JTWROS" and was signed by both. This agreement, too, established rights of survivorship in the account. Because both of these accounts were held with rights of survivorship, so too were the certificates issued from those accounts. Accordingly, we reverse the court of appeals' judgment as to these securities.

IV

CONCLUSION

The 1987 constitutional amendment and accompanying legislation sought to facilitate the creation of rights of survivorship in community property and eliminate the constitutional hurdles spouses faced when attempting to establish such rights. The Holmeses' account agreements clearly indicated their intent to create rights of survivorship in those accounts. The rights were not lost when the Holmeses later obtained some of their investments in certificate form. Pursuant to these survivorship agreements, each of the accounts and certificates at issue in this case passed to Thomas upon his wife's death, and then by will to Thomas's beneficiaries when he died. If the Holmeses had wished an alternate devise, they could have made appropriate provisions in their respective wills. As they did not, we reverse and render in part and affirm in part the court of appeals' judgment. Texas Rule of Appellate Procedure 60.2(a), (c).

Section D. Pour-Over Wills and Revocable Trusts in Estate Planning

Estates Code § 254.001. Devises to Trustees

(a) A testator may validly devise property in a will to the trustee of a trust established or to be established:

> (1) during the testator's lifetime by the testator, the testator and another person, or another person, including a funded or unfunded life insurance trust in which the settlor has reserved any or all rights of ownership of the insurance contracts; or
>
> (2) at the testator's death by the testator's devise to the trustee, regardless of the existence, size, or character of the corpus of the trust, if:

(A) the trust is identified in the testator's will; and

(B) the terms of the trust are in:

(i) a written instrument, other than a will, executed before, with, or after the execution of the testator's will; or

(ii) another person's will if that person predeceased the testator.

(b) A devise under Subsection (a) is not invalid because the trust:

(1) is amendable or revocable; or

(2) was amended after the execution of the will or the testator's death.

(c) Unless the testator's will provides otherwise, property devised to a trust described by Subsection (a) is not held under a testamentary trust of the testator. The property:

(1) becomes part of the trust to which the property is devised; and

(2) must be administered and disposed of according to the provisions of the instrument establishing the trust, including any amendment to the instrument made before or after the testator's death.

(d) Unless the testator's will provides otherwise, a revocation or termination of the trust before the testator's death causes the devise to lapse.

Section E. Joint Tenancies in Realty

Estates Code § 101.002. Effect of Joint Ownership of Property

If two or more persons hold an interest in property jointly and one joint owner dies before severance, the interest of the decedent in the joint estate:

(1) does not survive to the remaining joint owner or owners; and

(2) passes by will or intestacy from the decedent as if the decedent's interest had been severed.

Estates Code § 111.001. Right of Survivorship Agreements Authorized

(a) Notwithstanding Section 101.002, two or more persons who hold an interest in property jointly may agree in writing that the interest of a joint owner who dies survives to the surviving joint owner or owners.

(b) An agreement described by Subsection (a) may not be inferred from the mere fact that property is held in joint ownership.

Section F. Planning for Incapacity

Power of attorney may impose fiduciary duty to keep principal informed regarding material facts of transactions

JORDAN v. LYLES

Court of Appeals of Texas, Tyler
455 S.W.3d 785 (2015)

WORTHEN, C.J. Aaron Jordan, Michael Jordan, Heather Jordan, Gilbert Jordan, Phyllis Ann Woods, and Donna Joyce Curtis appeal the trial court's judgment notwithstanding the verdict entered in favor of Cynthia Kay Lyles. In two issues, Appellants argue that the trial court erroneously rendered judgment notwithstanding the jury's verdict and, alternatively, the evidence supports the jury's verdict for interference with inheritance rights. We reverse and render.

BACKGROUND

Melvin "Bud" Jordan and Joy Jordan married in the late 1960s. Both had children prior to their marriage to one another. Bud's three children are Harold Jordan, Gilbert Jordan, and Melvin Jordan Jr. Melvin, Jr. also had three children—Aaron Jordan, Michael Jordan, and Heather Jordan. Joy's children are Donna Curtis, Phyllis Woods, Cynthia "Cyndi" Lyles, Johnny Lyles, and Lynda Lyles. Cyndi lived with Bud and Joy from an early age and, by all accounts, had a very close relationship with Bud. On the other hand, Bud was estranged from his sons until they reconciled on his seventieth birthday in 1983.

In 2001, Bud and Joy executed wills that were, in pertinent part, identical to one another. By their wills, each left his or her estate to the other. In the event the decedent was not survived by a spouse, one-half of his or her estate would pass to the decedent's own children and one-half to the decedent's spouse's children. The wills further provided that if any child predeceased the decedent, that deceased child's share would go to the child's surviving descendants. On or about March 15, 2004, Bud executed a codicil changing the disposition of his estate in the event Joy predeceased him. Under the codicil, Bud left one-half of his estate to his two then-living sons as follows: 20% to Gilbert and 80% in trust to Melvin Jr. with Cyndi serving as trustee.

Joy died on December 14, 2004. The next day, Bud signed a power of attorney form appointing Cyndi as his attorney in fact.

In late January 2006, Bud executed change forms making Cyndi the sole beneficiary of three annuities worth in excess of $249,000. Cyndi filled out portions of the forms at Bud's direction and mailed them to the respective financial institutions after Bud signed them.

On February 25, 2009, Melvin Jr. died. Two days later, Bud, who had been ill, signed a new power of attorney form appointing Cyndi as his attorney in fact. That same day, Cyndi drove Bud to Bank Texas, where Bud and Melvin Jr. had maintained a joint money market account. Because Bud could not go inside due to his catheter, a bank employee came out to the car to assist him. As he sat in the car, Bud signed a form making Cyndi a joint account holder with right of survivorship.[6]

On March 1, 2009, Bud died. Cyndi used her beneficiary designations and right of survivorship to withdraw approximately $275,000 from Bud's annuities and bank accounts. Bud's probate estate comprised less than $30,000 in assets.

On February 25, 2011, Appellants filed the instant suit against Cyndi for breach of fiduciary duty and interference with inheritance rights. The matter proceeded to a jury trial. After considering the evidence, the jury determined that Cyndi failed to comply with her fiduciary duty to Bud and tortiously interfered with Appellants' inheritance rights. As a result, the jury awarded Appellants $156,016 in compensatory damages and $50,000 in exemplary damages.

Thereafter, Cyndi moved for judgment notwithstanding the verdict. On January 2, 2013, the trial court conducted a hearing on her motion. On January 14, 2013, the trial court granted Cyndi's motion and rendered judgment that Appellants take nothing by their suit. This appeal followed . . . .

CHALLENGE TO JUDGMENT NOTWITHSTANDING THE VERDICT

In their first issue, Appellants argue that the trial court erred in granting Cyndi's motion for judgment notwithstanding the verdict on their breach of fiduciary duty claim. . . . Absent an objection to the charge, we conduct our sufficiency review in light of the charge as given, even if that charge misstates the law or imposes a more rigorous burden of proof on a party

---

[6] Cyndi was previously listed on the account as a pay on death (POD) beneficiary.

than is required by the law. See Romero v. KPH Consolidation, Inc., 166 S.W.3d 212, 220–21 (Tex. 2005).

Governing Law

The elements of a breach of a fiduciary duty claim are (1) a fiduciary relationship between the plaintiff and defendant, (2) a breach by the defendant of her fiduciary duty to the plaintiff, and (3) an injury to the plaintiff or benefit to the defendant as a result of the defendant's breach. Lundy v. Masson, 260 S.W.3d 482, 501 (Tex. App.–Houston [14th Dist.] 2008, pet. denied). A power of attorney creates an agency relationship, which is a fiduciary relationship as a matter of law. Vogt v. Warnock, 107 S.W.3d 778, 782 (Tex. App.–El Paso 2003, pet. denied); In re Estate of Miller, 446 S.W.3d 445, 454–55 (Tex. App.–Tyler 2014, no pet.).

A fiduciary owes her principal a strict duty of good faith and candor, as well as the general duty of full disclosure respecting matters affecting the principal's interests. See Lesikar v. Rappeport, 33 S.W.3d 282, 296 (Tex. App.–Texarkana 2000, pet. denied). All transactions between a fiduciary and her principal are presumptively fraudulent and void; therefore, the burden lies on the fiduciary to establish the validity of any particular transaction in which she is involved. Id. at 298. Moreover, where a fiduciary relationship exists, the burden is on the fiduciary to show that she acted fairly and informed the principal of all material facts relating to the alleged transaction. See id. (citing Hoggett v. Brown, 971 S.W.2d 472, 487 (Tex. App.–Houston [14th Dist.] 1997, pet. denied)). Even in the case of a gift between parties with a fiduciary relationship, equity indulges the presumption of unfairness and invalidity, and requires proof at the hand of the party claiming validity of the transaction that it is fair and reasonable. Estate of Townes v. Townes, 867 S.W.2d 414, 417 (Tex. App.–Houston [14th Dist.] 1993, writ denied). In establishing the fairness of a transaction involving a fiduciary, some of the most important factors are (1) whether there was full disclosure regarding the transaction, (2) whether the consideration, if any, was adequate, and (3) whether the beneficiary had the benefit of independent advice. Id.

The Charge

We again note that, absent objection, we conduct our sufficiency review in light of the charge as given. See *Romero*, 166 S.W.3d at 220–21. In the instant case, the court's charge instructed the jury on breach of fiduciary duty as follows:

> You are instructed that the Defendant, CYNTHIA KAY LYLES, was in a fiduciary relationship with the Decedent, MELVIN "BUD" JORDAN, from December 14, 2005, the date of Joy's death, through the date of Bud's death on March 1, 2009. Under Texas law, a fiduciary owes its principal a high duty of good faith, fair dealing, honest performance, and strict accountability. A fiduciary must fulfill her duties with reasonable care, diligence, and good faith, and judgment, and if she fails to do so, she will be liable to [the] principal for the

> resulting damage. There is a general prohibition against the fiduciary's using the relationship to benefit her personal interest, except with the full knowledge and consent of the principal.

Question 1, which pertains to the issue of fiduciary duty, reads as follows:

Question No. 1

> Did CYNTHIA KAY LYLES comply with her fiduciary duty to MELVIN "BUD" JORDAN?
>
> Because a relationship of trust and confidence existed between them, CYNTHIA KAY LYLES owed MELVIN "BUD" JORDAN a fiduciary duty. To prove she complied with her duty, CYNTHIA KAY LYLES, must show:
>
> a. the transaction(s) in question were fair and equitable to MELVIN "BUD" JORDAN; and
>
> b. CYNTHIA KAY LYLES made reasonable use of the confidence that MELVIN "BUD" JORDAN placed in her; and
>
> c. CYNTHIA KAY LYLES acted in the utmost good faith and exercised the most scrupulous honesty toward MELVIN "BUD" JORDAN; and
>
> d. CYNTHIA KAY LYLES placed the interest of MELVIN "BUD" JORDAN before her own, did not use the advantage of her position to gain any benefit for herself at the expense of MELVIN "BUD" JORDAN, and did not place herself in any position where her self-interest might conflict with her obligations as a fiduciary . . . .
>
> Answer "Yes" or "No":

The jury answered in the negative, and Cyndi has not raised any cross issues on appeal challenging the court's charge. As a result, given the wording of the charge, the jury's finding must be upheld as long as there is more than a scintilla of evidence that Cyndi failed to comply with her fiduciary duty to Bud in any one transaction. See *Townes*, 867 S.W.2d at 417.

Breach of Fiduciary Duty—Annuities

Much of the relevant evidence admitted at trial pertained to the three annuities from ING, AIG, and Metlife.[7] The record reflects that the annuities were established by Joy, who listed

---

[7] Two of the remaining accounts at Wood County National Bank were established in the early 1990s, long before Cyndi entered into a fiduciary relationship with Bud. At the time of their creation, Cyndi was listed as a joint account holder with Joy and Bud and had right of survivorship in the accounts. Based on our review of the record, there is no evidence that

Bud as the primary beneficiary and Cyndi as the contingent beneficiary. The record further reflects that after Joy died and Cyndi became Bud's fiduciary, Bud had to elect whether to take a lump sum payment of the annuities or exercise a spousal continuation, i.e., step into Joy's shoes as an account holder. Cyndi testified that in January 2006, she assisted Bud in completing the forms to exercise a spousal continuation in the three annuities. These forms were admitted as exhibits. On each of the forms, Cyndi is designated as the primary beneficiary of the respective annuity. Cyndi further testified that anything she wrote on the forms was done at Bud's direction and in his presence. Cyndi stated that she did not coerce Bud into making her a beneficiary. Nonetheless, there is no evidence that Cyndi or anyone else specifically discussed these transactions with Bud and informed him of all material facts pertaining to them. See id.

Cyndi's Responsive Arguments

In her brief, Cyndi raises several arguments in support of the trial court's judgment notwithstanding the jury's verdict. We will address each of these arguments in turn.

Vogt v. Warnock

Cyndi first argues that the court of appeals' holding in *Vogt* supports the trial court's judgment notwithstanding the jury's verdict here. In that case, Dr. Warnock named Vogt, his much younger fiancé, his attorney in fact under a power of attorney. See *Vogt*, 107 S.W.3d at 780. Thereafter, he revoked a living trust that he and his late wife had established for their son, transferred four pieces of real property to Vogt, and named Vogt the beneficiary of his brokerage account and veteran's life insurance policy. See id. Later, Warnock prepared a codicil to his will, by which he left furniture, household goods, jewelry, and personal effects to Vogt, while making a number of specific bequests of a sentimental nature to his son. See id. at 780. An attorney/friend assisted Warnock and consulted with him on several occasions in making these changes to his estate plan to "insure that [he] understood and desired these transfers." Id. Following Warnock's death, the representative of his estate sued Vogt for breach of fiduciary duty. See id. at 781. The jury determined that some of the transfers to Vogt were "fair," while others were not fair.[8] See id. at 782. The court of appeals held that the evidence was uncontroverted that Warnock did what he wanted to do in transferring his property to Vogt, that he was competent at the time the transfers were made, and that Vogt did not exercise undue influence upon him to accomplish the transfers. See id. at 785.

Cyndi was involved in any transactions pertaining to these accounts during the period of her fiduciary relationship with Bud. There is also evidence concerning a Bank Texas money market account, wherein Bud changed Cyndi's status from pay on death beneficiary to joint account holder with right of survivorship. As a result of our analysis pertaining to the three annuities, we do not consider whether Cyndi breached her fiduciary duty to Bud in the Bank Texas transaction.

[8] The jury was instructed that "by the term 'fair' is meant transactions characterized by frankness, honesty, impartiality or candor; open, upright, reasonable, free from suspicion or bias; equitable, just; affording no undue advantage."

Here, Cyndi argues that the evidence of record closely resembles the evidence before the court in *Vogt*, and, therefore, conclusively establishes that the transactions at issue were fair to Bud. However, there is no indication that the jury in *Vogt* was instructed that transactions involving a fiduciary and her principal require proof of "full knowledge and consent" by the principal. See *Townes*, 867 S.W.2d at 417. Even so, in *Vogt*, there was very specific evidence that Warnock consulted numerous times with an attorney concerning the disposition of his estate. See *Vogt*, 107 S.W.3d at 785. Moreover, the court noted that Warnock's primary physician signed an affidavit stating that Warnock was able to perform the transfers and understood the consequences of his actions. See id. Accordingly, we conclude that facts of *Vogt* are distinguishable from the facts in the case at hand. The fact remains in this case that Cyndi failed to meet her burden of proving that she or anyone else specifically discussed the transactions at issue with Bud and informed him of all material facts relating to them.

Acts Not Undertaken in Fiduciary Capacity

Cyndi next asserts that her role was akin to that of a scrivener and there is no evidence that she acted under her power of attorney. In *Vogt*, the appellant made a similar argument that she could not have breached her fiduciary duty when there was no evidence that she used her power of attorney in some way. See id. at 778. The court of appeals disagreed, stating that a fiduciary's duty to her principal should be viewed by a "stringent standard undiluted by exceptions." See id. We, too, decline to dilute Cyndi's fiduciary duty with such an exception.

"Transactions"

Cyndi further argues that the relevant transactions were between Bud and the various financial institutions and, as a beneficiary, she was not a party to these transactions. Thus, she contends that there was no need to measure the fairness of Bud's transactions with the financial institutions and the jury's answer to Question 1 is rendered immaterial as a result. The term "transaction" means "a business agreement or exchange" or a "[c]ommunication involving two or more people that affects all those involved." [The American Heritage College Dictionary 1435 (3rd ed. 1997).] Although the communications initiating the transactions at issue were between Bud and the various financial institutions, by the broad common meaning of the term, Cyndi was nonetheless involved in these transactions.

Even assuming arguendo that Cyndi was not involved in the transactions at issue, this scenario would not render the jury's finding that Cyndi did not comply with her fiduciary duty to Bud immaterial as Cyndi suggests. Indeed, if Cyndi had objected to the court's charge on these grounds, she may have been successful in convincing the trial court that Question 1 should not place the burden of proof on her. See Navigant Consulting, Inc. v. Wilkinson, 508 F.3d 277, 295 (5th Cir. 2007) (where there is no transaction between fiduciary and principal, there is no presumption of unfairness, and burden of proof does not shift to fiduciary). But because Cyndi has not raised any issue on appeal concerning the court's charge, her argument concerning her involvement in the transactions at issue is of no consequence. See *Romero*, 166 S.W.3d at 220–21.

"Benefitting" from the Transactions

Finally, Cyndi argues that, ultimately, she did not benefit from her change in status by Bud's making her the primary beneficiary on the annuities where, before, she had been a secondary beneficiary, when he executed the spousal continuation forms. We disagree.

The term "benefit" is defined as "an advantage." [The American Heritage College Dictionary 127 (3rd ed. 1997).] An "advantage" is a "relatively favorable position." Id. at 19. Here, as a result of Bud's transactions, Cyndi remained the only person who would receive the funds therein upon his death. Her contention that she would have received these funds even had the status quo been maintained is novel. But, with regard to the annuities, there were only two scenarios—Bud could take a lump sum payment or he could step into Joy's shoes by executing a spousal continuation form. In either of these scenarios, the previous designations were of no further effect. Thus, when Bud again made Cyndi a beneficiary of the annuities, she benefitted.

Summation

In sum, the record contains no evidence that Cyndi or anyone else specifically discussed any of these three transactions with Bud and informed him of all material facts relating to the transactions. As a result, Cyndi failed to meet her burden of proving that she complied with her fiduciary duty to Bud. Because she failed to meet her burden, we hold that the trial court erred in granting Cyndi's motion for judgment notwithstanding the verdict. Appellants' first issue is sustained . . . .

DISPOSITION

Having sustained Appellants' first issue, we ***reverse*** the trial court's judgment and ***render*** judgment in accordance with the jury's verdict.

Chapter 8. Limits on Freedom of Disposition: Protection of the Spouse and Children

Section A. Miscellaneous Rights to Support

Property Code § 42.001. Personal Property Exemption

(a) Personal property, as described in Section 42.002, is exempt from garnishment, attachment, execution, or other seizure if:

(1) the property is provided for a family and has an aggregate fair market value of not more than $100,000, exclusive of the amount of any liens, security interests, or other charges encumbering the property; or

(2) the property is owned by a single adult, who is not a member of a family, and has an aggregate fair market value of not more than $50,000, exclusive of the amount of any liens, security interests, or other charges encumbering the property.

(b) The following personal property is exempt from seizure and is not included in the aggregate limitations prescribed by Subsection (a):

(1) current wages for personal services, except for the enforcement of court-ordered child support payments;

(2) professionally prescribed health aids of a debtor or a dependent of a debtor;

(3) alimony, support, or separate maintenance received or to be received by the debtor for the support of the debtor or a dependent of the debtor; and

(4) a religious bible or other book containing sacred writings of a religion that is seized by a creditor other than a lessor of real property who is exercising the lessor's contractual or statutory right to seize personal property after a tenant breaches a lease agreement for or abandons the real property.

(c) Except as provided by Subsection (b)(4), this section does not prevent seizure by a secured creditor with a contractual landlord's lien or other security in the property to be seized.

(d) Unpaid commissions for personal services not to exceed 25 percent of the aggregate limitations prescribed by Subsection (a) are exempt from seizure and are included in the aggregate.

(e) A religious bible or other book described by Subsection (b)(4) that is seized by a lessor of real property in the exercise of the lessor's contractual or statutory right to seize personal property after a tenant breaches a lease agreement for the real property or abandons the real property may not be included in the aggregate limitations prescribed by Subsection (a).

Property Code § 42.002. Personal Property

(a) The following personal property is exempt under Section 42.001(a):

(1) home furnishings, including family heirlooms;

(2) provisions for consumption;

(3) farming or ranching vehicles and implements;

(4) tools, equipment, books, and apparatus, including boats and motor vehicles used in a trade or profession;

(5) wearing apparel;

(6) jewelry not to exceed 25 percent of the aggregate limitations prescribed by Section 42.001(a);

(7) two firearms;

(8) athletic and sporting equipment, including bicycles;

(9) a two-wheeled, three-wheeled, or four-wheeled motor vehicle for each member of a family or single adult who holds a driver's license or who does not hold a driver's license but who relies on another person to operate the vehicle for the benefit of the nonlicensed person;

(10) the following animals and forage on hand for their consumption:

(A) two horses, mules, or donkeys and a saddle, blanket, and bridle for each;

(B) 12 head of cattle;

(C) 60 head of other types of livestock; and

(D) 120 fowl; and

(11) household pets.

. . .

Protection of the Spouse and Children

Estates Code § 102.002. Homestead Rights Not Affected by Character of the Homestead

The homestead rights and the respective interests of the surviving spouse and children of a decedent are the same whether the homestead was the decedent's separate property or was community property between the surviving spouse and the decedent.

Estates Code § 102.003. Passage of Homestead

The homestead of a decedent who dies leaving a surviving spouse descends and vests on the decedent's death in the same manner as other real property of the decedent and is governed by the same laws of descent and distribution.

Estates Code § 102.004. Liability of Homestead for Debts

If the decedent was survived by a spouse or minor child, the homestead is not liable for the payment of any of the debts of the estate, other than:

(1) purchase money for the homestead;

(2) taxes due on the homestead;

(3) work and material used in constructing improvements on the homestead if the requirements of Section 50(a)(5), Article XVI, Texas Constitution, are met;

(4) an owelty of partition imposed against the entirety of the property by a court order or written agreement of the parties to the partition, including a debt of one spouse in favor of the other spouse resulting from a division or an award of a family homestead in a divorce proceeding;

(5) the refinance of a lien against the homestead, including a federal tax lien resulting from the tax debt of both spouses, if the homestead is a family homestead, or from the tax debt of the decedent;

(6) an extension of credit on the homestead if the requirements of Section 50(a)(6), Article XVI, Texas Constitution, are met; or

(7) a reverse mortgage.

Estates Code § 102.005. Prohibitions on Partition of Homestead

The homestead may not be partitioned among the decedent's heirs:

(1) during the lifetime of the surviving spouse for as long as the surviving spouse elects to use or occupy the property as a homestead; or

(2) during the period the guardian of the decedent's minor children is permitted to use and occupy the homestead under a court order.

Estates Code § 102.006. Circumstances Under Which Partition of Homestead is Authorized

The homestead may be partitioned among the respective owners of the property in the same manner as other property held in common if:

(1) the surviving spouse dies, sells his or her interest in the homestead, or elects to no longer use or occupy the property as a homestead; or

(2) the court no longer permits the guardian of the minor children to use and occupy the property as a homestead.

Estates Code § 353.051. Exempt Property to be Set Aside

(a) Unless an application and verified affidavit are filed as provided by Subsection (b), immediately after the inventory, appraisement, and list of claims of an estate are approved or after the affidavit in lieu of the inventory, appraisement, and list of claims is filed, the court by order shall set aside:

(1) the homestead for the use and benefit of the decedent's surviving spouse and minor children; and

(2) all other exempt property described by Section 42.002(a), Property Code, for the use and benefit of the decedent's:

(A) surviving spouse and minor children;

(B) unmarried adult children remaining with the decedent's family; and

(C) each other adult child who is incapacitated.

(b) Before the inventory, appraisement, and list of claims of an estate are approved or, if applicable, before the affidavit in lieu of the inventory, appraisement, and list of claims is filed:

(1) the decedent's surviving spouse or any other person authorized to act on behalf of the decedent's minor children may apply to the court to have exempt property described by Subsection (a), including the homestead, set aside by filing an application and a verified affidavit listing all exempt property that the applicant claims is exempt property described by Subsection (a); and

(2) any of the decedent's unmarried adult children remaining with the decedent's family, any other adult child of the decedent who is incapacitated, or a person who is authorized to act on behalf of the adult incapacitated child may apply to the court to have all exempt property described by Subsection (a), other than the homestead, set aside by filing an application and a verified affidavit listing all the exempt property, other than the homestead, that the applicant claims is exempt property described by Subsection (a).

(c) At a hearing on an application filed under Subsection (b), the applicant has the burden of proof by a preponderance of the evidence. The court shall set aside property of the decedent's estate that the court finds is exempt.

Estates Code § 353.052. Delivery of Exempt Property

(a) This section only applies to exempt property described by Section 353.051(a).

(a-1) The executor or administrator of an estate shall deliver, without delay, exempt property that has been set aside for the decedent's surviving spouse and children in accordance with this section.

(b) If there is a surviving spouse and there are no children of the decedent, or if all the children, including any adult incapacitated children, of the decedent are also the children of the surviving spouse, the executor or administrator shall deliver all exempt property to the surviving spouse.

(c) If there is a surviving spouse and there are children of the decedent who are not also children of the surviving spouse, the executor or administrator shall deliver the share of those children in exempt property, other than the homestead, to:

(1) the children, if the children are of legal age;

(2) the children's guardian, if the children are minors; or

(3) the guardian of each of the children who is an incapacitated adult, or to another appropriate person, as determined by the court, on behalf of the adult incapacitated child if there is no guardian.

(d) If there is no surviving spouse and there are children of the decedent, the executor or administrator shall deliver exempt property, other than the homestead, to:

(1) the children, if the children are of legal age;

(2) the children's guardian, if the children are minors; or

(3) the guardian of each of the children who is an incapacitated adult, or to another appropriate person, as determined by the court, on behalf of the adult incapacitated child if there is no guardian.

(e) In all cases, the executor or administrator shall deliver the homestead to:

(1) the decedent's surviving spouse, if there is a surviving spouse; or

(2) the guardian of the decedent's minor children, if there is not a surviving spouse.

Estates Code § 353.053. Allowance in Lieu of Exempt Property

(a) If all or any of the specific articles of exempt property described by Section 353.051(a) are not among the decedent's effects, the court shall make, in lieu of the articles not among the effects, a reasonable allowance to be paid to the decedent's surviving spouse and children as provided by Section 353.054.

(b) The allowance in lieu of a homestead may not exceed $45,000, and the allowance in lieu of other exempt property may not exceed $30,000, excluding the family allowance for the support of the surviving spouse, minor children, and adult incapacitated children provided by Subchapter C.

Estates Code § 353.152. Distribution of Exempt Property of Solvent Estate

If on final settlement of an estate it appears that the estate is solvent, the exempt property, other than the homestead or any allowance made in lieu of the homestead, is subject to partition and distribution among the heirs of the decedent and the distributees in the same manner as other estate property.

Estates Code § 353.153. Title to Property of Insolvent Estate

If on final settlement an estate proves to be insolvent, the decedent's surviving spouse and children have absolute title to all property and allowances set aside or paid to them under this title. The distributees are entitled to distribution of any remaining exempt property held by the executor or administrator in the same manner as other estate property. The property and allowances set aside or paid to the decedent's surviving spouse or children, and any remaining exempt property held by the executor or administrator, may not be taken for any of the estate debts except as provided by Section 353.155.

Estates Code § 353.101. Family Allowance

(a) Unless an application and verified affidavit are filed as provided by Subsection (b), immediately after the inventory, appraisement, and list of claims of an estate are approved or after the affidavit in lieu of the inventory, appraisement, and list of claims is filed, the court shall fix a family allowance for the support of the decedent's surviving spouse, minor children, and adult incapacitated children.

(b) Before the inventory, appraisement, and list of claims of an estate are approved or, if applicable, before the affidavit in lieu of the inventory, appraisement, and list of claims is filed, the decedent's surviving spouse or any other person authorized to act on behalf of the decedent's minor children or adult incapacitated children may apply to the court to have the court fix the family allowance by filing an application and a verified affidavit describing:

(1) the amount necessary for the maintenance of the surviving spouse, the decedent's minor children, and the decedent's adult incapacitated children for one year after the date of the decedent's death; and

(2) the surviving spouse's separate property and any property that the decedent's minor children or adult incapacitated children have in their own right.

(c) At a hearing on an application filed under Subsection (b), the applicant has the burden of proof by a preponderance of the evidence. The court shall fix a family allowance for the support of the decedent's surviving spouse, minor children, and adult incapacitated children.

(d) A family allowance may not be made for:

(1) the decedent's surviving spouse, if the surviving spouse has separate property adequate for the surviving spouse's maintenance;

(2) the decedent's minor children, if the minor children have property in their own right adequate for the children's maintenance; or

(3) any of the decedent's adult incapacitated children, if:

(A) the adult incapacitated child has property in the person's own right adequate for the person's maintenance; or

(B) at the time of the decedent's death, the decedent was not supporting the adult incapacitated child.

Estates Code § 353.102. Amount and Method of Payment of Family Allowance

(a) The amount of the family allowance must be sufficient for the maintenance of the decedent's surviving spouse, minor children, and adult incapacitated children for one year from the date of the decedent's death.

(b) The allowance must be fixed with regard to the facts or circumstances then existing and the facts and circumstances anticipated to exist during the first year after the decedent's death.

(c) The allowance may be paid in a lump sum or in installments, as ordered by the court.

Estates Code § 353.105. Payment of Family Allowance

(a) The executor or administrator of an estate shall apportion and pay the family allowance in accordance with this section.

(b) If there is a surviving spouse and there are no minor children or adult incapacitated children of the decedent, the executor or administrator shall pay the entire family allowance to the surviving spouse.

(c) If there is a surviving spouse and all of the minor children and adult incapacitated children of the decedent are also the children of the surviving spouse, the executor or administrator shall pay the entire family allowance to the surviving spouse for use by the surviving spouse, the decedent's minor children, and adult incapacitated children.

(d) If there is a surviving spouse and some or all of the minor children or adult incapacitated children of the decedent are not also children of the surviving spouse, the executor or administrator shall pay:

(1) the portion of the entire family allowance necessary for the support of those minor children to the guardian of those children; and

(2) the portion of the entire family allowance necessary for the support of each of those adult incapacitated children to the guardian of the adult incapacitated child or another appropriate person, as determined by the court, on behalf of the adult incapacitated child if there is no guardian.

(e) If there is no surviving spouse and there are minor children or adult incapacitated children of the decedent, the executor or administrator shall pay the family allowance:

(1) for the minor children, to the guardian of those children; and

(2) for each adult incapacitated child, to the guardian of the adult incapacitated child or another appropriate person, as determined by the court, on behalf of the adult incapacitated child if there is no guardian.

Protection of the Spouse and Children

Trial court must set aside exempt personal property on hand and also award allowance in lieu of exempt personal property not on hand

Estate of RHEA

Court of Appeals of Texas, Fort Worth
257 S.W.3d 787 (2008)

GARDNER, J. Appellants Charlotte Bonner Barrett and Trenton Bonner, independent co-executors of the estate of Wanda Meacham Rhea, deceased, appeal from a trial court order awarding Appellee Charles Rhea a family allowance of $20,000; $5,000 in lieu of exempt property; and the use of Wanda's wedding ring during his lifetime. We modify the trial court's order and affirm the order as modified.

BACKGROUND

Charles, who is eighty-seven years old, and Wanda married late in life and had been married for just under nine years when Wanda died in June 2005 at the age of seventy-nine. Wanda left a will bequeathing $10,000 cash to each of her grandchildren and step-grandchildren, all of her jewelry and personal effects to Charlotte, and the remainder of her estate to Charlotte and Trenton.

In October 2005, Charlotte and Trenton notified Charles of their intent to remove Wanda's personal property from the marital home. Charles labeled some of the possessions in the home to mark his own separate property, then left the house from November 11 through November 14. Charlotte and Trenton spent those four days moving possessions out of the home; they estimated the value of the furniture and other possessions removed from the home at $50,000. Charles testified that they took towels, sheets, pillow cases, blankets, dishes, cooking utensils, pots and pans, and even toilet paper, half boxes of Kleenex, used bars of soap, and all but one or two books. They left him one chair, a television, a couple of table lamps, one set of glasses, one set of china, and some eating utensils. Charles testified that he was required to purchase a refrigerator, a bed, a table and chairs, a washer and dryer, a microwave oven, a vacuum cleaner, glasses, dishes, and pans "to maintain . . . some semblance of the same standard of living" to which he and Wanda had grown accustomed during their marriage. He said he spent $3,700 "to get back [to] where [he] could just exist there."

In December 2006, shortly after Charlotte and Trenton filed an inventory, appraisement, and list of claims, Charles filed (1) an application for a family allowance of $30,000 and (2) an application to set aside exempt property—including many of the items removed by Charlotte and Trenton—or, alternatively, for an allowance of $5,000 in lieu of the removed personal property. The trial court awarded Charles a $20,000 family allowance; $5,000 in lieu of exempt property; and use and possession of Wanda's wedding ring during his lifetime "as part of the exempt property." Charlotte and Trenton filed this appeal. . . .

FAMILY ALLOWANCE

In their first issue, Charlotte and Trenton argue that the trial court erred by granting Charles a $20,000 family allowance because Charles answered interrogatories showing that he had monthly income of $2,706 and monthly expenses of $1,570, thereby conclusively proving that he owned separate property adequate to provide for his maintenance.

Before a trial court approves an estate's inventory, appraisement, and list of claims, a surviving spouse may apply to the court to have the court fix a family allowance by filing an application and a verified affidavit describing the amount necessary for the maintenance of the surviving spouse for one year after the date of the death of the decedent and describing the spouse's separate property. Texas Probate Code § 286(b). The trial court must fix a family allowance for the support of the surviving spouse in an amount sufficient for the spouse's maintenance for one year from the time of the testator's death with regard to the facts or circumstances then existing and those anticipated to exist during the first year after such death. Id. §§ 286(b), 287. But when the surviving spouse has separate property adequate to the survivor's maintenance, the trial court may not award an allowance. Id. § 288. The applicant bears the burden of proof by a preponderance of the evidence at any hearing on the application. Id. § 286. When determining whether a surviving spouse is entitled to an allowance and, if so, in what amount, the trial court must consider the whole condition of the estate during the first year after the spouse's death, the necessities of the surviving spouse, and the circumstances to which he or she has been accustomed.

The inventory, appraisement, and list of claims filed by Charlotte and Trenton listed assets in Wanda's estate with a total value of $847,601 and no liabilities. In answers to interrogatories served by Charlotte and Trenton, Charles itemized his income and expenses, and his income of $2,706 exceeded his expenses of $1,570 by $1,136 per month. But it is undisputed that Charlotte and Trenton removed $50,000 worth of Wanda's possessions from the marital home, including necessities such as the beds, bedding, the refrigerator, dishes, cooking utensils, and most of the furniture—all of which figure into the calculus of the circumstances to which Charles was accustomed during Wanda's life. At the time of trial, Charles had spent $3,700 on necessities to "get back to where [he] could just exist" in the marital home. Moreover, he testified that before her death, Wanda contributed $2,000 per month to their joint checking account. To the extent the $50,000 of property removed from the marital home reflects the circumstances to which Charles was accustomed beyond mere necessities, his $1,136 per month—$13,632 per year—surplus income was inadequate to return him to those circumstances in the year following Wanda's death. . . .

Considering the evidence in the light most favorable to the trial court's allowance order, we hold that Charles's monthly surplus income was not—as Charlotte and Trenton contend—conclusive proof of means adequate to provide for his maintenance in the year following Wanda's death. Therefore, we overrule Charlotte's and Trenton's first issue.

ALLOWANCE IN LIEU OF EXEMPT PROPERTY AND THE WEDDING RING

In their second issue, Charlotte and Trenton argue that the trial court erred by awarding Charles both a $5,000 allowance in lieu of exempt personal property and use and possession of Wanda's wedding ring. They contend that a court may award a cash allowance in lieu of exempt property *or* set aside the property for the surviving spouse, but it may not do both.

Before the approval of the inventory, appraisement, and list of claims, a surviving spouse may apply to the court to have exempt property set aside. Texas Probate Code § 271(b). The trial court must award a monetary allowance for exempt property not among the decedent's effects:

> In case there should not be among the effects of the deceased all or any of the specific articles exempted from execution . . . , the court shall make a reasonable allowance in lieu thereof . . . . The allowance in lieu of a homestead shall in no case exceed $15,000 and the allowance for other exempted property shall in no case exceed $5,000 . . . .

Id. § 273.

Charlotte and Trenton argue that setting aside exempt property and a cash allowance in lieu thereof are mutually exclusive, alternative remedies; that is, they argue that if any exempt property *is* on hand, the trial court may not award an allowance in lieu of any exempt property that *is not* on hand. This interpretation is contrary to the plain meaning of section 273. Under that section, if *any* of the exempt property is not among the decedent's effects, the trial court must "make a reasonable allowance in lieu thereof." Id. In other words, the trial court must make an allowance for those exempt items that it cannot set aside because they are not on hand. If some exempt items are on hand, it must set those aside for the surviving spouse and award an allowance in lieu of those exempt items that are not on hand. . . .

Because section 273 authorized the trial court to set aside the exempt personal property that was on hand—the ring—*and* award Charles an allowance in lieu of the exempt personal property that was not on hand, we hold that the trial court did not err by so doing. We overrule Charlotte and Trenton's second issue.

LIFE ESTATE IN WANDA'S WEDDING RING

In their third issue, Charlotte and Trenton argue that the trial court erred by granting Charles a life estate in Wanda's wedding ring. The trial court ordered that "Charles Rhea shall have use and possession of the wedding ring worn by the Decedent during his lifetime as part of the exempt property. The Court makes no determination of ownership or of the character of the ownership of the ring." Charlotte and Trenton contend that the Probate Code authorizes a survivor's use and possession of exempt personal property only until final settlement of the estate.

Probate Code section 278 provides as follows:

> If, upon a final settlement of the estate, it shall appear that the same is solvent, the exempted property, except the homestead or any allowance in lieu thereof, shall be subject to partition and distribution among the heirs and distributees of such estate in like manner as the other property of the estate.

Texas Probate Code § 278. Thus, a surviving spouse can retain possession of tangible exempt property under the "use and benefit" provision of section 271, but when the administration terminates, the decedent's interest in these items must pass to the decedent's heirs or devisees.

The trial court's order is captioned in part "Order . . . Setting Aside Exempt Property . . . for Use and Benefit of Surviving Spouse." The only property set aside for Charles's use and benefit is the ring. Thus, the trial court clearly set aside the ring under Probate Code section 271, but section 278 precludes the grant of a life estate in exempt property set aside under section 271. See Texas Probate Code §§ 271, 278. Thus, the trial court erred by granting Charles a life estate in the ring under section 271.

Charles argues that the ring is presumptively community property because it was acquired during the marriage and that he is therefore entitled to a life estate in the ring. In fact, Charles testified that he bought the ring before the wedding and gave it to Wanda on their wedding day. He further testified that they purchased a diamond for the ring several months later, with each of them contributing half of the diamond's cost. But the trial court specifically reserved the question of the ring's ownership; therefore, the issue of whether Charles is entitled to a life estate in the ring because it is community property is not ripe for our review.

We sustain Charlotte and Trenton's third issue.

CONCLUSION

Having overruled Charlotte and Trenton's first and second issues and sustained their third issue, we strike the words "during his lifetime" from the part of the trial court's order granting Charles the use and possession of Wanda's wedding ring, and we affirm the order as modified.

Section B. Pretermitted Children

Estates Code § 255.051. Definition

In this subchapter, "pretermitted child" means a testator's child who is born or adopted:

(1) during the testator's lifetime or after the testator's death; and

(2) after the execution of the testator's will.

Estates Code § 255.052. Applicability and Construction

(a) Sections 255.053 and 255.054 apply only to a pretermitted child who is not:

(1) mentioned in the testator's will;

(2) provided for in the testator's will; or

(3) otherwise provided for by the testator.

(b) For purposes of this subchapter, a child is provided for or a provision is made for a child if a disposition of property to or for the benefit of the pretermitted child, whether vested or contingent, is made:

(1) in the testator's will, including a devise to a trustee under Section 254.001; or

(2) outside the testator's will and is intended to take effect at the testator's death.

Estates Code § 255.053. Succession by Pretermitted Child if Testator Has Living Child at Will's Execution

(a) If no provision is made in the testator's last will for any child of the testator who is living when the testator executes the will, a pretermitted child succeeds to the portion of the testator's separate and community estate, other than any portion of the estate devised to the pretermitted child's other parent, to which the pretermitted child would have been entitled under Section 201.001 if the testator had died intestate without a surviving spouse, except as limited by Section 255.056.

(b) If a provision, whether vested or contingent, is made in the testator's last will for one or more children of the testator who are living when the testator executes the will, a pretermitted child is entitled only to a portion of the disposition made to children under the will that is equal to the portion the child would have received if the testator had:

(1) included all of the testator's pretermitted children with the children on whom benefits were conferred under the will; and

(2) given an equal share of those benefits to each child.

(c) To the extent feasible, the interest in the testator's estate to which the pretermitted child is entitled under Subsection (b) must be of the same character, whether an equitable or legal life estate or in fee, as the interest that the testator conferred on the testator's children under the will.

Estates Code § 255.054. Succession by Pretermitted Child if Testator Has No Living Child at Will's Execution

If a testator has no child living when the testator executes the testator's last will, a pretermitted child succeeds to the portion of the testator's separate and community estate, other than any portion of the estate devised to the pretermitted child's other parent, to which the pretermitted child would have been entitled under Section 201.001 if the testator had died intestate without a surviving spouse, except as limited by Section 255.056.

Estates Code § 255.055. Ratable Recovery by Pretermitted Child from Portions Passing to Other Beneficiaries

(a) A pretermitted child may recover the share of the testator's estate to which the child is entitled from the testator's other children under Section 255.053(b) or from the testamentary beneficiaries under Sections 255.053(a) and 255.054, other than the pretermitted child's other parent, ratably, out of the portions of the estate passing to those persons under the will.

(b) In abating the interests of the beneficiaries described by Subsection (a), the character of the testamentary plan adopted by the testator must be preserved to the maximum extent possible.

Estates Code § 255.056. Limitation on Reduction of Estate Passing to Surviving Spouse

If a pretermitted child's other parent is not the surviving spouse of the testator, the portion of the testator's estate to which the pretermitted child is entitled under Section 255.053(a) or 255.054 may not reduce the portion of the testator's estate passing to the testator's surviving spouse by more than one-half.

Protection of the Spouse and Children

Individual named in will and subsequently adopted as an adult cannot claim a share as a pretermitted child

OZUNA v. WELLS FARGO BANK, N.A.

Court of Appeals of Texas, San Antonio
123 S.W.3d 429 (2003)

DUNCAN, J. The issue on appeal is whether an adult child adopted after execution of a will naming her as the beneficiary of a specific bequest is a pretermitted child for purposes of section 67(a) of the Texas Probate Code. We hold she is not and therefore affirm the trial court's judgment.

FACTUAL AND PROCEDURAL BACKGROUND

The material facts are undisputed. On May 26, 2000, Jack Gideon Putnam executed his Last Will and Testament. In his will, Putnam made specific bequests of varying amounts to nine related and unrelated persons; in the single largest bequest, Putnam's will made a specific bequest of $100,000 to Alma Ozuna. At the time, Ozuna and Putnam were not related. However, on October 31, 2000, Putnam adopted Ozuna in an adult adoption proceeding. Putnam did not revoke or change his will before he died on June 14, 2001.

On July 19, 2001, Putnam's executor, Wells Fargo Bank, filed an application to probate Putnam's will. Ozuna filed a contest and an application for letters of administration as Putnam's pretermitted child and heir. The parties filed cross-motions for summary judgment. The trial court ruled that Ozuna was not Putnam's pretermitted child for purposes of section 67(a) of the Texas Probate Code, granted the Bank's motion, and denied Ozuna's motion. Ozuna appealed. . . .

DISCUSSION

Ozuna argues she is Putnam's pretermitted child for purposes of section 67(a) of the Texas Probate Code because she was adopted after the execution of Putnam's will. We disagree.

A "pretermitted child," as used in section 67 of the Texas Probate Code, "means a child of a testator who, during the lifetime of the testator, or after his death, is born or adopted after the execution of the will of the testator." Texas Probate Code § 67(c). A pretermitted child "succeed[s] to a portion of the testator's estate as provided by Subsection (a)(1) or (a)(2)" of section 67 of the Texas Probate Code "[w]henever [the] pretermitted child is not mentioned in the testator's will, provided for in the testator's will, or otherwise provided for by the testator." Id. at § 67(a). "For the purposes of [section 67], a child is provided for or a provision is made for a child if a disposition of property to or for the benefit of the pretermitted child, whether vested or contingent, is made . . . in the testator's will. . . ." Id. at § 67(d)(1).

It is undisputed that Ozuna was adopted after Putnam's executed his will; and Putnam's will makes a disposition of property to Ozuna. Therefore, even if we assume Ozuna is Putnam's pretermitted child, the plain terms of section 67(d) preclude Ozuna from succeeding to a portion of Putnam's estate as Putnam's pretermitted child under section 67(a). Relying on cases from other jurisdictions, however, Ozuna argues that we should interpret section 67 to permit Ozuna's succession to a portion of Putnam's estate as a pretermitted child because Putnam's will does not provide for her "*as a child*." Brown v. Crawford, 699 P.2d 162 (Okla. Ct. App. 1984); see, e.g., In re Estate of Turkington, 147 Cal. App. 3d 590, 195 Cal. Rptr. 178 (1983); In re Will of Stier, 74 Misc. 2d 634, 345 N.Y.S.2d 913 (N.Y. Sur. Ct. 1973); In re Estate of Hamilton, 73 Wash. 2d 865, 441 P.2d 768 (1968). However, the Bank has provided us with authority dictating the opposite result; and, as the attorney ad litem points out, none of the cases cited by Ozuna involve or even mention a statutory scheme that contains a provision similar to section 67(d), which expressly states that a child who receives a bequest is "provided for" for purposes of section 67(a). Under these circumstances, we hold Ozuna is not a pretermitted child entitled to succeed to a portion of Putnam's estate pursuant to section 67(a) of the Texas Probate Code as a matter of law and therefore affirm the trial court's judgment.

Chapter 9. Trusts: Fiduciary Administration

Section A. Dealings with Third Persons

Property Code § 114.081. Protection of Person Dealing With Trustee

(a) A person who deals with a trustee in good faith and for fair value actually received by the trust is not liable to the trustee or the beneficiaries of the trust if the trustee has exceeded the trustee's authority in dealing with the person.

(b) A person other than a beneficiary is not required to inquire into the extent of the trustee's powers or the propriety of the exercise of those powers if the person:

(1) deals with the trustee in good faith; and

(2) obtains:

(A) a certification of trust described by Section 114.086; or

(B) a copy of the trust instrument.

(c) A person who in good faith delivers money or other assets to a trustee is not required to ensure the proper application of the money or other assets.

(d) A person other than a beneficiary who in good faith assists a former trustee, or who in good faith and for value deals with a former trustee, without knowledge that the trusteeship has terminated, is protected from liability as if the former trustee were still a trustee.

(e) Comparable protective provisions of other laws relating to commercial transactions or transfer of securities by fiduciaries prevail over the protection provided by this section.

Property Code § 114.082. Conveyance by Trustee

If property is conveyed or transferred to a trustee in trust but the conveyance or transfer does not identify the trust or disclose the names of the beneficiaries, the trustee may convey, transfer, or encumber the title of the property without subsequent question by a person who claims to be a beneficiary under the trust or who claims by, through, or under an undisclosed beneficiary.

Property Code § 114.0821. Liability of Trust Property

Although trust property is held by the trustee without identifying the trust or its beneficiaries, the trust property is not liable to satisfy the personal obligations of the trustee.

Property Code § 114.083. Rights and Liabilities for Committing Torts

(a) A personal liability of a trustee or a predecessor trustee for a tort committed in the course of the administration of the trust may be collected from the trust property if the trustee is sued in a representative capacity and the court finds that:

(1) the trustee was properly engaged in a business activity for the trust and the tort is a common incident of that kind of activity;

(2) the trustee was properly engaged in a business activity for the trust and neither the trustee nor an officer or employee of the trustee is guilty of actionable negligence or intentional misconduct in incurring the liability; or

(3) the tort increased the value of the trust property.

(b) A trust that is liable for the trustee's tort under Subdivision (3) of Subsection (a) is liable only to the extent of the permanent increase in value of the trust property.

(c) A plaintiff in an action against the trustee as the representative of the trust does not have to prove that the trustee could have been reimbursed by the trust if the trustee had paid the claim.

(d) Subject to the rights of exoneration or reimbursement under Section 114.062, the trustee is personally liable for a tort committed by the trustee or by the trustee's agents or employees in the course of their employment.

Property Code § 114.084. Contracts of Trustee

(a) If a trustee or a predecessor trustee makes a contract that is within his power as trustee and a cause of action arises on the contract, the plaintiff may sue the trustee in his representative capacity, and a judgment rendered in favor of the plaintiff is collectible by execution against the trust property. The plaintiff may sue the trustee individually if the trustee made the contract and the contract does not exclude the trustee's personal liability.

(b) The addition of "trustee" or "as trustee" after the signature of a trustee who is party to a contract is prima facie evidence of an intent to exclude the trustee from personal liability.

(c) In an action on a contract against a trustee in the trustee's representative capacity the plaintiff does not have to prove that the trustee could have been reimbursed by the trust if the trustee had paid the claim.

Property Code § 114.085. Partnerships

(a) To the extent allowed by law, a trustee who takes the place of a deceased partner in a general partnership in accordance with the articles of partnership is liable to third persons only to the extent of the:

(1) deceased partner's capital in the partnership; and

(2) trust funds held by the trustee.

(b) A trustee who contracts to enter a general partnership in its capacity as trustee shall limit, to the extent allowed by law, the trust's liability to:

(1) the trust assets contributed to the partnership; and

(2) other assets of the trust under the management of the contracting trustee.

(c) If another provision of this subtitle conflicts with this section, this section controls. This section does not exonerate a trustee from liability for negligence.

Property Code § 114.086. Certification of Trust

(a) As an alternative to providing a copy of the trust instrument to a person other than a beneficiary, the trustee may provide to the person a certification of trust containing the following information:

(1) a statement that the trust exists and the date the trust instrument was executed;

(2) the identity of the settlor;

(3) the identity and mailing address of the currently acting trustee;

(4) one or more powers of the trustee or a statement that the trust powers include at least all the powers granted a trustee by Subchapter A, Chapter 113;

(5) the revocability or irrevocability of the trust and the identity of any person holding a power to revoke the trust;

(6) the authority of cotrustees to sign or otherwise authenticate and whether all or less than all of the cotrustees are required in order to exercise powers of the trustee; and

(7) the manner in which title to trust property should be taken.

(b) A certification of trust may be signed or otherwise authenticated by any trustee.

(c) A certification of trust must state that the trust has not been revoked, modified, or amended in any manner that would cause the representations contained in the certification to be incorrect.

(d) A certification of trust:

(1) is not required to contain the dispositive terms of a trust; and

(2) may contain information in addition to the information required by Subsection (a).

(e) A recipient of a certification of trust may require the trustee to furnish copies of the excerpts from the original trust instrument and later amendments to the trust instrument that designate the trustee and confer on the trustee the power to act in the pending transaction.

(f) A person who acts in reliance on a certification of trust without knowledge that the representations contained in the certification are incorrect is not liable to any person for the action and may assume without inquiry the existence of the facts contained in the certification.

(g) If a person has actual knowledge that the trustee is acting outside the scope of the trust, and the actual knowledge was acquired by the person before the person entered into the transaction with the trustee or made a binding commitment to enter into the transaction, the transaction is not enforceable against the trust.

(h) A person who in good faith enters into a transaction relying on a certification of trust may enforce the transaction against the trust property as if the representations contained in the certification are correct. This section does not create an implication that a person is liable for acting in reliance on a certification of trust that fails to contain all the information required by Subsection (a). A person's failure to demand a certification of trust does not:

(1) affect the protection provided to the person by Section 114.081; or

(2) create an inference as to whether the person has acted in good faith.

(i) A person making a demand for the trust instrument in addition to a certification of trust or excerpts as described by Subsection (e) is liable for damages if the court determines that the person did not act in good faith in making the demand.

(j) This section does not limit the right of a person to obtain a copy of the trust instrument in a judicial proceeding concerning the trust.

(k) This section does not limit the rights of a beneficiary of the trust against the trustee.

Section B. Trustee's Powers

Property Code § 113.001. Limitation of Powers

A power given to a trustee by this subchapter does not apply to a trust to the extent that the instrument creating the trust, a subsequent court order, or another provision of this subtitle conflicts with or limits the power.

Property Code § 113.002. General Powers

Except as provided by Section 113.001, a trustee may exercise any powers in addition to the powers authorized by this subchapter that are necessary or appropriate to carry out the purposes of the trust.

Property Code § 113.003. Options

A trustee may:

(1) grant an option involving a sale, lease, or other disposition of trust property, including an option exercisable beyond the duration of the trust; or

(2) acquire and exercise an option for the acquisition of property, including an option exercisable beyond the duration of the trust.

Property Code § 113.004. Additions to Trust Assets

A trustee may receive from any source additions to the assets of the trust.

Property Code § 113.005. Acquisition of Undivided Interests

A trustee may acquire all or a portion of the remaining undivided interest in property in which the trust holds an undivided interest.

Property Code § 113.006. General Authority to Manage and Invest Trust Property

Subject to the requirements of Chapter 117, a trustee may manage the trust property and invest and reinvest in property of any character on the conditions and for the lengths of time as the trustee considers proper, notwithstanding that the time may extend beyond the term of the trust.

Property Code § 113.007. Temporary Deposits of Funds

A trustee may deposit trust funds that are being held pending investment, distribution, or the payment of debts in a bank that is subject to supervision by state or federal authorities.

However, a corporate trustee depositing funds with itself is subject to the requirements of Section 113.057 of this code.

Property Code § 113.008. Business Entities

A trustee may invest in, continue, or participate in the operation of any business or other investment enterprise in any form, including a sole proprietorship, partnership, limited partnership, corporation, or association, and the trustee may effect any change in the organization of the business or enterprise.

Property Code § 113.009. Real Property Management

A trustee may:

(1) exchange, subdivide, develop, improve, or partition real property;

(2) make or vacate public plats;

(3) adjust boundaries;

(4) adjust differences in valuation by giving or receiving value;

(5) dedicate real property to public use or, if the trustee considers it in the best interest of the trust, dedicate easements to public use without consideration;

(6) raze existing walls or buildings;

(7) erect new party walls or buildings alone or jointly with an owner of adjacent property;

(8) make repairs; and

(9) make extraordinary alterations or additions in structures as necessary to make property more productive.

Property Code § 113.010. Sale of Property

A trustee may contract to sell, sell and convey, or grant an option to sell real or personal property at public auction or private sale for cash or for credit or for part cash and part credit, with or without security.

Property Code § 113.011. Leases

(a) A trustee may grant or take a lease of real or personal property for any term, with or without options to purchase and with or without covenants relating to erection of buildings or renewals, including the lease of a right or privilege above or below the surface of real property.

(b) A trustee may execute a lease containing terms or options that extend beyond the duration of the trust.

Property Code § 113.012. Minerals

(a) A trustee may enter into mineral transactions, including:

(1) negotiating and making oil, gas, and other mineral leases covering any land, mineral, or royalty interest at any time forming a part of a trust;

(2) pooling and unitizing part or all of the land, mineral leasehold, mineral, royalty, or other interest of a trust estate with land, mineral leasehold, mineral, royalty, or other interest of one or more persons or entities for the purpose of developing and producing oil, gas, or other minerals, and making leases or assignments granting the right to pool and unitize;

(3) entering into contracts and agreements concerning the installation and operation of plans or other facilities for the cycling, repressuring, processing, or other treating or handling of oil, gas, or other minerals;

(4) conducting or contracting for the conducting of seismic evaluation operations;

(5) drilling or contracting for the drilling of wells for oil, gas, or other minerals;

(6) contracting for and making "dry hole" and "bottom hole" contributions of cash, leasehold interests, or other interests towards the drilling of wells;

(7) using or contracting for the use of any method of secondary or tertiary recovery of any mineral, including the injection of water, gas, air, or other substances;

(8) purchasing oil, gas, or other mineral leases, leasehold interests, or other interests for any type of consideration, including farmout agreements requiring the drilling or reworking of wells or participation therein;

(9) entering into farmout contracts or agreements committing a trust estate to assign oil, gas, or other mineral leases or interests in consideration for the drilling of wells or other oil, gas, or mineral operations;

(10) negotiating the transfer of and transferring oil, gas, or other mineral leases or interests for any consideration, such as retained overriding royalty interests of any nature, drilling or reworking commitments, or production interests; and

(11) executing and entering into contracts, conveyances, and other agreements or transfers considered necessary or desirable to carry out the powers granted in this section, whether or not the action is now or subsequently recognized or considered as a common or proper practice by those engaged in the business of prospecting for, developing, producing, processing, transporting, or marketing minerals, including entering into and executing division orders, oil, gas, or other mineral sales contracts, exploration agreements, processing agreements, and other contracts relating to the processing, handling, treating, transporting, and marketing of oil, gas, or other mineral production from or accruing to a trust and receiving and receipting for the proceeds thereof on behalf of a trust.

(b) A trustee may enter into mineral transactions that extend beyond the term of the trust.

Property Code § 113.013. Insurance

A trustee may purchase insurance of any nature, form, or amount to protect the trust property and the trustee.

Property Code § 113.014. Payment of Taxes

A trustee may pay taxes and assessments levied or assessed against the trust estate or the trustee by governmental taxing or assessing authorities.

Property Code § 113.015. Authority to Borrow

A trustee may borrow money from any source, including a trustee, purchase property on credit, and mortgage, pledge, or in any other manner encumber all or any part of the assets of the trust as is advisable in the judgment of the trustee for the advantageous administration of the trust.

Property Code § 113.016. Management of Securities

A trustee may:

(1) pay calls, assessments, or other charges against or because of securities or other investments held by the trust;

(2) sell or exercise stock subscription or conversion rights;

(3) vote corporate stock, general or limited partnership interests, or other securities in person or by general or limited proxy;

(4) consent directly or through a committee or other agent to the reorganization, consolidation, merger, dissolution, or liquidation of a corporation or other business enterprise; and

(5) participate in voting trusts and deposit stocks, bonds, or other securities with any protective or other committee formed by or at the instance of persons holding similar securities, under such terms and conditions respecting the deposit thereof as the trustee may approve; sell any stock or other securities obtained by conversion, reorganization, consolidation, merger, liquidation, or the exercise of subscription rights free of any restrictions upon sale otherwise contained in the trust instrument relative to the securities originally held; assent to corporate sales, leases, encumbrances, and other transactions.

Property Code § 113.017. Corporate Stock or Other Securities Held in Name of Nominee

A trustee may:

(1) hold corporate stock or other securities in the name of a nominee;

(2) under Subchapter B, Chapter 161, or other law, employ a bank incorporated in this state or a national bank located in this state as custodian of any corporate stock or other securities held in trust; and

(3) under Subchapter C, Chapter 161, or other law, deposit or arrange for the deposit of securities with a Federal Reserve Bank or in a clearing corporation.

Property Code § 113.018. Employment of Agents

A trustee may employ attorneys, accountants, agents, including investment agents, and brokers reasonably necessary in the administration of the trust estate.

Property Code § 113.019. Claims

A trustee may compromise, contest, arbitrate, or settle claims of or against the trust estate or the trustee.

Property Code § 113.020. Burdensome or Worthless Property

A trustee may abandon property the trustee considers burdensome or worthless.

Property Code § 113.021. Distribution to Minor or Incapacitated Beneficiary

(a) A trustee may make a distribution required or permitted to be made to any beneficiary in any of the following ways when the beneficiary is a minor or a person who in the judgment of the trustee is incapacitated by reason of legal incapacity or physical or mental illness or infirmity:

(1) to the beneficiary directly;

(2) to the guardian of the beneficiary's person or estate;

(3) by utilizing the distribution, without the interposition of a guardian, for the health, support, maintenance, or education of the beneficiary;

(4) to a custodian for the minor beneficiary under the Texas Uniform Transfers to Minors Act (Chapter 141) or a uniform gifts or transfers to minors act of another state;

(5) by reimbursing the person who is actually taking care of the beneficiary, even though the person is not the legal guardian, for expenditures made by the person for the benefit of the beneficiary; or

(6) by managing the distribution as a separate fund on the beneficiary's behalf, subject to the beneficiary's continuing right to withdraw the distribution.

(b) The written receipts of persons receiving distributions under Subsection (a) of this section are full and complete acquittances to the trustee.

Property Code § 113.022. Power to Provide Residence and Pay Funeral Expenses

A trustee of a trust that is not a charitable remainder unitrust, annuity trust, or pooled income fund that is intended to qualify for a federal tax deduction under Section 664, Internal Revenue Code, after giving consideration to the probable intention of the settlor and finding that the trustee's action would be consistent with that probable intention, may:

(1) permit real estate held in trust to be occupied by a beneficiary who is currently eligible to receive distributions from the trust estate;

(2) if reasonably necessary for the maintenance of a beneficiary who is currently eligible to receive distributions from the trust estate, invest trust funds in real property to be used for a home by the beneficiary; and

(3) in the trustee's discretion, pay funeral expenses of a beneficiary who at the time of the beneficiary's death was eligible to receive distributions from the trust estate.

Property Code § 113.023. Ancillary Trustee

(a) If trust property is situated outside this state, a Texas trustee may name in writing an individual or corporation qualified to act in the foreign jurisdiction in connection with trust property as ancillary trustee.

(b) Within the limits of the authority of the Texas trustee, the ancillary trustee has the rights, powers, discretions, and duties the Texas trustee delegates, subject to the limitations and directions of the Texas trustee specified in the instrument evidencing the appointment of the ancillary trustee.

(c) The Texas trustee may remove an ancillary trustee and appoint a successor at any time as to all or part of the trust assets.

(d) The Texas trustee may require security of the ancillary trustee, who is answerable to the Texas trustee for all trust property entrusted to or received by the ancillary trustee in connection with the administration of the trust.

(e) If the law of the foreign jurisdiction requires a certain procedure or a judicial order for the appointment of an ancillary trustee or to authorize an ancillary trustee to act, the Texas trustee and the ancillary trustee must satisfy the requirements.

Property Code § 113.024. Implied Powers

The powers, duties, and responsibilities under this subtitle do not exclude other implied powers, duties, or responsibilities that are not inconsistent with this subtitle.

Property Code § 113.025. Powers of Trustee Regarding Environmental Laws

(a) A trustee or a potential trustee may inspect, investigate, cause to be inspected, or cause to be investigated trust property, property that the trustee or potential trustee has been asked to hold, or property owned or operated by an entity in which the trustee or potential trustee holds or has been asked to hold any interest or for the purpose of determining the potential application of environmental law with respect to the property. This subsection does not grant any person the right of access to any property. The taking of any action under this subsection with respect to a trust or an addition to a trust is not evidence that a person has accepted the trust or the addition to the trust.

(b) A trustee may take on behalf of the trust any action before or after the initiation of an enforcement action or other legal proceeding that the trustee reasonably believes will help to prevent, abate, or otherwise remedy any actual or potential violation of any environmental law affecting property held directly or indirectly by the trustee.

Section C. Coexecutors and Cotrustees

Estates Code § 307.002. Joint Executors or Administrators

(a) Except as provided by Subsection (b), if there is more than one executor or administrator of an estate at the same time, the acts of one of the executors or administrators in that capacity are valid as if all the executors or administrators had acted jointly. If one of the executors or administrators dies, resigns, or is removed, a co-executor or co-administrator of the estate shall proceed with the administration as if the death, resignation, or removal had not occurred.

(b) If there is more than one executor or administrator of an estate at the same time, all of the qualified executors or administrators who are acting in that capacity must join in the conveyance of real estate unless the court, after due hearing, authorizes fewer than all to act.

Property Code § 113.085. Exercise of Powers by Multiple Trustees

(a) Cotrustees may act by majority decision.

(b) If a vacancy occurs in a cotrusteeship, the remaining cotrustees may act for the trust.

(c) A cotrustee shall participate in the performance of a trustee's function unless the cotrustee:

> (1) is unavailable to perform the function because of absence, illness, suspension under this code or other law, disqualification, if any, under this code, disqualification under other law, or other temporary incapacity; or
>
> (2) has delegated the performance of the function to another trustee in accordance with the terms of the trust or applicable law, has communicated the delegation to all other cotrustees, and has filed the delegation in the records of the trust.

(d) If a cotrustee is unavailable to participate in the performance of a trustee's function for a reason described by Subsection (c)(1) and prompt action is necessary to achieve the efficient administration or purposes of the trust or to avoid injury to the trust property or a beneficiary, the remaining cotrustee or a majority of the remaining cotrustees may act for the trust.

(e) A trustee may delegate to a cotrustee the performance of a trustee's function unless the settlor specifically directs that the function be performed jointly. Unless a cotrustee's delegation under this subsection is irrevocable, the cotrustee making the delegation may revoke the delegation.

Property Code § 114.006. Liability of Cotrustees for Acts of Other Cotrustees

(a) A trustee who does not join in an action of a cotrustee is not liable for the cotrustee's action, unless the trustee does not exercise reasonable care as provided by Subsection (b).

(b) Each trustee shall exercise reasonable care to:

> (1) prevent a cotrustee from committing a serious breach of trust; and
>
> (2) compel a cotrustee to redress a serious breach of trust.

(c) Subject to Subsection (b), a dissenting trustee who joins in an action at the direction of the majority of the trustees and who has notified any cotrustee of the dissent in writing at or before the time of the action is not liable for the action.

Inability of cotrustees to cooperate does not justify appointment of receiver over trust property

ELLIOTT v. WEATHERMAN
Court of Appeals of Texas, Austin
396 S.W.3d 224 (2013)

FIELD, J. This is an interlocutory appeal from a trial court order concerning the Glen L. Weatherman and Mildred S. Weatherman Revocable Living Trust. See Texas Civil Practice & Remedies Code § 51.014(a)(1) (providing for interlocutory review of order appointing receiver). Sarah W. Elliot and Margaret W. Clem, successor cotrustees, contend that the trial court abused its discretion by appointing a receiver over certain trust assets. We will reverse the order of the trial court.

BACKGROUND

In 1997, Glen L. Weatherman and Mildred Weatherman created a revocable living trust and named themselves as cotrustees. The Weathermans later amended the trust, designating their three adult children as joint successor cotrustees upon their "death, resignation, or incapacity." The trust also provides that upon the death of the Weathermans, the trustees shall distribute the trust assets as directed in the trust.[1] When the Weathermans passed away in 2010 the trust assets valued approximately 1.2 million dollars. Other than a few household goods and personal effects, the largest trust assets consist of two parcels of real property located in McCulloch County and two bank accounts.

On March 9, 2012, the Weathermans' daughters, Elliot and Clem, sued their brother and cotrustee, Jerald G. Weatherman. Elliot and Clem asserted that Weatherman had violated the terms of the trust, breached his fiduciary duties as a trustee, and converted trust property. Elliot and Clem sought declaratory relief, actual damages, exemplary damages, and attorney's fees. In addition, Elliot and Clem asked the court to issue a temporary injunction enjoining Weatherman from exercising independent, unauthorized control over any of the trust assets and from interfering with the marketing and sale of the real property. Elliot and Clem also requested that the court permit Elliot and Clem to make decisions on behalf of

[1] According to Elliot and Clem, the trust names the three Weatherman children as the trust beneficiaries and, because there are no outstanding debts, requires them as cotrustees to distribute the assets equally between themselves.

the trust during the pendency of the suit without having to first obtain Weatherman's consent. In response, Weatherman filed a countersuit for declaratory relief and for an accounting of trust assets. Weatherman also requested that the court issue a temporary injunction enjoining Elliot and Clem from exercising control over the trust assets.

On April 23, 2012, the trial court held an evidentiary hearing to determine whether it should issue any of the requested temporary injunctions.[2] At the hearing, Elliot and Clem presented testimony that Weatherman had refused to cooperate in the administration of the trust and had prevented performance of the trust's function, specifically preventing the sale of trust property. Conversely, Weatherman testified that Elliot and Clem had made decisions on behalf of the trust and withdrawn money from the trust bank account without his consent, including money for the payment of their legal fees.

At the conclusion of the evidence, the parties orally presented their closing arguments to the trial court. First, Elliot and Clem argued that they had sufficiently shown that the ability of the parties "to work unanimously has not been practical" and requested that they be allowed, by majority rule, to make decisions necessary to maintain the trust property during the pendency of the suit, citing section 113.085 of the Texas Trust Code.[3]

---

[2] During the same hearing, the trial court also considered Elliot and Clem's motion to expunge a lis pendens filed by Weatherman. However, the trial court's ruling on that motion is not currently before this Court.

[3] Section 113.085 of the Texas Trust Code provides:

> (a) Cotrustees may act by majority decision.
>
> (b) If a vacancy occurs in a cotrusteeship, the remaining cotrustees may act for the trust.
>
> (c) A cotrustee shall participate in the performance of a trustee's function unless the cotrustee:
>
>> (1) is unavailable to perform the function because of absence, illness, suspension under this code or other law, disqualification, if any, under this code, disqualification under other law, or other temporary incapacity; or
>>
>> (2) has delegated the performance of the function to another trustee in accordance with the terms of the trust or applicable law, has communicated the delegation to all other cotrustees, and has filed the delegation in the records of the trust.
>
> (d) If a cotrustee is unavailable to participate in the performance of a trustee's function for a reason described by Subsection (c)(1) and prompt action is necessary to achieve the efficient administration or purposes of the trust or to avoid injury to the trust property or a beneficiary, the remaining cotrustee or a majority of the remaining

Elliot and Clem also argued that the court could, alternatively, issue an order that would allow for a variety of simple maintenance and ongoing management issues to be addressed without prior approval of the court.

In response, Weatherman argued that the majority rule proposed by Elliot and Clem was unworkable and that the trial court had two other options. First, Weatherman suggested that the court could order that the trustors be allowed to withdraw up to a specified amount of money each month as necessary to maintain trust assets without court approval. Alternatively, Weatherman suggested that the trial court could appoint "a receiver or some kind of an independent Trustee to get us to the finish line[,] . . . [l]eave on hand whatever cash is needed, kind of reasonable expectation of getting the Trust administered, get the property sold, and do this thing with the property that's been sold."

Following the hearing, the trial court neither expressly granted nor denied the parties' requests for temporary injunctive relief. Instead, the trial court "consider[ed] the request of [Weatherman] for the appointment of a receiver" and issued a written order appointing a receiver over certain trust assets. Specifically, the order authorized the named receiver to take control of the trust bank accounts and real property, manage the sale of the real property, and "distribute the proceeds of sale in a manner set forth in future orders of [the] Court."

On May 19, 2012, the trial court issued the following findings of fact and conclusions of law:

1. On October 15, 1997, Glen L. Weatherman and Mildred S. Weatherman created the Glen L. Weatherman and Mildred S. Weatherman Revocable Living Trust with themselves as co-trustees.

2. On October 25, 2008, Mr. and Mrs. Weatherman executed an amendment appointing [Weatherman], [Elliot], and [Clem] as joint successor trustees.

3. Glen L. Weatherman died on June 9, 2010, and Mildred S. Weatherman died on December 21, 2010.

---

cotrustees may act for the trust.

(e) A trustee may delegate to a cotrustee the performance of a trustee's function unless the settlor specifically directs that the function be performed jointly. Unless a cotrustee's delegation under this subsection is irrevocable, the cotrustee making the delegation may revoke the delegation.

Texas Property Code § 113.085.

4. The Trust does not designate any particular management technique for the joint successor trustees.

5. Unanimous decision management has become unworkable.

6. Two of the joint successor trustees are likely aligned.

. . .

There is a significant likelihood of future party alignment wherein exercise of co-trustees['] decisions by majority decision would not lead to a just and timely division of trust assets. It is just and equitable to appoint a neutral receiver to manage the fair distribution of trust assets in a timely and equitable manner.

In two issues on appeal, Elliot and Clem argue that the trial court abused its discretion in appointing a receiver. First, Elliot and Clem argue that the trial court abused its discretion in appointing the receiver without providing notice, without considering "less harsh remedies," and without requiring a "showing of immediate harm, or risk of material loss of trust assets." Second, Elliot and Clem argue that the trial court abused its discretion because it did not have statutory authority to appoint a receiver without a finding of breach of duty by the trustees . . . .

ANALYSIS

A court may appoint a receiver over trust property under certain circumstances. . . . The remedy of receivership, however, is an extraordinary remedy that must be cautiously applied. *Benefield*, 266 S.W.3d at 31; Rowe v. Rowe, 887 S.W.2d 191, 200 (Tex. App.-Fort Worth 1994, writ denied). Even if a specific statutory provision authorizes a receivership, a trial court should not appoint a receiver if another remedy exists at law or in equity that is adequate and complete. *Benefield*, 266 S.W.3d at 31; see also Fortenberry v. Cavanaugh, No. 03–04–00816–CV, 2005 WL 1412103, at *2 (Tex. App.-Austin June 16, 2005, no pet.) (mem. op).

Moreover, the appointment of a receiver without notice is an especially drastic action and "should be exercised with extreme caution and only where great emergency or imperative necessity requires it. . . ." Krumnow v. Krumnow, 174 S.W.3d 820, 828 (Tex. App.-Waco 2005, pet. denied) (citing Best Inv. Co. v. Whirley, 536 S.W.2d 578, 581 (Tex. Civ. App.-Dallas 1976, no writ)). Courts have "uniformly been reluctant to grant such harsh relief." Id. In addition, Rule 695 of the Texas Rules of Civil Procedure specifically provides:

> Except where otherwise provided by statute, no receiver shall be appointed without notice to take charge of property which is fixed and immovable. When an application for appointment of a receiver to take possession of this type is filed, the judge or court shall set the same down for hearing and notice of such hearing shall be given to

> the adverse party by serving notice thereof not less than three days prior to such hearing.

Texas Rule of Civil Procedure 695. Thus, appointment of a receiver over real property without notice is expressly forbidden . . . .

The threshold issue before this court is whether Elliot and Clem received proper notice of Weatherman's request for appointment of a receiver. In making this determination, we first examine whether Weatherman pled such relief prior to the temporary-injunction hearing in April. At the time of the hearing, Weatherman's sole pleading before the trial court was his counterpetition. In his counterpetition, Weatherman asserts that the trust had expired by its terms and seeks a declaration to this effect. Weatherman also requests that the court direct the trustees to distribute the contents of the trust. Nowhere in his pleadings does Weatherman use the term "receiver" or request that the court transfer control of trust assets to a third party. Accordingly, we conclude that Weatherman has not pled an application for receivership, and there is nothing in the record suggesting that Elliot and Clem otherwise had notice prior to the hearing that Weatherman would request such relief.

Next, we consider whether Weatherman's oral request for receivership at the conclusion of the temporary-injunction hearing constitutes sufficient notice. We recognize that there is some authority for the proposition that an oral request for receivership, such as the oral request made by Weatherman at the hearing, could be construed as a sufficient "application" to appoint a receiver. See O & G Carriers, Inc. v. Smith Energy 1986–A P'ship, 826 S.W.2d 703, 707 n. 2 (Tex. App.-Houston [1st Dist.] 1992, no writ). However, Weatherman did not make his oral request until after the close of evidence at the hearing, and the record does not show that his request for receivership was ever separately set for hearing. Thus, even assuming that Weatherman's oral request for a receivership at the temporary-injunction hearing constitutes an "application," Elliot and Clem clearly were not provided a hearing upon three-days notice, as required for a receivership over real property. See Texas Rule of Civil Procedure 695. Therefore, the trial court abused its discretion in appointing a receiver over the real property held by the trust.

Upon review of the record, we also conclude that the evidence is insufficient to justify the appointment of a receiver over the trust bank accounts without notice and the opportunity to be heard. The burden of proof to show the existence of circumstances justifying the appointment of a receiver rests on the party seeking the appointment. *Benefield*, 266 S.W.3d at 32. Here, the record fails to support a finding that other remedies, available either at law or in equity, were inadequate to temporarily maintain the status of the property and the parties' rights pending a hearing on Weatherman's request for a receiver. See *Krumnow*, 174 S.W.3d at 829 (noting that appointment without notice to adverse party should only be exercised "when the status of the property cannot be maintained and the rights of applicants protected pending a hearing by restraining order or temporary injunction or any less drastic remedy"). For instance, there is nothing in the record, including Weatherman's own pleadings, demonstrating that Weatherman's interest in the trust account could not be adequately protected by an injunction limiting the parties' ability to withdraw funds from the trust bank accounts pending a hearing. Further, there is nothing in the record suggesting that Weatherman's request for a receiver could not have been expeditiously set for a hearing. See *Whirley*, 536 S.W.2d at 583 (holding that trial court erred in appointing receiver without notice and noting that "no reason is shown why the application could not have been set down for prompt hearing within a few days and the appellants given a reasonable opportunity to appear and show cause why the receivership should not be granted"). Accordingly, we cannot conclude that a compelling reason exists to justify "the harsh and stringent remedy of an appointment of a receiver without notice" and the opportunity to be heard. See id. The trial court abused its discretion in appointing a receiver over the trust bank accounts.

Having concluded that the trial court abused its discretion in appointing a receiver over the specified property, we sustain Elliot and Clem's first issue on appeal. Therefore, we need not address Elliot and Clem's second issue regarding statutory authority. See Texas Rule of Appellate Procedure 47.1.

CONCLUSION

We reverse and vacate the trial court's order appointing a receiver, and we remand the cause to the trial court for further proceedings consistent with this opinion.

Section D. Directed Trusts and Trust Protectors

Property Code § 114.0031. Directed Trusts; Advisors

(a) In this section:

(1) "Advisor" includes protector.

(2) "Investment decision" means, with respect to any investment, the retention, purchase, sale, exchange, tender, or other transaction affecting the ownership of the investment or rights in the investment and, with respect to a nonpublicly traded investment, the valuation of the investment.

(b) This section does not apply to a charitable trust as defined by Section 123.001.

(c) For purposes of this section, an advisor with authority with respect to investment decisions is an investment advisor.

(d) A protector has all the power and authority granted to the protector by the trust terms, which may include:

(1) the power to remove and appoint trustees, advisors, trust committee members, and other protectors;

(2) the power to modify or amend the trust terms to achieve favorable tax status or to facilitate the efficient administration of the trust; and

(3) the power to modify, expand, or restrict the terms of a power of appointment granted to a beneficiary by the trust terms.

(e) If the terms of a trust give a person the authority to direct, consent to, or disapprove a trustee's actual or proposed investment decisions, distribution decisions, or other decisions, the person is considered to be an advisor and a fiduciary when exercising that authority except that the trust terms may provide that an advisor acts in a nonfiduciary capacity.

(f) A trustee who acts in accordance with the direction of an advisor, as prescribed by the trust terms, is not liable, except in cases of wilful misconduct on the part of the trustee so directed, for any loss resulting directly or indirectly from that act.

(g) If the trust terms provide that a trustee must make decisions with the consent of an advisor, the trustee is not liable, except in cases of wilful misconduct or gross negligence on the part of the trustee, for any loss resulting directly or indirectly from any act taken or not taken as a result of the advisor's failure to provide the required consent after having been requested to do so by the trustee.

(h) If the trust terms provide that a trustee must act in accordance with the direction of an advisor with respect to investment decisions, distribution decisions, or other decisions of the trustee, the trustee does not, except to the extent the trust terms provide otherwise, have the duty to:

(1) monitor the conduct of the advisor;

(2) provide advice to the advisor or consult with the advisor; or

(3) communicate with or warn or apprise any beneficiary or third party concerning instances in which the trustee would or might have exercised the trustee's own discretion in a manner different from the manner directed by the advisor.

(i) Absent clear and convincing evidence to the contrary, the actions of a trustee pertaining to matters within the scope of the advisor's authority, such as confirming that the advisor's directions have been carried out and recording and reporting actions taken at the advisor's direction, are presumed to be administrative actions taken by the trustee solely to allow the trustee to perform those duties assigned to the trustee under the trust terms, and such administrative actions are not considered to constitute an undertaking by the trustee to monitor the advisor or otherwise participate in actions within the scope of the advisor's authority.

Section E. The Duty of Loyalty

Failure to provide beneficiary with disclosures and options not required by trust does not constitute bad faith, gross negligence, or fraud

TEXAS COMMERCE BANK, N.A. v. GRIZZLE
Supreme Court of Texas
96 S.W.3d 240 (2002)

ENOCH, J. In this putative class action, The Frost National Bank ("Frost"), Texas Commerce Bank, N.A. ("TCB"), and their respective parent corporations, defendants in the trial court, challenge that part of the court of appeals' judgment reversing the trial court's summary judgment rendered in their favor. The court of appeals held that a trust instrument's exculpatory clause cannot, as a matter of public policy, exonerate Frost and TCB, as trustees of various trusts invested in each bank's respective stock, from Grizzle's claim that the banks engaged in self-dealing by merging and liquidating trust funds which caused the trusts to suffer losses. . . . We disagree with the court of appeals . . . . Accordingly, we reverse in part that court's judgment and render judgment that Grizzle take nothing against the TCB and Frost defendants. . . .

I. BACKGROUND

A. The Brentley G. Grizzle Trust

On October 30, 1992, a Dallas County district court rendered a decree designating Frost as trustee for the Brentley G. Grizzle Trust (the "Grizzle Trust"). The Grizzle Trust was established under Texas Property Code chapter 142 to receive and administer settlement proceeds received by Brentley, a minor, from a wrongful death claim asserted when her father died. The Grizzle Trust was created with $200,000 in cash settlement proceeds. Frost, as trustee, invested that money in its own common stock and taxable fixed income funds, as permitted by federal law, state law, and the Grizzle Trust.

The Grizzle Trust states that "[t]he broad powers herein conferred upon the Trustee shall always be exercised only in a fiduciary capacity, and nothing herein shall be construed to limit the fiduciary obligation of the Trustee." The Grizzle Trust also contains an exculpatory clause which states:

> This instrument shall always be construed in favor of the validity of any act or omission of any Trustee, and a Trustee shall not be liable for any act or omission except in the case of gross negligence, bad faith, or fraud.

In addition, the Grizzle Trust permits a successor corporate trustee through the purchase of, or merger or consolidation with, the original trustee, Frost. The successor trustee succeeds to all "the rights, duties, and powers" of the original trustee.

B. Frost and TCB Exchange Banks

On April 14, 1994, TCB and its parent corporation, Texas Commerce Equity Holdings, Inc., and Frost and its parent corporation, the New Galveston Company, entered into what the parties call a merger or a bank swap. We will refer to the transaction as a merger. The merger consisted of Frost transferring its Dallas bank to TCB, and TCB transferring its Corpus Christi bank to Frost. By this transfer, the two banks exchanged all assets including their trusts. TCB accordingly became trustee of the Grizzle Trust.

The day after the merger, Richard W. Phillips, TCB's Senior Vice-President and Trust Officer, sent a letter apprizing TCB's new trust customers, including Grizzle, of the merger and TCB's new role as trustee. The letter states, in part:

> As we previously announced, Texas Commerce Bank and Cullen/Frost Bank of Dallas, N.A., have merged and we are pleased to welcome you to Texas Commerce.
>
> Texas Commerce and Cullen/Frost share the same customer-oriented culture, and we look forward to working together to ensure that your relationship with Texas Commerce is a very positive one. Here is a brief summary of what you can expect:
>
> No changes are required to administer your trust account(s). You can count on receiving the same high quality service and attention from your trust administrator/relationship manager.
>
> It will not be necessary to make any adjustments to your trust documents or agreements defining your account. . . .
>
> As service enhancements or other developments are planned, you will be notified well in advance.

Soon after this letter was sent, TCB liquidated the Frost stock and income funds it had acquired from the merger into cash on April 30, 1994. Frost did the same thing with the TCB stock and income funds it had acquired from the merger. TCB and Frost assert that they did this because federal law and regulations prohibit banks, acting as trustees, from investing in common trust funds managed by another bank.

On May 6, 1994, TCB placed the liquidated funds into a short-term investment earning interest. A few weeks later, TCB reinvested those funds in fixed income and common stock funds managed by TCB. Because market forces had caused the Grizzle Trust funds' value to decrease when the merger occurred, liquidating the Frost funds resulted in the Grizzle Trust realizing a long-term capital tax loss of $5,508.70.

C. Linda Grizzle Files Suit

On April 11, 1996, Linda Grizzle, as next friend of her daughter Brentley, brought suit individually and on behalf of a putative class of trust beneficiaries against the TCB and Frost defendants. The suit was based on alleged damages sustained by the trusts, including the Grizzle Trust, as a result of the merger. Grizzle asserted numerous claims including breach of fiduciary duty, deceptive trade practices, negligence, gross negligence, fraud, conspiracy, and breach of contract.

On December 27, 1996, the Frost defendants moved for summary judgment, asserting among other grounds, that the Grizzle Trust's exculpatory clause precluded liability. On January 13, 1997, the TCB defendants filed a similar motion for summary judgment. Grizzle opposed the summary judgment motions and filed her own affidavit, which she subsequently amended. In her amended affidavit, she stated that her daughter's loss included audit fees and other charges allegedly netted against the liquidation proceeds allocable to the Grizzle Trust. Grizzle further stated that she was never provided the option of allowing another bank in the Frost banking system to continue administering the Grizzle Trust.

On February 10, 1997, the trial court heard the summary judgment motions. On February 17, 1997, Grizzle filed a first amended petition that sought to add, among other things, claims that the TCB and Frost defendants had engaged in self-dealing. . . .

[Grizzle subsequently amended her petitions to attempt to add additional plaintiffs, but the trial court granted summary judgment to defendants.] Grizzle and the other individuals who attempted to join the lawsuit appealed, asserting that the trial court erred in rendering summary judgment for the TCB and Frost defendants. The court of appeals affirmed in part and reversed in part, remanding the case to the trial court for further proceedings.

Citing other courts of appeals' decisions, the court of appeals here concluded that the Grizzle Trust's exculpatory clause could not, as a matter of public policy, vitiate a claim for, among other things, self-dealing. The court of appeals held that self-dealing included misapplying or mishandling trust funds and failing to promptly reinvest substantial sums of trust monies. The court of appeals held there was evidence that TCB failed to promptly reinvest liquidated funds, which was evidence of mishandling of trust funds included within the meaning of self-dealing. The court of appeals concluded that because a fact issue existed about whether TCB and Frost had engaged in self-dealing, the exculpatory clause did not support the trial court's summary judgment.

The court of appeals further held that the summary judgment evidence raised a fact question about whether the Frost defendants' failure to disclose the consequences of the merger and liquidation amounted to a misrepresentation. The court of appeals also concluded that the summary judgment could not be upheld based on the Frost defendants' argument that Grizzle was not entitled to a separate recovery on a fraud claim because there were no damages attributed to fraud rather than contract. According to the court of appeals, Grizzle's fraud claim arose from TCB's letter notifying her of the merger and telling her that no changes were required in administering the trust, no adjustments to the trust documents were necessary, and as other developments were planned, beneficiaries would be notified in advance. The court of appeals concluded that Grizzle's fraud claim arose from being induced to accept the change in trusteeship based on TCB's assurances that no change in the trust agreements or their administration was necessary.

The court of appeals further held that the summary judgment evidence presented a fact issue about whether audit and other fees were assessed against the trusts. The court of appeals noted that 12 C.F.R. § 9.18(b)(12) (now § 9.18(b)(10)) provides that "[t]he bank shall absorb the costs of establishing or reorganizing a collective investment fund," and that audit fees could fall within that provision. Thus, the court of appeals concluded that § 9.18 supported Grizzle's argument that federal banking regulations did not excuse TCB's failure to mitigate any damages, such as charging expenses related to the liquidation and reinvestment of the funds after the merger. . . .

We granted the TCB and Frost defendants' petitions for review to determine, among other things, whether a trust's exculpatory clause can, without violating public policy, exonerate a corporate trustee from liability for self-dealing defined as the misapplication or mishandling of trust funds, including the failure to promptly reinvest trust monies. In addition to briefing from the parties, we received an amicus brief from Texas Bankers Association, Independent Bankers Association of Texas, and Texas Savings & Community Bankers Association.

II. ANALYSIS

A. The Exculpatory Clause's Effect

The TCB and Frost defendants argue that the court of appeals erred in holding that the Grizzle Trust's exculpatory clause did not exonerate them from liability. The TCB and Frost defendants contend that the court of appeals erroneously held there was evidence that TCB failed to promptly reinvest the liquidated funds which, in turn, was evidence of mishandling trust funds, which fell within the meaning of self-dealing. The TCB and Frost defendants assert that the court of appeals' broad self-dealing exception is not authorized by the Texas Trust Code,[4] which sets forth the only self-dealing exceptions to exculpatory clauses the Legislature deemed appropriate.[5] The TCB and Frost defendants further assert that, even if such a self-dealing exception is appropriate the federally-approved merger and subsequent

---

[4] Texas Property Code §§ 111.001-115.017.
[5] Id. § 113.059(b).

liquidations of trust funds required by federal law cannot constitute self-dealing as a matter of law.

Grizzle responds with numerous arguments, including that public policy prohibits an exculpatory clause from exonerating a trustee from liability for self-dealing to further its own financial interests. Additionally, Grizzle asserts that the court of appeals correctly recognized that self-dealing includes mishandling of trust funds and unreasonable delay in making investments. Grizzle also contends that Trust Code section 113.059, which authorizes exculpatory clauses, does not apply to the Grizzle Trust because the Grizzle Trust was created under Texas Property Code chapter 142, which is not part of the Trust Code.

As an initial matter, we disagree with Grizzle's argument that Trust Code section 113.059 does not apply to trusts created under Property Code chapter 142. The Trust Code applies to "express trusts" created on or after January 1, 1984.[6] The Trust Code states that it does not apply to a resulting trust, a constructive trust, a business trust, or a security instrument.[7] But the Trust Code does not say that it does not apply to trusts created under Property Code chapter 142.

Instead, the Trust Code defines an "express trust" as:

> a fiduciary relationship with respect to property which arises as a manifestation by the settlor [the person who creates the trust[8]] of an intention to create the relationship and which subjects the person holding title to the property to equitable duties to deal with the property for the benefit of another person.[9]

Property Code section 142.002 provides that a court may render a decree creating a trust to manage funds for a minor's benefit.[10] Thus, we conclude that a trust created under Property Code chapter 142 by the court acting as settlor is an "express trust" to which the Trust Code applies.[11]

Next, we agree with the TCB and Frost defendants that a trust instrument's exculpatory clause can relieve a corporate trustee of liability for self-dealing defined as the misapplication or mishandling of trust funds, including the failure to promptly reinvest trust monies. We base our decision on the Trust Code's express language. . . .

While the Trust Code imposes certain obligations on a trustee—including all duties imposed by the common law[12]—the Trust Code also permits the settlor to modify those

---

[6] Id. §§ 111.003, 111.006(1).
[7] Id. § 111.003.
[8] Id. § 111.004(14).
[9] Id. § 111.004(4).
[10] Id. § 142.002(a).
[11] See Brownsville-Valley Reg'l Med. Ctr., Inc. v. Gamez, 894 S.W.2d 753, 756 (Tex. 1995).
[12] Id. § 113.051.

obligations in the trust instrument. Indeed, Trust Code section 113.059 broadly states that a settlor may relieve a corporate trustee from a "duty, liability, or restriction imposed by this subtitle," except for those contained in sections 113.052 and 113.053.[13] The Trust Code contains no other limitations on relieving a corporate trustee from liability for self-dealing in a trust instrument. Thus, we conclude that the Trust Code allows an exculpatory clause to relieve a corporate trustee from liability for self-dealing defined as misapplying or mishandling trust funds, including failing to promptly reinvest trust monies, unless those activities violate the prohibitions in sections 113.052 and 113.053.[14] We disapprove [earlier decisions] to the extent they suggest otherwise. We further hold that the court of appeals

---

[13] Id. § 113.059.

[14] After the Texas Supreme Court's decision in *Grizzle*, the legislature enacted the following provision of the Texas Trust Code:

> § 114.007. Exculpation of Trustee. (a) A term of a trust relieving a trustee of liability for breach of trust is unenforceable to the extent that the term relieves a trustee of liability for:
>
> (1) a breach of trust committed:
>
> (A) in bad faith;
>
> (B) intentionally; or
>
> (C) with reckless indifference to the interest of a beneficiary; or
>
> (2) any profit derived by the trustee from a breach of trust.
>
> (b) A term in a trust instrument relieving the trustee of liability for a breach of trust is ineffective to the extent that the term is inserted in the trust instrument as a result of an abuse by the trustee of a fiduciary duty to or confidential relationship with the settlor.
>
> (c) This section applies only to a term of a trust that may otherwise relieve a trustee from liability for a breach of trust. Except as provided in Section 111.0035, this section does not prohibit the settlor, by the terms of the trust, from expressly:
>
> (1) relieving the trustee from a duty or restriction imposed by this subtitle or by common law; or
>
> (2) directing or permitting the trustee to do or not to do an action that would otherwise violate a duty or restriction imposed by this subtitle or by common law.

—Ed.

here erred in holding that the Grizzle Trust's exculpatory clause could not relieve the TCB and Frost defendants from liability for misapplying and mishandling trust funds when there was no claim that, by doing so, the TCB and Frost defendants violated sections 113.052 or 113.053.

That does not end our inquiry though. The Grizzle Trust exonerates TCB and Frost from liability as trustee for any act or omission "except in the case of gross negligence, bad faith, or fraud." We therefore must decide whether the TCB and Frost defendants are entitled to judgment as a matter of law because their actions did not constitute gross negligence, bad faith, or fraud.

The TCB and Frost defendants argue that the facts supporting Grizzle's purported damages are that the TCB and Frost defendants: (1) converted the Grizzle Trust's investments into cash, causing the trust to realize a long-term capital loss of $5,508.70 due to a prior market decrease in the investments' value; (2) delayed reinvesting the trust funds, causing the trust to lose income that otherwise would have been realized; and (3) charged audit and other fees that were applied to the Grizzle Trust. According to the TCB and Frost defendants, those facts, even if true, constituted no more than mere failures to exercise the degree of judgment required under the circumstances. They did not amount to gross negligence, bad faith, or fraud.

The TCB and Frost defendants assert that federal law required TCB to liquidate the trust's investment in Frost funds,[15] and it was not gross negligence or bad faith to comply with federal law. They argue that the brief delay in reinvesting the funds was not even a simple breach of trust, much less gross negligence or bad faith. And charging audit fees was not gross negligence or bad faith, particularly when the Grizzle Trust authorized the trustee to charge fees.

The TCB and Frost defendants also argue that Grizzle's fraud allegations are without merit. Grizzle bases her fraud claim on the letter from TCB's Vice-President welcoming her as a new customer. The TCB and Frost defendants argue that the statements made in that letter cannot support a fraud claim as a matter of law. Moreover, the TCB and Frost defendants assert, Grizzle admitted that she did not rely on the letter. The court of appeals nevertheless determined that "Grizzle's fraud claim arises from being induced to accept the change in trusteeship resulting from the merger on [the letter's] assurances that no change in the trust agreements or their administration was necessary. . . ."[16] The TCB and Frost defendants argue that the letter was sent after the merger and, as a matter of federal law, substituting TCB as trustee was automatic. Thus, they contend that the court of appeals erred in holding that the letter induced Grizzle to accept the change in trusteeship.

Grizzle responds that the TCB and Frost defendants could have avoided this lawsuit by giving their customers advance notice of the merger and its ramifications and allowing

---

[15] See 12 C.F.R. § 9.18.

[16] 38 S.W.3d at 283.

their customers to move their trust accounts to other branches within the same bank system. Grizzle asserts that the TCB and Frost defendants' conduct in how they structured and consummated their merger qualifies as an intentional adverse act and reckless indifference about the beneficiaries' best interests. According to Grizzle, only their trust customers' interests should have guided the TCB and Frost defendants' decisions, not whether the merger would be to their own economic advantage. She claims that the TCB and Frost defendants acted in bad faith and with gross negligence by looking out for their own interests at the beneficiaries' expense, thus violating the duties of loyalty, candor, and fidelity.

Grizzle also argues that TCB's welcome letter was affirmatively misleading because it implied that TCB's takeover as trustee had nothing but positive results for the former Frost trust customers. Therefore, Grizzle concludes that the court of appeals properly held that "the summary judgment evidence raises a fact issue on whether the Frost defendants' failure to disclose the consequences of the merger and liquidation amounted to misrepresentation."[17]

Summary judgment is appropriate only when there are no disputed issues of material fact and the moving party is entitled to judgment as a matter of law.[18] In reviewing a traditional motion for summary judgment, such as the one granted to the TCB and Frost defendants, the reviewing court must resolve every doubt and indulge every reasonable inference in the nonmovant's favor. All evidence favorable to the nonmovant will be taken as true.

We begin our analysis of whether, as a matter of law, the TCB and Frost defendants are exculpated from liability for their actions by focusing on the Grizzle Trust's provisions, as the Trust Code instructs us to do. Those provisions state, in part:

> Any corporation that shall succeed (by purchase, merger, consolidation, or otherwise) to all or the greater part of the assets of any corporate Trustee shall succeed to all the rights, duties, and powers of such corporate Trustee, as Trustee of this trust.
>
> The Trustee shall also be reimbursed for all reasonable expenses incurred in connection with the administration of the trust.
>
> The Trustee may buy, sell, or trade any security of any nature (including stocks, stock rights, warrants, bonds, debentures, notes, certificates of interest, certificates of indebtedness, and options) or any other things of value issued by any person, firm, association, trust, corporation, or body politic whatsoever. In addition, the Trustee may invest the trust assets in the Trustee's common trust funds.
>
> The Trustee may sell, exchange, alter, mortgage, pledge, or otherwise dispose of trust property . . . pay all reasonable expenses . . . join in, by deposit, pledge, or

---

[17] 38 S.W.3d at 282.

[18] D. Houston, Inc. v. Love, 92 S.W.3d 450 (Tex. 2002).

> otherwise, any plan of reorganization or readjustment of any investments of the trust, and vest in a protective committee or other legal entity such power as in the Trustee's opinion may be desirable; and sell for cash and/or credit all or any part of the trust estate.
>
> The Trustee may employ and compensate agents and other employees, including attorneys, accountants, and investment advisers. . . .
>
> Stock dividends and capital gains shall be treated as corpus. Except as herein otherwise specifically provided, the Trustee shall determine the manner in which expenses are to be borne and receipts credited between corpus and income. . . .
>
> The Trustee shall confer with the Beneficiary, or the Beneficiary's legal guardian or other legal representative if the Beneficiary is a minor or incapacitated person, from time to time concerning the needs of the Beneficiary and shall consider (but shall not be bound by) the requests of the Beneficiary or the Beneficiary's legal guardian or other legal representative, as the case may be, concerning the administration of the trust, including, but not limited to, the investment and distribution of the trust assets.

Given these provisions, we conclude that the TCB and Frost defendants cannot be held liable for their actions in this case. For example, Grizzle complains that the TCB and Frost defendants did not give her advance notice of the merger or offer her the option to move the Grizzle Trust to another bank. While we recognize that Grizzle has a strong interest in protecting her daughter's trust assets, the Grizzle Trust contains no provision requiring such disclosures and options. And we decline to read such a provision into the trust.[19] Accordingly, the trustee's failure to provide such disclosures and options does not amount to gross negligence, bad faith, or fraud.

We likewise conclude that TCB's brief delay in reinvesting the liquidated funds does not give rise to liability under the Grizzle Trust. Within several days following the merger, TCB placed the funds into an interest-bearing account. Within a few weeks thereafter, TCB had reinvested the funds into its own common stock funds. We accordingly agree with the Supreme Judicial Court of Massachusetts that:

> [a]t most, these [delays] were no more than failures to exercise the degree of judgment required in the circumstances. They did not amount to bad faith or to intentional breaches of trust or to reckless indifference to the interest of the beneficiaries.[20]

We next decide whether the TCB and Frost defendants can be held liable under the Grizzle Trust for imposing audit fees and other expenses incurred from liquidating trust assets and reinvesting them. We note that if there had been no merger and Frost had decided

---

[19] See Danciger Oil & Ref. Co. of Tex. v. Powell, 137 Tex. 484, 154 S.W.2d 632, 635 (1941).
[20] New England Trust Co. v. Paine, 317 Mass. 542, 59 N.E.2d 263, 272 (1945).

to sell the Grizzle Trust's assets, liquidate them into cash, and reinvest them in other assets, there would be no liability under the trust solely because that transaction caused the trust to realize tax consequences and incur audit and other fees. The Grizzle Trust gives its trustee broad authority to manage the trust, including the authority to sell assets and reinvest them. The Grizzle Trust recognizes that such transactions may produce tax consequences and result in fees being charged to the trust. And the Grizzle Trust authorizes the trustee to pay all reasonable expenses incurred in administering the trust, including expenses incurred in selling the assets. Therefore, absent some assertion that the investments themselves were made with gross negligence, in bad faith, or fraudulently, the trustee cannot be held liable under the Grizzle Trust for exercising the authority and discretion given to it.

We see no reason to reach a different result simply because, in this case, the sale of assets and the consequences that followed resulted from the trustee's decision to enter into a merger. The Grizzle Trust contemplates that a merger or other transaction may occur that results in a new trustee. And Grizzle does not argue that Frost could not enter into the merger; nor does she complain about the investments TCB made as the new trustee. Instead, she complains about the audit and other fees charged to the trust because of the merger.

But the fees resulted from Frost exercising its discretion under the Grizzle Trust to merge with TCB. Once that occurred, TCB, as the new trustee, was authorized to liquidate the Frost stock in which the Grizzle Trust was invested and reinvest that money in TCB stock. Grizzle does not contend otherwise. And the Grizzle Trust contemplates that fees may be incurred in such a situation and authorizes the trustee to pay them.

Grizzle argued below that 12 C.F.R. § 9.18(b)(12) (now § 9.18(b)(10)) demonstrated that federal law did not excuse TCB's failure to mitigate damages such as charging expenses related to the merger. Section 9.18 states that a "bank shall absorb the expenses of establishing or reorganizing a collective investment fund,"[21] which is defined, in part, as "[a] fund maintained by the bank . . . exclusively for the collective investment and reinvestment of money contributed to the fund by the bank . . . in its capacity as trustee. . . ."[22] This begs the question of whether Grizzle could assert a claim based on the federal regulations. But Grizzle did not argue or brief this question here or below. We therefore decline to address it. And as we have otherwise discussed, the Grizzle Trust authorizes its trustee to pay the reasonable expenses incurred in administering the trust, including expenses incurred from liquidating funds and investing in others. We accordingly decline to hold, under the circumstances, that assessing fees in connection with the merger amounted to gross negligence, bad faith, or fraud.

Moreover, TCB's letter to Grizzle informing her of the merger did not raise a fact question with respect to Grizzle's fraud claim, either by its statements or its omissions. The court of appeals concluded that Grizzle's fraud claim arose from "being induced to accept

[21] 12 C.F.R. § 9.18(b)(10).

[22] Id. § 9.18(a)(1).

the change in trusteeship resulting from the merger."[23] But the Grizzle Trust did not provide Grizzle with approval authority over a change in the trusteeship. Further, Grizzle does not complain about TCB becoming the new trustee except for the fact that she was not informed of the consequences that flowed from that change. As we have said, those consequences, and the Frost and TCB defendants' failure to inform her of them, do not constitute gross negligence, bad faith, or fraud.

In short, Grizzle failed to create a fact issue that TCB or Frost acted or failed to act as a result of gross negligence, bad faith, or fraud. We accordingly hold that the TCB and Frost defendants are entitled to judgment as a matter of law on Grizzle's individual claims against them. We therefore need not reach the TCB and Frost defendants' other arguments about why they are entitled to summary judgment on Grizzle's claims. . . .

III. CONCLUSION

We conclude that the Grizzle Trust's exculpatory clause exonerated the TCB and Frost defendants from liability on Grizzle's claims. Thus, the trial court properly granted summary judgment for the TCB and Frost defendants. The court of appeals erred in concluding that the Grizzle Trust's exculpatory clause could not, as a matter of public policy, exonerate the TCB and Frost defendants from liability for allegedly mishandling trust funds when their actions did not constitute self-dealing under the Trust Code or amount to gross negligence, bad faith, or fraud for which the trustee is liable under the Grizzle Trust. . . . We accordingly reverse the court of appeals' judgment in part and render judgment that Grizzle take nothing against the TCB and Frost defendants.

Property Code § 113.051. General Duty

The trustee shall administer the trust in good faith according to its terms and this subtitle. In the absence of any contrary terms in the trust instrument or contrary provisions of this subtitle, in administering the trust the trustee shall perform all of the duties imposed on trustees by the common law.

Property Code § 113.052. Loan of Trust Funds to Trustee

(a) Except as provided by Subsection (b) of this section, a trustee may not lend trust funds to:

(1) the trustee or an affiliate;

---

[23] 38 S.W.3d at 283.

(2) a director, officer, or employee of the trustee or an affiliate;

(3) a relative of the trustee; or

(4) the trustee's employer, employee, partner, or other business associate.

(b) This section does not prohibit:

(1) a loan by a trustee to a beneficiary of the trust if the loan is expressly authorized or directed by the instrument or transaction establishing the trust; or

(2) a deposit by a corporate trustee with itself under Section 113.057 of this Act.

Property Code § 113.053. Purchase or Sale of Trust Property by Trustee

(a) Except as provided by Subsections (b), (c), (d), (e), (f), and (g), a trustee shall not directly or indirectly buy or sell trust property from or to:

(1) the trustee or an affiliate;

(2) a director, officer, or employee of the trustee or an affiliate;

(3) a relative of the trustee; or

(4) the trustee's employer, partner, or other business associate.

(b) A national banking association or a state-chartered corporation with the right to exercise trust powers that is serving as executor, administrator, guardian, trustee, or receiver may sell shares of its own capital stock held by it for an estate to one or more of its officers or directors if a court:

(1) finds that the sale is in the best interest of the estate that owns the shares;

(2) fixes or approves the sales price of the shares and the other terms of the sale; and

(3) enters an order authorizing and directing the sale.

(c) If a corporate trustee, executor, administrator, or guardian is legally authorized to retain its own capital stock in trust, the trustee may exercise rights to purchase its own stock if increases in the stock are offered pro rata to shareholders.

(d) If the exercise of rights or the receipt of a stock dividend results in a fractional share holding and the acquisition meets the investment standard required by this subchapter, the trustee may purchase additional fractional shares to round out the holding to a full share.

(e) A trustee may:

(1) comply with the terms of a written executory contract signed by the settlor, including a contract for deed, earnest money contract, buy/sell agreement, or stock purchase or redemption agreement; and

(2) sell the stock, bonds, obligations, or other securities of a corporation to the issuing corporation or to its corporate affiliate if the sale is made under an agreement described in Subdivision (1) or complies with the duties imposed by Chapter 117.

(f) A national banking association, a state-chartered corporation, including a state-chartered bank or trust company, a state or federal savings and loan association that has the right to exercise trust powers and that is serving as trustee, or such an institution that is serving as custodian with respect to an individual retirement account, as defined by Section 408, Internal Revenue Code, or an employee benefit plan, as defined by Section 3(3), Employee Retirement Income Security Act of 1974 (29 U.S.C. Section 1002(3)), regardless of whether the custodial account is, or would otherwise be, considered a trust for purposes of this subtitle, may, subject to its fiduciary duties:

(1) employ an affiliate or division within a financial institution to provide brokerage, investment, administrative, custodial, or other account services for the trust or custodial account and charge the trust or custodial account for the services;

(2) unless the instrument governing the fiduciary relationship expressly prohibits the purchase or charge, purchase insurance underwritten or otherwise distributed by an affiliate, a division within the financial institution, or a syndicate or selling group that includes the financial institution or an affiliate and charge the trust or custodial account for the insurance premium, provided that:

(A) the person conducting the insurance transaction is appropriately licensed if required by applicable licensing and regulatory requirements administered by a functional regulatory agency of this state; and

(B) the insurance product and premium are the same or similar to a product and premium offered by organizations that are not an affiliate, a division within the financial institution, or a syndicate or selling group that includes the financial institution or an affiliate; and

(3) receive a fee or compensation, directly or indirectly, on account of the services performed or the insurance product sold by the affiliate, division within the financial institution, or syndicate or selling group that includes the financial institution or an affiliate, whether in the form of shared commissions, fees, or otherwise, provided that any amount charged by the affiliate, division, or syndicate or selling group that includes the financial institution or an affiliate for the services or insurance product is disclosed and does not exceed the customary or prevailing amount that is charged by

the affiliate, division, or syndicate or selling group that includes the financial institution or an affiliate, or a comparable entity, for comparable services rendered or insurance provided to a person other than the trust.

(g) In addition to other investments authorized by law for the investment of funds held by a fiduciary or by the instrument governing the fiduciary relationship, and notwithstanding any other provision of law and subject to the standard contained in Chapter 117, a bank or trust company acting as a fiduciary, agent, or otherwise, in the exercise of its investment discretion or at the direction of another person authorized to direct the investment of funds held by the bank or trust company as fiduciary, may invest and reinvest in the securities of an open-end or closed-end management investment company or investment trust registered under the Investment Company Act of 1940 (15 U.S.C. Sec. 80a-1 et seq.) if the portfolio of the investment company or investment trust consists substantially of investments that are not prohibited by the governing instrument. The fact that the bank or trust company or an affiliate of the bank or trust company provides services to the investment company or investment trust, such as those of an investment advisor, custodian, transfer agent, registrar, sponsor, distributor, manager, or otherwise, and receives compensation for those services does not preclude the bank or trust company from investing or reinvesting in the securities if the compensation is disclosed by prospectus, account statement, or otherwise. An executor or administrator of an estate under a dependent administration or a guardian of an estate shall not so invest or reinvest unless specifically authorized by the court in which such estate or guardianship is pending.

Property Code § 113.054. Sales From One Trust to Another

A trustee of one trust may not sell property to another trust of which it is also trustee unless the property is:

(1) a bond, note, bill, or other obligation issued or fully guaranteed as to principal and interest by the United States; and

(2) sold for its current market price.

Property Code § 113.055. Purchase of Trustee's Securities

(a) Except as provided by Subsection (b) of this section, a corporate trustee may not purchase for the trust the stock, bonds, obligations, or other securities of the trustee or an affiliate, and a noncorporate trustee may not purchase for the trust the stock, bonds, obligations, or other securities of a corporation with which the trustee is connected as director, owner, manager, or any other executive capacity.

(b) A trustee may:

(1) retain stock already owned by the trust unless the retention does not satisfy the requirements prescribed by Chapter 117; and

(2) exercise stock rights or purchase fractional shares under Section 113.053 of this Act.

Section F. The Duty of Prudence

Texas has adopted both the Uniform Prudent Investor Act and the Uniform Principal and Income Act. Since these are discussed in detail in national casebooks, they are not reproduced here.

Arbitration clause in inter vivos trust is enforceable against trust beneficiaries

RACHAL v. REITZ
Supreme Court of Texas
403 S.W.3d 840 (2013)

GUZMAN, J. Federal and state policies favor arbitration for its efficient method of resolving disputes, and arbitration has become a mainstay of the dispute resolution process. Today we determine whether these policies render an arbitration provision contained in an *inter vivos* trust enforceable against the trust beneficiaries. The trust here contained a provision requiring all disputes regarding the trust and the trustee to proceed to arbitration. When a trust beneficiary sued the trustee, the trustee moved to compel arbitration. The trial court denied the motion. The court of appeals, sitting *en banc,* affirmed, concluding that the provision could not be enforced under the Texas Arbitration Act (TAA) because there was no agreement to arbitrate trust disputes. We conclude that the arbitration provision contained in the trust at issue is enforceable against the beneficiary for two reasons. First, the settlor determines the conditions attached to her gifts, and we enforce trust restrictions on the basis of the settlor's intent. The settlor's intent here was to arbitrate any disputes over the trust. Second, the TAA requires enforcement of written agreements to arbitrate, and an agreement requires mutual assent, which we have previously concluded may be manifested through the doctrine of direct benefits estoppel. Thus, the beneficiary's acceptance of the benefits of the trust and suit to enforce its terms constituted the assent required to form an enforceable agreement to arbitrate under the TAA. We reverse the judgment of the court of appeals and remand to the trial court to enter an order consistent with this opinion.

I. Background

Andrew Francis Reitz established the A.F. Reitz Trust in 2000, naming his sons, James and John, as sole beneficiaries and himself as trustee. The trust was revocable during Andrew's lifetime and irrevocable after his death. Upon Andrew's death, Hal Rachal, Jr., the attorney who drafted the trust, became the successor trustee.

In 2009, John Reitz sued Rachal individually and as successor trustee, alleging that Rachal had misappropriated trust assets and failed to provide an accounting to the beneficiaries as required by law. Reitz sought a temporary injunction, Rachal's removal as trustee, and damages.

Rachal generally denied the allegations and later moved to compel arbitration of the dispute under the TAA, relying on the trust's arbitration provision. That provision states:

> *Arbitration.* Despite anything herein to the contrary, I intend that as to any dispute of any kind involving this Trust or any of the parties or persons concerned herewith (e.g., beneficiaries, Trustees), arbitration as provided herein shall be the sole and exclusive remedy, and no legal proceedings shall be allowed or given effect except as they may relate to enforcing or implementing such arbitration in accordance herewith. Judgment on any arbitration award pursuant hereto shall be binding and enforceable on all said parties.

The trust further provided that "[t]his agreement shall extend to and be binding upon the Grantor, Trustees, and beneficiaries hereto and on their respective heirs, executors, administrators, legal representatives, and successors."

The trial court denied Rachal's motion to compel and Rachal filed this interlocutory appeal. See Texas Civil Practice & Remedies Code § 171.098(a)(1) (authorizing interlocutory appeal for orders denying applications to compel arbitration). A divided court of appeals, sitting *en banc*, affirmed the trial court's order. 347 S.W.3d 305, 312. The court of appeals held that a binding arbitration provision must be the product of an enforceable contract between the parties, reasoning that such a contract does not exist in the trust context, in part because there is no consideration and in part because the trust beneficiaries have not consented to such a provision. Id. at 308, 310–11. The court further concluded that because there is no contractual agreement to arbitrate in this context, it is for the Legislature, rather than the courts, to decide "whether and to what extent the settlor of this type of a trust should have the power to bind the beneficiaries of the trust to arbitrate." Id. at 311–12.

The four dissenting Justices reasoned that further legislation is not necessarily required because a trust can be "a written agreement to arbitrate" within the meaning of the TAA even without the signatures of the beneficiaries and successor trustee. 347 S.W.3d at 312–13 (Murphy, J., dissenting) (quoting Texas Civil Practice & Remedies Code § 171.001(a)). The dissent notes that the TAA does not require a formal contract to arbitrate but only a written agreement, a broader term that includes legal contracts but also less formal agreements. Id. The dissent concludes that, because the Legislature chose the broader term "agreement" in the TAA, rulings in other jurisdictions that arbitration provisions in trusts are unenforceable are inapplicable to arbitration provisions under the TAA. Id. at 313–14. We granted the trustee's petition to decide whether an arbitration provision under the TAA in an *inter vivos* trust is enforceable against trust beneficiaries.

II. Discussion

A. Standard of Review

Rachal moved to compel arbitration under the TAA, which provides that a "written agreement to arbitrate" is enforceable if it provides for arbitration of either an existing controversy or one that arises "between the parties after the date of the agreement." Texas Civil Practice & Remedies Code § 171.001(a). As a threshold matter, a party seeking to compel arbitration must establish the existence of a valid arbitration agreement and the existence of a dispute within the scope of the agreement. Meyer v. WMCO–GP, LLC, 211 S.W.3d 302, 305 (Tex. 2006).

We review de novo whether an arbitration agreement is enforceable. In re Labatt Food Serv., L.P., 279 S.W.3d 640, 643 (Tex. 2009). When reviewing a denial of a motion to compel arbitration, we defer to the trial court's factual determinations that are supported by evidence but review the trial court's legal determinations de novo. Id.

This case also requires us to construe a statute. Our primary goal in construing a statute is to give effect to the Legislature's intent. Texas Mut. Ins. Co. v. Ruttiger, 381 S.W.3d 430, 452 (Tex. 2012); TGS–NOPEC Geophysical Co. v. Combs, 340 S.W.3d 432, 439 (Tex. 2011). We defer to the plain meaning of a statute as the best indication of the Legislature's intent unless a different meaning is apparent from the context of the statute or the plain meaning would yield absurd results. Molinet v. Kimbrell, 356 S.W.3d 407, 411 (Tex. 2011). Moreover, we determine legislative intent from the entire act, not merely from isolated portions. *Ruttiger,* 381 S.W.3d at 454; *TGS–NOPEC,* 340 S.W.3d at 439.

B. Trusts and the TAA

Rachal echoes the dissenting justices' view that the TAA does not require a formal contract but rather only an agreement to arbitrate future disputes. Reitz argues that even if the TAA requires only an agreement to arbitrate—as opposed to a formal contract—the trust instrument here does not meet that less exacting standard because it lacks mutual assent and unity in thought between its parties. We agree with Rachal.

1. Settlor's Intent

Generally, Texas courts endeavor to enforce trusts according to the settlor's intent, which we divine from the four corners of unambiguous trusts. Frost Nat'l Bank of San Antonio v. Newton, 554 S.W.2d 149, 153 (Tex. 1977); see also Huffman v. Huffman, 161 Tex. 267, 339 S.W.2d 885, 888 (1960) ("Assuming that there is a valid will to be construed, it is the place of the court to find the meaning of such will, and not under guise of construction or under general powers of equity to assume to correct or redraft the will in which testator has expressed his intentions." (quotation marks omitted)). We enforce the settlor's intent as expressed in an unambiguous trust over the objections of beneficiaries that disagree with a trust's terms. *Newton,* 554 S.W.2d at 153. For example, in *Newton,* a trust provided for a portion of the trust to be distributed for the education of certain student beneficiary relatives, with excess income paid during the life of the trust to other relatives who would receive the ultimate distribution when the trust terminated. Id. at 151–52. The trust provided that the trustee could terminate the trust if the income was insufficient. Id. at 151. When the student beneficiaries completed their education, the ultimate beneficiaries argued the trust should be terminated because its primary purpose had been accomplished. Id. at 153. But we noted the additional purpose of the trust was the payment of excess income to those ultimate beneficiaries and refused to distinguish between the two purposes as primary or secondary because it would require venturing beyond the settlor's intent in the express language of the trust. Id. at 154. Accordingly, we enforced the trust with the restriction that the settlor intended: that the trust only terminate when the income was insufficient. Id.; see also Moore v. Smith, 443 S.W.2d 552, 555–56 (Tex. 1969) (assessing settlor's intent by examining the four corners of the trust).

Here, the settlor unequivocally stated his requirement that all disputes be arbitrated. He specified that, "[d]espite anything herein to the contrary," arbitration would be "the sole and exclusive remedy" for "any dispute of any kind involving this Trust or any of the parties or persons connected herewith (e.g., beneficiaries, Trustees) . . . ." Because this language is unambiguous, we must enforce the settlor's intent and compel arbitration if the arbitration provision is valid and the underlying dispute is within the provision's scope. *Meyer,* 211 S.W.3d at 305.

2. The TAA

The TAA provides that a "written *agreement* to arbitrate is valid and enforceable if the *agreement* is to arbitrate a controversy that: (1) exists at the time of the *agreement;* or (2) arises between the parties after the date of the *agreement.*" Texas Civil Practice & Remedies Code § 171.001(a) (emphases added). The TAA further states that a "party may revoke the agreement only on a ground that exists at law or in equity for the revocation of a *contract.*" Id. § 171.001(b) (emphasis added). The Legislature specifically chose to enforce "agreements" to arbitrate. Id. § 171.001(a). It knew how to enforce only "contracts;" it selected that term to specify the grounds for revoking an agreement to arbitrate. Id. § 171.001(b). The language of the TAA indicates legislative intent to enforce arbitration provisions in agreements. If the Legislature intended to only enforce arbitration provisions within a contract, it could have said so. See id.; *TGS–NOPEC,* 340 S.W.3d at 441 ("The meaning of a word that appears ambiguous when viewed in isolation may become clear when the word is analyzed in light of the terms that surround it.").

Because the TAA does not define agreement, we must look to its generally accepted definition. *TGS–NOPEC,* 340 S.W.3d at 439. Black's Law Dictionary defines an agreement as "a manifestation of mutual assent by two or more persons." Black's Law Dictionary 78 (9th ed. 2009). Contract treatises have made similar observations. Williston commented:

> An agreement, as the courts have said, "is nothing more than a manifestation of mutual assent by two or more legally competent persons to one another." In some respects, the

term agreement is a broader term than contract, and even broader than the term bargain or promise. It covers executed sales, gifts, and other transfers of property.

1 Samuel Williston & Richard A. Lord, A Treatise on the Law of Contracts § 1:3, at 13–14 (4th ed. 1990) (citations omitted); see also 3 Stephen's Commentaries on the Laws of England 4 (Edward Jenks ed., 17th ed.1922) ("The term 'agreement,' although frequently used as synonymous with the word 'contract,' is really an expression of greater breadth of meaning and less technicality. Every contract is an agreement; but not every agreement is a contract. In its colloquial sense, the term 'agreement' would include any arrangement between two or more persons intended to affect their relations (whether legal or otherwise) to each other."). Thus, although an agreement need not meet all the formal requirements of a contract, it must be supported by mutual assent.[24] Black's Law Dictionary 78 (9th ed.2009); 1 Samuel Williston & Richard A. Lord, A Treatise on the Law of Contracts § 1:3, at 13–14 (4th ed.1990).

We therefore address whether the trust here was supported by the mutual assent required to render the trust an agreement and the arbitration provision valid. Typically, a party manifests its assent by signing an agreement. See Mid–Continent Cas. Co. v. Global Enercom Mgmt., Inc., 323 S.W.3d 151, 157 (Tex. 2010) (holding that, in formal contract negotiations, signing the contract is not required so long as there is assent). But we have also found assent by nonsignatories to arbitration provisions when a party has obtained or is seeking substantial benefits under an agreement under the doctrine of direct benefits estoppel.[25] For example, in the case of *In re FirstMerit Bank, N.A.,* the de los Santos plaintiffs purchased a mobile home for their daughter and her husband (the Alvarezes, their co-plaintiffs) under a retail installment financing agreement with the seller. 52 S.W.3d 749, 752 (Tex. 2001). The agreement contained an arbitration addendum. Id. at 752. The de los Santoses signed the agreement but the Alvarezes did not. Id. at 752, 755. The seller assigned the contract to FirstMerit Bank, and the de los Santoses ceased making payments when the seller failed to make certain repairs. Id. at 753. FirstMerit took possession of the home, the de los Santoses and the Alvarezes both sued, and FirstMerit moved to compel arbitration. Id. We stated: "a litigant who sues based on a contract subjects him or herself to the contract's terms." Id. at 755. We thus held that, even though the Alvarezes did not sign the contract containing the

---

[24] We acknowledge that we have previously discussed arbitration agreements under contract principles. See J.M. Davidson, Inc. v. Webster, 128 S.W.3d 223, 227–28 (Tex. 2003) ("Arbitration agreements are interpreted under traditional contract principles. Thus, an employer attempting to enforce an arbitration agreement must show the agreement meets all requisite contract elements." (citations omitted)). Those holdings are not in tension with our analysis here in light of Rachal's arguments, our long-standing deference to the settlor's intent, and the unique requirements of the TAA.

[25] We have noted that there are at least six theories in contract and agency law that may bind nonsignatories to arbitration agreements: (1) incorporation by reference; (2) assumption; (3) agency; (4) alter ego; (5) equitable estoppel; and (6) third-party beneficiary. In re Kellogg Brown & Root, Inc., 166 S.W.3d 732, 739 (Tex. 2005). Direct benefits estoppel, discussed herein, is a type of equitable estoppel. Id.

arbitration clause, their suit on the contract was their assent to the contract's terms, including the arbitration provision. Id. at 755–56. We later noted that in addition to filing suit on the contract, the Alvarezes' occupancy of the home and planned future ownership of it further indicated their acceptance of the contract. In re Weekley Homes, L.P., 180 S.W.3d 127, 134 (Tex. 2005).

We expressly adopted the federal doctrine of direct benefits estoppel in the context of arbitration agreements under state law in *In re Kellogg Brown & Root, Inc.,* where we held that a non-signatory who is seeking the benefits of a contract or seeking to enforce it "is estopped from simultaneously attempting to avoid the contract's burdens, such as the obligation to arbitrate disputes." 166 S.W.3d 732, 739 (Tex. 2005). As the Fourth Circuit described it, "the doctrine recognizes that a party may be estopped from asserting that the lack of his signature on a written contract precludes enforcement of the contract's arbitration clause when he has consistently maintained that other provisions of the same contract should be enforced to benefit him." Int'l Paper Co. v. Schwabedissen Maschinen & Anlagen GMBH, 206 F.3d 411, 418 (4th Cir. 2000) (quoted in *Kellogg Brown & Root,* 166 S.W.3d at 739). We noted in *Kellogg Brown & Root* that if the claims are based on the agreement, they must be arbitrated, but if the claims can stand independently of the agreement, they may be litigated. 166 S.W.3d at 739–40; see also In re U.S. Home Corp., 236 S.W.3d 761, 765 (Tex. 2007) (per curiam).

In *Weekley Homes,* we addressed the circumstances under which direct benefits estoppel binds parties for actions other than filing suit. 180 S.W.3d at 131–32. There, we stated that a "nonparty may be compelled to arbitrate if it deliberately seeks and obtains substantial benefits from the contract itself" during the performance of the agreement. Id. at 132–33. We likened the situation to promissory estoppel, where a promisor induces substantial action or forbearance by another and estoppel requires enforcing the promise to prevent injustice. Id. at 133. There, the plaintiff never signed the agreement to purchase the newly constructed home but claimed the authority of the agreement in directing the construction and repair of the home, submitted reimbursement claims for expenses incurred during repairs, and conducted settlement negotiations with the builder. Id. We held that these were sufficiently substantial actions demanding the builder comply with the contract to equitably estop the plaintiff from resisting the agreement's arbitration provision. Id.

We must examine here whether the direct benefits estoppel doctrine applies to an arbitration provision in a trust. A beneficiary may disclaim an interest in a trust. See Texas Property Code § 112.010; see also Aberg v. First Nat'l Bank, 450 S.W.2d 403, 407 (Tex. App.–Dallas 1970, writ ref'd n.r.e.) (stating the well-settled rule that a trust beneficiary who has not manifested his acceptance of a beneficial interest may disclaim such interest). And a beneficiary is also free to challenge the validity of a trust: conduct that is incompatible with the idea that she has consented to the instrument. See Rapid Settlements, Ltd. v. SSC Settlements, LLC, 251 S.W.3d 129, 148 (Tex. App.–Tyler 2008, no pet.) (holding direct benefits estoppel inapplicable when a nonsignatory filed suit for a declaration that an arbitration agreement was not binding on it). Thus, beneficiaries have the opportunity to opt out of the arrangement proposed by the settlor.

On the other hand, a beneficiary who attempts to enforce rights that would not exist without the trust manifests her assent to the trust's arbitration clause. For example, a beneficiary who brings a claim for breach of fiduciary duty seeks to hold the trustee to her obligations under the instrument and thus has acquiesced to its other provisions, including its arbitration clause. In such circumstances, it would be incongruent to allow a beneficiary to hold a trustee to the terms of the trust but not hold the beneficiary to those same terms.

Here, Reitz both sought the benefits granted to him under the trust and sued to enforce the provisions of the trust. On the death of the settlor, Reitz did not disclaim an interest in the trust, and his suit directly seeks actual damages for any amounts inappropriately taken from the trust. See Texas Property Code § 112.010 (presuming a beneficiary accepts an interest in a trust and establishing time period to disclaim that interest). Reitz also sued to enforce the trust's provisions against the trustee. The trust specifically prohibited the trustee from making "any distribution to or for the benefit of himself which is not subject to an ascertainable standard under the Code" and contained a number of other powers of and restrictions on the trustee. Reitz claimed Rachal "has materially violated the terms of the Trust and his fiduciary duty by failing to account to the beneficiary and . . . has materially violated th[e] terms of the Trust by his conversion of the Trust assets which has resulted in material financial loss to the Trust." Reitz further claimed, among other things, he was "entitled to any profits that would accrue to the trust estate if there had been no breach of trust." In accepting the benefits of the trust and suing to enforce its terms against the trustee so as to recover damages, Reitz's conduct indicated acceptance of the terms and validity of the trust.[26] In sum, we hold the doctrine of direct benefits estoppel applies to bar Reitz's claim that the arbitration provision in the trust is invalid. See *Weekley Homes,* 180 S.W.3d at 131–32; *Kellogg Brown & Root,* 166 S.W.3d at 739–40; *FirstMerit Bank,* 52 S.W.3d at 755–56.

Reitz argues, however, that direct benefits estoppel cannot apply here because there is no underlying contract. We have generally applied direct benefits estoppel when there is an underlying contract the claimant did not sign, but we have never held a formal contract is required for direct benefits estoppel to apply. Indeed, in *Weekley Homes,* we likened direct benefits estoppel to the defensive theory of promissory estoppel. 180 S.W.3d at 133. "[T]he promissory-estoppel doctrine presumes no contract exists." Subaru of Am., Inc. v. David McDavid Nissan, Inc., 84 S.W.3d 212, 226 (Tex. 2002) (citing Wheeler v. White, 398 S.W.2d 93, 96–97 (Tex. 1965)); see also Restatement (Second) of Contracts § 90 & ch. 4, topic 2, intro. note (1981) (addressing promissory estoppel as one of several types of contracts that need not be supported by consideration to be enforceable). As equitable defensive theories, direct benefits estoppel and promissory estoppel promote fairness by holding a party to its position in the performance of an agreement or in bringing litigation. See *Weekley Homes,* 180 S.W.3d at 133; *Kellogg Brown & Root,* 166 S.W.3d at 740–41; *FirstMerit Bank,* 52 S.W.3d at 755.

---

[26] Although we specified in *Kellogg Brown & Root* that claims are only subject to arbitration if they are based on the agreement containing the arbitration provision, the parties do not dispute here that the claims refer to and depend upon the trust. 166 S.W.3d at 739–40.

A valid, underlying contract is not required under these theories, nor is it required here; thus, Reitz's argument is without merit. See *Subaru of Am.,* 84 S.W.3d at 226.[27]

3. Other Jurisdictions

Reitz points to the holdings of two courts in sister states that support his view that arbitration provisions in trusts are unenforceable. There is a dearth of authority as to the validity of an arbitration provision in a trust, and the opinions Reitz relies on have been superseded. The two courts—both intermediate courts—that considered this precise issue declined to enforce mandatory arbitration provisions in trusts. See Diaz v. Bukey, 125 Cal. Rptr. 3d 610, 615 (Ct. App. 2011), pet. granted, 257 P.3d 1129 (Cal. 2011), remanded with directions, 287 P.3d 67 (Cal. 2012); Schoneberger v. Oelze, 96 P.3d 1078, 1079 (Ariz. Ct. App. 2004), superseded by statute, Arizona Revised Statutes § 14–10205. These courts generally concluded that a trust's arbitration provision is not enforceable because a trust is not a contract between the grantor, trustee, and beneficiary and thus does not bind those who do no sign the instrument to arbitrate future trust disputes. This bright-line distinction between trusts and contracts was first discussed in *Schoneberger,* where an Arizona court of appeals explained:

> Arbitration rests on an exchange of promises. Parties to a contract may decide to exchange promises to substitute an arbitral for a judicial forum . . . . In contrast, a trust does not rest on an exchange of promises. A trust merely requires a trustor to transfer a beneficial interest in property to a trustee who, under the trust instrument . . . holds that interest for the beneficiary. The undertaking between trustor and trustee does not stem from the premise of mutual assent to an exchange of promises and is not properly characterized as contractual.

96 P.3d at 1083 (internal citations and quotations omitted). A California intermediate court later adopted the Arizona court's explication. *Diaz,* 125 Cal. Rptr. 3d at 615. The court of appeals here followed the analysis in *Schoneberger.* 347 S.W.3d at 310–11.

But the Arizona Legislature superseded *Schoneberger* and the California Supreme Court vacated *Diaz.* Unlike the TAA's requirement that the arbitration provision be in an "agreement," the Arizona statute at issue in *Schoneberger* required the arbitration provision to be "in a written contract."[8] 96 P.3d at 1082. The Arizona Legislature superseded *Schoneberger,* providing that: "A trust instrument may provide mandatory, exclusive and reasonable procedures to resolve issues between the trustee and interested persons or among interested persons with regard to the administration or distribution of the trust." Arizona Revised Statutes § 14–10205.[9]

---

[27] Reitz has not asserted, and we thus need not decide, whether the doctrine of unclean hands bars Rachal from relying on the equitable doctrine of direct benefits estoppel.

A California appellate court followed *Schoneberger* in refusing to enforce an arbitration provision in a trust. The California statute at issue, like the Texas statute, addresses arbitration provisions in "written agreements." California Civil Procedure Code § 1281.1 ("[A]ny request to arbitrate . . . shall be considered as made pursuant to a written agreement to submit a controversy to arbitration."). The California Supreme Court instructed the court of appeals to vacate its decision and reconsider the case in light of Pinnacle Museum Tower Association v. Pinnacle Market Development (US), LLC, 282 P.3d 1217 (Cal. 2012). Diaz v. Bukey, 287 P.3d 67, 67 (Cal. 2012). In *Pinnacle,* a condominium developer included a mandatory arbitration provision in the recorded declaration of restrictions, which also provided for the creation of an owners' association. Id. at 1221–22. The association sued the developer for construction defects, and the developer moved to compel arbitration based on the provision in the declaration of restrictions. Id. at 1223. The California Supreme Court held that the Federal Arbitration Act applied to the provision in question, which refers to arbitration provisions "in . . . a contract." Id. (quoting 9 U.S.C. § 2). The court held that the recorded declaration was contractual in nature, despite the fact that the individual owners—not the owners' association—agreed to be bound by the declaration, and that enforcing the arbitration provision against the owners' association was not unconscionable. Id. at 1228–29, 1233–34. The court of appeals has yet to issue its new opinion in light of *Pinnacle.*

We note that other courts, while not addressing the precise issue raised here, have nonetheless favorably viewed arbitration provisions in trusts. See, e.g., Radian Ins., Inc. v. Deutsche Bank Nat'l Trust Co., 638 F. Supp .2d 443, 458 (E.D. Pa. 2009) (remanding a trust dispute involving a rescission claim to arbitration while retaining jurisdiction over questions of interpretation that arise during the arbitration); Roehl v. Ritchie, 54 Cal. Rptr. 3d 185, 187 (Ct. App. 2007) (determining that judicial confirmation of an open-ended arbitration award in a trust dispute did not bar a subsequent arbitration to resolve undetermined issues); see also New S. Fed. Sav. Bank v. Anding, 414 F. Supp. 2d 636, 643 (S.D. Miss. 2005) (noting that an arbitration provision in deed of trust is "not unenforceable solely because it is one-sided").

C. Scope

Having determined the arbitration provision at issue is enforceable against Reitz, Rachal must also establish that the dispute is within the scope of the agreement. *Meyer,* 211 S.W.3d at 305. Once a valid arbitration agreement is established, a "strong presumption favoring arbitration arises" and we resolve doubts as to the agreement's scope in favor of arbitration. Ellis v. Schlimmer, 337 S.W.3d 860, 862 (Tex. 2011). Reitz asserts that his lawsuit falls outside the scope of the agreement because the trust's terms indicate the settlor's intent to exempt trustee misconduct claims from the scope of the arbitration provision. We disagree.

When determining whether claims fall within the scope of the arbitration agreement, we look to the factual allegations, not the legal claims. *FirstMerit Bank,* 52 S.W.3d at 754. The arbitration provision here requires that:

> Despite anything herein to the contrary, I intend that as to any dispute of any kind involving this Trust or any of the parties or persons concerned herewith (e.g., beneficiaries, Trustees), arbitration as provided herein shall be the sole and exclusive remedy, and no legal proceedings shall be allowed or given effect except as they may relate to enforcing or implementing such arbitration in accordance herewith.

Reitz's suit against Rachal to enforce the trust's restrictions qualifies as "any dispute of any kind involving this Trust or any of the parties or persons connected herewith."

Reitz nonetheless argues that a subsequent provision in the trust regarding exoneration of trustees indicates an intent to allow for litigation of disputes with the trustee. The provision Reitz relies on refers to a trustee's liability for unintentional misconduct and permits the trustee to fund litigation or dispute related costs from the trust, providing that a beneficiary who initiates the proceedings without good faith shall have the defense costs deducted from his share of the trust income and assets. This provision does not defeat the arbitration requirement for two reasons. First, to the extent the two provisions conflict, the arbitration provision—by its own terms—prevails over "anything herein to the contrary." Second, the trustee exoneration provision, when read in conjunction with the arbitration provision, still has meaning. Even if the arbitration provision requires that all disputes over the trust be resolved in arbitration, the trustee exoneration provision is effective in at least two situations: (1) when a claim filed in court is then sent to arbitration, and (2) when a claim is filed in, and stays in, court because direct benefits estoppel or another doctrine that would compel arbitration does not apply. Under the first scenario, the trustee exoneration provision simply acknowledges that some claims that belong in arbitration will be initiated in court and determines how these defense costs are paid. Under the second scenario, not all claims initiated in court can be compelled to arbitration. We previously noted that the doctrine of direct benefits estoppel will not provide the mutual assent necessary to compel arbitration in all circumstances. One who does not accept benefits under a trust and contests its validity could not be compelled to arbitrate the trust dispute under the doctrine of direct benefits estoppel. In such a case, the trustee exoneration provision determines how these defense costs are paid. Our construction of the arbitration and trustee exoneration privileges gives meaning to both provisions. Universal C.I.T. Credit Corp. v. Daniel, 243 S.W.2d 154, 158 (Tex. 1951). In sum, Rachal demonstrated the existence of a valid arbitration agreement that covers the claims at issue.

III. Conclusion

Beneficiary Reitz sued trustee Rachal to require him to comply with the terms of the trust at issue, which contains an arbitration provision. The TAA requires arbitration provisions to be in written agreements. Reitz's assent to the trust is reflected in his acceptance of the benefits of the trust and his suit to compel the trustee to comply with the trust's terms. Reitz's claims that Rachal violated the terms of the trust are within the scope of the arbitration provision, which requires the arbitration of "any dispute of any kind involving this Trust." Thus,

Rachal carried his burden of demonstrating that the trust contains a valid arbitration agreement that covers Reitz's claims. We reverse the judgment of the court of appeals and remand to the trial court to enter an order consistent with this opinion.

Property Code § 113.029. Discretionary Powers; Tax Savings

(a) Notwithstanding the breadth of discretion granted to a trustee in the terms of the trust, including the use of terms such as "absolute," "sole," or "uncontrolled," the trustee shall exercise a discretionary power in good faith and in accordance with the terms and purposes of the trust and the interests of the beneficiaries.

(b) Subject to Subsection (d), and unless the terms of the trust expressly indicate that a requirement provided by this subsection does not apply:

> (1) a person, other than a settlor, who is a beneficiary and trustee, trustee affiliate, or discretionary power holder of a trust that confers on the trustee a power to make discretionary distributions to or for the trustee's, the trustee affiliate's, or the discretionary power holder's personal benefit may exercise the power only in accordance with an ascertainable standard relating to the trustee's, the trustee affiliate's, or the discretionary power holder's individual health, education, support, or maintenance within the meaning of Section 2041(b)(1)(A) or 2514(c)(1), Internal Revenue Code of 1986; and
>
> (2) a trustee may not exercise a power to make discretionary distributions to satisfy a legal obligation of support that the trustee personally owes another person.

(c) A power the exercise of which is limited or prohibited by Subsection (b) may be exercised by a majority of the remaining trustees whose exercise of the power is not limited or prohibited by Subsection (b). If the power of all trustees is limited or prohibited by Subsection (b), the court may appoint a special fiduciary with authority to exercise the power.

(d) Subsection (b) does not apply to:

> (1) a power held by the settlor's spouse who is the trustee of a trust for which a marital deduction, as defined by Section 2056(b)(5) or 2523(e), Internal Revenue Code of 1986, was previously allowed;
>
> (2) any trust during any period that the trust may be revoked or amended by its settlor; or

(3) a trust if contributions to the trust qualify for the annual exclusion under Section 2503(c), Internal Revenue Code of 1986.

(e) In this section, "discretionary power holder" means a person who has the sole power or power shared with another person to make discretionary decisions on behalf of a trustee with respect to distributions from a trust.

Property Code § 114.007. Exculpation of Trustee

(a) A term of a trust relieving a trustee of liability for breach of trust is unenforceable to the extent that the term relieves a trustee of liability for:

(1) a breach of trust committed:

(A) in bad faith;

(B) intentionally; or

(C) with reckless indifference to the interest of a beneficiary; or

(2) any profit derived by the trustee from a breach of trust.

(b) A term in a trust instrument relieving the trustee of liability for a breach of trust is ineffective to the extent that the term is inserted in the trust instrument as a result of an abuse by the trustee of a fiduciary duty to or confidential relationship with the settlor.

(c) This section applies only to a term of a trust that may otherwise relieve a trustee from liability for a breach of trust. Except as provided in Section 111.0035, this section does not prohibit the settlor, by the terms of the trust, from expressly:

(1) relieving the trustee from a duty or restriction imposed by this subtitle or by common law; or

(2) directing or permitting the trustee to do or not to do an action that would otherwise violate a duty or restriction imposed by this subtitle or by common law.

Section G. The Duty to Inform and Account

Property Code § 113.151. Demand for Accounting

(a) A beneficiary by written demand may request the trustee to deliver to each beneficiary of the trust a written statement of accounts covering all transactions since the last accounting or since the creation of the trust, whichever is later. If the trustee fails or refuses to deliver the statement on or before the 90th day after the date the trustee receives the demand or after a longer period ordered by a court, any beneficiary of the trust may file suit to compel the trustee to deliver the statement to all beneficiaries of the trust. The court may require the trustee to deliver a written statement of account to all beneficiaries on finding that the nature of the beneficiary's interest in the trust or the effect of the administration of the trust on the beneficiary's interest is sufficient to require an accounting by the trustee. However, the trustee is not obligated or required to account to the beneficiaries of a trust more frequently than once every 12 months unless a more frequent accounting is required by the court. If a beneficiary is successful in the suit to compel a statement under this section, the court may, in its discretion, award all or part of the costs of court and all of the suing beneficiary's reasonable and necessary attorney's fees and costs against the trustee in the trustee's individual capacity or in the trustee's capacity as trustee.

(b) An interested person may file suit to compel the trustee to account to the interested person. The court may require the trustee to deliver a written statement of account to the interested person on finding that the nature of the interest in the trust of, the claim against the trust by, or the effect of the administration of the trust on the interested person is sufficient to require an accounting by the trustee.

Property Code § 113.152. Contents of Accounting

A written statement of accounts shall show:

(1) all trust property that has come to the trustee's knowledge or into the trustee's possession and that has not been previously listed or inventoried as property of the trust;

(2) a complete account of receipts, disbursements, and other transactions regarding the trust property for the period covered by the account, including their source and nature, with receipts of principal and income shown separately;

(3) a listing of all property being administered, with an adequate description of each asset;

(4) the cash balance on hand and the name and location of the depository where the balance is kept; and

(5) all known liabilities owed by the trust.

Communications between the trustee and his attorney are protected from disclosure to beneficiaries

HUIE v. DeSHAZO

Supreme Court of Texas
922 S.W.2d 920 (1995)

PHILLIPS, C.J. The issue presented in this original mandamus proceeding is whether the attorney-client privilege protects communications between a trustee and his or her attorney relating to trust administration from discovery by a trust beneficiary. We hold that, notwithstanding the trustee's fiduciary duty to the beneficiary, only the trustee, not the trust beneficiary, is the client of the trustee's attorney. The beneficiary therefore may not discover communications between the trustee and attorney otherwise protected under Texas Rule of Civil Evidence 503. Because the trial court ruled otherwise, we conditionally grant writ of mandamus.

I

Harvey K. Huie, the relator, is the executor of the estate of his deceased wife, who died in 1980. Huie is also the trustee of three separate testamentary trusts created under his wife's will for the primary benefit of the Huies' three daughters. One of the daughters, Melissa Huie Chenault, filed the underlying suit against Huie in February 1993 for breach of fiduciary duties relating to her trust.[28] Chenault claims that Huie mismanaged the trust, engaged in self-dealing, diverted business opportunities from the trust, and commingled and converted trust property. Huie's other two daughters have not joined in the lawsuit.

Chenault noticed the deposition of Huie's lawyer, David Ringer, who has represented Huie in his capacity as executor and trustee since Mrs. Huie's death. Ringer has also represented Huie in many other matters unrelated to the trusts and estate during that period. Before Chenault filed suit, Ringer was compensated from trust and estate funds for his fiduciary representation. Since the suit, however, Huie has personally compensated Ringer for all work.

Although Ringer appeared for deposition, he refused to answer questions about the management and business dealings of the trust, claiming the attorney-client and attorney-work-product privileges. Chenault subsequently moved to compel responses, and Huie moved for a protective order. After an evidentiary hearing, the trial court held that the attorney-client privilege did not prevent beneficiaries of the trust from discovering pre-lawsuit communications between Huie and Ringer relating to the trust. The court's order, signed July 19, 1995, does not cite to any of the exceptions under Texas Rule of Civil

---

[28] Chenault sued individually, as next friend of her minor daughter, and as next friend of her minor niece, who is under Chenault's conservatorship. Chenault also named several business associates of Huie as additional defendants.

Evidence 503 or otherwise disclose the court's rationale.[29] The court held that the attorney-client privilege protected only communications made under the following circumstances: 1) a litigious dispute existed between Chenault and Huie; 2) Huie obtained legal advice to protect himself against charges of misconduct; and 3) Huie paid for the legal counsel without reimbursement from the estate or trust. The court accordingly ordered Ringer to answer questions relating to events before February 1993, when suit was filed and Huie began personally compensating Ringer. The court also held that the attorney-work-product privilege did not apply to communications made before Chenault filed suit, again without stating its reasoning.

The court of appeals, after granting Huie's motion for leave to file petition for writ of mandamus, subsequently vacated that order as improvidently granted, denying relief. After Huie sought mandamus relief from this Court, we stayed Ringer's deposition pending our consideration of the merits.

II

The attorney-client privilege protects from disclosure confidential communications between a client and his or her attorney "made for the purpose of facilitating the rendition of professional legal services to the client. . . ." Texas Rule of Civil Evidence 503(b). This privilege allows "unrestrained communication and contact between an attorney and client in all matters in which the attorney's professional advice or services are sought, without fear that these confidential communications will be disclosed by the attorney, voluntarily or involuntarily, in any legal proceeding." West v. Solito, 563 S.W.2d 240, 245 (Tex. 1978). The privilege thus "promote[s] effective legal services," which "in turn promotes the broader societal interest of the effective administration of justice." Republic Ins. Co. v. Davis, 856 S.W.2d 158, 160 (Tex. 1993).

The Texas Trust Code provides that "[a] trustee may employ attorneys . . . reasonably necessary in the administration of the trust estate." Texas Property Code § 113.018. Chenault does not dispute that Huie employed Ringer to assist Huie in the administration of the Chenault trust. Indeed, Chenault does not seriously dispute that an attorney-client relationship existed between Huie and Ringer about trust matters.[30] Further, Rule 503 contains no exception to the privilege for fiduciaries and their counsel. Chenault nonetheless contends that communications between Huie and Ringer regarding trust matters cannot be privileged as to Chenault, a trust beneficiary, even if the elements of Rule 503 are

[29] The trial court initially relied on Texas Rule of Civil Evidence 503(d)(5), which creates an exception to the attorney-client privilege as between joint clients of an attorney regarding matters of common interest to the clients. The court, however, later amended its order to delete this reference.

[30] Chenault argues for the first time in a post-submission brief that Ringer represented the trust itself as an entity, rather than Huie as trustee. This argument is addressed in section III-B below.

otherwise met. Chenault's primary argument is that Huie's fiduciary duty of disclosure overrides any attorney-client privilege that might otherwise apply.

Trustees and executors owe beneficiaries "a fiduciary duty of full disclosure of all material facts known to them that might affect [the beneficiaries'] rights." Montgomery v. Kennedy, 669 S.W.2d 309, 313 (Tex. 1984). See also Texas Property Code § 113.151(a) (requiring trustee to account to beneficiaries for all trust transactions). This duty exists independently of the rules of discovery, applying even if no litigious dispute exists between the trustee and beneficiaries.

Chenault argues that the trustee's duty of disclosure extends to any communications between the trustee and the trustee's attorney. The fiduciary's affairs are the beneficiaries' affairs, according to Chenault, and thus the beneficiaries are entitled to know every aspect of Huie's conduct as trustee, including his communications with Ringer. We disagree.

The trustee's duty of full disclosure extends to all *material facts* affecting the beneficiaries' rights. Applying the attorney-client privilege does not limit this duty. In Texas, the attorney-client privilege protects confidential communications between a client and attorney made for the purpose of facilitating the rendition of professional legal services to the client. See Texas Rule of Civil Evidence 503(b). While the privilege extends to the entire communication, including facts contained therein, See GAF Corp. v. Caldwell, 839 S.W.2d 149, 151 (Tex. App.-Houston [14th Dist.] 1992, orig. proceeding); 1 Steven Goode et al., Texas Practice: Guide to the Texas Rules of Evidence: Civil and Criminal, § 503.5 n. 15 (1993), a person cannot cloak a material fact with the privilege merely by communicating it to an attorney. See, e.g., National Tank Co. v. Brotherton, 851 S.W.2d 193, 199 (Tex. 1993).

This distinction may be illustrated by the following hypothetical example: Assume that a trustee who has misappropriated money from a trust confidentially reveals this fact to his or her attorney for the purpose of obtaining legal advice. The trustee, when asked at trial whether he or she misappropriated money, cannot claim the attorney-client privilege. The act of misappropriation is a material fact of which the trustee has knowledge independently of the communication. The trustee must therefore disclose the fact (assuming no other privilege applies), even though the trustee confidentially conveyed the fact to the attorney. However, because the attorney's only knowledge of the misappropriation is through the confidential communication, the attorney cannot be called on to reveal this information.

Our holding, therefore, in no way affects Huie's duty to disclose all material facts and to provide a full trust accounting to Chenault, even as to information conveyed to Ringer. In the underlying litigation, Chenault may depose Huie and question him fully regarding his handling of trust property and other factual matters involving the trust. Moreover, the attorney-client privilege does not bar Ringer from testifying about factual matters involving the trust, as long as he is not called on to reveal confidential attorney-client communications.

The *communications* between Ringer and Huie made confidentially and for the purpose of facilitating legal services are protected. The attorney-client privilege serves the same important purpose in the trustee-attorney relationship as it does in other attorney-client relationships. A trustee must be able to consult freely with his or her attorney to obtain the best possible legal guidance. Without the privilege, trustees might be inclined to forsake legal advice, thus adversely affecting the trust, as disappointed beneficiaries could later pore over the attorney-client communications in second-guessing the trustee's actions. Alternatively, trustees might feel compelled to blindly follow counsel's advice, ignoring their own judgment and experience. . . .

Chenault . . . relies on a study by the Section of Real Property, Probate and Trust Law of the American Bar Association, entitled *Report of the Special Study Committee on Professional Responsibility—Counselling the Fiduciary.* See 28 Real Prop., Prob. & Tr. J. 823 (1994). This study concludes that, while counsel retained by a fiduciary ordinarily represents only the fiduciary, the counsel should be allowed to disclose confidential communications relating to trust administration to the beneficiaries. Id. at 849-850. The study reasoned as follows:

> The fiduciary's duty is to administer the estate or trust for the benefit of the beneficiaries. A lawyer whose assignment is to provide assistance to the fiduciary during administration is also working, in tandem with the fiduciary, for the benefit of the beneficiaries, and the lawyer has the discretion to reveal such information to the beneficiaries, if necessary to protect the trust estate. The interests of the beneficiaries should not be compromised by a barrier of confidentiality.

Id. Several English common-law cases, and treatises citing those cases, also support this view. See, e.g., In re Mason, 22 Ch.D. 609 (1883); Talbot v. Marshfield, 2 Dr. & Sm. 549 (1865); Wynne v. Humbertson, 27 Beav. 421 (1858). See also Bogart, The Law of Trusts and Trustees, § 961 (2nd ed. 1983); Scott, The Law of Trusts, § 173 (3rd ed. 1967).

We decline to adopt this approach. We find the countervailing arguments supporting application of the privilege, discussed previously, more persuasive. Moreover, Rule 503 contains no exception applicable to fiduciaries and their attorneys. If the special role of a fiduciary does justify such an exception, it should be instituted as an amendment to Rule 503 through the rulemaking process. Ringer testified that he had the "fullest expectation" that his communications with Huie would be privileged. This expectation was justified considering the express language of Rule 503 protecting confidential attorney-client communications. We should not thwart such legitimate expectations by retroactively amending the rule through judicial decision.

We thus hold that, while a trustee must fully disclose material facts regarding the administration of the trust, the attorney-client privilege protects confidential communications between the trustee and his or her attorney under Rule 503.[31]

III

A

We also reject the notion that the attorney-client privilege does not apply because there was no true attorney-client relationship between Huie and Ringer. This argument finds support in some other jurisdictions, where courts have held that an attorney advising a trustee in connection with the trustee's fiduciary duties in fact represents the trust beneficiaries. Accordingly, the trustee has no privilege to withhold confidential communications from the beneficiaries. . . .

We conclude that, under Texas law at least, the trustee who retains an attorney to advise him or her in administering the trust is the real client, not the trust beneficiaries. See Thompson v. Vinson & Elkins, 859 S.W.2d 617 (Tex. App.-Houston [1st Dist.] 1993, writ denied) (beneficiary lacked standing to sue trustee's attorney for malpractice, as no attorney-client relationship existed between them). "Client" is defined under Rule 503 as

> a person, public officer, or corporation, association, or other organization or entity, either public or private, who is rendered professional legal services by a lawyer, or who consults a lawyer with a view to obtaining professional legal services from him.

Texas Rule of Civil Evidence 503(a)(1). It is the trustee who is empowered to hire and consult with the attorney and to act on the attorney's advice. While Huie owes fiduciary duties to Chenault as her trustee, he did not retain Ringer to represent Chenault, but to represent himself in carrying out his fiduciary duties. Ringer testified, for example, that he has "never given any legal advice to Mrs. Chenault," and in fact had only seen her on a few isolated occasions. It would strain reality to hold that a trust beneficiary, who has no direct professional relationship with the trustee's attorney, is the real client. See In re Prudence-Bonds Corp., 76 F. Supp. 643 (E.D.N.Y. 1948); Shannon v. Superior Court, 217 Cal. App. 3d 986, 266 Cal. Rptr. 242, 246 (1990). We thus hold that Huie, rather than Chenault, was Ringer's client for purposes of the attorney-client privilege.

---

[31] Chenault also argues that Huie, by accepting the appointment as trustee with knowledge of his duty of disclosure, impliedly waived the protection of the attorney-client privilege. Because we conclude that a trustee does not violate the duty of full disclosure by invoking the attorney-client privilege, we reject this waiver argument.

B

Chenault also advances an argument on post-submission brief to this Court that the *trust* itself was Ringer's real client. This approach, however, is inconsistent with the law of trusts. Mrs. Huie created the testamentary trusts by devising property to *Huie* as trustee. See Texas Property Code § 112.001(3). It is Huie that holds the trust property for the benefit of Chenault, and it is Huie that is authorized to hire counsel. See Texas Property Code § 113.018. The term "trust" refers not to a separate legal entity but rather to the *fiduciary relationship* governing the trustee with respect to the trust property. See Texas Property Code § 111.004. Ringer thus represented Huie in his capacity as trustee, not the "trust" as an entity.

IV

Chenault also argues that communications between Ringer and Huie should be disclosed under the crime-fraud exception to the attorney-client privilege. See Texas Rule of Civil Evidence 503(d)(1). Chenault does not argue that the alleged breaches of trust for which she is suing are crimes or fraud within this exception; rather, she contends that the failure to disclose communications in and of itself is fraud. Because we have held that the trustee's invocation of the attorney-client privilege does not violate his or her duty of full disclosure, we find Chenault's crime-fraud argument to be without merit.

V

A

The party resisting discovery bears the burden of proving any applicable privilege. See State v. Lowry, 802 S.W.2d 669, 671 (Tex. 1991). Chenault argues that even if the attorney-client privilege is otherwise available, Huie failed to carry his evidentiary burden to establish its applicability in this case. . . .

The trial court's ruling is based on its conclusion that the attorney-client privilege does not apply to any pre-litigation communications between a trustee and the trustee's attorney, a contention we have rejected. In light of this holding, we believe the trial court should have an opportunity to consider, in the first instance, whether Huie has carried his evidentiary burden as to each of the certified questions for which Ringer claimed, on Huie's behalf, the attorney-client privilege. The court may, in its discretion, receive further evidence from the parties.

B

Chenault further argues that many of the certified questions relate to federal tax returns filed by the estate. Relying on cases interpreting the federal attorney-client privilege, she contends that the privilege does not apply when an attorney is employed to prepare tax returns, as the attorney is primarily performing accounting, rather than legal, services. . . . The attorney-client privilege embodied in Rule 503 requires that the communication be "made for the purpose of facilitating the rendition of professional legal services to the client. . . ." The trial court, in considering whether Huie has met his evidentiary burden, should in the first instance determine whether this element is satisfied as to each of the certified questions.

VI

The trial court also overruled Huie's attorney-work-product objections as to communications made before the date Chenault filed suit. Huie contends that the work-product privilege protects communications made after 1988, the time when he contends that he anticipated litigation.

An attorney's "work product" refers to "specific documents, reports, communications, memoranda, mental impressions, conclusions, opinions, or legal theories, prepared and assembled in actual anticipation of litigation or for trial." National Tank Co. v. Brotherton, 851 S.W.2d 193, 200 (Tex. 1993). The trial court did not rule on Huie's claims of work-product privilege independently of his claims of attorney-client privilege; rather, the court summarily overruled both of these claims as to all pre-litigation communications. It thus appears that the trial court concluded, as it did for the attorney-client privilege, that the work-product privilege simply does not apply in the fiduciary-attorney relationship prior to the time suit is actually filed.

We disagree with this conclusion. The policy reasons supporting the attorney-client privilege in the context of the fiduciary-attorney relationship support even more strongly the work-product privilege, as the latter protects the confidentiality of work prepared in anticipation of litigation. There can be little dispute that a fiduciary must be allowed some measure of confidentiality in defending against an anticipated suit for breach of fiduciary duty. Further, we do not believe it is determinative that Ringer was compensated from trust funds, rather than by Huie personally, before Chenault filed suit. The determinative factor for the work-product privilege is instead whether litigation was anticipated. While we express no opinion on whether it was *proper* for Ringer to be compensated from trust funds for any work that may have been done in anticipation of litigation, we hold that any such impropriety would not abrogate the work-product privilege. See Lasky, Haas, Cohler & Munter v. Superior Court, 172 Cal. App. 3d 264, 218 Cal. Rptr. 205 (1985) (public policy underlying full disclosure by trustee does not overcome work-product privilege, even where attorney is compensated from trust corpus).

Because the trial court concluded that the work-product privilege did not apply to materials or communications generated prior to the time suit was filed and Huie began personally compensating Ringer, it appears that the court never reached the issue of when Huie anticipated litigation. The court should therefore reconsider Huie's work-product objections in accordance with this opinion.

VII

Chenault argues that because the legal question confronting the trial court was an issue of first impression in Texas, the court could not have "abused its discretion" in resolving the issue, and thus mandamus relief is inappropriate. We disagree. "A trial court has no 'discretion' in determining what the law is or applying the law to the facts." Walker v. Packer, 827 S.W.2d 833, 840 (Tex. 1992). Consequently, the trial court's erroneous legal conclusion, even in an unsettled area of law, is an abuse of discretion. See Lunsford v. Morris, 746 S.W.2d 471 (Tex. 1988). Moreover, because the trial court's order compels the disclosure of potentially privileged information, Huie lacks an adequate remedy by appeal. See *Walker*, 827 S.W.2d at 843.

We therefore conditionally grant the writ of mandamus and direct the trial court to vacate its July 19, 1995, discovery order. The trial court shall reconsider Huie's claims of attorney-client and attorney-work-product privilege in accordance with this opinion. The court may in its discretion receive additional evidence from the parties.

Chapter 10. Trusts: Alienation and Modification

Section A. Spendthrift Trusts

Property Code § 112.035. Spendthrift Trusts

(a) A settlor may provide in the terms of the trust that the interest of a beneficiary in the income or in the principal or in both may not be voluntarily or involuntarily transferred before payment or delivery of the interest to the beneficiary by the trustee.

(b) A declaration in a trust instrument that the interest of a beneficiary shall be held subject to a "spendthrift trust" is sufficient to restrain voluntary or involuntary alienation of the interest by a beneficiary to the maximum extent permitted by this subtitle.

(c) A trust containing terms authorized under Subsection (a) or (b) of this section may be referred to as a spendthrift trust.

(d) If the settlor is also a beneficiary of the trust, a provision restraining the voluntary or involuntary transfer of the settlor's beneficial interest does not prevent the settlor's creditors from satisfying claims from the settlor's interest in the trust estate. A settlor is not considered a beneficiary of a trust solely because:

> (1) a trustee who is not the settlor is authorized under the trust instrument to pay or reimburse the settlor for, or pay directly to the taxing authorities, any tax on trust income or principal that is payable by the settlor under the law imposing the tax; or
>
> (2) the settlor's interest in the trust was created by the exercise of a power of appointment by a third party.

(e) A beneficiary of the trust may not be considered a settlor merely because of a lapse, waiver, or release of:

> (1) a power described by Subsection (f); or
>
> (2) the beneficiary's right to withdraw a part of the trust property to the extent that the value of the property affected by the lapse, waiver, or release in any calendar year does not exceed the greater of the amount specified in:
>
> > (A) Section 2041(b)(2) or 2514(e), Internal Revenue Code of 1986; or

(B) Section 2503(b), Internal Revenue Code of 1986.

(f) A beneficiary of the trust may not be considered to be a settlor, to have made a voluntary or involuntary transfer of the beneficiary's interest in the trust, or to have the power to make a voluntary or involuntary transfer of the beneficiary's interest in the trust, merely because the beneficiary, in any capacity, holds or exercises:

(1) a presently exercisable power to:

(A) consume, invade, appropriate, or distribute property to or for the benefit of the beneficiary, if the power is:

(i) exercisable only on consent of another person holding an interest adverse to the beneficiary's interest; or

(ii) limited by an ascertainable standard, including health, education, support, or maintenance of the beneficiary; or

(B) appoint any property of the trust to or for the benefit of a person other than the beneficiary, a creditor of the beneficiary, the beneficiary's estate, or a creditor of the beneficiary's estate;

(2) a testamentary power of appointment; or

(3) a presently exercisable right described by Subsection (e)(2).

(g) For the purposes of this section, property contributed to the following trusts is not considered to have been contributed by the settlor, and a person who would otherwise be treated as a settlor or a deemed settlor of the following trusts may not be treated as a settlor:

(1) an irrevocable inter vivos marital trust if:

(A) the settlor is a beneficiary of the trust after the death of the settlor's spouse; and

(B) the trust is treated as:

(i) qualified terminable interest property under Section 2523(f), Internal Revenue Code of 1986; or

(ii) a general power of appointment trust under Section 2523(e), Internal Revenue Code of 1986;

(2) an irrevocable inter vivos trust for the settlor's spouse if the settlor is a beneficiary of the trust after the death of the settlor's spouse; or

(3) an irrevocable trust for the benefit of a person:

(A) if the settlor is the person's spouse, regardless of whether or when the person was the settlor of an irrevocable trust for the benefit of that spouse; or

(B) to the extent that the property of the trust was subject to a general power of appointment in another person.

(h) For the purposes of Subsection (g), a person is a beneficiary whether named a beneficiary:

(1) under the initial trust instrument; or

(2) through the exercise of a limited or general power of appointment by:

(A) that person's spouse; or

(B) another person.

Family Code § 154.005. Payments of Support Obligation by Trust

(a) The court may order the trustees of a spendthrift or other trust to make disbursements for the support of a child to the extent the trustees are required to make payments to a beneficiary who is required to make child support payments as provided by this chapter.

(b) If disbursement of the assets of the trust is discretionary, the court may order child support payments from the income of the trust but not from the principal.

Beneficiary, upon termination of trust, may assign interest subject to spendthrift clause

FAULKNER v. BOST
Court of Appeals of Texas, Tyler
137 S.W.3d 254 (2004)

DeVASTO, J. Appellant Cheryl Faulkner ("Faulkner"), Trustee of the Stephen and Hilda Hefner Trust, appeals a summary judgment granted in favor of Appellee, Sharon Tanner Evans Bost ("Bost"), individually and as former trustee of the Hattie M. Tanner Trust. In two issues, Faulkner contends that the trial court erred in granting Bost's motion for summary judgment and denying her own motion for partial summary judgment. We reverse and remand.

BACKGROUND

In 1992, Hilda Hefner ("Hefner") and her husband created a trust, The Stephen F. & Hilda T. Freeman-Hefner Trust ("Hefner Trust"). Hefner named her daughter, Faulkner, as trustee of the Hefner Trust. On April 15, 1993, Hefner assigned any future interests she might inherit from her mother, Hattie M. Tanner ("Tanner"), to Faulkner in her capacity as trustee of the Hefner Trust. In 1994, Tanner conveyed all of her property to Hattie M. Tanner, Trustee of The Hattie M. Tanner Trust ("Tanner Trust"). Tanner created the Tanner Trust for her own benefit until her death. She named her three daughters—Hefner, Bost, and Glenda Murff Todd—as beneficiaries of the trust following her death. In 1998, Tanner appointed Bost as trustee of the Tanner Trust.

Tanner died on June 23, 2001. On July 18, 2002, Hefner executed an affidavit and affirmation of prior conveyance, which provided, in part, as follows:

1. I executed the Stephen F. & Hilda T. Freeman-Hefner Trust (1992) documents as Grantor at the time of its creation on July 19, 1992. I also executed an assignment of all estate or inheritance properties which I might have and/or be thereafter conveyed, whether by instrument and/or operation of law, conveying such properties to the said Hefner Trust on April 15, 1993, above-described. . . . It was my intent on April 15, 1993, that such assignment would include all property, of whatever nature, kind and/or character, whether real, personal and/or mixed, and whether in fee simple, undivided interests, as joint tenants and/or tenants in common, and/or otherwise, which I might own on April 15, 1993, and /or which [I] might later (after April 15, 1993) inherit, and/or might be conveyed to me by any means, including the property of my mother, Hattie Marie McLemore Tanner. . . .

2. At all times since April 15, 1993, I have considered all of the above-described property, including, but not limited to the property conveyed to me by my mother in the Trust mentioned above, I have considered all of said property represented thereby, including, but not limited to, any claims, causes of action, choses in action, and/or any and all other interests to be owned in fee simple absolute and/or otherwise by the Stephen F. & Hilda T. Freeman-Hefner Trust (1992).

3. In the event that it might be determined at any time that I might have retained any property and/or interest which, although assumed by me to have been convey[ed] to the said Stephen F. & Hilda T. Freeman-Hefner Trust (1992), then, and in the event, I do hereby reaffirm, confirm, and convey any such alleged omitted interest of any nature, kind, and/or character to the said Stephen F. & Hilda T. Freeman-Hefner Trust (1992). This conveyance, if any, shall relate back to April 15, 1993, regardless of the date I may be determined to be the owner of and/or entitled to any and/or all such interests.

After Tanner's death, Faulkner requested a full and complete accounting of the Tanner Trust on several occasions. Hefner, as agent for Faulkner, also asked Bost for an accounting several times. Bost refused to comply. After Bost refused a demand for an accounting by Faulkner's attorney, Faulkner filed the suit upon which this appeal is based. In her action against Bost, Faulkner requested a full and complete accounting of the Tanner Trust, a declaratory judgment, attorneys' fees and costs, and damages. The action was filed August 5, 2002.

Bost filed an answer and request for declaratory judgment on October 16, 2002, and a traditional motion for summary judgment on October 22. In response, Faulkner filed a counter motion for a partial summary judgment and a response to Bost's motion. The trial court held a hearing on the motions. In its final judgment, the court granted Bost's motion for summary judgment, finding that:

1. Faulkner is not a beneficiary of the Tanner Trust as a matter of law;

2. Faulkner has no rights to the Tanner Trust; and

3. Faulkner does not have standing to bring suit.

The court also denied Faulkner's motion for partial summary judgment. This appeal followed. . . .

TRUST ADMINISTRATION AND STANDING

A trust is a method used to transfer property. Jameson v. Bain, 693 S.W.2d 676, 680 (Tex. App.-San Antonio 1985, no writ). "[W]hen a valid trust is created, the beneficiaries become the owners of the equitable or beneficial title to the trust property and are considered the real owners." City of Mesquite v. Malouf, 553 S.W.2d 639, 644 (Tex. Civ. App.-Texarkana 1977, writ ref'd n.r.e.). The trustee is merely the depository of the bare legal title. Id. The trustee is vested with legal title and right of possession of the trust property but holds it for the benefit of the beneficiaries, who are vested with equitable title to the trust property. *Jameson*, 693 S.W.2d at 680.

A trustee must administer the trust according to its terms and section 113.051 of the Texas Property Code. Generally, in the absence of any contrary terms in the trust instrument, the trustee shall perform all of the duties imposed on trustees by the common law. Texas Property Code § 113.051. A trustee shall maintain a complete and accurate accounting of the administration of the trust. See Shannon v. Frost Nat'l Bank of San Antonio, 533 S.W.2d 389, 393 (Tex. Civ. App.-San Antonio 1975, writ ref'd n.r.e.).

Standing deals with whether a litigant is the proper person to bring a lawsuit, not whether that party can ultimately prevail on the claims asserted. See Prostok v. Browning, 112 S.W.3d 876, 921-22 (Tex. App.-Dallas, 2003). Standing consists of some interest peculiar to the person. See id. The general test for standing requires that there "(a) shall be a real controversy between the parties, which (b) will be actually determined by the judicial declaration sought." Texas Ass'n of Bus. v. Texas Air Control Bd., 852 S.W.2d 440, 446 (Tex. 1993) (quoting Board of Water Eng'rs v. City of San Antonio, 155 Tex. 111, 114, 283 S.W.2d 722, 724 (1955)). In this case, the Texas Property Code governs who has standing. In Texas, an "interested person" may file suit to compel a trustee to provide an accounting. Texas Property Code § 113.151(b). The court may require the trustee to deliver a written statement of account to the interested person after finding that the nature of the interest in the trust of the interested person is sufficient to require an accounting by the trustee. Id. The Property Code defines "interested person" as "a trustee, beneficiary, *or any other person having an interest in or a claim against the trust or any person who is affected by the administration of the trust.*" Texas Property Code § 111.004(7) (emphasis added).

BOST'S MOTION FOR SUMMARY JUDGMENT

In her first issue, Faulkner contends that the trial court erred in granting Bost's motion for summary judgment. Bost filed a motion for summary judgment asserting that 1) Faulkner has no rights under the Tanner Trust agreement, including the right to bring this suit, and 2) Hefner is estopped to deny that she is a beneficiary. The trial court granted Bost's motion based on standing and did not address estoppel. When the trial court grants summary judgment on grounds that dispose of all the non-movant's claims, the judgment becomes final, regardless of whether the trial court rules on the other grounds. Cincinnati Life Ins. Co. v. Cates, 927 S.W.2d 623, 625 (Tex. 1996). Here, the summary judgment on standing disposes of all of Faulkner's claims. Therefore, the judgment is final. Furthermore, if the trial court's order explicitly specifies the ground relied on for the summary judgment ruling, the summary judgment can be affirmed only if the theory relied on by the trial court is meritorious. State Farm Fire & Cas. Co. v. S.S., 858 S.W.2d 374, 380 (Tex. 1993). Because the trial court's order expressly states standing as the basis for summary judgment, we do not address estoppel.

Bost's Burden and Summary Judgment Evidence

Lack of standing is an affirmative defense. See Coppock & Teltschik v. Mayor, Day & Caldwell, 857 S.W.2d 631, 635 (Tex. App.-Houston [1st Dist.] 1993, writ denied). A defendant who moves for summary judgment on its affirmative defense must prove the defense as a matter of law. City of Houston v. Clear Creek Basin Auth., 589 S.W.2d 671, 678 (Tex. 1979). Therefore, to prevail on the standing issue in her motion for summary judgment, Bost was required to prove that she is entitled to judgment as a matter of law that Faulkner is not an "interested person" as that term is defined in the Property Code. Id. In support of her motion, Bost attached a certified copy of the document creating the Tanner Trust. This document establishes as a matter of law that Tanner did not name Faulkner as a trustee or a beneficiary of the Tanner Trust. Bost also relied on the following provision in the trust document:

> This trust is a spendthrift trust. No beneficiary shall have any right to transfer, encumber, or otherwise alienate any interest in any trust, nor shall any such interest be

> subject to any obligation of any beneficiary. This spendthrift provision shall apply to any trust established pursuant to this instrument.

According to Bost, Faulkner cannot be an "interested person" because this spendthrift provision prohibited Hefner from assigning her interest in the Tanner Trust. Consequently, she concludes, Faulkner has no standing to bring her suit.

Spendthrift Provision

Bost, as trustee of the Tanner Trust, held bare legal title and the right to possession of the trust assets. However, it is "the beneficiary [who] is considered the real owner of the property, holding equitable or beneficial title." Hallmark v. Port/Cooper-T. Smith Stevedoring Co., 907 S.W.2d 586, 589 (Tex. App.-Corpus Christi 1995, no writ). As a named beneficiary, Hefner held equitable or beneficial title to her interest in the Tanner Trust.

A trust beneficiary who has capacity to transfer property has the power to transfer her equitable interest, unless restricted by the terms of the trust. See Moody v. Moody Nat'l Bank of Galveston, 522 S.W.2d 710, 715-16 (Tex. App.-Houston [14th Dist.] 1975, writ ref'd n.r.e.). Hefner's capacity to transfer property has not been questioned; thus she held the power to convey her equitable interest to the Hefner Trust, unless restricted by the terms of the Tanner Trust. Bost contends that the spendthrift provision constitutes such a restriction.

Beneficial interests in trusts are generally assignable; however, assignments of such interests are invalid when they are subject to a spendthrift provision in the trust. See Texas Property Code § 112.035(a) (spendthrift provision prevents the voluntary transfer of a beneficial interest in a trust); Dierschke v. Central Nat'l Branch of First Nat'l Bank at Lubbock, 876 S.W.2d 377, 380 (Tex. App.-Austin, 1994, no writ). However, a spendthrift provision terminates with the termination of the trust. Clarke v. Clarke, 121 Tex. 165, 46 S.W.2d 658, 663 (Tex. 1932) (spendthrift provisions of trust are no longer operative after termination of trust and legal and equitable titles have merged in beneficiaries); see also Long v. Long, 252 S.W.2d 235, 247 (Tex. Civ. App. 1952, writ ref'd n.r.e.) (spendthrift trusts must be based on active trusts). At oral argument, Bost conceded the trust terminated upon Tanner's death. Additionally, the Property Code provides that a trust terminates if, by its terms, the trust is to continue only until the happening of a certain event and that event has occurred. Texas Property Code § 112.052. Even when the trust permits the trustee a reasonable period of time to wind up the affairs of the trust, the continued exercise of the trustee's powers after termination does not affect the vested rights of the beneficiaries of the trust. Sorrel v. Sorrel, 1 S.W.3d 867, 870 (Tex. App.-Corpus Christi 1999, no pet.). Therefore, upon Tanner's death, the trust as well as the spendthrift provision terminated, and Hefner could assign her interest.

Summary judgment may be rendered only if the pleadings, depositions, admissions, and affidavits show (1) there is no genuine issue as to any material fact and (2) the moving party is entitled to judgment as a matter of law. Texas Rule of Civil Procedure 166a(c); Nixon v. Mr. Prop. Mgmt. Co., 690 S.W.2d 546, 548 (Tex. 1985). It is axiomatic that the spendthrift provision prevented Hefner from assigning her interest in the Tanner Trust only so long as the provision was in effect. Tanner died on June 23, 2001. On July 18, 2002, Hefner executed an affidavit and affirmation of her prior conveyance of any property that she might inherit from Tanner. Bost's summary judgment proof did not establish that the spendthrift provision prevented Hefner from assigning her interest following the termination of the Tanner Trust. Thus, Bost failed to establish that she is entitled to summary judgment as a matter of law. See Gibbs v. Gen. Motors Corp., 450 S.W.2d 827, 828 (Tex. 1970). We sustain Faulkner's first issue.

Faulkner's Motion for Partial Summary Judgment

In her second issue, Appellant contends that the trial court erred in denying her motion for partial summary judgment. Before a court of appeals may review an order denying a cross motion for summary judgment not covered by an interlocutory appeal statute, both parties must have sought final judgment in their motions for summary judgment. See CU Lloyd's of Texas v. Feldman, 977 S.W.2d 568, 569 (Tex. 1998). Faulkner's motion for partial summary judgment did not seek a final judgment. Therefore, we lack appellate jurisdiction to review the trial court's denial of this motion. Id. Consequently, we do not address Faulkner's second issue.

CONCLUSION

Bost did not prove as a matter of law that she is entitled to summary judgment, and we are without jurisdiction to review the denial of Faulkner's motion for partial summary judgment. Therefore, trial court's judgment is reversed and this cause is remanded to the trial court for further proceedings consistent with this opinion.

Section B. Modification and Termination

Property Code § 112.051. Revocation, Modification, or Amendment by Settlor

(a) A settlor may revoke the trust unless it is irrevocable by the express terms of the instrument creating it or of an instrument modifying it.

(b) The settlor may modify or amend a trust that is revocable, but the settlor may not enlarge the duties of the trustee without the trustee's express consent.

(c) If the trust was created by a written instrument, a revocation, modification, or amendment of the trust must be in writing.

Property Code § 112.052. Termination

A trust terminates if by its terms the trust is to continue only until the expiration of a certain period or until the happening of a certain event and the period of time has elapsed or the event has occurred. If an event of termination occurs, the trustee may continue to exercise the powers of the trustee for the reasonable period of time required to wind up the affairs of the trust and to make distribution of its assets to the appropriate beneficiaries. The continued exercise of the trustee's powers after an event of termination does not affect the vested rights of beneficiaries of the trust.

Property Code § 112.054. Judicial Modification or Termination of Trusts

(a) On the petition of a trustee or a beneficiary, a court may order that the trustee be changed, that the terms of the trust be modified, that the trustee be directed or permitted to do acts that are not authorized or that are forbidden by the terms of the trust, that the trustee be prohibited from performing acts required by the terms of the trust, or that the trust be terminated in whole or in part, if:

(1) the purposes of the trust have been fulfilled or have become illegal or impossible to fulfill;

(2) because of circumstances not known to or anticipated by the settlor, the order will further the purposes of the trust;

(3) modification of administrative, nondispositive terms of the trust is necessary or appropriate to prevent waste or avoid impairment of the trust's administration;

(4) the order is necessary or appropriate to achieve the settlor's tax objectives and is not contrary to the settlor's intentions; or

(5) subject to Subsection (d):

(A) continuance of the trust is not necessary to achieve any material purpose of the trust; or

(B) the order is not inconsistent with a material purpose of the trust.

(b) The court shall exercise its discretion to order a modification or termination under Subsection (a) in the manner that conforms as nearly as possible to the probable intention of the settlor. The court shall consider spendthrift provisions as a factor in making its decision whether to modify or terminate, but the court is not precluded from exercising its discretion to modify or terminate solely because the trust is a spendthrift trust.

(c) The court may direct that an order described by Subsection (a)(4) has retroactive effect.

(d) The court may not take the action permitted by Subsection (a)(5) unless all beneficiaries of the trust have consented to the order or are deemed to have consented to the order. A minor, incapacitated, unborn, or unascertained beneficiary is deemed to have consented if a person representing the beneficiary's interest under Section 115.013(c) has consented or if a guardian ad litem appointed to represent the beneficiary's interest under Section 115.014 consents on the beneficiary's behalf.

Property Code § 112.057. Division and Combination of Trusts

(a) The trustee may, unless expressly prohibited by the terms of the instrument establishing the trust, divide a trust into two or more separate trusts without a judicial proceeding if the result does not impair the rights of any beneficiary or adversely affect achievement of the purposes of the original trust. The trustee may make a division under this subsection by:

(1) giving written notice of the division, not later than the 30th day before the date of a division under this subsection, to each beneficiary who might then be entitled to receive distributions from the trust or may be entitled to receive distributions from the trust once it is funded; and

(2) executing a written instrument, acknowledged before a notary public or other person authorized to take acknowledgements of conveyances of real estate stating that the trust has been divided pursuant to this section and that the notice requirements of this subsection have been satisfied.

(b) A trustee, in the written instrument dividing a trust, shall allocate trust property among the separate trusts on a fractional basis, by identifying the assets and liabilities passing to each separate trust, or in any other reasonable manner. The trustee shall allocate undesignated trust property received after the trustee has divided the trust into separate trusts in the manner provided by the written instrument dividing the trust or, in the absence of a provision in the written instrument, in a manner determined by the trustee.

(c) The trustee may, unless expressly prohibited by the terms of the instrument establishing a trust, combine two or more trusts into a single trust without a judicial proceeding if the result does not impair the rights of any beneficiary or adversely affect achievement of the purposes of one of the separate trusts. The trustee shall complete the trust combination by:

(1) giving a written notice of the combination, not later than the 30th day before the effective date of the combination, to each beneficiary who might then be entitled to receive distributions from the separate trusts being combined or to each beneficiary who might be entitled to receive distributions from the separate trusts once the trusts are funded; and

(2) executing a written instrument, acknowledged before a notary public or other person authorized to take acknowledgments of conveyances of real estate stating that

the trust has been combined pursuant to this section and that the notice requirements of this subsection have been satisfied.

(d) The trustee may divide or combine a testamentary trust after the will establishing the trust has been admitted to probate, even if the trust will not be funded until a later date. The trustee may divide or combine any other trust before it is funded.

(e) A beneficiary to whom written notice is required to be given under this section may waive the notice requirement in a writing delivered to the trustee. If all beneficiaries to whom notice would otherwise be required to be given under this section waive the notice requirement, notice is not required.

(f) Notice required under this section shall be given to a guardian of the estate, guardian ad litem, or parent of a minor or incapacitated beneficiary. A guardian of the estate, guardian ad litem, or parent of a minor or incapacitated beneficiary may waive the notice requirement in accordance with this section on behalf of the minor or incapacitated beneficiary.

Property Code § 112.059. Termination of Uneconomic Trust

(a) After notice to beneficiaries who are distributees or permissible distributees of trust income or principal or who would be distributees or permissible distributees if the interests of the distributees or the trust were to terminate and no powers of appointment were exercised, the trustee of a trust consisting of trust property having a total value of less than $50,000 may terminate the trust if the trustee concludes after considering the purpose of the trust and the nature of the trust assets that the value of the trust property is insufficient to justify the continued cost of administration.

(b) On termination of a trust under this section, the trustee shall distribute the trust property in a manner consistent with the purposes of the trust.

(c) A trustee may not exercise a power described by Subsection (a) if the trustee's possession of the power would cause the assets of the trust to be included in the trustee's estate for federal estate tax purposes.

(d) This section does not apply to an easement for conservation or preservation.

Settlor's "confusion" does not constitute an unanticipated circumstance that would justify judicial termination of trust

In re WHITE INTERVIVOS TRUSTS
Court of Appeals of Texas, San Antonio
248 S.W.3d 340 (2007)

MARION, J. J.D. White and Connie White (collectively, "grantors") established the following four irrevocable trusts naming their minor grandchildren as beneficiaries: (1) in December 1992, the David Paul White Irrevocable Trust; (2) in December 1992, the Scott L. and Jake R. White Irrevocable Trust; (3) in December 1994, the Jacob Michael White Irrevocable Trust; and (4) in November 1997, the Samantha Walker White Irrevocable Trust. The grantors' two adult children, Larry J. White and David M. White, were named as trustees of each of the trusts. In February 2006, Larry and David (collectively, "the trustees") filed their Petition for Termination of White Intervivos Trusts. Scott and Jake (who are now adults) entered appearances, waived service and citation, and agreed that the trial court could hear and determine the cause without any further notice to them. Jon William West was appointed guardian ad litem to represent the interests of the minors, David, Samantha, and Jacob.

In their petition to terminate the trusts, the trustees alleged (1) the grantors' intent "was to provide assets in each of the" trusts for the benefit of the trustees, (2) the grantors were not advised that the trustees were not "distributees of the income and principal" of the trusts during their lifetimes, and (3) the purpose of the trusts was not satisfied. Therefore, the trustees concluded that based on circumstances unknown to the grantors, termination of the trusts furthered the purpose of the trusts as intended by the grantors. At a hearing on the petition, the court heard the testimony of one of the grantors, J.D. White, who stated he did not understand the difference between a "trustee" and a "beneficiary" and he intended Larry and David to be the beneficiaries of the trusts. He agreed that termination of the trusts would further the purpose of the trusts. On cross-examination, Mr. White admitted his attorney drafted the various trust documents. Other than Mr. White's testimony and admission of the trust documents into evidence, no other evidence was offered in support of the petition. Following the hearing, the trial court terminated the trusts and distributed the trust assets equally to the two trustees, who are the appellees before this court. This appeal was brought by the guardian ad litem on behalf of the minor grandchildren. We reverse that portion of the judgment terminating the trusts of David, Samantha, and Jacob.

DISCUSSION

Each of the four trusts state the trust is irrevocable. Additionally, each of the four trust agreements clearly and unambiguously designate the grantors' grandchildren as beneficiaries of their respective trusts, and each clearly and unambiguously designate Larry and David as trustees. The 1992 trust agreements for David Paul White and Scott and Jake White state as follows: "This trust shall terminate on the death of both Grantors and both initial Trustees. Thereafter the Trustee shall distribute the remaining corpus per stirpes to the beneficiary named after each beneficiary attains 25 years of age. The beneficiary of this trust is [David Paul White and Scott and Jake White, respectively]." The 1994 and 1997 trust agreements for Jacob Michael White and Samantha Walker White designate Jacob and Samantha as beneficiaries at least three times in the documents and provide that their trusts "shall continue until the Primary Beneficiary attains the age of thirty (30) years."

All of the trust agreements admitted into evidence, except the one for Jacob, were signed by the grantors and Larry and David. In each case, Larry and David signed the trust documents as "trustees." Each trust document clearly and unambiguously states the trust is irrevocable. Despite signing the documents as trustees and despite the clear designation of the grandchildren as beneficiaries, the trustees waited until 2006 to petition the court alleging they were the intended beneficiaries. The only evidence of this intent was Mr. White's testimony that he did not understand the difference between a trustee and a beneficiary. Based on this testimony and in the face of the unambiguous language of the documents, the trial court found that "[a] mistake was made in drafting" the trust agreements. The trial court found that the grantors' intent "was to provide assets in each of the [trusts] for the benefit of" Larry and David and the "purpose of the [trusts] was not satisfied by each of the Trust Indentures creating the [trusts]." The court concluded "the termination of the [trusts] will further the purpose of the [trusts] as intended by [the grantors]" and the "continuance of the [trusts] is not necessary to achieve any material purpose of the [trusts]." On appeal, appellant asserts the evidence at trial established no legal basis for the termination of the trusts. We agree.

A settlor may not revoke a trust if "it is irrevocable by the express terms of the instrument creating it . . . ." Texas Property Code § 112.051(a). However, an irrevocable trust, such as the ones at issue here, may be judicially terminated under proper circumstances. In 2005, the Texas Legislature amended the Texas Property Code to provide that "a court may order that . . . the trust be terminated in whole or in part, if . . . because of circumstances not known to or anticipated by the settlor, the order will further the purposes of the trust." Id. § 112.054(a)(2). The court has "discretion to order a modification or termination under Subsection (a) in the manner that conforms as nearly as possible to the probable intention of the settlor." Id. § 112.054(b). The 2005 amendment to subsection (a)(2) "liberalized the rules governing modification and early termination of trusts." Stanley M. Johanson, Johanson's Texas Probate Code Ann., Texas Property Code § 112.054, commentary (2007 ed.). While the former law[1] allowed early termination of a trust only to permit "the removal of obstacles to carrying out the trust purposes"; the new law made termination easier "by authorizing modifications that enhance the attainment of the settlor's trust purposes." Id.

Although the amendment to subsection (a)(2) may have made termination of an irrevocable trust easier to achieve, there must still be evidence of "circumstances not known

---

[1] The former version read: "because of circumstances not known to or anticipated by the settlor, compliance with the terms of the trust would defeat or substantially impair the accomplishment of the purposes of the trust."

to or anticipated by the settlor" presented to the court that supports terminating an irrevocable trust. Here, the unknown circumstance was Mr. White's "confusion."[2] He did not testify that this "confusion" stemmed from any misrepresentations made to him, from a lack of legal advice, or from a lack of awareness regarding the terms of the trust documents. He did not testify that he never intended to establish four separate irrevocable trusts over a period of five years. And no one explained why almost fourteen years had to pass before the "mistake" was realized. We conclude that this record cannot support a finding of "circumstances not known to or anticipated by the settlor." Accordingly, the trial court erred in terminating the trusts.

CONCLUSION

Because we conclude the trial court erred in terminating the trusts, we reverse that portion of the trial court's judgment terminating the David Paul White Irrevocable Trust, the Jacob Michael White Irrevocable Trust, and the Samantha Walker White Irrevocable Trust and we reverse that portion of the judgment distributing the assets of these trusts to Larry J. White and David M. White. Because no appeal was taken from the termination of the Scott L. and Jake R. White Irrevocable Trust, we affirm that portion of the judgment. The judgment is affirmed in all other respects.

Section C. Trustee Removal

Property Code § 113.081. Resignation of Trustee

(a) A trustee may resign in accordance with the terms of the trust instrument, or a trustee may petition a court for permission to resign as trustee.

(b) The court may accept a trustee's resignation and discharge the trustee from the trust on the terms and conditions necessary to protect the rights of other interested persons.

Property Code § 113.082. Removal of Trustee

(a) A trustee may be removed in accordance with the terms of the trust instrument, or, on the petition of an interested person and after hearing, a court may, in its discretion, remove a trustee and deny part or all of the trustee's compensation if:

(1) the trustee materially violated or attempted to violate the terms of the trust and the violation or attempted violation results in a material financial loss to the trust;

---

[2] Mr. White testified, "I was more than confused."

(2) the trustee becomes incapacitated or insolvent;

(3) the trustee fails to make an accounting that is required by law or by the terms of the trust; or

(4) the court finds other cause for removal.

(b) A beneficiary, cotrustee, or successor trustee may treat a violation resulting in removal as a breach of trust.

(c) A trustee of a charitable trust may not be removed solely on the grounds that the trustee exercised the trustee's power to adjust between principal and income under Section 113.0211.

Property Code § 113.083. Appointment of Successor Trustee

(a) On the death, resignation, incapacity, or removal of a sole or surviving trustee, a successor trustee shall be selected according to the method, if any, prescribed in the trust instrument. If for any reason a successor is not selected under the terms of the trust instrument, a court may and on petition of any interested person shall appoint a successor in whom the trust shall vest.

(b) If a vacancy occurs in the number of trustees originally appointed under a valid charitable trust agreement and the trust agreement does not provide for filling the vacancy, the remaining trustees may fill the vacancy by majority vote.

Mere hostility or ill will between trustee and beneficiaries does not qualify as cause for removal of trustee

AKIN v. DAHL
Supreme Court of Texas
661 S.W.2d 911 (1983)

WALLACE, J. This is a suit seeking removal of a trustee from office and termination of the power of appointment. The court of appeals reversed the judgment of the trial court, holding that removal of the trustee was not warranted and the power of appointment was not voided. We affirm the judgment of the court of appeals.

George Dahl was, at all times pertinent to this appeal, Trustee of the Lille E. Dahl Trust, a discretionary trust established by Mr. Dahl's late wife. The beneficiaries under the trust include George Dahl, his daughter, Gloria Dahl Akin, her husband, Ted Akin, and the children of the Akins and their spouses. The instrument generally provides that the trust income and corpus would go to the Trustee, Mr. Dahl, if his accustomed life style could not be supported from other income sources, and that disbursements to the other beneficiaries would be at the discretion of the Trustee, including support, maintenance and education of the other beneficiaries. This cause of action was tried in connection with a malicious prosecution suit brought by Mr. Dahl against the Akins arising from guardianship and incompetency proceedings brought against him by the Akins. In answer to two special issues, the jury found that Mr. Dahl had developed such hostility toward Mrs. Akin and her children (presumably from the guardianship and incompetency proceedings) that in administering the Lille E. Dahl Trust, Mr. Dahl would probably be influenced adversely to the interest of Gloria Akin and her children. Specifically those two special issues read as follows:

> Do you find from a preponderance of the evidence that Mr. Dahl has developed such hostility toward Gloria Akin that his decisions as Trustee in administering the funds of the Lille E. Dahl Trust will probably be influenced adversely to the interest of Gloria Akin?
>
> Answer: We do.
>
> Do you find from a preponderance of the evidence that Mr. Dahl has developed such hostility toward the Akin children that his decisions as Trustee in administering the funds of the Lille E. Dahl Trust will probably be influenced adversely to the interest of Gloria Akin?
>
> Answer: We do.

The trial court subsequently removed George Dahl as Trustee, apparently on the basis of the two jury findings and due to a determination by the trial court that Mr. Dahl had, as a matter of law, acted improperly with the trust funds.

Three issues are presented for our determination:

(1) Is removal of the trustee from office an act of discretion of the trial court and to be judged only by the "arbitrary and unreasonable" standard applicable to the charge that the trial court abused its discretion?

(2) Was mismanagement or improper conduct by the trustee established as a matter of law and was removal of the trustee therefore justified?

(3) Were the two jury findings regarding hostility between the trustee and the beneficiaries sufficient cause to remove the trustee from office?

Gloria Akin urges that Section 39 of the Texas Trust Act allows removal of a trustee to be at the discretion of the trial court, and that review of the trial court's action should be the "arbitrary or unreasonable" standard applicable to trial court rulings alleged to be an abuse of discretion. Landry v. Travelers Ins. Co., 458 S.W.2d 649, 651 (Tex. 1970). Texas Revised Civil Statutes Annotated art. 7425b-39, which is a portion of what is commonly known as the Texas Trust Act, reads in pertinent part as follows:

> Art. 7425b-39. Removal of trustee
>
> Trustees having materially violated (or attempted to violate) any express trust resulting in an actual financial loss to the trust, or becoming incompetent or insolvent, or of whose solvency or that of the sureties there is reasonable doubt, or for other cause, in the discretion of the court having jurisdiction, may . . . be removed by such court . . . .

This section of the Act indicates that the phrase "in the discretion of the court having jurisdiction," is meant to insure that the number of grounds for removal of a trustee is not expressly limited to those enumerated in the section, but rather may include those that the trial court, in its discretion, deems necessary and proper. The section does not make removal of a trustee a discretionary act on the part of the trial court and hence subject upon review to the "arbitrary and unreasonable" standard.[3] Having rejected the abuse-of-discretion standard of review urged by petitioner, we now turn to the apparent finding by the trial court that Mr. Dahl had acted improperly as trustee as a matter of law.

The trial court rendered judgment for Gloria Akin, removing George Dahl as Trustee. Because there was no issue submitted to the jury concerning Mr. Dahl's mismanagement of trust funds, the trial court had of necessity to find as a matter of law that such improper conduct had occurred in order to remove him for impropriety. We agree with the court of appeals that no such mismanagement or improper conduct was established as a matter of law. Each assertion of mismanagement or improper conduct of such magnitude as to require removal was controverted or denied, giving rise to a question of fact to be submitted to the jury. Since no issue was submitted to the jury, the point was waived unless established as a matter of law, which we hold was not done. See Glens Falls Ins. Co. v. Peters, 386 S.W.2d 529, 531 (Tex. 1965); Texas Rule of Civil Procedure 279.

There then remains the question of whether or not the jury findings concerning hostility justify removal of the trustee. Ill will or hostility between a trustee and the beneficiaries of the trust, is, standing alone, insufficient grounds for removal of the trustee from office. White v. White, 15 S.W.2d 1090, 1093 (Tex. Civ. App.-Texarkana 1929, writ dism'd), 25 S.W.2d 826 (Tex. Comm'n App. 1930). Article 7425b-39 of the Texas Trust Act sets out circumstances which warrant the removal of a trustee from office. Should the trier of fact affirmatively find that one of the enumerated circumstances has occurred, the trustee will be removed. Additionally, should the trier of fact find that hostility, ill will, or other factors have affected the trustee so that he cannot properly serve in his capacity, the trustee

---

[3] In 2003, the legislature amended this provision to specify that "a court may, in its discretion, remove a trustee and deny part or all of the trustee's compensation" if certain specified conditions are met. See Texas Trust Code § 113.082(a). —Ed.

will be removed. In the present case, the jury found in essence that George Dahl could probably not serve as trustee. This is insufficient. Just as there must be an affirmative finding that an enumerated circumstance has occurred under Article 7425b-39, not merely probably had or probably will occur, there likewise must be a finding that the trustee's hostility does or will affect his performance in the office. The jury must decide by preponderance of the evidence that George Dahl could not properly serve as trustee due to the hostility between him and the Akins. The jury did not make this finding and as a consequence Mr. Dahl may not be removed as trustee. We note that the hostility herein was primarily created by the beneficiaries. Preservation of the trust and assurance that its purpose be served is of paramount importance in the law and this Court will not sanction the creation of hostility by a beneficiary in order to effectuate the removal of a trustee.

The Court also notes that a serious conflict of interest may be present between Mr. Dahl as Trustee of the Lille E. Dahl Trust, while at the same time being a judgment creditor of the beneficiaries of the trust. This is particularly true where the beneficiaries must seek funds from the Trustee in order to satisfy a judgment held against them by the Trustee individually. This point has, however, not been presented to this Court.

We affirm the judgment of the court of appeals, holding that the Trustee remain in office and continuation of the power of appointment.

ROBERTSON, J., not sitting.

Court must follow settlor's direction in appointing successor trustee following removal

CONTE v. DITTA
Court of Appeals of Texas, Houston
312 S.W.3d 951 (2010)

HANKS, J. This appeal is before us on remand from the Supreme Court of Texas. Having reversed our Court's earlier judgment that this trustee-removal suit was barred by the four-year statute of limitations applicable to a breach-of-fiduciary-duty claim, the Supreme Court remanded the case for consideration of the merits of the appeal.

Appellee, Louis M. Ditta ("Ditta"), acting in his capacity as the Guardian of the Estate of Doris L. Conte ("Doris"), an Incapacitated Person, filed suit seeking the removal of appellant, Susan C. Conte ("Susan"), as trustee of the Conte Family Trust. After a bench trial, the probate court ruled in Ditta's favor and issued two orders. The first order removed Susan as trustee, and the second order modified the terms of the Conte Family Trust and appointed a successor trustee. In three issues, Susan argues that the probate court erred in (1) removing her from her position as trustee, (2) modifying the trust's prescribed method of appointing successor trustees, and (3) appointing a successor trustee. We affirm in part and reverse and remand in part for orders consistent with this opinion.

BACKGROUND

In 1987, Joseph and Doris Conte created the Joseph P. Conte Family Trust, an inter vivos trust that became irrevocable on the earlier of Joseph or Doris's death. The Trust agreement named Joseph the original trustee. Upon Joseph's death in 1993, per the terms of the Trust, Doris began serving as co-trustee along with her two children, Susan and Joseph, Jr. The co-trustees were obliged to create and fund three separate trusts for the primary benefit of Doris, during her lifetime. The co-trustees were to distribute quarterly income from a management trust to Doris, as well as principal amounts requested by Doris for "her comfort, health, support and maintenance, in order to maintain" the equivalent lifestyle to which Doris was accustomed at the time of Joseph's death.

Initially, Joseph, Jr. managed the Trust's day-to-day affairs. About two years later, Susan and Doris discovered that Joseph, Jr. was not administering the Trust in accordance with its terms. This discovery heralded a proliferation of litigation, including eight separate lawsuits between Susan and Joseph, Jr.[4] In the course of one of these suits, Doris was

---

[4] Generally described, these suits were as follows:

1. A suit for declaratory judgment, filed by Doris and Susan, seeking a declaration that a separate suit, filed by both Doris and Susan, to remove Joseph, Jr. as co-trustee would not violate the "no contest" clause in the Trust agreement.

2. A suit filed by Susan seeking a protective order against Joseph, Jr. subsequent to an incident of family violence and assault.

3. A suit filed by Joseph, Jr., against Susan and Doris, alleging that the two women had no authority, in their capacities as co-trustees, to direct the affairs of Joe Conte Toyota, Inc.

4. A suit filed by Susan against Joseph, Jr. for fraud, conversion, and breach of fiduciary duty.

5. A suit for declaratory judgment, filed by Susan alone, seeking a declaration that a suit by Susan to remove Joseph, Jr. as trustee would not violate the "no contest" clause of the Trust agreement.

6. A suit filed by Susan against Joseph, Jr. and his attorneys for conversion and interference with the conduct of the day-to-day administration of the Trust.

7. A suit filed by Joseph, Jr., against Susan and Doris, seeking the rescission of a settlement agreement entered into by the co-trustees and a trust accounting.

declared mentally incapacitated. In an agreed order, Susan was appointed guardian of Doris's person, and Louis Ditta, appellee in this case and an attorney, was appointed guardian of Doris's estate. Due to the declaration of incapacity, Doris was removed from her position as a co-trustee of the Trust, leaving Susan and Joseph, Jr. with the joint responsibility of administering and managing the Trust.

In August 1998, Ditta sought appointment of a receiver to take over the Trust, claiming that the discord between Joseph, Jr. and Susan was materially injuring the Trust assets. Instead of appointing a receiver, the probate court entered an agreed order appointing a temporary successor trustee, Paula Miller. Pursuant to the order, the trustee powers of both Susan and Joseph, Jr. were temporarily suspended. In June 2000, Miller filed an accounting for the Trust with the court that covered March 8, 1993 (the date of Joseph's death) to December 31, 1999. The accounting revealed that both Susan and Joseph, Jr. had become significantly indebted to the Trust by using Trust assets for personal expenses. The Trust agreement did not authorize payment of personal expenses of a trustee out of the Trust funds.

Susan initially contested the accounting, but the parties eventually entered into an agreed judgment in January 2001. The agreed judgment approved Miller's accounting that Susan owed the Trust $420,423.32, plus accrued interest on the indebtedness at a rate of 6% per annum, and Joseph, Jr. also owed a larger debt to the Trust. The agreed judgment provided that collection of the amounts owed by Susan and Joseph, Jr. would be deferred during Doris's lifetime, unless the probate court later found that Doris's "financial needs" required earlier repayment. Miller continued to serve for more than six years as temporary successor trustee under the supervision of the court. Miller was charged with funding the three separate trusts, as expressed in the Trust, a task which Joseph, Jr. and Susan never completed during their administration of the Trust. Miller's subsequent accountings brought the records up-to-date through September 2004. As of September 2004, with the accumulation of interest, Susan owed $515,534.32, Joseph, Jr. owed $899,529.80, and Conte Investments (a company held half by Susan and half by Joseph, Jr.) owed $702,276.34.

In January 2003, Ditta persuaded the probate court to remove Joseph, Jr. as trustee based on his violations of the Trust agreement. Thereafter, only Susan (whose trustee powers were suspended) and Miller (the temporary successor trustee) remained as trustees. On April 5, 2004, Ditta filed this suit, seeking Susan's removal as trustee. On both April 27 and November 3 of that same year, Susan and Joseph, Jr., in their capacity as beneficiaries of

---

8. An application filed by Joseph, Jr. for the appointment of a temporary guardian for Doris and a motion contesting that application filed by Susan.

the Trust, signed documents, pursuant to the terms of the Trust,[5] to reappoint Susan as trustee if she were removed by the court in the removal proceeding initiated by Ditta.

Following a bench trial, the probate court removed Susan as trustee, modified the terms of the Trust regarding trustee succession, and appointed Frost Bank as successor trustee. This appeal followed. At some point during the pendency of the appeal, Frost Bank resigned from its position as trustee. The parties, including Ditta, entered into an agreed order appointing Susan temporarily as substitute successor trustee under a $1 million bond and supervised by the court as a dependent administrator. Despite Frost Bank's resignation, the parties are in agreement that the case is not moot because controversies still exist as to the propriety of the trial court's removal of Susan as trustee, its modification of the terms of the Trust, and its power to appoint a successor trustee.

On appeal, this Court reversed, holding that the trial court erred in removing Susan as trustee because Ditta's removal action was barred by the four-year statute of limitations governing breach-of-fiduciary-duty claims. Additionally, our Court held that the probate court erred in modifying the terms of the Trust and appointing a successor trustee because it took those actions based on a time-barred petition. On discretionary review, the Texas Supreme Court held that "[n]o statute of limitations period applies in a trustee-removal suit." Ditta v. Conte, 298 S.W.3d 187, 192 (Tex. 2009). On remand from the Texas Supreme Court, we consider the issues we did not reach.

DISCUSSION

A. Removal of Susan as Trustee

Susan argues that the trial court erred in removing her from her position as the sole remaining trustee of the Trust. Specifically, she argues that there is no evidence supporting the trial court's stated reasons for her removal and the removal action was barred by the doctrines of election of remedies and waiver.

1. Bar on Removal Action

Susan argues that the removal action is barred or waived because of an earlier settlement. Susan points to a settlement agreement between the parties relating to her indebtedness to the Trust for money used on personal expenses. Susan contends that the settlement was an "election of remedies" precluding or waiving removal action.

---

[5] The Trust provided that, should the position of trustee become vacant, a series of persons would have an opportunity to appoint the successor trustee. If neither Joseph Conte, Sr. nor Doris Conte appointed a successor in the first sixty days after the position of trustee was vacated, the majority of adult beneficiaries had a thirty-day window within which they could appoint a successor trustee.

We reject this argument because, as the Supreme Court held, the removal action seeks to prevent future injury, which is distinguishable from a monetary settlement remedying past injury. Id. The Supreme Court rejected Susan's earlier claim that the statute of limitations for breach of fiduciary duty applies to a trustee-removal action. Id. Because the removal suit seeks to prevent future harm to the Trust, Susan's past settlement of monetary claims does not preclude or waive removal actions to prevent future harm. See id.

2. Merits of Susan's Removal

Additionally, Susan argues that there was no evidence supporting the trial court's stated reasons for her removal. At Susan's request, the trial court issued findings of fact and conclusions of law, which provided in part:

1. As co-trustee of the Trust, Susan C. Conte materially violated the terms of the Trust by paying her personal expenses out of the Trust.

2. Susan C. Conte's violation of the terms of the Trust resulted in a material financial loss to the Trust.

3. Susan C. Conte's violation of the terms of the Trust resulting in her removal is a breach of trust.

4. Susan C. Conte is personally indebted to the Trust, therefore, her personal interests are adverse and in conflict with her duties as trustee.

5. Extensive litigation and hostility between Susan C. Conte and Joseph P. Conte, Jr. adversely affected their ability as co-trustees to administer the Trust consistent with its purpose.

Susan concedes that the stated reasons for her removal are proper grounds but argues that there is no evidence supporting the court's stated reasons.

a) Standard of Review

A court may, in its discretion, remove a trustee on the petition of an interested person and after hearing if "the trustee materially violated or attempted to violate the terms of the trust and the violation or attempted violation results in a material financial loss to the trust" or "in the discretion of the court, for other cause." Act of May 22, 2003, 78th Leg., R.S., ch. 550, 2003 Tex. Gen. Laws 1871, 1872 (amended 2005) (current version at Texas Property Code § 113.082(a)). Accordingly, we review a court's removal of a trustee under an abuse of discretion standard. Id.; See, e.g., Kappus v. Kappus, 284 S.W.3d 831, 838 (Tex. 2009).

b) Analysis

The probate court gave three reasons for removing Susan: (1) Susan's prior use of Trust funds to pay personal expenses materially violated the terms of the Trust, resulting in a material loss to the trust; (2) Susan's indebtedness to the Trust and concurrent responsibility to collect on that debt if Doris needed the funds created an inherent and continuing conflict of interest; and (3) Susan's tenuous relationship with Joseph, Jr. impaired the performance of her trustee duties. Susan argues that the record does not support these conclusions.

First, Susan argues that there is no evidence that she materially violated the terms of the Trust in a manner that caused a material financial loss to the Trust. Contrary to Susan's assertion, Paula Miller provided testimony and accounting schedules that showed Susan's use of Trust money for personal expenses. Specifically, due to disputes over the Trust, Doris, Susan, and Joseph, Jr. entered into an agreed order appointing Paula Miller as temporary successor trustee to conduct an accounting of the Trust. Miller testified at trial that her accounting of the Trust revealed that Susan used money from the Trust to pay personal expenses during her tenure as a co-trustee. Miller documented these expenses in a schedule that was admitted at trial. Miller determined that Susan used a total of $420,423.32 of Trust money on personal expenses. Miller also discovered that money from the Trust was impermissibly used by Conte Investments, Inc., a company owned 50/50 by Susan and Joseph, Jr.

As of September 2004, due to the accrual of interest, the amount owed to the Trust by Susan amounted to $515,534.32 for her personal expenses and $702,276.34 for impermissible lending of Trust money to Conte Investments. The Trust did not allow for Susan, as a trustee, to use money from the Trust to pay for personal expenses. Nor do the terms of the Trust permit a trustee to lend funds of the Trust to himself or to an entity owned by the trustee personally.

All parties, including Susan, signed an agreed judgment approving of Miller's accounting, acknowledging Susan's indebtedness to the Trust for her misuse of funds, and deferring collection of the indebtedness during Doris's lifetime, unless her financial needs required collection. The "Agreed Final Judgment on Accounting," which Susan approved, conclusively shows that she is indebted to the Trust for improper use of Trust funds while serving as a co-trustee. At the time of trial in February 2005, Miller estimated the liquid assets of the Trust to be less than $200,000 and anticipated those assets would be exhausted by the end of May 2005.

Susan argues that, because she entered into the agreed judgment acknowledging her indebtedness, the amounts cannot be classified as a loss to the Trust. Susan argues that the assets cannot be considered a loss until a demand for payment is refused. Susan cites no authority to support her position.

Susan's argument presumes that her acknowledgement of indebtedness to the Trust cures any harm to the extent that we cannot consider the misappropriations a loss. In essence, she asserts that the previous agreed judgment precludes us from considering her indebtedness as a loss. If the statute were interpreted in the way Susan suggests, a monetary recovery for a trustee's breach would preclude removal under Section 113.082(a)(1) for a material violation of the trust resulting in material financial loss. See Texas Property Code § 113.082(a). Such a narrow interpretation of the statute would be in conflict with the Supreme Court's opinion. See *Ditta*, 298 S.W.3d at 192. Specifically, Susan's emphasis on the accounting characterization and resolution of the past harm is misplaced; removal actions "exist to prevent the trustee from engaging in further behavior that could potentially harm the trust." Id. The Supreme Court explained, "[a]ny prior breaches or conflicts on the part of the trustee indicate that the trustee could repeat her behavior and harm the trust in the future." Id.

Initially Susan denied that she was indebted to the Trust, and had it not been for Miller's accounting, the misuse of funds likely would have gone undiscovered. Susan's acknowledgement of her indebtedness after being caught does not cure the harm to the trust relationship. Additionally, we observe that Susan's indebtedness to the trust is not a documented loan, nor is it a secured loan. Susan has not attempted to repay the amounts owed. It was within the trial judge's discretion to conclude that the money was a loss, as it was taken out of the Trust and has not been repaid.

Susan also argues without supporting authority that, if there was a loss to the Trust, it was not material. Susan points to the fees charged by Miller for serving as a temporary successor trustee in comparison to the amount of her debt. Susan draws this comparison in an effort to minimize the amount she owes to the Trust. But the propriety of Miller's services is uncontested in this proceeding.

We conclude that the trial court did not abuse its discretion in concluding that Susan materially violated the terms of the Trust. Similarly, the court did not abuse its discretion in finding that there was material financial loss to the Trust as a result of the breach.

Because we conclude that the trial court was within its discretion in removing Susan as trustee, we need not address the trial court's other grounds supporting the removal.

We overrule Susan's first issue.

B. Modification of Trust and Appointment of Successor Trustee

In her second point, Susan argues that the trial court erred in appointing a successor trustee. Specifically, Susan argues that the trial court erred by modifying the terms of the Trust to allow the court to deviate from the Trust's terms for appointing a successor trustee.

In the court's findings of fact and conclusions of law, the court concluded, in relevant part:

6. This Court has the equitable power to deviate from the terms of the Trust agreement and the statutory power to modify the terms of the Trust agreement due to changes in circumstances since the creation of the Trust by the grantors.

7. It is in the best interests of the Trust and Doris L. Conte to deviate from the terms of the Trust agreement and modify the terms of the Trust agreement for appointing a successor trustee as a result of Susan C. Conte's removal, due to changed circumstances, including the following, (i) improper use of funds of the Trust by Susan C. Conte and Joseph P. Conte, Jr. to pay their personal expenses while serving as co-trustees, (ii) substantial indebtedness owed to the Trust by Susan C. Conte and Joseph P. Conte, Jr., (iii) lack of sufficient liquidity of the Trust to meet the needs of the primary beneficiary of the Trust, Doris L. Conte, and (iv) extensive litigation between Susan C. Conte and Joseph P. Conte, Jr., while serving as co-trustees which interfered with the proper administration of the Trust.

8. Further, under the circumstances set forth above, it is impractical, inexpedient, and would substantially impair the accomplishment of the purposes of the Trust to permit Susan C. Conte and Joseph P. Conte, Jr., to re-appoint Susan C. Conte as trustee upon her removal.

9. Further, given this Court's familiarity with the administration of the Trust for over six and one-half years, and the concurrent jurisdiction of this court with the Harris County Texas District Court in matters involving inter vivos trusts, it is in the best interest of the Trust for this Court to appoint the successor trustee rather than a district judge of Harris County, Texas.

The Texas Trust Code requires that, on the removal of a sole trustee, a successor trustee must be appointed by the court in accordance with the terms of the trust instrument. Texas Property Code § 113.083(a). In this case, the terms of the Trust provided that, in the event that the position of trustee became vacant, a series of persons would have an opportunity to appoint the successor trustee. The Trust gave the power of appointment first to Joseph, Sr., and if not exercised by Joseph, Sr. within 30 days, then Doris had the opportunity to appoint a successor. If neither Joseph Conte, Sr. nor Doris Conte appointed a successor in the first sixty days after the position of trustee was vacated, the majority of adult beneficiaries had a thirty-day window within which they could appoint a successor trustee.

The Trust in this case clearly shows the grantor's intent to leave decisions regarding the management of the Trust to his wife and children. The Trust also states that "[n]o individual Trustee shall receive any compensation for serving under this instrument." However, the Trust provides for "fair and reasonable compensation" for a corporate trustee.

The court is permitted to modify the terms of a trust if, due to circumstances not known to or anticipated by the settler, compliance with the terms of the trust would defeat or substantially impair accomplishment of the purposes of the trust. Act of May 9, 1985,

69th Leg., R.S., ch. 149, § 1, 1985 Tex. Gen. Laws 676 (amended 2005) (current version at Texas Property Code § 112.054(a)(2)). The court, however, does not have unfettered discretion to modify the Trust in any way it chooses. If the court finds that modification is proper, the court must exercise its discretion to modify "in the manner that conforms as nearly as possible to the intention of the settlor."[6] Id. (current version at Texas Property Code § 112.054(b)).

In the court's conclusions of law, it concluded that it would be "impractical, inexpedient, and would substantially impair the accomplishment of the purposes of the Trust to permit Susan C. Conte and Joseph P. Conte, Jr., to re-appoint Susan C. Conte as trustee upon her removal." It appears that the trial court justified its modification of the Trust on the presumption that under the Trust's terms, Susan and Joseph, Jr., as a majority of the adult beneficiaries, would have the power to appoint a successor trustee and they would use that power to reappoint Susan.

As previously noted, the Trust expresses the grantor's clear intention to leave the power to appoint a successor trustee to his wife and children. The preceding paragraph in the Trust addresses resignation of a trustee, requiring that notice be given to the grantors or beneficiaries. Notably, this paragraph specifies that "if the person entitled to receive notice is a minor or an incompetent, such notice shall be delivered to . . . such incompetent's guardian." This provision shows that the grantor anticipated the possibility of guardianship in drafting the Trust agreement. Significantly, while the guardian is entitled to receive notice on behalf of the ward, the Trust agreement does not provide that the guardian can exercise a ward's power of appointment.[7] After reviewing the language of the Trust, it is clear from the terms that the grantor did not intend the power to appoint a successor trustee to be exercisable by a guardian on the ward's behalf. The omission of language giving the guardian power is significant given the specific inclusion of such language in the paragraph directly before. Because we must interpret the document in such a way that gives effect to each and every provision without rendering any parts meaningless, we cannot interpret a grant of power to "the Wife" to extend to the wife's guardian. See Alpert v. Riley, 274 S.W.3d 277, 288 (Tex. App.-Houston [1st Dist.] 2008, pet. denied).

Because Doris was unable to exercise the power to appoint, that power would have been left to "a majority of the adult Beneficiaries." It can be inferred from the trial court's conclusions of law that it also arrived at this interpretation. The court went on to conclude that it would be "impractical, inexpedient, and would substantially impair the

---

[6] For the purposes of this opinion, we use the terms "grantor" and "settlor" interchangeably. We note that in the Trust agreement, Joseph, Sr. refers to himself as the "grantor." The Trust Code uses the term "settlor" to mean creator of a trust, but also provides that the terms "grantor" and "testor" mean the same as "settlor." Texas Property Code § 111.004.

[7] We note that Ditta serves as guardian of Doris's estate, giving him the power to manage her property. Susan serves as guardian of Doris's person, giving her power over Doris's care, supervision, protection, and medical decisions.

accomplishment of the purposes of the Trust to permit Susan C. Conte and Joseph P. Conte, Jr., to re-appoint Susan C. Conte as trustee upon her removal." Based on this conclusion, the court determined it was in the best interest of the Trust for the court to appoint a successor.

We agree with the court that Susan's removal as trustee rendered her unqualified to serve as trustee. In determining whether a trustee should be removed, the court can consider prior breaches or conflicts, without limitation, so long as potential harm exists. *Ditta*, 298 S.W.3d at 192 ("Any prior breaches or conflicts on the part of the trustee indicate that the trustee could repeat her behavior and harm the trust in the future."). Accordingly, we observe that reappointment cannot be utilized to reinstate a trustee that the court previously removed.

However, the trial court erred in giving itself the power to appoint a successor trustee. Upon finding that it was not feasible for Susan to be reappointed, the court should have modified the terms of the Trust "in the manner that conforms as nearly as possible to the intention of the settlor," as required by Section 112.054(b) of the Property Code. Act of May 9, 1985, 69th Leg., R.S., ch. 149, § 1, 1985 Tex. Gen. Laws 676 (amended 2005). Rather than limiting its exercise of discretion in light of the grantor's intentions, the court modified the Trust by depriving Susan and Joseph, Jr. the opportunity to suggest a suitable trustee. Rather than of making its own determination of what would be best, the court's modification should have been guided by the grantor's clear intention to allow the beneficiaries to appoint a successor trustee. See Texas Property Code § 112.054(b) (providing that court should modify trust "in the manner that conforms as nearly as possible to the intention of the settlor").

While Susan's removal disqualified her from reappointment as trustee, her missteps in her fiduciary role as trustee do not strip away her rights as a beneficiary. Per the terms of the Trust, the power to appoint a successor trustee was left to "a majority of the adult Beneficiaries." The grounds for Susan's removal as trustee have no bearing on her rights as a beneficiary. The court should have allowed Susan and Joseph, Jr. to select a successor trustee and simply modified the Trust by restricting their choice of successor trustee to someone whom it had not previously removed. Such a restriction would address the problem recognized by the court, while still giving effect to the grantor's intentions.

While we agree modification was necessary, the trial court erred by not exercising its discretion in a manner that conformed to the grantor's intent. See Texas Property Code § 112.054(b). We conclude that that the trial court abused its discretion in modifying the terms of the Trust and by appointing the successor trustee because the court should not have given itself the authority to appoint a successor in place of a majority of the adult beneficiaries.

We sustain Susan's second issue.

CONCLUSION

We affirm the trial court's judgment, in part, as to the removal of Susan as trustee. We reverse, in part, as to the modification of the terms of the Trust and the court's appointment of a successor trustee, and remand for orders consistent with this opinion.

Chapter 11. Trusts: Charitable Purposes, Cy Pres, and Supervision

Section A. Modification of Charitable Trusts

Property Code § 113.026. Authority to Designate New Charitable Beneficiary

(a) In this section:

(1) "Charitable entity" has the meaning assigned by Section 123.001.

(2) "Failed charitable beneficiary" means a charitable entity that is named as a beneficiary of a trust and that:

(A) does not exist at the time the charitable entity's interest in the trust becomes vested;

(B) ceases to exist during the term of the trust; or

(C) ceases to be a charitable entity during the term of the trust.

(b) This section applies only to an express written trust created by an individual with a charitable entity as a beneficiary. If the trust instrument provides a means for replacing a failed charitable beneficiary, the trust instrument governs the replacement of a failed charitable beneficiary, and this section does not apply.

(c) The trustee of a trust may select one or more replacement charitable beneficiaries for a failed charitable beneficiary in accordance with this section.

(d) Each replacement charitable beneficiary selected under this section by any person must:

(1) be a charitable entity and an entity described under Sections 170(b)(1)(A), 170(c), 2055(a), and 2522(a) of the Internal Revenue Code of 1986, as amended; and

(2) have the same or similar charitable purpose as the failed charitable beneficiary.

(e) If the settlor of the trust is living and not incapacitated at the time a trustee is selecting a replacement charitable beneficiary, the trustee shall consult with the settlor concerning the selection of one or more replacement charitable beneficiaries.

(f) If the trustee and the settlor agree on the selection of one or more replacement charitable beneficiaries, the trustee shall send notice of the selection to the attorney general. If the attorney general determines that one or more replacement charitable beneficiaries do not have the same or similar charitable purpose as the failed charitable beneficiary, not later than the 21st day after the date the attorney general receives notice of the selection, the attorney general shall request in writing that a district court in the county in which the trust was created review the selection. If the court agrees with the attorney general's determination, any remaining replacement charitable beneficiary agreed on by the trustee and the settlor is the replacement charitable beneficiary. If there is not a remaining replacement charitable beneficiary agreed on by the trustee and the settlor, the court shall select one or more replacement charitable beneficiaries. If the court finds that the attorney general's request for a review is unreasonable, the replacement charitable beneficiary is the charitable beneficiary agreed on by the trustee and the settlor, and the court may require the attorney general to pay all court costs of the parties involved. Not later than the 30th day after the date the selection is final, the trustee shall provide to each replacement charitable beneficiary selected notice of the selection by certified mail, return receipt requested.

(g) If the trustee and the settlor cannot agree on the selection of a replacement charitable beneficiary, the trustee shall send notice of that fact to the attorney general not later than the 21st day after the date the trustee determines that an agreement cannot be reached. The attorney general shall refer the matter to a district court in the county in which the trust was created. The trustee and the settlor may each recommend to the court one or more replacement charitable beneficiaries. The court shall select a replacement charitable beneficiary and, not later than the 30th day after the date of the selection, provide to each charitable beneficiary selected notice of the selection by certified mail, return receipt requested.

Property Code § 123.001. Definitions

In this chapter:

(1) "Charitable entity" means a corporation, trust, community chest, fund, foundation, or other entity organized for scientific, educational, philanthropic, or environmental purposes, social welfare, the arts and humanities, or another civic or public purpose described by Section 501(c)(3) of the Internal Revenue Code of 1986 (26 U.S.C. 501(c)(3)).

(2) "Charitable trust" means a charitable entity, a trust the stated purpose of which is to benefit a charitable entity, or an inter vivos or testamentary gift to a charitable entity.

(3) "Proceeding involving a charitable trust" means a suit or other judicial proceeding the object of which is to:

(A) terminate a charitable trust or distribute its assets to other than charitable donees;

(B) depart from the objects of the charitable trust stated in the instrument creating the trust, including a proceeding in which the doctrine of cy-pres is invoked;

(C) construe, nullify, or impair the provisions of a testamentary or other instrument creating or affecting a charitable trust;

(D) contest or set aside the probate of an alleged will under which money, property, or another thing of value is given for charitable purposes;

(E) allow a charitable trust to contest or set aside the probate of an alleged will;

(F) determine matters relating to the probate and administration of an estate involving a charitable trust; or

(G) obtain a declaratory judgment involving a charitable trust.

(4) "Fiduciary or managerial agent" means an individual, corporation, or other entity acting either as a trustee, a member of the board of directors, an officer, an executor, or an administrator for a charitable trust.

Trust to enrich the American public financially does not qualify as charitable

MARSH v. FROST NATIONAL BANK
Court of Appeals of Texas, Corpus Christi-Edinburg
129 S.W.3d 174 (2004)

RODRIGUEZ, J. This is a declaratory judgment action. Appellants, Anna Spohn Welch Marsh, Noel Marsh, and Holly McKee, appeal from a probate order that modified a provision in the will of Charles Vartan Walker, deceased. Appellants raise four issues on appeal: (1) whether the trial court properly applied the cy pres doctrine to reform a will provision; (2) whether the trial court correctly ruled that tract 3 with its associated income, rather than the proceeds of the sale of that land, should be conveyed to the charitable beneficiary based on the cy pres reformation; (3) whether the abatement provisions of the order are appealable, and if so, whether those provisions were correct;[1] and (4) whether the trial court properly awarded attorney's fees to the Attorney General. We reverse and remand.

I. FACTUAL BACKGROUND

Charles Walker died on March 13, 2000, leaving a holographic will. The will named appellee, Frost National Bank (Frost Bank), as independent executor. On July 11, 2000, Frost Bank filed an original petition for declaratory judgment for clarification of several probate matters including the construction of Article V of the Charles Walker will, the provision at issue in this appeal. Article V reads in relevant part:

> I hereby direct my Executor to sell tract 3 of the V.M. Donigan 456.80 Partition for cash and to invest the proceeds in safe and secure tax-free U.S. government bonds or insured tax-free municipal bonds. This trust is to be called the James Madison Fund to honor our fourth President, the Father of the Constitution. The ultimate purpose of this fund is to provide a million dollar trust fund for every American 18 years or older. At 6% compound interest and a starting figure of $1,000,000.00, it would take approximately 346 years to provide enough money to do this. My executor will head the Board of Trustees. . . . When the Fund reaches $15,000,000 my Executor's function will cease, and the money will be turned over to the Sec. of the Treasury for management by the federal government. The President of the U.S., the Vice President of the U.S., and the Speaker of the U.S. House of Representatives shall be permanent Trustees of the Fund. The Congress of the United States shall make the final rules and regulations as to how the money will be distributed. No one shall be denied their share because of race, religion, marital status, sexual preference, or the amount of their wealth or lack thereof. . . .

Appellants filed an answer to the petition for declaratory judgment alleging that Article V of the will is void under the rule against perpetuities. Appellee, John Cornyn, Texas Attorney General, intervened in this action pursuant to section 123.002 of the Texas Property Code,[2] alleging that a general charitable intent could be found and that Article V of the will created a charitable trust. See Texas Property Code § 123.002. The Attorney General then moved for the application of the cy pres doctrine to Article V. After a hearing on this issue, the trial court found in relevant part that: (1) the will evidenced a general charitable intent; (2) Article V of the will established a valid charitable trust not subject to the rule against perpetuities;

[1] We will not address issue three on appeal for two reasons: (1) the issue calls upon this Court to issue an advisory opinion, which we have no authority to do . . . and (2) a review of the record reveals that no objection to the abatement provisions was ever made to the trial court and, therefore, appellants have not preserved any error for review. Texas Rule of Appellate Procedure 33.1(a); See Wal-Mart Stores, Inc. v. McKenzie, 997 S.W.2d 278, 280 (Tex. 1999).

[2] Section 123.002 designates the attorney general as a proper party who may intervene on behalf of the interest of the general public in a proceeding involving a charitable trust. Texas Property Code § 123.002.

(3) the Attorney General's request to have the court exercise its cy pres powers should be granted; and (4) attorney's fees should be awarded to the Attorney General. The order was signed with the modification of the trust and charitable beneficiary to be determined after a second hearing. The second hearing was held before a different judge. After reconsidering the previous order, the second judge confirmed and ratified that order and signed a final judgment establishing the modifications of Article V. This appeal ensued.

II. INTERPRETATION OF ARTICLE V

In their first issue, appellants argue that Article V does not show a charitable intent and therefore is not subject to reformation under the cy pres doctrine. Furthermore, appellants argue that because Article V violates the rule against perpetuities and cannot be legally reformed, it is void, and the proceeds of the land that would fund the trust should pass through intestate succession.

In Texas, under the rule against perpetuities, an interest is not good unless it must vest, if at all, not later than twenty-one years after some life in being at the time of the creation of the interest, plus a period of gestation. Id. § 112.036; See Foshee v. Republic Nat'l Bank, 617 S.W.2d 675, 677 (Tex. 1981). Both perpetual trusts and trusts for an indefinite duration violate the rule against perpetuities and are void. Atkinson v. Kettler, 372 S.W.2d 704, 711 (Tex. Civ. App.-Dallas 1963), aff'd, 383 S.W.2d 557 (Tex. 1964). The rule against perpetuities does not, however, apply to charitable trusts. See Texas Property Code § 112.036; *Foshee*, 617 S.W.2d at 677. Therefore, we must first address whether Article V of the will establishes a trust for a charitable purpose.

Whether or not a given purpose is "charitable" is a question of law for the court to decide. Frost Nat'l Bank v. Boyd, 188 S.W.2d 199, 206 (Tex. Civ. App.-San Antonio 1945), aff'd, 145 Tex. 206, 196 S.W.2d 497 (1946). When an issue turns on a pure question of law, we apply a de novo standard of review, Tenet Health Ltd. v. Zamora, 13 S.W.3d 464, 468 (Tex. App.-Corpus Christi 2000, pet. dism'd w.o.j.) (citing State v. Heal, 917 S.W.2d 6, 9 (Tex. 1996)), and we are not obligated to give any deference to legal conclusions reached by the trial court. Id. at 468-69.

Where the question of whether a given purpose is or is not charitable arises, the words "charitable purpose" have a definite ascertainable meaning in law, and a judicial determination may be made with satisfactory certainty in every case. See Boyd v. Frost Nat'l Bank, 145 Tex. 206, 196 S.W.2d 497, 501-03 (1946). Legal concepts of what are "charitable purposes" are categorized in section 368 of the Restatement Second of Trusts.[3] Id. at 502. Section 368 provides as follows:

---

[3] The Restatement now addresses "charitable purposes" in section 28 of the Restatement Third of Trusts. See Restatement (Third) of Trusts § 28 (2003). It provides no substantive changes. See id.

> Charitable purposes include
>
> (a) the relief of poverty;
>
> (b) the advancement of education;
>
> (c) the advancement of religion;
>
> (d) the promotion of health;
>
> (e) governmental or municipal purposes;
>
> (f) other purposes the accomplishment of which is beneficial to the community.

Restatement (Second) of Trusts § 368 (1959); see *Boyd*, 196 S.W.2d at 502.[4]

Article V of the will clearly states that the purpose of the fund is to provide a million dollar trust fund for every American eighteen years or older with no one being denied his share due to race, religion, marital status, sexual preference, or the amount of his wealth. Thus, it is clear from the language of Article V that if the purpose is to be found charitable, it must fall under the broad category (f) of section 368 of the Restatement; other purposes the accomplishment of which is beneficial to the community. Restatement (Second) of Trusts § 368 (1959). To be included in category (f), the purpose set out in Article V must go beyond merely providing financial enrichment to the individual members of the community; the purpose must promote the social interest of the community as a whole. See Restatement (Second) of Trusts § 374 cmt. a, f (1959).[5] The Restatement provides this Court with the following illustration applicable to the facts of this case:

> [I]f a large sum of money is given in trust to apply the income each year in paying a certain sum to every inhabitant of a city, whether rich or poor, the trust is not charitable, since although each inhabitant may receive a benefit, the social interest of the community as such is not thereby promoted.

---

[4] The *Boyd* court also set out other sources for use in determining what is a charitable purpose, including: (1) Bogart, Trusts and Trustees, section 361 et seq.; (2) Zollman, American Law of Charities, section 184 et seq.; (3) 14 C.J.S., Charities, p. 410 et seq.; and (4) 10 Am. Jur., Charities, p. 584 et seq. Boyd v. Frost Nat'l Bank, 145 Tex. 206, 196 S.W.2d 497, 502 (1946).

[5] The discussion in the Restatement Third of Trusts regarding purposes beneficial to the community, parallels the material in section 374 of the prior Restatement. See Restatement (Third) of Trusts § 28 cmt. 1 (2003). The observations in section 374 of the Restatement Second of Trusts are equally apt today. See id.

Id. § 374 cmt. f.[6] Furthermore, trusts created to distribute money out of liberality or generosity, without regard to the need of the donees and the effect of the gifts, do not have the requisite public benefit necessary to a charity. See G. Bogart, The Law of Trusts and Trustees § 379 (1991). With these concepts in mind, we analyze Article V.

Charles Walker expressly states in Article V that "[t]he ultimate purpose of this fund is to provide a million dollar trust fund for every American 18 years or older." From this language, it is obvious Walker intended nothing more than to financially enrich the American public. While this act is generous and benevolent, it is not necessarily beneficial to the community. There is no evidence referenced or argument made by appellees to persuade us that the effect of the trust contemplated by Walker would promote the social interest of the community. See Restatement (Second) of Trusts § 374 cmt. a (1959). Article V does not place restrictions or limitations on the beneficiaries of the trust, which would allow them to use the funds for any purpose, whether it be one that benefits the community or one that burdens it. The trust would provide a personal, individual benefit to each beneficiary but would fail to promote the social interest of the community as a whole. See id. § 374 cmt. a, f. Furthermore, the trust is established without regard to the need of the beneficiaries or the effect of the trust and as a result lacks the requisite public benefit necessary to a charity. See G. Bogart, The Law of Trusts and Trustees § 379 (1991). The trust created by Walker is nothing more than a generous distribution of money with no contemplation or recognition of public benefit. We conclude the trust established by Walker is devoid of any charitable intent or purpose and is therefore not charitable as defined by law.

Appellees argue that Texas courts have a long history of favoring charitable bequests and use liberal rules of construction to fulfill the intent of the testator. They also urge that where a bequest is open to two constructions, the interpretation that gives the charity effect should be adopted, and that which will defeat the charity should be rejected. In support of their arguments, appellees cite *Boyd*; Blocker v. State, 718 S.W.2d 409 (Tex. App.-Houston [1st Dist.] 1986, writ ref'd n.r.e.); Taysum v. El Paso Nat'l Bank, 256 S.W.2d 172 (Tex. Civ. App.-El Paso 1952, writ ref'd); and Eldridge v. Marshall Nat'l Bank, 527 S.W.2d 222 (Tex. Civ. App.-Houston [14th Dist.] 1975, writ ref'd n.r.e.). We agree with appellees' contentions and the cases cited in support thereof. However, we find these cases distinguishable and the specific propositions stated inapplicable. In the cases cited, the courts, after finding an existing charitable intent as defined by law, used liberal rules of construction to sustain the charitable trust. In this case, however, we find no charitable

---

[6] Appellees argue that Texas courts have not followed nor adopted the Restatement, much less a comment, as even persuasive authority. We note that in many of the Texas cases addressing the issue of charitable trusts the Restatement is cited and used as guidance. In some cases courts have also cited to specific comments of the Restatement. E.g., Powers v. First Nat. Bank of Corsicana, 138 Tex. 604, 161 S.W.2d 273, 279 (1942) (citing comment d of the Restatement (Second) of Trusts § 371 in determining whether a trust is charitable); Foshee v. Republic Nat'l Bank, 617 S.W.2d 675, 677 (Tex. 1981) (citing comment h of the Restatement (Second) of Trusts § 374 as a source used in determining the existence of a charitable purpose).

intent or purpose. Therefore, these rules of law do not apply. Appellees would have us use these rules to create a charitable intent where none exists. We decline to do so.

Having concluded Article V of the will does not establish a charitable trust, the rule against perpetuities is applicable. In this case, the trust is of indefinite duration and therefore violates the rule against perpetuities. See *Atkinson*, 372 S.W.2d at 711. Accordingly, appellants' first issue is sustained.

III. REFORMATION OF NONCHARITABLE TRUSTS

When a noncharitable trust is in violation of the rule against perpetuities, a trial court is authorized to reform the trust pursuant to section 5.043 of the Texas Property Code. Texas Property Code § 5.043. A court has the power to reform or construe the trust according to the doctrine of cy pres by giving effect to the general intent of the testator within the limits of the rule. Id. § 5.043(b). It is clear from the language in Article V that Walker's general intent in creating the trust was to financially enrich the American public. Therefore, application of section 5.043 requires the court to reform or construe Article V within the limits of the rule against perpetuities and consistent with this intent. If reformation is not possible however, the trust is void as being in violation of the rule.

Appellants contend in their second issue that the court erred in not selling tract 3 of the V.M. Donigan 456.80 partition for cash as stated in Article V. Because of the disposition of appellants' first issue, we need not address their second issue. However, as noted above, reformation under section 5.043, if possible, provides for the court to give effect to the general intent and specific directives of the creator. Texas Property Code § 5.043(b). The selling of the land provided for under Article V would constitute a specific directive and should be given effect in any reformation contemplated by the court.

Therefore, we remand this case to the trial court to consider the feasibility of reformation of Article V under section 5.043.

IV. ATTORNEY'S FEES

In their fourth issue, appellants complain that the court improperly awarded attorney's fees to the Attorney General. The trial court awarded reasonable and necessary attorney's fees totaling $24,500 to be paid out of the Estate of Charles Walker.

In proceedings under both the Texas Trust Code and the Uniform Declaratory Judgments Act, the trial court may award such costs and reasonable and necessary attorney's fees as are equitable and just. Texas Property Code § 114.064; Texas Civil Practice & Remedies Code § 37.009. In this case, the attorney's fees were awarded pursuant to both the trust code and the declaratory judgment act. Because we are reversing the trial court's judgment interpreting Article V as having a general charitable intent, the trial court may wish to reconsider the award of attorney's fees to the Attorney General. . . . Appellants' fourth issue is sustained.

V. CONCLUSION

Accordingly, we reverse the trial court's judgment to the extent it established a charitable trust and remand this case for further proceedings consistent with this opinion. We also reverse the trial court's award of attorney's fees and remand this issue to the trial court for further consideration.

Section B. Supervision of Charitable Trusts

Property Code § 114.003. Powers to Direct; Charitable Trusts

(a) In this section, "charitable trust" has the meaning assigned by Section 123.001.

(a-1) The terms of a charitable trust may give a trustee or other person a power to direct the modification or termination of the trust.

(b) If the terms of a charitable trust give a person the power to direct certain actions of the trustee, the trustee shall act in accordance with the person's direction unless:

(1) the direction is manifestly contrary to the terms of the trust; or

(2) the trustee knows the direction would constitute a serious breach of a fiduciary duty that the person holding the power to direct owes to the beneficiaries of the trust.

(c) A person, other than a beneficiary, who holds a power to direct with respect to a charitable trust is presumptively a fiduciary required to act in good faith with regard to the purposes of the trust and the interests of the beneficiaries. The holder of a power to direct with respect to a charitable trust is liable for any loss that results from a breach of the person's fiduciary duty.

Property Code § 123.002. Attorney General's Participation

For and on behalf of the interest of the general public of this state in charitable trusts, the attorney general is a proper party and may intervene in a proceeding involving a charitable trust. The attorney general may join and enter into a compromise, settlement agreement, contract, or judgment relating to a proceeding involving a charitable trust.

Property Code § 123.003. Notice

(a) Any party initiating a proceeding involving a charitable trust shall give notice of the proceeding to the attorney general by sending to the attorney general, by registered or certified mail, a true copy of the petition or other instrument initiating the proceeding involving a charitable trust within 30 days of the filing of such petition or other instrument, but no less than 25 days prior to a hearing in such a proceeding. This subsection does not apply to a proceeding that is initiated by an application that exclusively seeks the admission of a will to probate, regardless of whether the application seeks the appointment of a personal representative, if the application:

(1) is uncontested; and

(2) is not subject to Section 83, Texas Probate Code.

(b) Notice shall be given to the attorney general of any pleading which adds new causes of action or additional parties to a proceeding involving a charitable trust in which the attorney general has previously waived participation or in which the attorney general has otherwise failed to intervene. Notice shall be given by sending to the attorney general by registered or certified mail a true copy of the pleading within 30 days of the filing of the pleading, but no less than 25 days prior to a hearing in the proceeding.

(c) The party or the party's attorney shall execute and file in the proceeding an affidavit stating the facts of the notice and shall attach to the affidavit the customary postal receipts signed by the attorney general or an assistant attorney general.

Property Code § 123.004. Voidable Judgment or Agreement

(a) A judgment in a proceeding involving a charitable trust is voidable if the attorney general is not given notice of the proceeding as required by this chapter. On motion of the attorney general after the judgment is rendered, the judgment shall be set aside.

(b) A compromise, settlement agreement, contract, or judgment relating to a proceeding involving a charitable trust is voidable on motion of the attorney general if the attorney general is not given notice as required by this chapter unless the attorney general has:

(1) declined in writing to be a party to the proceeding; or

(2) approved and joined in the compromise, settlement agreement, contract, or judgment.

Members of charitable organization lack special interest standing

NACOL v. STATE
Court of Appeals of Texas, Houston
792 S.W.2d 810 (1990)

ROBERTSON, J. This case arises out of a suit brought by the State of Texas seeking the appointment of a receiver for ARMS of America (Multiple Sclerosis Research) Limited ("ARMS") and injunctive relief. Within two years after being funded with over $1 million, ARMS maintained a cash balance of $100,000 with expenses of $50,000 per month. The attorney general sought to place ARMS in receivership to determine if the organization could be restructured. The receiver found that ARMS could not be restructured and should be dissolved. In fourteen points of error, Nacol and Blackwell, members of ARMS, challenge (1) the attorney general's authority to file suit in Harris County, (2) the trial court's order striking their pleas in intervention, (3) the ARMS president's authority to sign the agreed order to appoint a receiver, and (4) the constitutionality of article 4412a of the Revised Civil Statutes, now codified as sections 123.001 through 123.005 of the Property Code.

The attorney general of Texas filed an original petition for appointment of a receiver and injunctive relief against ARMS to protect and conserve the assets of ARMS and to prevent disposal or concealment of property, assets, or records of ARMS. The petition recited that ARMS was created to receive charitable donations from the public to fund multiple sclerosis research. In 1985, ARMS was funded with $1,067,092.97. By September 30, 1985, the balance was $393,831 and by March 27, 1986, the balance was approximately $100,000 with expenses of $50,000 per month.

In an agreed order, dated March 31, 1986, Ronald J. Sommers was appointed receiver for ARMS. The agreed order was signed by ARMS's president and stated that, "all assets of the corporation, which was organized solely for charitable purposes, are deemed impressed with a charitable trust by virtue of the expressed declaration of the corporation's purpose." The receiver filed his report finding (1) the affairs of ARMS had been mismanaged, (2) there were inadequate financial controls, excessive expenditures, and unreasonable salaries, (3) there was a pattern of self-dealing between the board of directors, executive committee, and the officers of the corporation, (4) all fund raising, but one event, resulted in losses, and (5) the expenditures authorized by the ARMS board were inappropriate. The receiver further recommended that ARMS be liquidated.

The court accepted the report of the receiver and ordered the liquidation of ARMS. Three days later, Mae Nacol filed her plea in intervention. Nacol also filed a motion to set aside the order accepting the receiver's report and the agreed order appointing the receiver, and a motion to dismiss the original petition seeking appointment of a receiver. Several months later, Gene Blackwell filed his plea in intervention. The trial judge struck Nacol's and Blackwell's pleas and denied Nacol's motions. Nacol and Blackwell appeal from those rulings.

Because points of error eight and nine are dispositive of this appeal, we will address only those points. Nacol and Blackwell claim the trial court improperly struck their pleas in intervention. After final judgment in this case, Nacol and Blackwell filed pleas in intervention claiming they were members of ARMS of America and, as such, had standing to intervene pursuant to the Non-Profit Corporation Act. Texas Revised Civil Statutes art. 1396-1.01 et seq. The attorney general moved to strike those pleas, alleging Nacol and Blackwell had no greater interest in ARMS than the general public and, therefore, did not have standing to intervene. The trial court struck the pleas.

Because Nacol and Blackwell have no special interest different from that of the general public they have no standing to institute or maintain a suit to enforce a public charitable trust. See Coffee v. William Marsh Rice University, 403 S.W.2d 340, 341 (Tex. 1966). The attorney general is the representative of the public and is the proper party to maintain such a suit. Gray v. Saint Matthews Cathedral Endowment Fund, Inc., 544 S.W.2d 488, 490 (Tex. Civ. App.-Texarkana 1976, writ ref'd n.r.e.). Where a charity is for the benefit of the public at large or a considerable portion of it, and the language of its creation is such that no particular individuals can be pointed out as the objects to be benefited by it, the official representative of the public is the only party capable of vindicating the public's rights in connection with that charity. Id.

Nacol and Blackwell argue that ARMS is not a charitable trust and is therefore not subject to the attorney general's authority to enforce public charitable trusts. Article 4412a of the Texas Revised Civil Statutes, however, includes in a charitable trust "all gifts and trusts for charitable purposes." A public charity is defined to include any organization with a purpose benefitting a large and indefinite group of people. Powers v. First Nat'l Bank of Corsicana, 161 S.W.2d 273, 280 (Tex. 1942). In its articles of incorporation, ARMS states the purposes for which the corporation is organized:

(1) To operate exclusively for charitable, educational and scientific purposes as referred to in Sections 501(c)(3) and 170(c)(2) of the Internal Revenue Code[.]

(2) To promote all research necessary to find the cause, cure and prevention of Multiple Sclerosis and aid and improve the condition of those suffering from it and publish the results of such research for the benefit of the public.

(3) To collect, analyze and collate information relating thereto and to exchange such information with other affinitive bodies, to treat and determine upon all questions relating to Multiple Sclerosis and publish the results of such research for the benefit of the public.

We conclude that, based on its stated purposes, ARMS is a charitable trust under article 4412a.

Under Texas Rule of Civil Procedure 60, an individual may intervene if the intervenor's interest is such that, if the original action had never been commenced, and he had first brought it as a sole plaintiff, he would have been entitled to recover to the extent of at least a part of the relief sought; if the action had been brought against him, he would be able to defeat recovery, or some part thereof. Intercontinental Consolidated v. University Sav. Ass'n, 793 S.W.2d 652 (Tex. 1990). Whether an intervention should be struck is in the discretion of the trial court and its exercise of that discretion is subject to review for abuse of discretion. Texas Supply Center, Inc. v. Daon Corp., 641 S.W.2d 335, 337 (Tex. App.-Dallas 1982, writ ref'd n.r.e.). The attorney general is the representative of the public and he is the individual who may bring suit for the benefit of the public. Nacol and Blackwell have no greater interest than the members of the public the attorney general represents. Nacol and Blackwell are not proper parties to the suit; therefore, the trial court did not abuse its discretion in striking the pleas in intervention.

Moreover, Nacol's and Blackwell's pleas were not timely filed. The pleas were filed after the trial court signed the judgment. Where a petition in intervention is filed after judgment, rule 60 does not apply. Comal County Rural High School District No. 705 v. Nelson, 314 S.W.2d 956, 957 (Tex. 1958). The filing of Nacol's and Blackwell's pleas in intervention was not proper under rule 60, and the pleas had no effect on the court's final judgment. Points of error eight and nine are overruled.

Nacol's and Blackwell's right to intervene is dispositive of this appeal. Intervention is a mechanism where one not an original party to pending legal proceedings becomes a party thereto for the protection of some right or interest to be affected by the proceedings. Whitman v. Willis, 51 Tex. 421, 424 (1879). By definition, one who seeks to intervene is not a party to the proceedings. Therefore, once Nacol's and Blackwell's pleas in intervention were properly struck, they were not parties and had no standing to challenge the attorney general's actions. See Road Dist. No. 5 v. McElwrath, 64 S.W.2d 1109 (Tex. Civ. App.-San Antonio 1933, no writ) (Third parties who unsuccessfully tried to intervene after rendition of final judgment held not parties and not entitled to appeal). Points of error one through seven and ten through fourteen are overruled.

The trial court's judgment is affirmed.

Chapter 12. Trusts: Powers of Appointment

Section A. Exercise of a Power of Appointment

Court approval is not a prerequisite to vesting of power of appointment

FOSTER v. FOSTER
Court of Appeals of Texas, Dallas
884 S.W.2d 497 (1993)

KINKEADE, J. William Dee Foster appeals from a trial court order approving the administrator's account for final settlement and denying his application for partition of assets. In two points of error, he argues that the trial court erred in concluding that a document signed by his brother, Billy A. Foster, was not a valid and enforceable exercise of a power of appointment granting him a one-half interest in the assets of the estate of his other brother, Bryant Foster. Because the trial court's conclusions that the document was not a valid and enforceable exercise of the power of appointment were incorrect, we reverse the trial court's judgment.

FACTUAL AND PROCEDURAL HISTORY

Bryant Foster died on August 24, 1985. He left a will dated March 24, 1985. Pursuant to the will, he appointed his brother, Billy Foster, executor of his estate. He left one dollar to each of his two sons. The rest of the estate was to be divided by Billy Foster "equally as he sees fit." The will did not mention Bryant Foster's other brother, William Foster. On September 12, 1985, Billy Foster filed an application in county court to probate the will. On October 7, 1985, he filed a request for a declaratory judgment in the same action, requesting the court to construe the will as granting him a general power of appointment to distribute the assets of his brother's estate.

After requesting the declaratory judgment but before the court acted on his request, Billy Foster consulted an attorney and signed an "Exercise of Power of Appointment" on November 23, 1985. That document provided:

> I, BILLY A. FOSTER, the donee of a power of appointment given to me under the Last Will and Testament of Bryant F. Foster, dated March 24, 1985, which was admitted to probate in Cause No. 22566 styled "Estate of Bryant F. Foster,

> Deceased" in the Probate Court of Grayson County, Texas, Sitting in Probate, by Order dated September 27, 1985, hereby expressly exercise the aforesaid power by appointing one-half of the assets subject to it to my brother, William Foster, whose permanent address is Route 2, Box 275, West Monroe, Louisiana 71291.

The document was never filed with the court.

In response to Billy Foster's request for declaratory judgment, the court issued an order on February 5, 1986, construing the will. It held that the will created:

> . . . a generally exercisable power of appointment of the residuary property of the Estate of Bryant F. Foster, Deceased, granted to Billy A. Foster as donee, in which Billy A. Foster shall have the current power to appoint all of such residuary estate to such persons, including himself, Billy A. Foster, and in such estate, interest and proportions as Billy A. Foster shall determine.

Billy Foster later filed a cumulative accounting of the assets of Bryant Foster's estate. The accounting showed that Billy Foster equally divided some but not all of the estate's assets between himself and William Foster. On January 8, 1992, William Foster filed an application for partition and distribution of the estate. He claimed that he was entitled to an undivided one-half of the assets of the estate under the exercise of the power of appointment signed by Billy Foster on November 23, 1985. Billy Foster moved for dismissal of the application. On April 24, 1992, Billy Foster filed an account for final settlement of the estate in which he exercised his power of appointment to give all the estate's remaining assets to himself.

The court entered an order on June 29, 1992, approving Billy Foster's cumulative accounting and his account for final settlement and denying William Foster's application for partition of assets. The court concluded that (1) the document signed by Billy Foster on November 23, 1985, was premature, (2) the court's declaratory judgment of February 5, 1986, declaring that Bryant Foster's intent was to give Billy Foster an unlimited power of appointment, required Billy Foster to ratify the November 23, 1985 document before that document became effective, (3) Billy Foster's failure to ratify the November 23, 1985 document operated as a de facto revocation of that document, and (4) any distributions made by Billy Foster to persons other than himself were gifts of the estate made pursuant to Billy Foster's unlimited power of appointment under the will as construed by the court.

POWER OF APPOINTMENT

In his first point of error, William Foster contends that the court erred in concluding that the document signed by Billy Foster on November 23, 1985, was not a valid and enforceable exercise of his power of appointment granted in the will. William Foster argues that Billy Foster's power of appointment under the will was created by the will and vested in Billy Foster when Bryant Foster died on August 24, 1985. He further argues that the November 23, 1985 document signed by Billy Foster met the criteria for exercising that power of appointment as set out in Republic National Bank v. Fredericks, 155 Tex. 79, 283 S.W.2d 39,

47 (1955). Since the power of appointment under the will was vested in Billy Foster at the time he signed the November 23, 1985 document and that document met the *Fredericks* criteria, William Foster concludes that the November 23, 1985 document was a valid assignment of an undivided one-half interest in the estate to him. We agree. . . .

Vesting of the Power of Appointment

We first address the issue of when the power of appointment granted to Billy Foster vested. When an individual delegates to another person the power of designating or selecting how that individual's property will be divided upon death, that individual has granted a power of appointment. See *Fredericks*, 283 S.W.2d at 46. The person granting the power, such as a testator through a will, is the "donor." See G.A.C. Halff Found. v. Calvert, 281 S.W.2d 178, 182 n. 1 (Tex. Civ. App.-San Antonio 1955, writ ref'd n.r.e.). The person receiving the power is the "donee." Id. Those who receive property from the donee are "appointees." Id.

Billy Foster argues that the power of appointment did not vest in him until the date the trial court construed the will as granting him a general power of appointment. Since that date was after the date he signed the exercise of the power of appointment, he argues the document was not effective until he ratified it, which he never did. Billy Foster's argument ignores the express language of section 37 of the Texas Probate Code. That section states:

> When a person dies, leaving a lawful will, all of his estate devised or bequeathed by such will, and all powers of appointment granted in such will, shall vest immediately in the devisees and legatees of such estate and the donees of such powers . . . .

Texas Probate Code § 37. Based upon section 37, Billy Foster was vested with the power of appointment granted to him in the will immediately upon Bryant Foster's death on August 24, 1985; therefore, he could and did exercise that power as of November 23, 1985.

Exercise of the Power of Appointment

We next address the issue of whether the November 23, 1985 document was a valid exercise of Billy Foster's power of appointment. In *Fredericks*, the Texas Supreme Court prescribed the following three criteria for determining if an instrument purporting to be an exercise of a power of appointment is valid:

(1) did the instrument reference the power,

(2) did the instrument reference the property subject to execution under the power of appointment, and

(3) would the provisions of the instrument executed by the donee otherwise be ineffectual; i.e., would have no operation except as an execution of the power.

Fredericks, 283 S.W.2d at 47. When we apply these three criteria, the November 23, 1985 document exercised Billy Foster's power of appointment under the will. The document referenced the power of appointment granted under Bryant Foster's will and stated that Billy Foster was expressly exercising that power. The document referred to the property subject to execution under the power of appointment and specifically stated that Billy Foster appointed one-half of the assets subject to the power of appointment to William Foster. The document titled "Exercise of Power of Appointment" specifically provided that Billy Foster was exercising the power of appointment granted to him under Bryant Foster's will.

Billy Foster contends that the document was not valid because it was never filed with the county court. Contrary to that argument, the court in *Fredericks* did not include filing with the court as a criterion for determining whether a power of appointment was valid. Billy Foster cites no authority and we find none requiring that an exercise of a power of appointment be filed with the court in order to be effective.

Standing and Limitations

In the alternative, Billy Foster contends that, assuming the November 23, 1985 document was a valid exercise of his power of appointment, William Foster lacked standing to file his application for partition and distribution of the estate. He argues that once the court construed the will as granting him a general power of appointment, William Foster no longer qualified as an "interested person" pursuant to section 3(r) of the Texas Probate Code with the right to complain about how the estate's assets were divided because William Foster was not a beneficiary under the will. Billy Foster's interpretation of section 3(r) is incorrect.

Section 3(r) defines interested persons as "heirs, devisees, spouses, creditors, or any others having a property right in, or claim against, the estate being administered . . . ." Texas Probate Code § 3(r). William Foster claimed a property right in one-half of the assets of the estate by virtue of the November 23, 1985 exercise of the power of appointment. He was, therefore, an interested party as defined by section 3(r) and had standing to file his application.

Also in the alternative and assuming the November 23, 1985 document was valid and enforceable, Billy Foster contends that William Foster's claim was for breach of the document and was barred by limitations because he did not assert it within four years of the date the document was signed. He argues, therefore, that the trial court was required to disapprove the claim pursuant to section 298(c) of the Texas Probate Code. This argument fails for two reasons. First, a claim for breach of contract accrues when the contract is breached, not when the contract is signed. See Hoover v. Gregory, 835 S.W.2d 668, 677 (Tex. App. Dallas 1992, writ denied). Second, section 298 addresses money claims against a testator or intestate, such as those of a creditor, that were already in existence before death. Texas Probate Code § 298(a). That section does not concern claims dealing with the final division of the estate to devisees or appointees, as William Foster's claim in this case. See Texas Probate Code § 298.

CONCLUSION

Based upon section 37 of the Texas Probate Code and the criteria set out in *Fredericks*, the power of appointment granted to Billy Foster under Bryant Foster's will vested in Billy Foster at the time of Bryant Foster's death on August 24, 1985, and the November 23, 1985 document was a valid and enforceable exercise of that power. Accordingly, the court's conclusions that the document was invalid and unenforceable were incorrect because the trial court improperly applied the law to the facts. Because the exercise of the power of appointment was valid and enforceable, we conclude there is no other theory on which to affirm the court's order. We, therefore, sustain William Foster's first point of error. Because of our disposition of his first point of error, we need not reach his second point of error.

We reverse the court's order approving Billy Foster's account for final settlement and denying William Foster's application for partition of assets and remand the case to the court for further proceedings consistent with this opinion.

Section B. Release of a Power of Appointment

Property Code § 181.051. Authority of Donee to Release Power

Unless the instrument creating the power specifically provides to the contrary, a donee may at any time:

(1) completely release the power;

(2) release the power as to any property subject to the power;

(3) release the power as to a person in whose favor a power may be exercised; or

(4) limit in any respect the extent to which the power may be exercised.

Property Code § 181.052. Requisites of Release

(a) A partial or complete release of a power, with or without consideration, is valid if the donee executes and acknowledges, in the manner required by law for the execution and recordation of deeds, an instrument evidencing an intent to make the release, and the instrument is delivered:

(1) to the person or in the manner specified in the instrument creating the power;

(2) to an adult, other than the donee releasing the power, who may take any of the property subject to the power if the power is not exercised or in whose favor it may be exercised after the partial release;

(3) to a trustee or cotrustee of the property subject to the power; or

(4) to an appropriate county clerk for recording.

(b) An instrument releasing a power may be recorded in a county in this state in which:

(1) property subject to the power is located;

(2) a donee in control of the property resides;

(3) a trustee in control of the property resides;

(4) a corporate trustee in control of the property has its principal office; or

(5) the instrument creating the power is probated or recorded.

Chapter 13. Trusts: Construction and Future Interests

Section A. Classification of Future Interests

Right of reentry is not distinguishable from possibility of reverter for purposes of inverse condemnation claim

EL DORADO LAND CO. v. CITY OF McKINNEY
Supreme Court of Texas
395 S.W.3d 798 (2013)

DEVINE, J. The issue in this inverse condemnation lawsuit is whether a reversionary interest, consisting of the grantor's right to purchase real property on the occurrence of a future event, is a sufficient property interest to support an inverse condemnation claim. The trial court concluded it was not and dismissed the case. The court of appeals affirmed the trial court's judgment, holding that the grantor's retained right was not a compensable property interest under the Takings Clause of the Texas Constitution. 349 S.W.3d 215, 216, 218 (Tex. App.-Dallas 2011) (citing Texas Constitution art I, § 17). Because we conclude that the reversionary interest here is a compensable property interest, we reverse and remand. . . .

I

In 1999, El Dorado Land Company sold several acres of land to the City of McKinney for use as a park. El Dorado's special warranty deed provided that the conveyance was "subject to the requirement and restriction that the property shall be used only as a Community Park." If the City decided not to use the property for that purpose, the deed further granted El Dorado the right to purchase the property. The deed labeled this right an option and set the option's price at the amount the City paid or the property's current market value, whichever was less. El Dorado also had the right to inspect the property and to close on the purchase within ninety days after inspection.

Ten years after acquiring the property, the City built a public library on part of the land. The City did not offer to sell the property to El Dorado or otherwise give notice before building the library. After learning about the library, El Dorado notified the City by letter that it intended to exercise its option to purchase. El Dorado's letter further asked the City within ten days to acknowledge its obligations under the deed and to suggest an acceptable closing date.

After the City failed to acknowledge El Dorado's rights under the deed, El Dorado sued for inverse condemnation. The City responded with a plea to the jurisdiction. In its plea, the City argued that El Dorado's claim did not involve a compensable taking of property but a mere breach of contract for which the City's governmental immunity had not been waived. The trial court agreed, sustaining the City's plea and dismissing El Dorado's lawsuit. The court of appeals similarly agreed and affirmed the trial court's judgment. 349 S.W.3d 215.

II

The dispute here continues over the nature of El Dorado's interest in this land. El Dorado argues that its right to purchase this property is a real property interest, in the nature of a reversionary interest, and more particularly described as a right of reentry. The City, on the other hand, contends that El Dorado's option is not a real property interest but a mere contract right. As such, the City argues that the option is unenforceable against it absent an express waiver of the City's governmental immunity. Because the Legislature has not chosen to waive governmental immunity for this particular type of contract claim, the City concludes that the court of appeals correctly affirmed the dismissal of El Dorado's claim.

The court of appeals similarly reasoned that the deed restriction and option were merely contract rights that were not compensable against a governmental entity under the Texas Constitution. See 349 S.W.3d at 218 (observing that inverse condemnation claims have "traditionally involved interests in real property and not the alleged taking of property interests created under contract"). The court accordingly "reject[ed] El Dorado's argument that, pursuant to the deed provision, it held a reversionary interest or the 'possibility of reverter' in the property." Id. While we agree that the deed did not create a possibility of reverter, we disagree that El Dorado did not retain another type of reversionary interest in the property.

El Dorado refers to its reversionary interest as a right of reentry. A right of reentry is a "future interest created in the transferor that [may] become possessory upon the termination of a fee simple subject to a condition subsequent." Restatement (Third) of Property: Wills and Other Donative Transfers § 25.2 cmt. b (hereafter Restatement (Third) of Property); see also Davis v. Vidal, 105 Tex. 444, 151 S.W. 290, 292-93 (1912) (describing a right of reentry as "a contingent reversionary interest in the premises resulting from the conveyance of an estate upon a condition subsequent where there has been an infraction of such condition").

Under the deed, El Dorado's possessory interest was contingent on the property's use. If the City violated the deed restriction, El Dorado retained the power to terminate the City's estate.[1] The deed referred to this power or right as an option, but it effectively

[1] This power, referred to in the deed as the option to purchase, is also known at common law by other names, such as a right of entry for condition broken, a right of reentry for breach of condition subsequent, or a power of termination. See 3 Richard R. Powell, Powell

functioned as a power of termination, or as El Dorado labels it, a right of reentry. El Dorado's deed conveyed a defeasible estate ("a fee simple subject to a condition subsequent")[2] to the City with El Dorado retaining a conditional future interest—the power to terminate the City's defeasible estate on the occurrence of a condition subsequent.[3] We have previously equated this right to an estate or interest in land. *Davis*, 151 S.W. at 293; See also Restatement of Property § 153(1)(a) & cmt. a (noting that the term future interest includes an interest in land which "may become a present interest" and is "sufficiently broad to include . . . powers of termination").

Contrary to the court of appeals, we conclude that El Dorado retained a reversionary interest in the property. We likewise disagree with the court of appeals' analysis of El Dorado's claim as a contract right dependent on a statutory waiver of the City's governmental immunity. A statutory waiver of immunity is unnecessary for a takings claim because the Texas Constitution waives "governmental immunity for the taking, damaging or destruction of property for public use." Steele v. City of Houston, 603 S.W.2d 786, 791 (Tex. 1980).

El Dorado's claim is that the City took or destroyed its reversionary interest in the property by refusing either to convey the property or to condemn El Dorado's interest. The issue then is whether El Dorado's reversionary interest can support a takings claim under the Texas Constitution. Texas Constitution art. I § 17. El Dorado submits that it can under our decision in Leeco Gas & Oil Co. v. Nueces County, 736 S.W.2d 629 (Tex. 1987).

III

Leeco, like this case, involved a restricted conveyance of land to a governmental entity that later sought to avoid the deed restriction. The land in that case was donated to Nueces County for use as a park, and the deed included a restrictive covenant requiring that use. *Leeco*, 736 S.W.2d at 630. The grantor retained a reversionary interest, described as a possibility of reverter,[4] in the event the land was not used as a park. Id.

---

on Real Property § 20.01[1] (2000) ("The term 'power of termination' is used by the Restatement and by some courts, but most courts and most lawyers employ the term 'right of entry for condition broken.'"); see also 34 Tex. Jur. 3d Estates § 8 at 546 (2010) (noting that "a future interest" may be "characterized as a right of reentry for breach of condition subsequent or, in other words, an estate subject to a power of termination").

[2] Restatement (Third) of Property § 25.2 cmt. b.

[3] See Restatement of Property § 155 (defining a power of termination as "the future interest created in the transferor . . . by a transfer of either an estate in land or an analogous interest in a thing other than land, subject to a condition subsequent").

[4] A possibility of reverter is a term of art for a future interest retained by a grantor that conveys a determinable fee; "it is the grantor's right to fee ownership in the real property reverting to him if the condition terminating the determinable fee occurs." Luckel v. White, 819 S.W.2d 459, 464 (Tex. 1991).

Nueces County subsequently decided to use the land for another purpose and sought to condemn the grantor's reversionary interest. Although the land was worth millions of dollars, the trial court awarded only nominal damages for the grantor's reversionary interest, and the court of appeals affirmed that award. Id. We reversed and remanded, concluding that the grantor's reversionary interest was worth more than nominal damages. Id. at 631-32.

Relying on the Restatement of Property, we observed that a possibility of reverter was a protected property interest, the value of which depended upon the imminence of possession. Id. We explained that a nominal valuation would be appropriate for the government taking such property only "when the event upon which the possessory estate in fee simple defeasible is to end is not probable within a reasonably short period of time." Id. at 631. Conversely, we explained that nominal damages would be inappropriate if the defeasible event was reasonably certain to occur in the near future or had already occurred. Id. Under those circumstances, we said the compensable value of the reversionary interest should be measured by the amount "the value of the unrestricted fee exceeds the value of the restricted fee." Id. at 631-32. *Leeco* thus recognizes that a future interest in real property is compensable under the Takings Clause, Texas Constitution art. I, § 17, and that the owner of such an interest is entitled to a condemnation award. Id. at 631 (citing Restatement of Property § 53).

The court of appeals' opinion does not directly address *Leeco*, but arguably attempts to distinguish the decision by observing that the deed in this case did not include a possibility of reverter. 349 S.W.3d at 218. While we agree it did not, as previously explained, we do not accept the court's further conclusion that El Dorado's deed did not create a reversionary interest. See id. (rejecting El Dorado's argument that "it held a reversionary interest or the 'possibility of reverter' in the property"). As El Dorado argues, the deed restriction and option created in El Dorado a right of reentry, which is a reversionary interest, albeit of a different type than the possibility of reverter reserved in *Leeco*.

The City argues that *Leeco* is distinguishable on this ground because a possibility of reverter is materially different from the right or option reserved by El Dorado. At oral argument, the City elaborated on the distinction, explaining that Leeco's reversionary interest was different because it was self-executing, whereas the right retained by El Dorado was not. While we agree that Leeco's possibility of reverter and El Dorado's right of reentry are different types of reversionary interests, it is not apparent why their technical differences make one a compensable property interest and the other a worthless right. In both, the termination of the possessory estate rests on the occurrence of a condition subsequent imposed upon the conveyance. That a right of reentry requires its holder to make an election does not make it any less a property right, particularly where as here the holder has made the required election.

Historically, the law divided future interests into five types: (1) remainders, (2) executory interests, (3) reversions, (4) possibilities of reverter, and (5) rights of entry. Restatement (Third) of Property § 25.2 cmt. a. Remainders and executory interests are future interests created in persons other than the grantor. 3 Richard R. Powell, Powell on Real Property § 20.01 [2] (2000). Reversions, possibilities of reverter, and rights of entry are interests that remain with the grantor. Id.; see also Restatement (Third) of Property § 25.2 cmt. b (noting their classification "as reversionary future interests, because they were retained by the transferor"). . . . The latest Restatement dispenses with the historical parsing of future interests, recognizing only reversions and remainders. Restatement (Third) of Property § 25.2. It thus abandons distinctions that previously differentiated a possibility of reverter from a right of entry because, in its view, no legal consequences attach to such distinctions. See id. § 25.2 cmt. a ("Today, no legal consequences depend upon placing a future interest in one category or another.").

We likewise see no reason to distinguish between the reversionary interest in *Leeco* and the one in this case. Under Texas law, the possibility of reverter and the right of reentry are both freely assignable like other property interests. James v. Dalhart Consol. Indep. Sch. Dist., 254 S.W.2d 826, 829 (Tex. Civ. App.-Amarillo 1952, writ ref'd). And, although the earlier Restatement individually identified automatic reversions and other interests, like El Dorado's power of termination or right of reentry, it nevertheless grouped them as reversionary interests. See Restatement of Property § 153 cmt. a. Simply put, both the possibility of reverter and the right of reentry are future interests in real property. See Lewis M. Simes & Allan F. Smith, The Law of Future Interests § 1 (2d ed. 1956) (defining a future interest as "an interest in land or other things in which the privilege of possession or of enjoyment is future and not present"). And *Leeco* recognizes that a future interest in real property is compensable under the Takings Clause. 736 S.W.2d at 631-32 (citing Restatement of Property § 53). We accordingly reject the City's argument that *Leeco* is distinguishable merely because it involved a different type of reversionary interest . . . .

In summary, we conclude that the reversionary interest retained by El Dorado in its deed to the City is a property interest capable of being taken by condemnation. We express no opinion, however, on whether a taking has occurred in this case. We reverse and remand to the trial court for it to determine whether the City violated its deed restrictions by building a public library on a part of the land dedicated for use as a community park and, if so, to what extent the City has taken El Dorado's interest in the restricted property.

Section B. Construction of Trust Instruments

Property Code § 5.042. Abolition of Common-Law Rules

(a) The common-law rules known as the rule in Shelley's case, the rule forbidding a remainder to the grantor's heirs, the doctrine of worthier title, and the doctrine or rule prohibiting an existing lien upon part of a homestead from extending to another part of the homestead not charged with the debts secured by the existing lien upon part of the homestead do not apply in this state.

(b) A deed, will, or other conveyance of property in this state that limits an interest in the property to a particular person or to a class such as the heirs, heirs of the body, issue, or next of kin of the conveyor or of a person to whom a particular interest in the same property is limited is effective according to the intent of the conveyor.

(c) Status as an heir or next of kin of a conveyor or the failure of a conveyor to describe a person in a conveyance other than as a member of a class does not affect a person's right to take or share in an interest as a conveyee.

(d) Subject to the intention of a conveyor, which controls unless limited by law, the membership of a class described in this section and the participation of a member in a property interest conveyed to the class are determined under this state's laws of descent and distribution.

(e) This section does not apply to a conveyance taking effect before January 1, 1964.

Spendthrift provision does not preclude devise of vested remainder

In re TOWNLEY BYPASS UNIFIED CREDIT TRUST
Court of Appeals of Texas, Texarkana
252 S.W.3d 715 (2008)

CARTER, J. Does a spendthrift provision in a trust preclude the remainder beneficiary from devising by a will his interest in the assets of the trust estate?

1. FACTS AND BACKGROUND

W.D. Townley's will contained a trust leaving a life estate to Josie Townley, his wife. Upon her death, the trust was to terminate and the remainder of the assets was to be split between the two children, Billy Ray Townley and Jimmy LaRue Wilson. The will contained a spendthrift provision which prohibited any beneficiary from assigning or transferring any income or principal before receiving it. W.D. Townley's will made no provision if either child predeceased his or her mother, the very thing that occurred when Billy Ray died before his mother. Several years later when Josie died, it was uncontroverted the daughter, Jimmy LaRue Wilson, was entitled to one half of the estate, but since Billy Ray predeceased his mother, the trial court was requested to determine how the other one half was to be distributed. The trial court determined that the son's one-half interest was vested and thus transferred through his will to his widow rather than by intestacy. We will affirm the judgment of the trial court.

2. STANDARD OF REVIEW

The construction of a written instrument is a question of law for the court, and we are to review such de novo. MCI Telecomm. Corp. v. Tex. Utils. Elec. Co., 995 S.W.2d 647, 650-51 (Tex. 1999). Here, the facts are not in dispute, but only the application of the law to those facts.

3. IS THIS A VESTED REMAINDER INTEREST?

Typically, a remainder interest occurs when a possessory interest in property (often a life estate) is given to one person, with a subsequent taking of the estate in another person. Here, the trust document created the trust for the benefit of the mother, with all income, and potentially all corpus, to be utilized for her benefit as determined to be appropriate by the trustee. Upon the mother's death, the trust terminated and directed that the corpus then be distributed to the son and daughter.[5]

If a remainder interest is in an ascertainable person, and no condition precedent exists other than the termination of prior estates, then it is a vested remainder. "Texas courts will not construe a remainder as contingent when it can reasonably be taken as vested." McGill v. Johnson, 799 S.W.2d 673, 675 (Tex. 1990); see also Pickering v. Miles, 477 S.W.2d 267, 270 (Tex. 1972).

It is settled that a remainder is vested when there is a person in being at the creation of the interest who would have a right to immediate possession upon termination of the intermediate estate. Chadwick v. Bristow, 146 Tex. 481, 208 S.W.2d 888, 891 (1948); Bradford v. Rain, 562 S.W.2d 514, 518 (Tex. Civ. App.-Texarkana 1978, no writ); Reilly v. Huff, 335 S.W.2d 275, 278 (Tex. Civ. App.-San Antonio 1960, no writ). In this case, the son met this criteria, and his remainder interest can reasonably be taken as vested. In fact, there is no substantial basis in the record for any other conclusion. See Shearrer v. Holley, 952 S.W.2d 74, 79 (Tex. App.-San Antonio 1997, no writ).

It is argued that, because the amount that might ultimately pass by the remainder interest was uncertain, it could not vest. There is no authority provided supporting that position, and a number of the cases cited above involve similar facts—a life estate, with remainder interest to another. The fact that the estate might, in part or whole, be consumed, is not a factor. In *Bradford*, this Court held explicitly that the character of a remainder as vested is not affected by an uncertainty as to the question of a quantum which will be received by the remainderman when he or she becomes entitled to possession. *Bradford*, 562 S.W.2d at 518.

---

[5] We note that other terms describing the son's interest would be more traditionally correct, such as secondary beneficiary, or a tertiary beneficiary. However, the current version of the Texas Trust Code identifies such as a "remainder beneficiary," and we will utilize that terminology from this point forward.

The remainder interest was vested. Under normal circumstances, then, it could be transferred from its owner to another person.

4. THE SPENDTHRIFT PROVISION

At trial, and now on appeal, the focus by the parties and the trial court was on the proper application of a spendthrift clause within the bypass trust. The clause reads as follows:

> (E) *Spendthrift Clause.* No Beneficiary of the trust shall have the right or power to anticipate by assignment or otherwise any income or principal given to such beneficiary of this Trust Agreement, or in advance of actually receiving the same, have the right or power to sell, transfer, encumber or in anywise charge same; nor shall such income or principal, or any portion of same, be subject to any execution, garnishment, attachment or legal sequestration, levy or sale, or in any event or manner be applicable or subject, voluntarily or involuntarily to the payment of such Beneficiary's debts.[6]

As previously noted, under general rules of law, Texas favors a construction that allows vesting at the earliest possible time. See *McGill*, 799 S.W.2d at 675; *Chadwick*, 208 S.W.2d at 891. Such a construction has been uniformly held to be in the public interest because it provides for a more complete disposition of property interests and provides for greater legal effectiveness. See Rust v. Rust, 147 Tex. 181, 211 S.W.2d 262, 266 (1948), aff'd, 147 Tex. 181, 214 S.W.2d 462 (1948); *Chadwick*, 208 S.W.2d at 891.

We agree with the trial court that an interest had vested in the son before his death. However, at the time of that vesting, the only interest was, at best, an expectancy that might or might not ripen into the right of possession of anything at all, as the corpus could have been consumed by the trust for the mother's benefit before he had any right to actually receive under the trust terms.[7]

Under the Texas Trust Act, a "beneficiary" includes, in the case of a decedent's estate, an heir, legatee, and devisee and, in the case of a trust, an income beneficiary and a remainder beneficiary. Texas Property Code § 116.002(2). A remainder beneficiary is later defined as a "person entitled to receive principal when an income interest ends." Texas Property Code § 116.002(11). The more general definition is found in Section 111.004(2) of the Texas Property Code, which states broadly that a beneficiary is a person for whose

---

[6] Section 112.035(1) of the Texas Property Code states that spendthrift provisions in trusts are lawful, providing that a settlor may provide a term stating that the interest of a beneficiary in income or principal "may not be voluntarily or involuntarily transferred before payment or delivery of the interest to the beneficiary by the trustee." Texas Property Code § 112.035(1).

[7] Restatement (Third) of Trusts § 49 (2003) states that, except as limited by law or public policy, the extent of the interest of a trust beneficiary depends upon the intention manifested by the settlor.

benefit property is held in trust, regardless of the nature of the interest. Texas Property Code § 111.004(2). Under either of these definitions, the son was a beneficiary of the trust, and it appears that he also qualified as a remainder beneficiary under the statute.

Under the express terms of the testamentary bypass trust, after the mother died, the trust terminated, with directions to the trustee to distribute the corpus to the son and daughter. Thus, the corpus became part of the son's estate upon the mother's death. The question is then, was the corpus to be distributed under the terms of his will, or does the spendthrift provision require distribution under the laws of intestacy?

The language of the spendthrift provision states that the beneficiary had no right or power to "anticipate" any principal given under the trust agreement or, in advance of actually receiving it, have the right or power to transfer any principal given under the trust agreement. The clause prevents creditors from reaching the trust.

Appellant argues that the son's will leaving his property to his wife is necessarily a transfer and falls within the spendthrift trust's restriction. Consequently, it is argued the trial court erred in determining that the son's remainder interest passed to his devisee, his widow. Neither of the parties has cited any Texas precedent on this issue, and we have found none. Therefore, we turn to other sources for guidance.

Some analogous situations are helpful. In the case of In re Estate of Campbell, 48 Haw. 1, 394 P.2d 784 (1964), a somewhat similar situation was presented. The issue there was whether a deceased beneficiary could leave income that had accumulated, but not distributed, before death to a devisee by will even though the trust included a spendthrift provision. The spendthrift provision of the trust stated that all payments "shall be valid and effectual only when made to the beneficiary, devisee or legatee, in person, to whom the same shall appertain and belong, and upon his or her individual receipt." Welsh v. Campbell, 42 Haw. 490, 495 (Haw. 1958).

The court stated, "The purpose of the inclusion of the spendthrift clause in the will was to protect an improvident beneficiary against his own folly by insulating him against overreaching creditors. It does not evidence intent to restrict the amount of income for a beneficiary's maintenance." Id. (citing Cromwell v. Converse, 108 Conn. 412, 143 A. 416 (1928)). "The spendthrift provisions should not be taken to cut off benefits which would in the absence of such provisions be conferred by the will." Id. Further, the Hawaii court quoted from a second edition of Scott's treatise on trusts. The same provision of that treatise is now found at IIA Austin Wakeman Scott & William Franklin Fratcher, The Law of Trusts § 158.1 (4th ed. 1987):

> Where the income of a trust estate is payable to a beneficiary and he dies, his personal representatives are entitled to the income that has accrued at the time of his death and that has not been paid to him, unless it is otherwise provided by the terms of the trust. Even though it is provided by the terms of the trust or by statute that the interest of the beneficiary shall not be transferable by him or subject to the claims of

> his creditors, the beneficiary's interest in such accrued income passes on his death to his personal representatives, if it would so pass in the absence of such a restraint on alienation. The purpose of the restraint on alienation is to protect the beneficiary, and when he dies he no longer needs such protection. The purpose is not to deprive the beneficiary's estate of the income which was payable to him but that had not been paid at the time of his death. Whatever is thus received by the personal representatives is a part of his estate and is subject to the claims of his creditors. Unless the claims of creditors preclude it, the beneficiary can dispose by will of his right to the income accruing up to the time of his death.

Id. (footnote omitted).

Appellant cites Cowdery v. Northern Trust Co., 321 Ill. App. 243, 53 N.E.2d 43 (Ill. App. Ct. 1944). In that case, the spendthrift trust directed that the beneficiary was to have no control of any of the trust's income "until after actual receipt thereof by such actual beneficiary." Once again, the issue of distribution of income that had accumulated during the beneficiary's lifetime, but had not been distributed before death, was before the court. The Illinois court held that the spendthrift provision precluded the distribution of the income to the beneficiary's estate:

> Whatever may be the purpose, generally, of restraint on alienation in spendthrift trusts, the terms used in the trust herein involved go further than mere protection of the beneficiary during his lifetime. They exclude control of such income by any beneficiary until same is actually received by the actual beneficiary, not his or her representative, and bar claims of creditors after, as well as before, the death of beneficiaries.

Id.

This discussion, while relevant, is not directly on point since it involves income accumulated, but not distributed, before the beneficiary's death, rather than property received after the beneficiary's death.

The Restatement of Trusts also has some discussion of this topic. In general comment (g) of Section 58(2) of the Restatement (Third) of Trusts it is stated that, on the death of the beneficiary of a spendthrift trust, his or her executor or administrator is entitled to accrued income. Further, in the reporter's notes to that general comment to that subsection, Scott's treatise is cited for the proposition that interests, other than accrued income, may pass by will of the beneficiary despite the spendthrift trust provision.

> '[S]pendthrift trusts are upheld on the ground that it is not against public policy to permit the settlor in creating the trust to protect the beneficiary against his own improvidence. When the beneficiary dies, the need for such protection ceases. There would seem no reason, therefore, why on his death his creditors should not be able to reach his interest under the trust if his interest has not ceased on his death.' *A*

> *continuing income or remainder interest in the trust*, despite the spendthrift provision, is transferable by will or intestacy for the same reason, and also because the right to pass the continuing interest on to others is a natural feature of such an interest as it was given to the beneficiary by the settlor.

Restatement (Third) of Trusts § 58 reporter's notes, cmt. g (2003) (emphasis added).

Unlike the other authorities cited, the Restatement appears to address not only income that was accumulated during the lifetime of the beneficiary, but also a remainder interest in the trust.

We recognize that these are not controlling authorities, but, having found none, we will follow the logic and reasoning of the Restatement. We agree that the purpose of the spendthrift provision is to protect the beneficiary from his or her own folly, a purpose that cannot be promoted after the beneficiary's death. Further, Texas law recognizes that a person of sound mind has a perfect legal right to dispose of his or her property as that person wishes. Rothermel v. Duncan, 369 S.W.2d 917, 923 (Tex. 1963).

For the reasons stated, we affirm the judgment of the trial court.

Chapter 14. The Rule Against Perpetuities and Trust Duration

Section A. The Common Law Rule

Texas Constitution art. I, § 26. Perpetuities and monopolies; primogeniture or entailments

Sec. 26. Perpetuities and monopolies are contrary to the genius of a free government, and shall never be allowed, nor shall the law of primogeniture or entailments ever be in force in this State.

Property Code § 112.036. Rule Against Perpetuities

The rule against perpetuities applies to trusts other than charitable trusts. Accordingly, an interest is not good unless it must vest, if at all, not later than 21 years after some life in being at the time of the creation of the interest, plus a period of gestation. Any interest in a trust may, however, be reformed or construed to the extent and as provided by Section 5.043.

Section B. Perpetuities Reform

Property Code § 5.043. Reformation of Interests Violating Rule Against Perpetuities

(a) Within the limits of the rule against perpetuities, a court shall reform or construe an interest in real or personal property that violates the rule to effect the ascertainable general intent of the creator of the interest. A court shall liberally construe and apply this provision to validate an interest to the fullest extent consistent with the creator's intent.

(b) The court may reform or construe an interest under Subsection (a) of this section according to the doctrine of cy pres by giving effect to the general intent and specific directives of the creator within the limits of the rule against perpetuities.

(c) If an instrument that violates the rule against perpetuities may be reformed or construed under this section, a court shall enforce the provisions of the instrument that do not violate the rule and shall reform or construe under this section a provision that violates or might violate the rule.

(d) This section applies to legal and equitable interests, including noncharitable gifts and trusts, conveyed by an inter vivos instrument or a will that takes effect on or after September

1, 1969, and this section applies to an appointment made on or after that date regardless of when the power was created.

Table of Cases

CASES

Table of Cases

Table of Statutes

STATUTES

Constitution of the State of Texas

Texas Estates Code

Table of Statutes

Table of Statutes

Texas Family Code

Texas Property Code